Yamada-kun and the Seven Witches

16

MIKI YOSHIKAWA

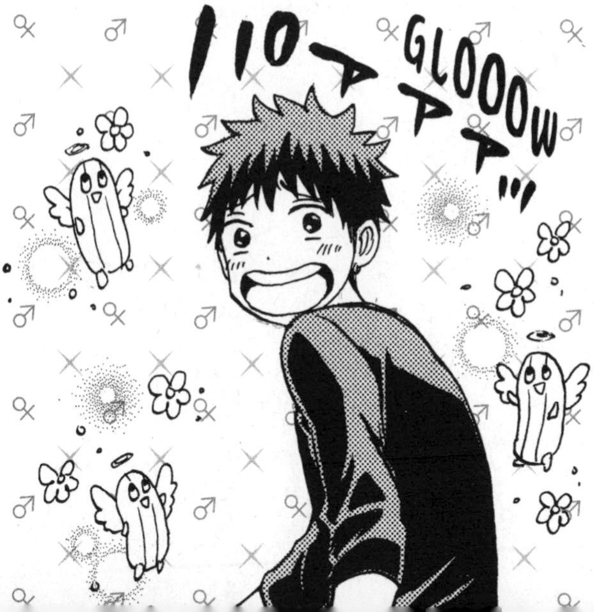
GLOOOW

Ryu Yamada

A second-year at Suzaku High School, member of the Supernatural Studies Club, and secretary of the Student Council. He's known as the "Copy Guy" and possesses the ability to copy the power of whichever witch he kisses. The brilliant genius Takuma is currently messing with him.

Urara Shiraishi

A second-year at Suzaku High School and president of the Supernatural Studies Club. She used to be known as the "Switch Witch," and through various events, she became Yamada's girlfriend. At her New Year's shrine visit with her club mates, she secretly bought a love charm.

Toranosuke Miyamura

A second-year at Suzaku High School and president of the Student Council. He's constantly joking around, but he can make incredibly clear-headed decisions when it counts!

Nene Odagiri

A second-year at Suzaku High School and clerk for the Student Council. She used to be the "Charm Witch." She has feelings for Yamada, but it seems that she's still embarrassed to express those feelings directly to Yamada.

Shinichi Tamaki

A second-year at Suzaku High School and treasurer for the Student Council. He's known as the "Capture Guy" and steals the power of the witch whom he kisses. He's a bit pretentious, but also easily feels lonely.

Miyabi Itou

A second-year at Suzaku High School and member of the Supernatural Studies Club. Her hobby is collecting occult paraphernalia. It seems she's fallen under the spell of one of the new witches!

Jin Kurosaki

A first-year at Suzaku High School and one of the vice-presidents of the Student Council. Although he doesn't talk much, he's steadily been opening up more these days. He has an extreme reverence for Miyamura.

Midori Arisugawa

A first-year at Suzaku High School and one of the vice-presidents of the Student Council. A carefree girl who also has an ambitious side. She's good at provoking Kurosaki.

Mikoto Asuka

A third-year at Suzaku High School and former vice-president of the Student Council. She used to be the "Invisible Witch" and now serves as the president of the Shogi Club.

Ushio Igarashi

A second-year at Suzaku High School and vice-president of the Shogi Club. He used to be Odagiri's loyal servant. He was Yamada's friend in junior high school.

Kentaro Tsubaki

A second-year at Suzaku High School and member of the Supernatural Studies Club. He's a cheerful guy who used to live abroad and livens up the mood in the club!

Rui Takuma

A second-year Suzaku High School student and the Seventh Witch of another sphere of witches separate from Nancy. He's at the top of his class. He's anemic.

Kotori Moegi

A second-year Suzaku High School student and one of the new witches. She can read minds by having her doll kiss the person in question.

Nancy

A second-year at Suzaku High School and the Seventh Witch who belongs to the Light Music Club. For some reason, she cooperates with Yamada.

CONTENTS

CHAPTER 129: That's all.

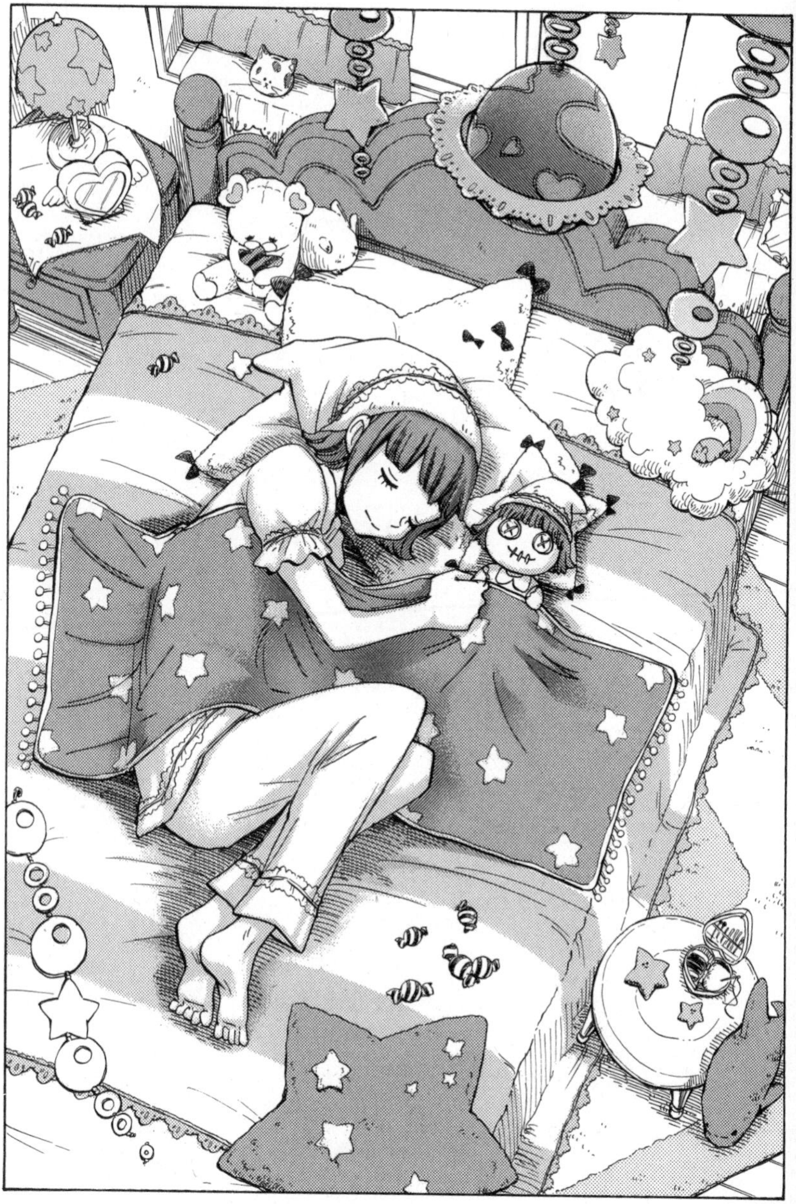

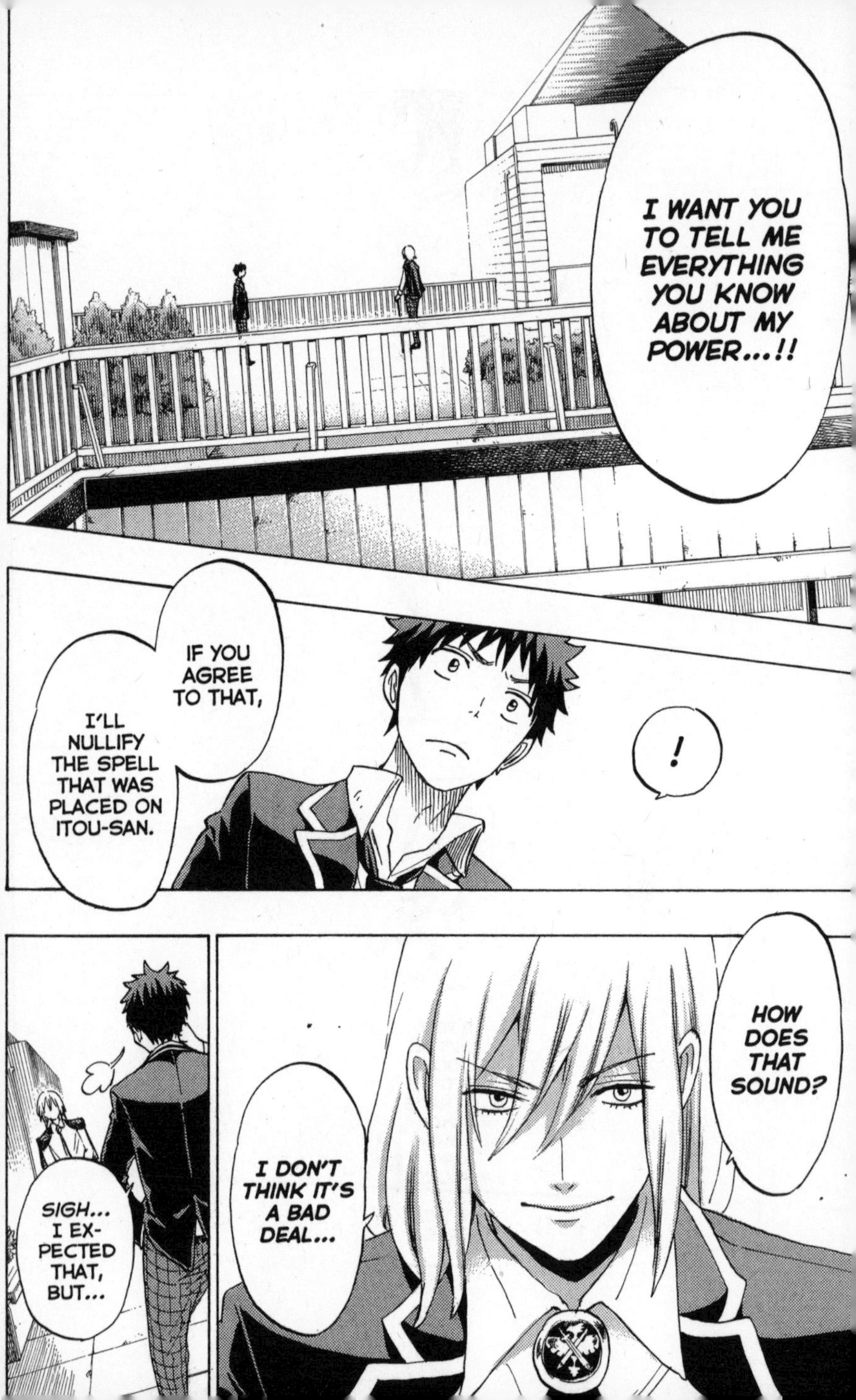
I WANT YOU TO TELL ME EVERYTHING YOU KNOW ABOUT MY POWER...!!
IF YOU AGREE TO THAT,
I'LL NULLIFY THE SPELL THAT WAS PLACED ON ITOU-SAN.
!
HOW DOES THAT SOUND?
I DON'T THINK IT'S A BAD DEAL...
SIGH... I EX-PECTED THAT, BUT...

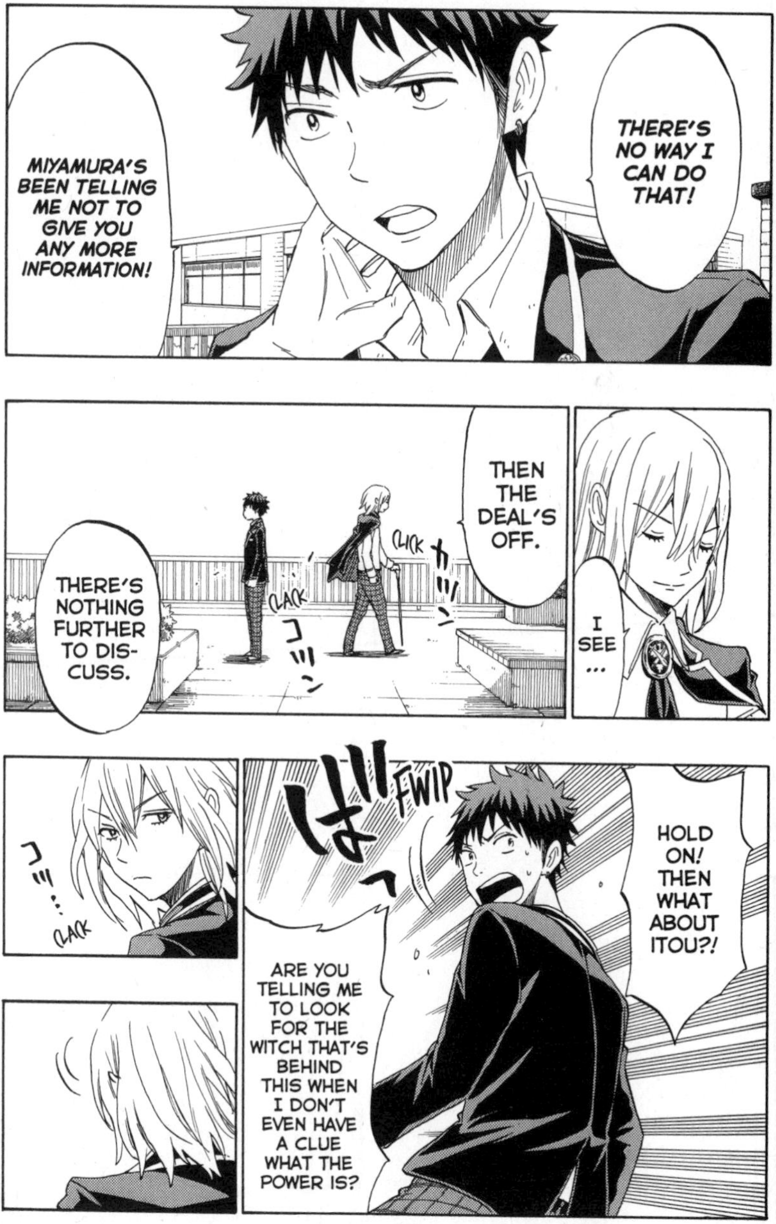
THERE'S NO WAY I CAN DO THAT!
MIYAMURA'S BEEN TELLING ME NOT TO GIVE YOU ANY MORE INFORMATION!
I SEE...
THEN THE DEAL'S OFF.
CLICK
カツン
CLACK
コツン
THERE'S NOTHING FURTHER TO DISCUSS.
HOLD ON! THEN WHAT ABOUT ITOU?!
FWIP
はッ
ARE YOU TELLING ME TO LOOK FOR THE WITCH THAT'S BEHIND THIS WHEN I DON'T EVEN HAVE A CLUE WHAT THE POWER IS?
コツ…
CLACK

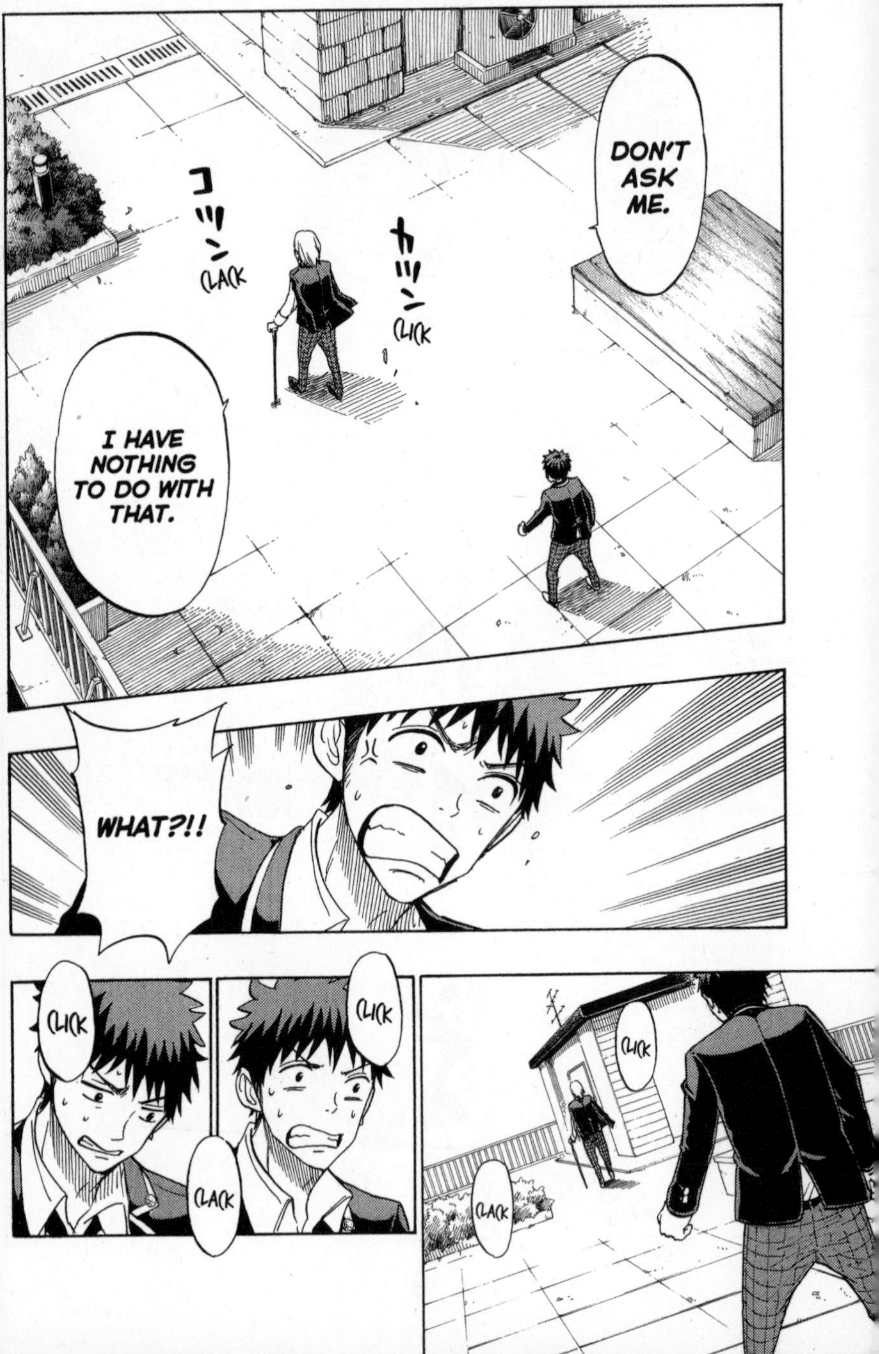
DON'T ASK ME.
カツン
CLICK
コツン
CLACK
I HAVE NOTHING TO DO WITH THAT.
WHAT?!!
CLICK
CLACK
CLICK
CLACK
CLICK
CLACK

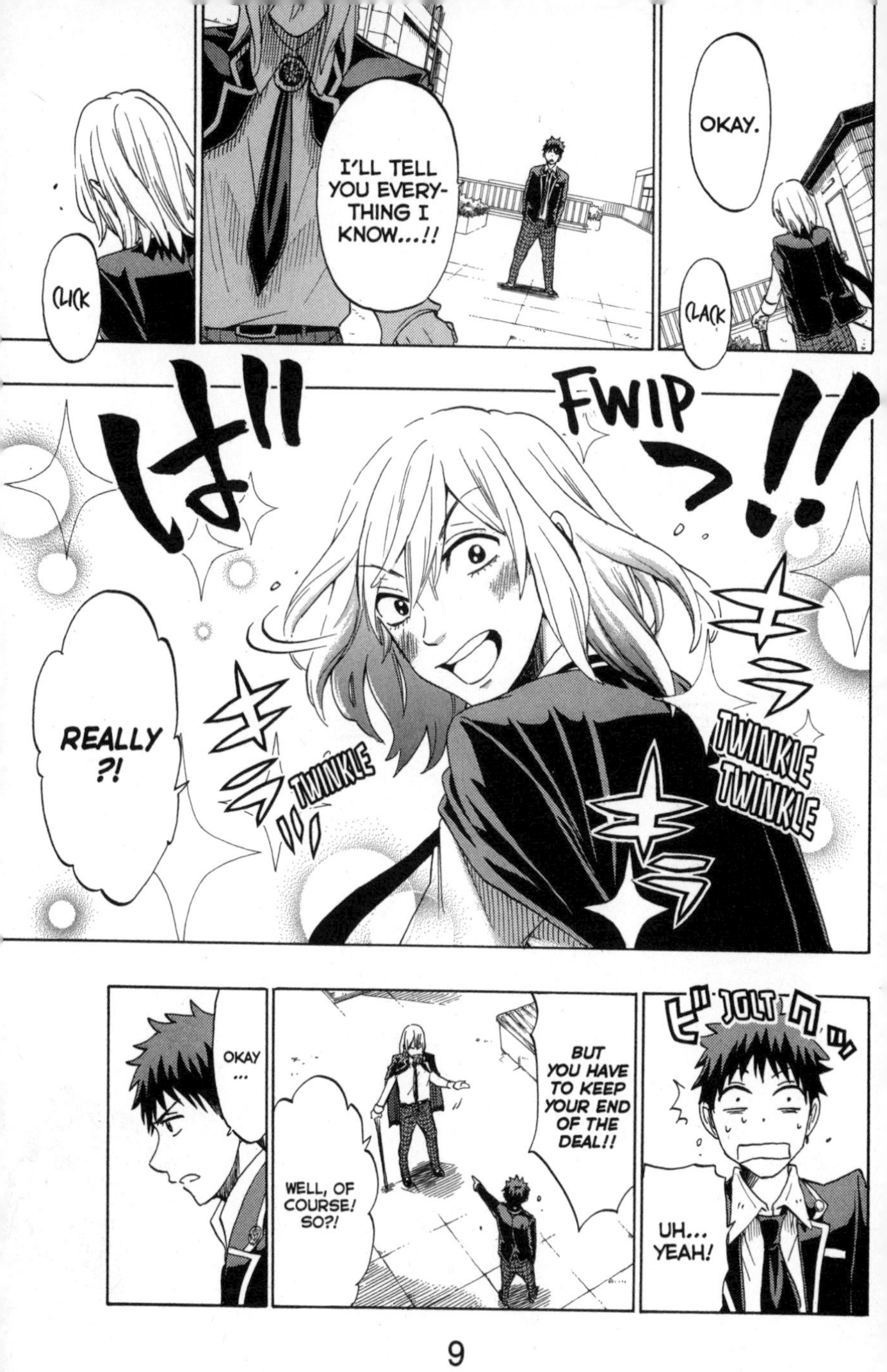
OKAY.
CLACK
I'LL TELL YOU EVERY-THING I KNOW...!!
CLICK
FWIP
っ!!
TWINKLE TWINKLE
TWINKLE
REALLY ?!
は!!
ビ JOLT クッ
UH... YEAH!
BUT YOU HAVE TO KEEP YOUR END OF THE DEAL!!
WELL, OF COURSE! SO?!
OKAY ...

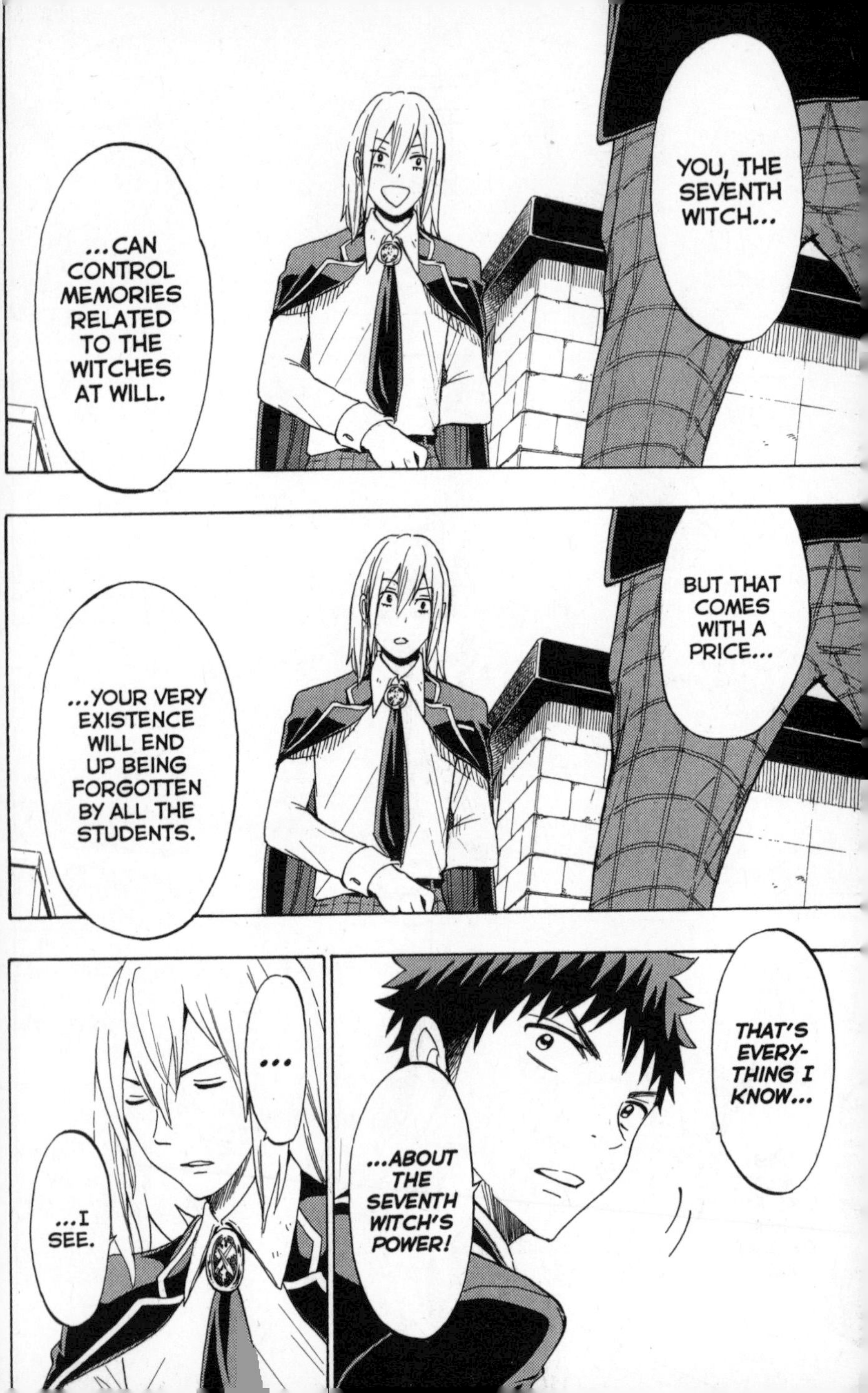
YOU, THE SEVENTH WITCH...
...CAN CONTROL MEMORIES RELATED TO THE WITCHES AT WILL.
BUT THAT COMES WITH A PRICE...
...YOUR VERY EXISTENCE WILL END UP BEING FORGOTTEN BY ALL THE STUDENTS.
THAT'S EVERY-THING I KNOW...
...ABOUT THE SEVENTH WITCH'S POWER!
...
...I SEE.

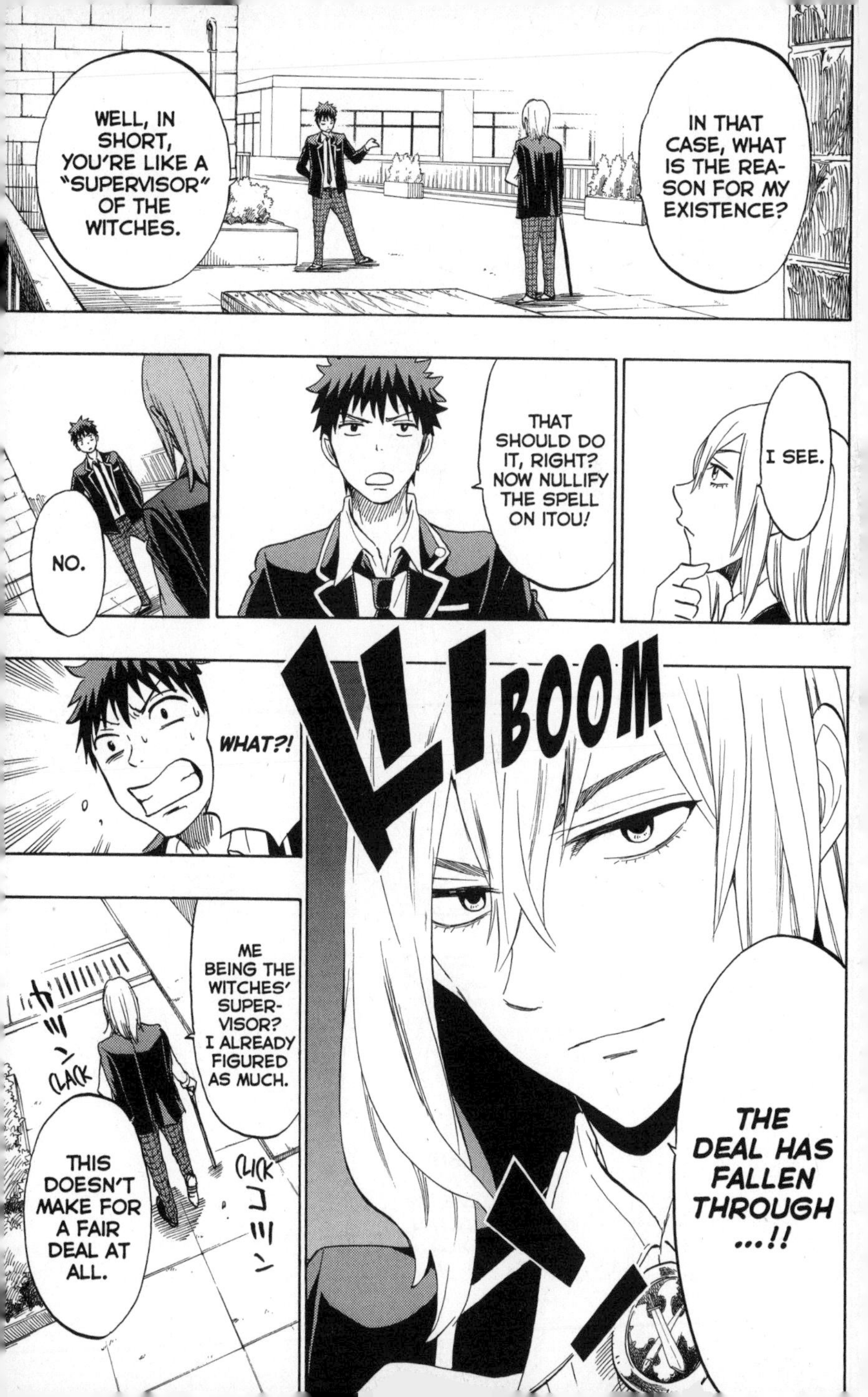
IN THAT CASE, WHAT IS THE REASON FOR MY EXISTENCE?
WELL, IN SHORT, YOU'RE LIKE A "SUPERVISOR" OF THE WITCHES.
I SEE.
THAT SHOULD DO IT, RIGHT? NOW NULLIFY THE SPELL ON ITOU!
NO.
BOOM
THE DEAL HAS FALLEN THROUGH ...!!
WHAT?!
ME BEING THE WITCHES' SUPERVISOR? I ALREADY FIGURED AS MUCH.
CLACK
THIS DOESN'T MAKE FOR A FAIR DEAL AT ALL.
CLICK

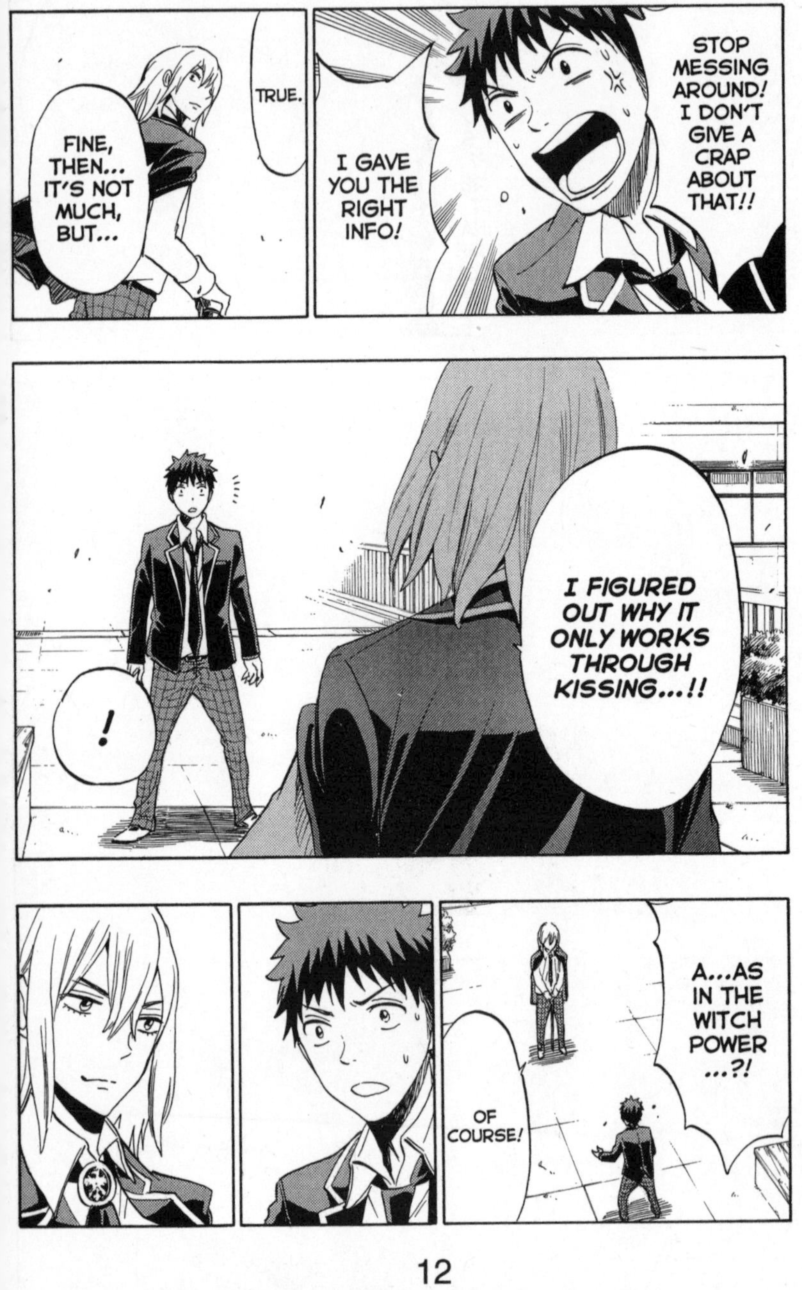
STOP MESSING AROUND! I DON'T GIVE A CRAP ABOUT THAT!!
I GAVE YOU THE RIGHT INFO!
TRUE.
FINE, THEN... IT'S NOT MUCH, BUT...
I FIGURED OUT WHY IT ONLY WORKS THROUGH KISSING...!!
!
A...AS IN THE WITCH POWER ...?!
OF COURSE!

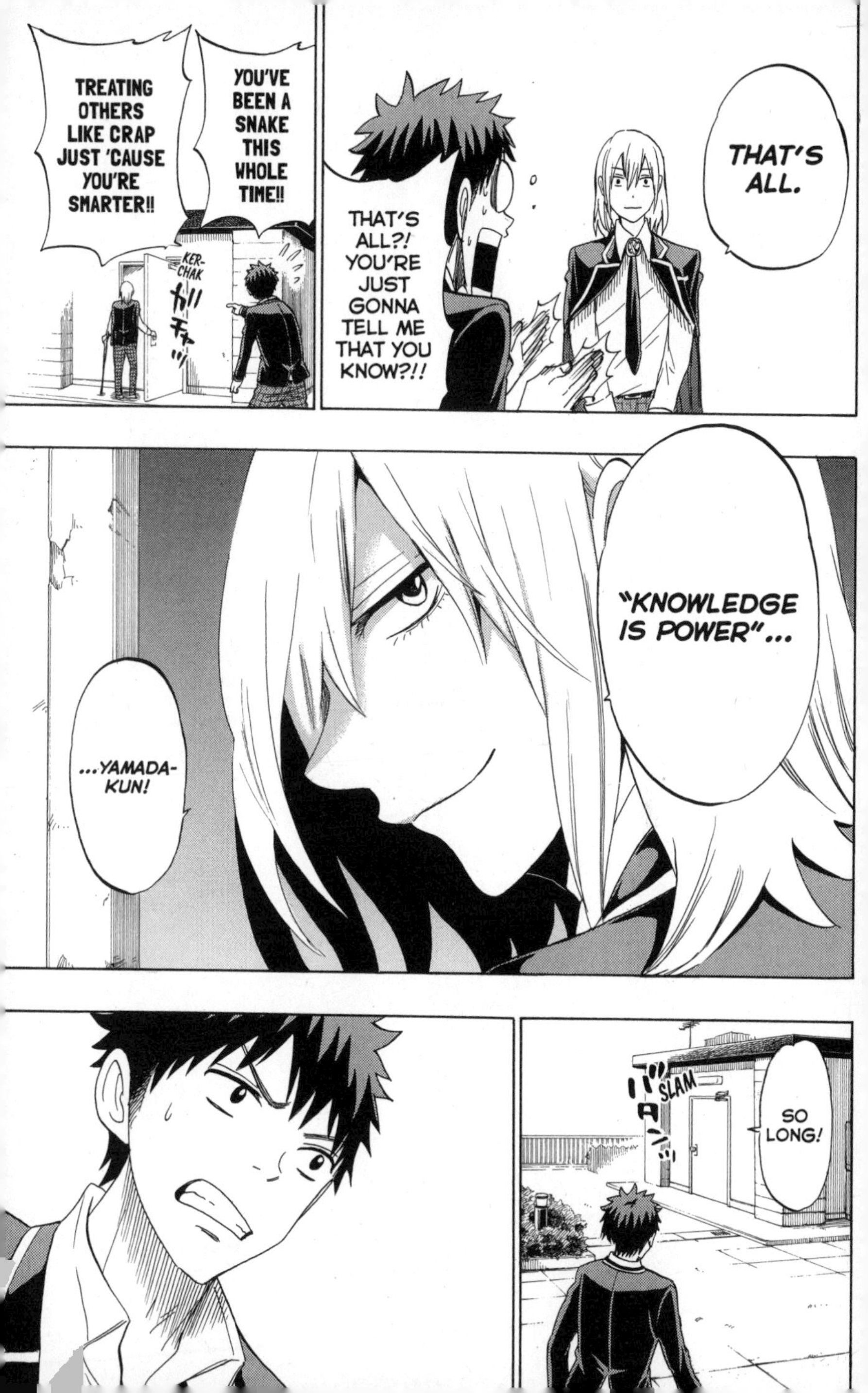
THAT'S ALL.
THAT'S ALL?! YOU'RE JUST GONNA TELL ME THAT YOU KNOW?!!
YOU'VE BEEN A SNAKE THIS WHOLE TIME!!
TREATING OTHERS LIKE CRAP JUST 'CAUSE YOU'RE SMARTER!!
KER-CHAK
"KNOWLEDGE IS POWER"...
...YAMADA-KUN!
SLAM
SO LONG!

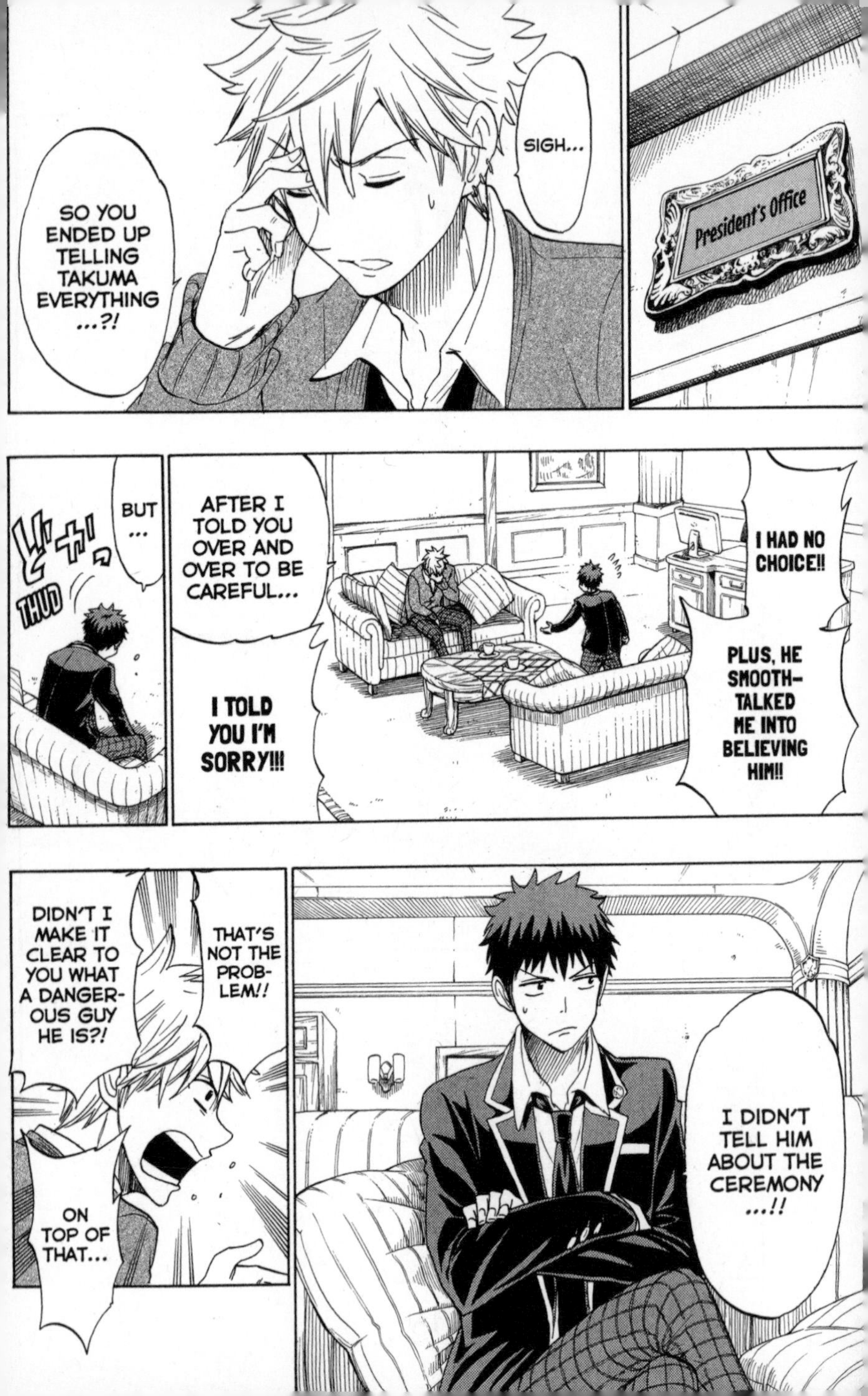
President's Office
SIGH...
SO YOU ENDED UP TELLING TAKUMA EVERYTHING ...?!
I HAD NO CHOICE!!
AFTER I TOLD YOU OVER AND OVER TO BE CAREFUL...
PLUS, HE SMOOTH-TALKED ME INTO BELIEVING HIM!!
I TOLD YOU I'M SORRY!!!
BUT ...
THUD
I DIDN'T TELL HIM ABOUT THE CEREMONY ...!!
THAT'S NOT THE PROB-LEM!!
DIDN'T I MAKE IT CLEAR TO YOU WHAT A DANGER-OUS GUY HE IS?!
ON TOP OF THAT...

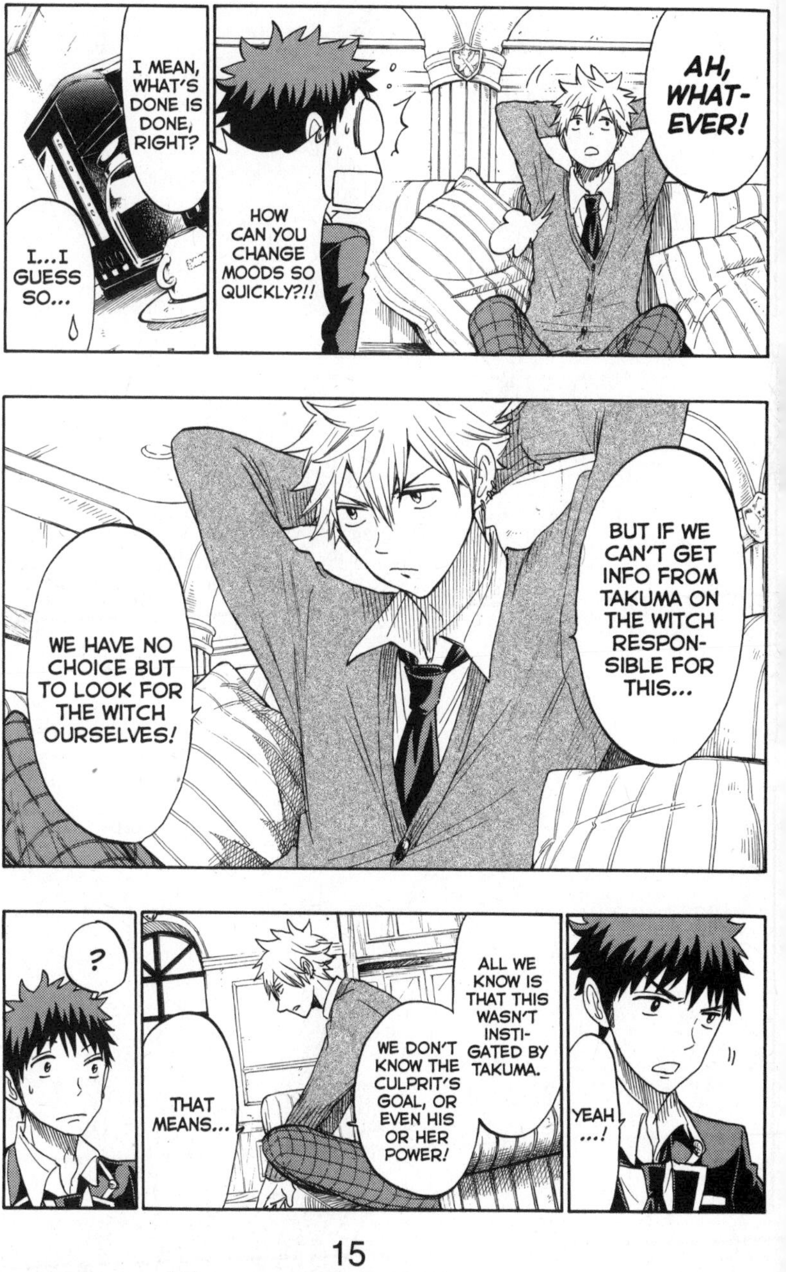
AH, WHATEVER!
HOW CAN YOU CHANGE MOODS SO QUICKLY?!!
I MEAN, WHAT'S DONE IS DONE, RIGHT?
I...I GUESS SO...
BUT IF WE CAN'T GET INFO FROM TAKUMA ON THE WITCH RESPONSIBLE FOR THIS...
WE HAVE NO CHOICE BUT TO LOOK FOR THE WITCH OURSELVES!
YEAH...!
ALL WE KNOW IS THAT THIS WASN'T INSTIGATED BY TAKUMA.
WE DON'T KNOW THE CULPRIT'S GOAL, OR EVEN HIS OR HER POWER!
THAT MEANS...
?

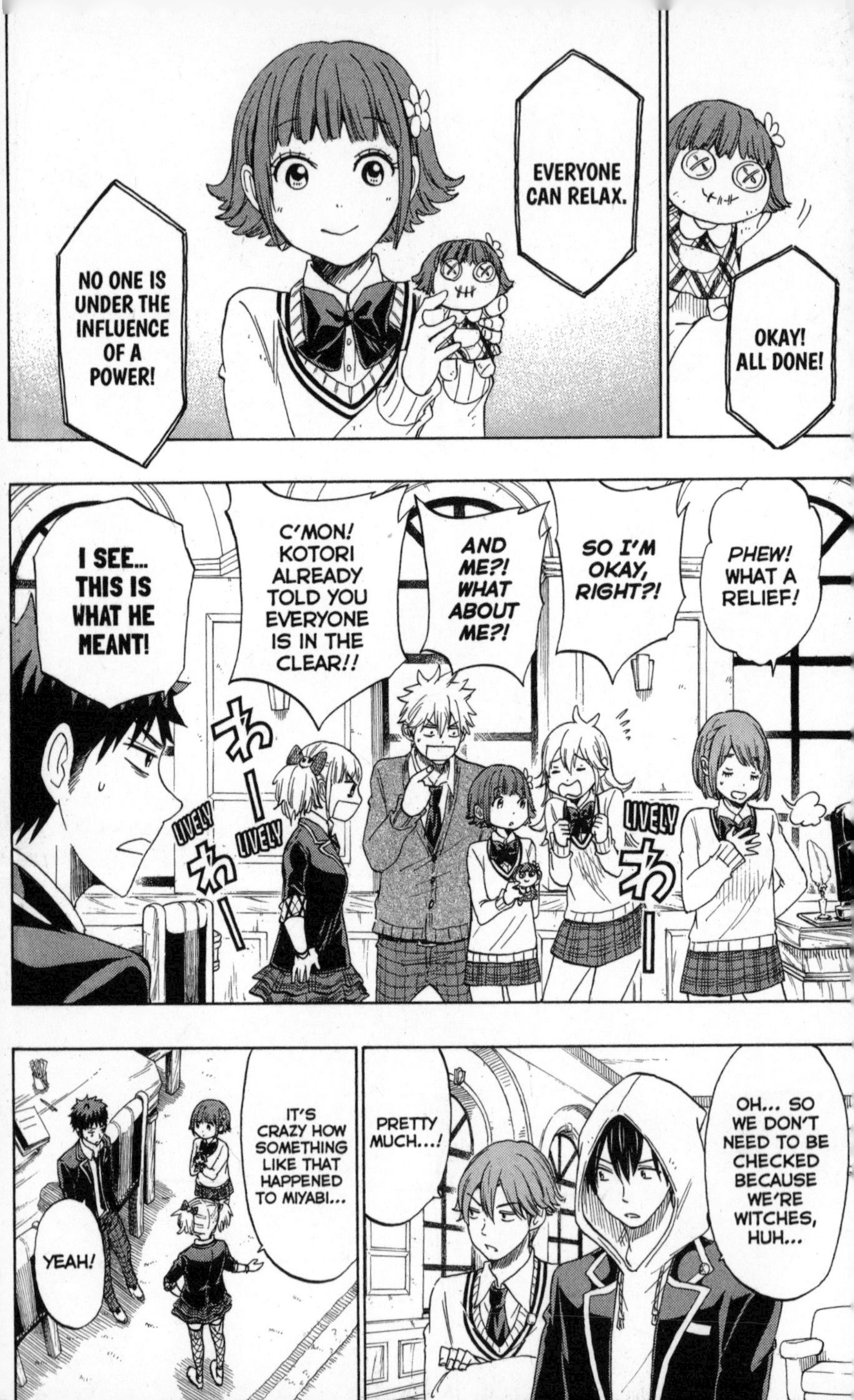
OKAY! ALL DONE!
EVERYONE CAN RELAX.
NO ONE IS UNDER THE INFLUENCE OF A POWER!
PHEW! WHAT A RELIEF!
SO I'M OKAY, RIGHT?!
AND ME?! WHAT ABOUT ME?!
C'MON! KOTORI ALREADY TOLD YOU EVERYONE IS IN THE CLEAR!!
LIVELY
LIVELY
LIVELY
I SEE... THIS IS WHAT HE MEANT!
OH... SO WE DON'T NEED TO BE CHECKED BECAUSE WE'RE WITCHES, HUH...
PRETTY MUCH...!
IT'S CRAZY HOW SOMETHING LIKE THAT HAPPENED TO MIYABI...
YEAH!

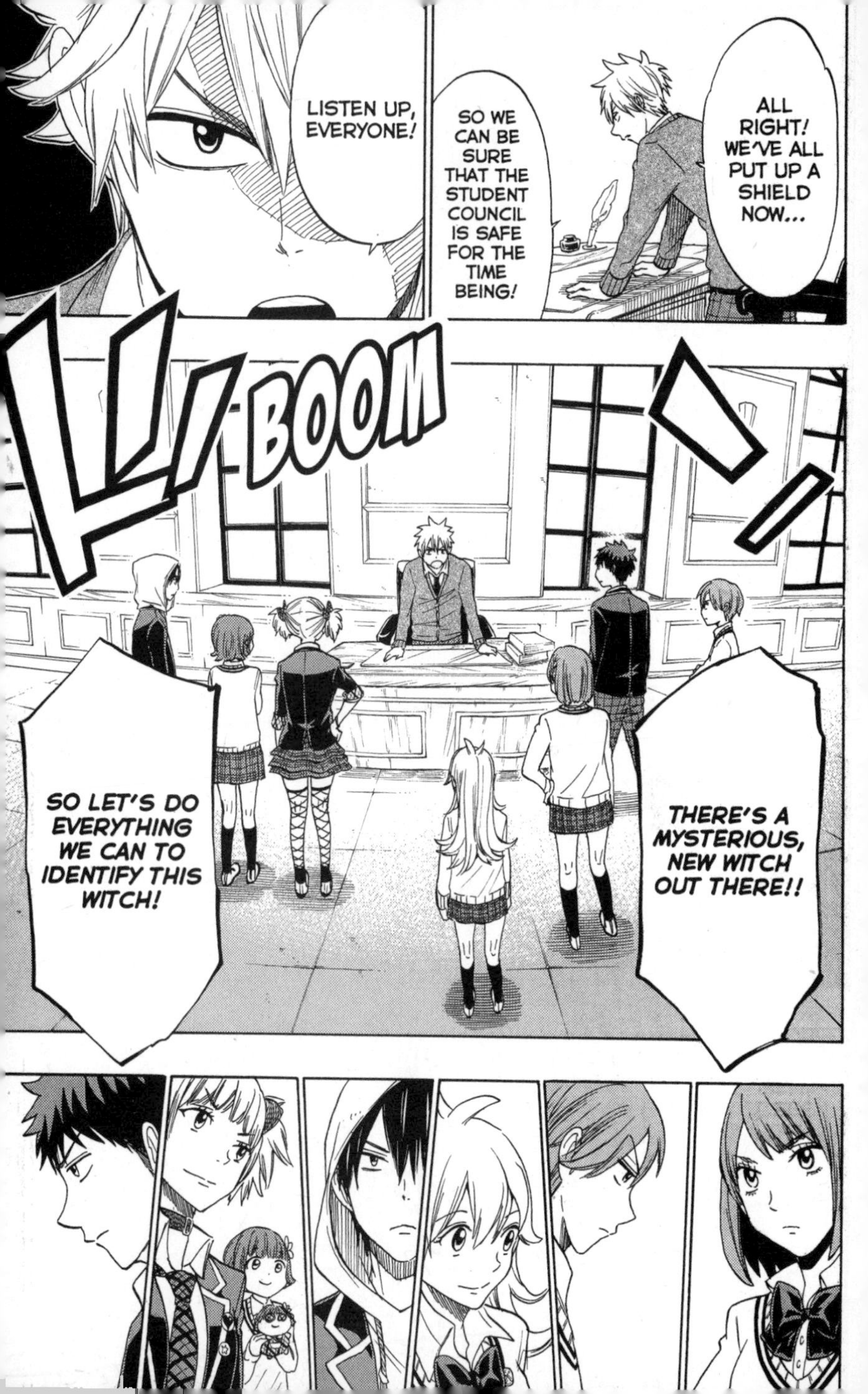
ALL RIGHT! WE'VE ALL PUT UP A SHIELD NOW...
SO WE CAN BE SURE THAT THE STUDENT COUNCIL IS SAFE FOR THE TIME BEING!
LISTEN UP, EVERYONE!
BOOM
THERE'S A MYSTERIOUS, NEW WITCH OUT THERE!!
SO LET'S DO EVERYTHING WE CAN TO IDENTIFY THIS WITCH!

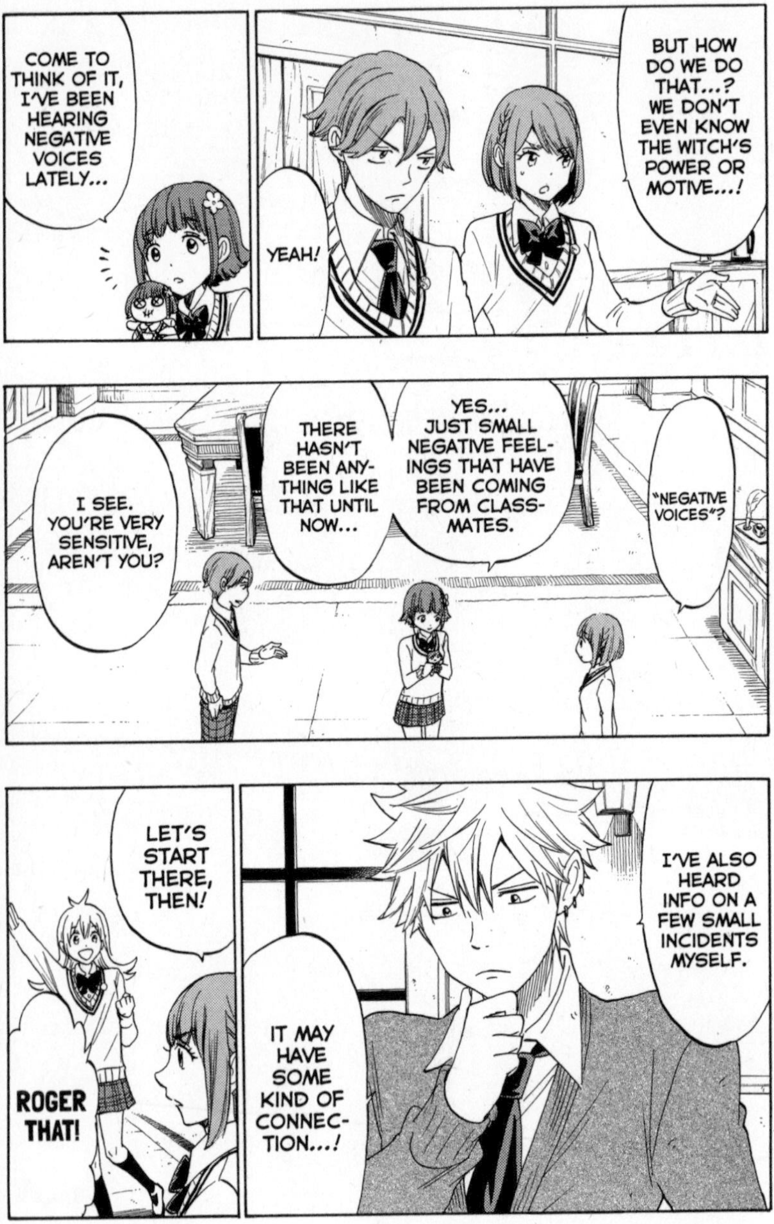
BUT HOW DO WE DO THAT...? WE DON'T EVEN KNOW THE WITCH'S POWER OR MOTIVE...!
YEAH!
COME TO THINK OF IT, I'VE BEEN HEARING NEGATIVE VOICES LATELY...
"NEGATIVE VOICES"?
YES... JUST SMALL NEGATIVE FEELINGS THAT HAVE BEEN COMING FROM CLASSMATES.
THERE HASN'T BEEN ANYTHING LIKE THAT UNTIL NOW...
I SEE. YOU'RE VERY SENSITIVE, AREN'T YOU?
I'VE ALSO HEARD INFO ON A FEW SMALL INCIDENTS MYSELF.
IT MAY HAVE SOME KIND OF CONNECTION...!
LET'S START THERE, THEN!
ROGER THAT!

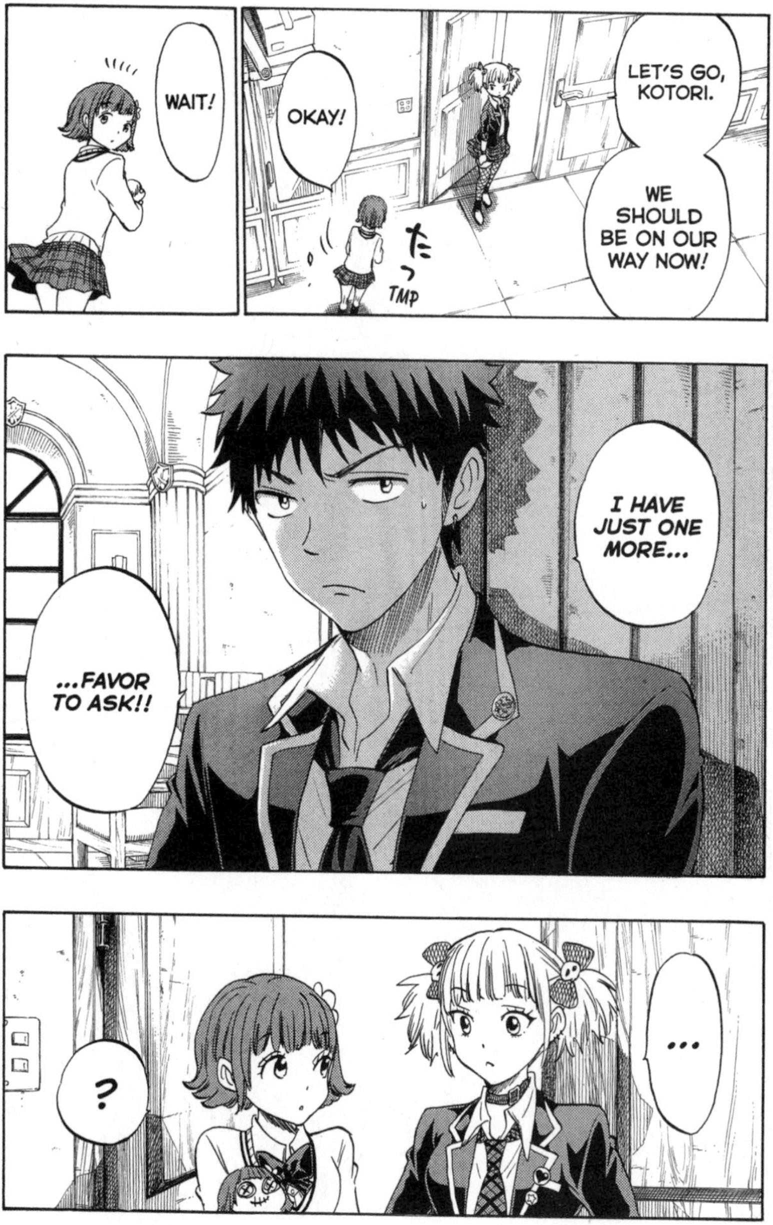
LET'S GO, KOTORI.
WE SHOULD BE ON OUR WAY NOW!
OKAY!
たっ
TMP
WAIT!
I HAVE JUST ONE MORE...
...FAVOR TO ASK!!
...
?

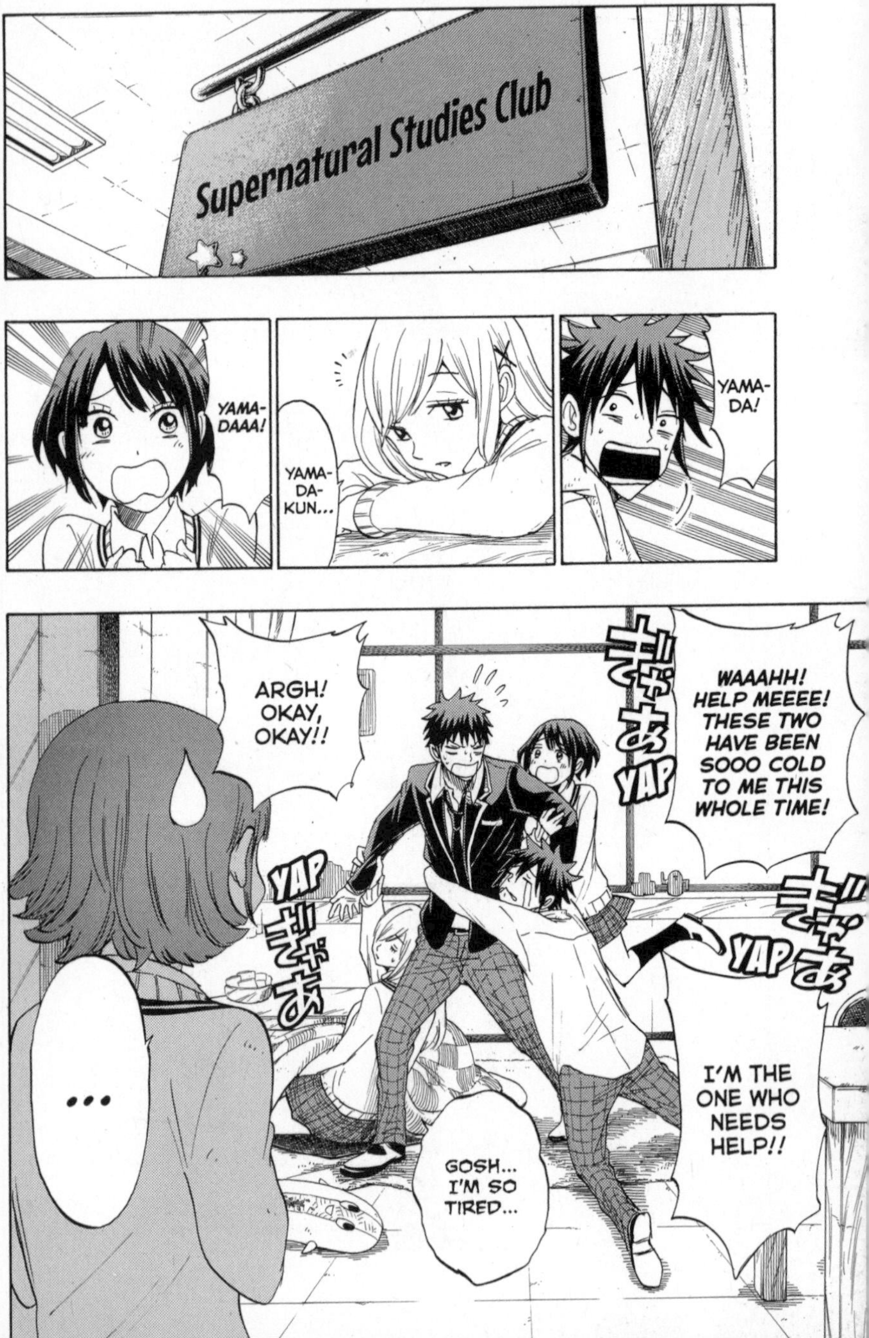
Supernatural Studies Club
YAMA-DA!
YAMA-DA-KUN...
YAMA-DAAA!
ぎゃあ YAP
WAAAHH! HELP MEEEE! THESE TWO HAVE BEEN SOOO COLD TO ME THIS WHOLE TIME!
ARGH! OKAY, OKAY!!
ぎゃあ YAP
I'M THE ONE WHO NEEDS HELP!!
YAP ぎゃあ
GOSH... I'M SO TIRED...
...

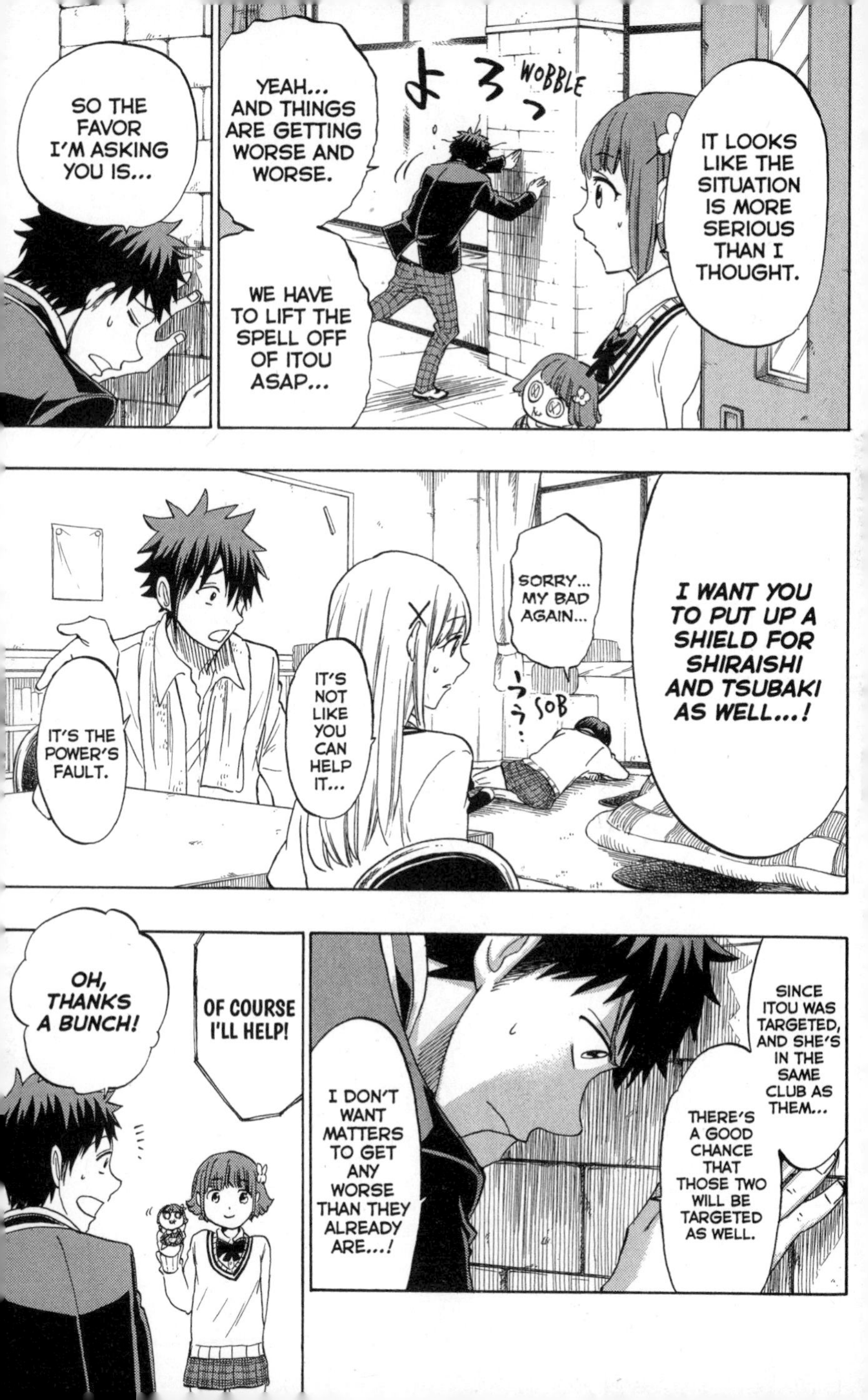
IT LOOKS LIKE THE SITUATION IS MORE SERIOUS THAN I THOUGHT.
WOBBLE
YEAH... AND THINGS ARE GETTING WORSE AND WORSE.
WE HAVE TO LIFT THE SPELL OFF OF ITOU ASAP...
SO THE FAVOR I'M ASKING YOU IS...
I WANT YOU TO PUT UP A SHIELD FOR SHIRAISHI AND TSUBAKI AS WELL...!
SORRY... MY BAD AGAIN...
SOB
IT'S NOT LIKE YOU CAN HELP IT...
IT'S THE POWER'S FAULT.
SINCE ITOU WAS TARGETED, AND SHE'S IN THE SAME CLUB AS THEM...
THERE'S A GOOD CHANCE THAT THOSE TWO WILL BE TARGETED AS WELL.
I DON'T WANT MATTERS TO GET ANY WORSE THAN THEY ALREADY ARE...!
OF COURSE I'LL HELP!
OH, THANKS A BUNCH!

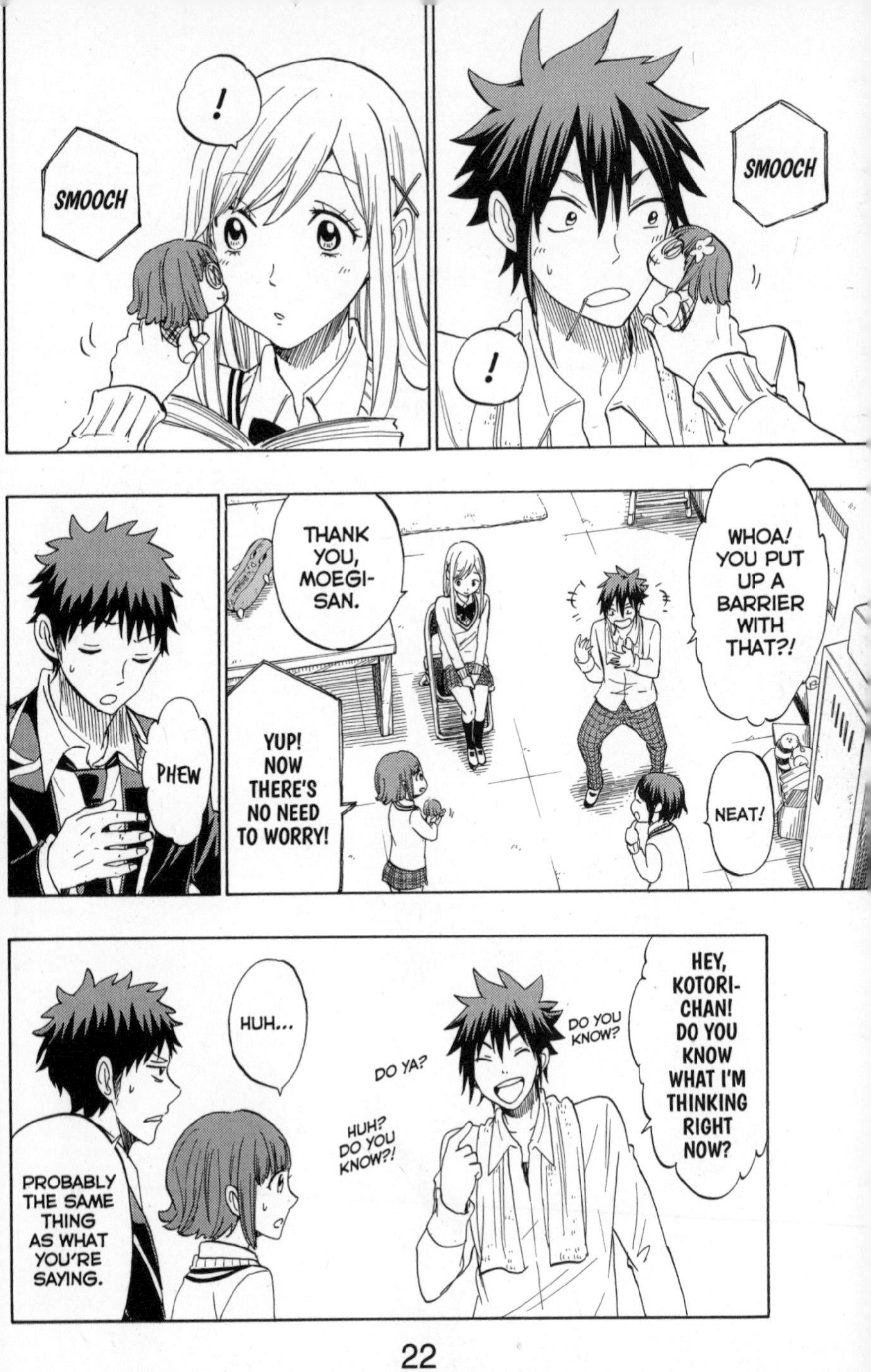
SMOOCH
!
!
SMOOCH
WHOA! YOU PUT UP A BARRIER WITH THAT?!
THANK YOU, MOEGI-SAN.
NEAT!
YUP! NOW THERE'S NO NEED TO WORRY!
PHEW
HEY, KOTORI-CHAN! DO YOU KNOW WHAT I'M THINKING RIGHT NOW?
DO YOU KNOW?
DO YA?
HUH? DO YOU KNOW?!
HUH...
PROBABLY THE SAME THING AS WHAT YOU'RE SAYING.

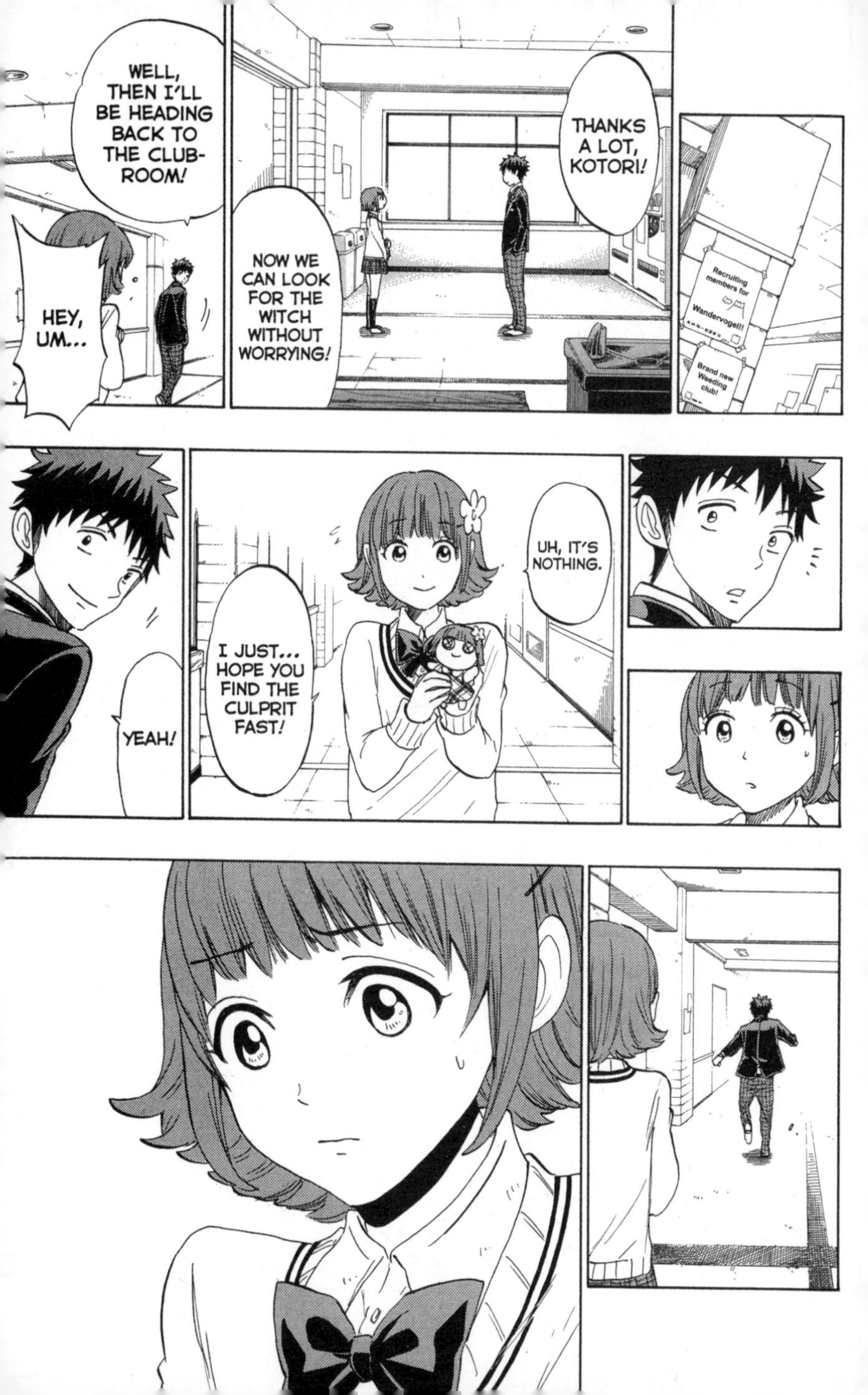
Recruiting members for
Wandervogel!!
Brand new Weeding club!
THANKS A LOT, KOTORI!
NOW WE CAN LOOK FOR THE WITCH WITHOUT WORRYING!
WELL, THEN I'LL BE HEADING BACK TO THE CLUB-ROOM!
HEY, UM...
UH, IT'S NOTHING.
I JUST... HOPE YOU FIND THE CULPRIT FAST!
YEAH!

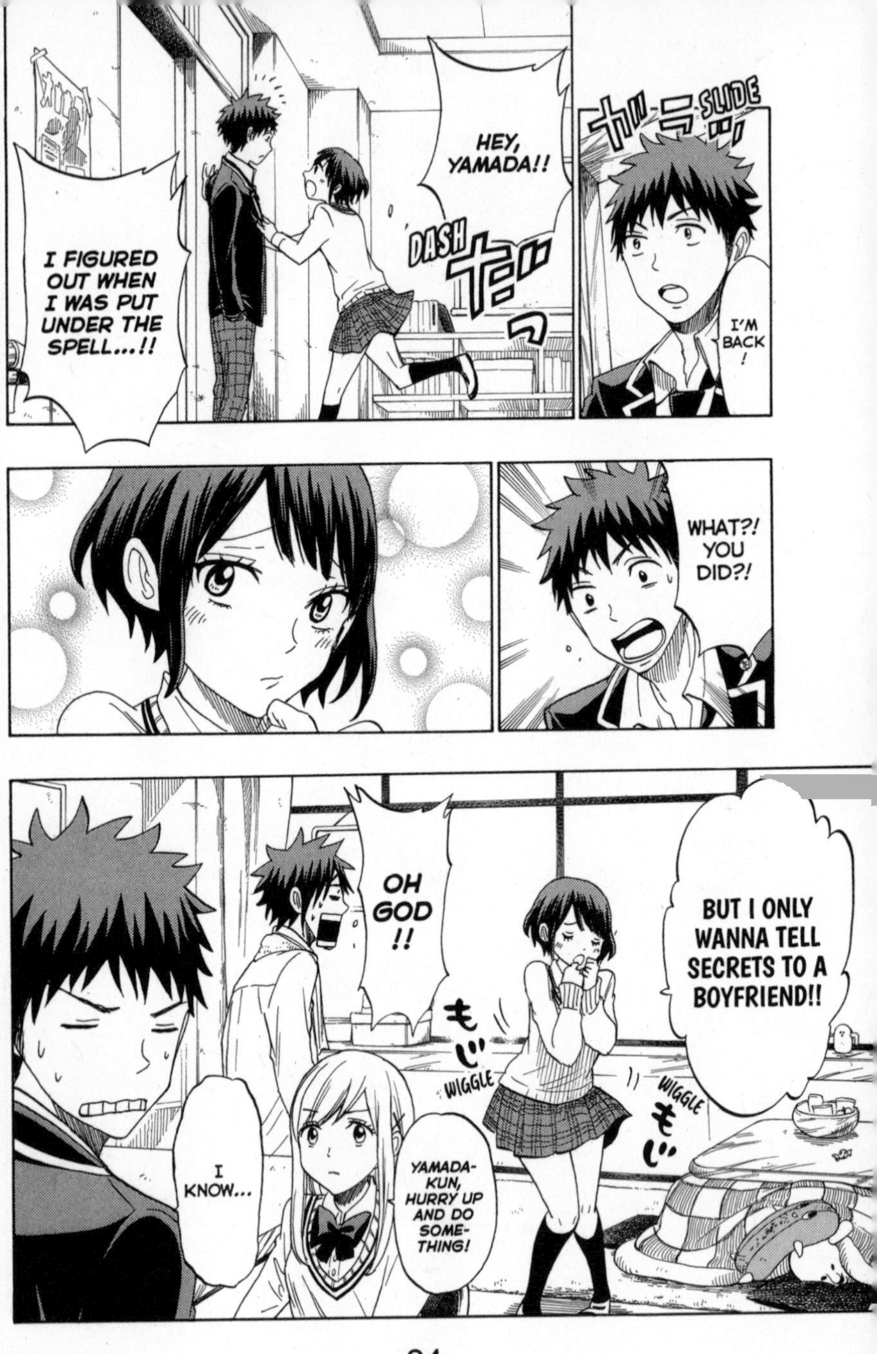
SLIDE
I'M BACK!
HEY, YAMADA!!
DASH
I FIGURED OUT WHEN I WAS PUT UNDER THE SPELL...!!
WHAT?! YOU DID?!
BUT I ONLY WANNA TELL SECRETS TO A BOYFRIEND!!
WIGGLE
WIGGLE
OH GOD!!
YAMADA-KUN, HURRY UP AND DO SOME-THING!
I KNOW...

CHAPTER 130: A lot on my mind!

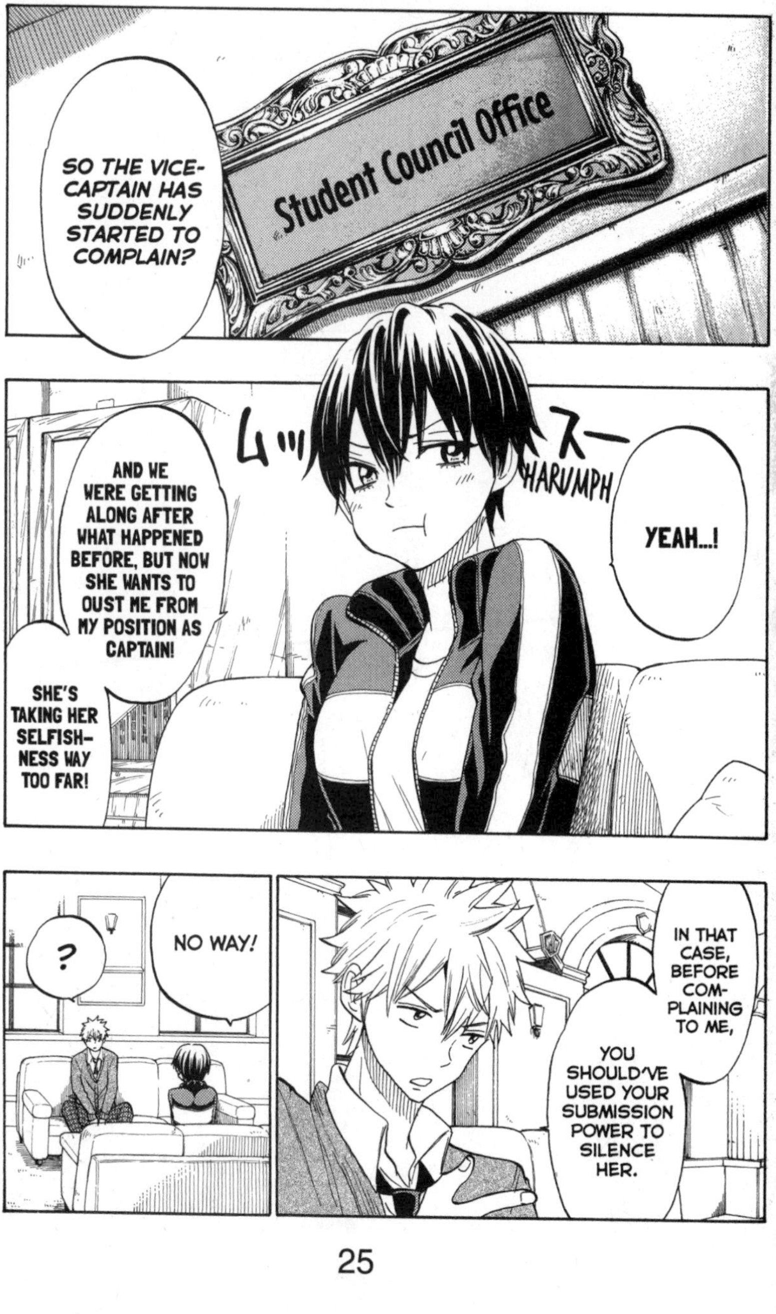
Student Council Office
SO THE VICE-CAPTAIN HAS SUDDENLY STARTED TO COMPLAIN?
スー
HARUMPH
YEAH...!
ムッ
AND WE WERE GETTING ALONG AFTER WHAT HAPPENED BEFORE, BUT NOW SHE WANTS TO OUST ME FROM MY POSITION AS CAPTAIN!
SHE'S TAKING HER SELFISHNESS WAY TOO FAR!
IN THAT CASE, BEFORE COMPLAINING TO ME,
YOU SHOULD'VE USED YOUR SUBMISSION POWER TO SILENCE HER.
NO WAY!
?

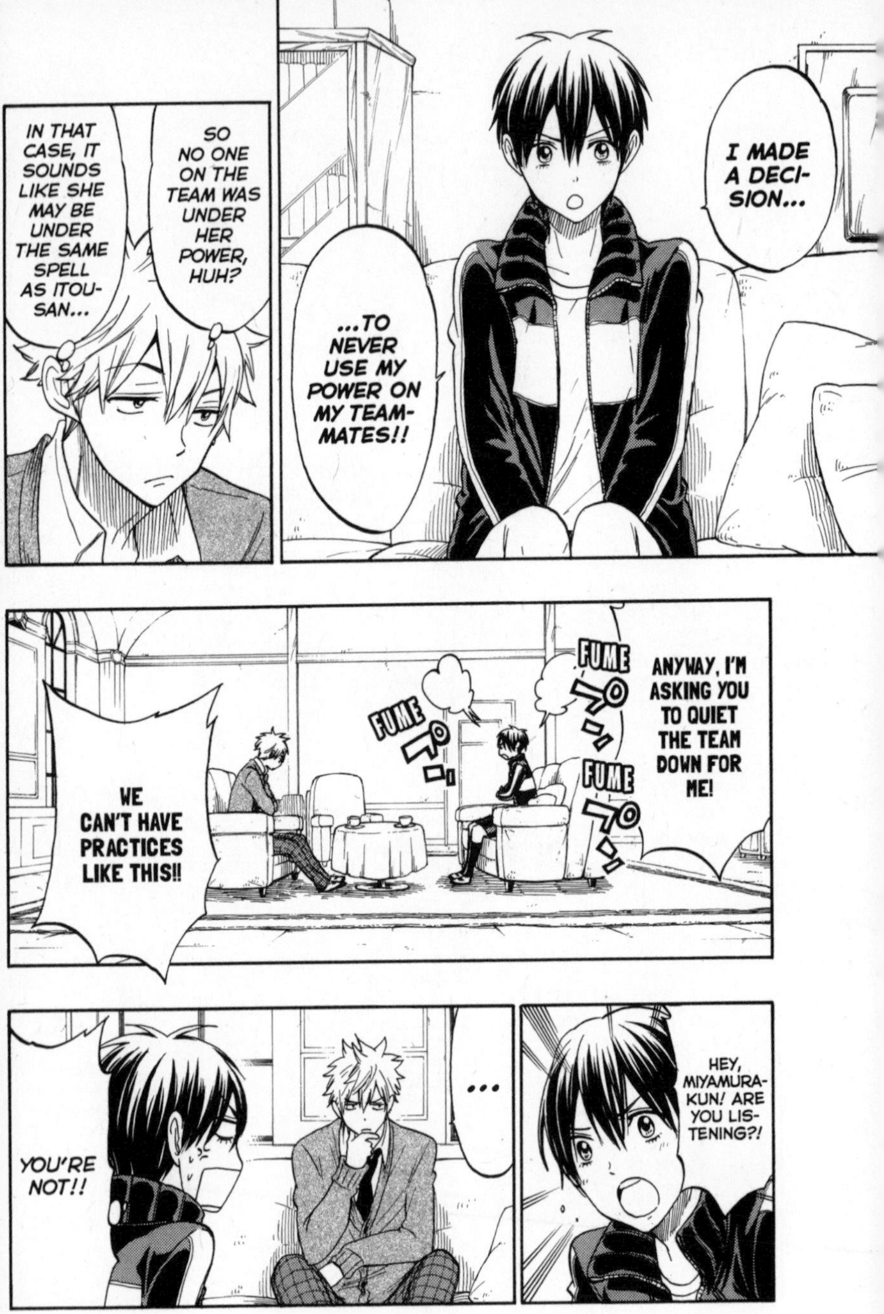
I MADE A DECISION...
...TO NEVER USE MY POWER ON MY TEAMMATES!!
SO NO ONE ON THE TEAM WAS UNDER HER POWER, HUH?
IN THAT CASE, IT SOUNDS LIKE SHE MAY BE UNDER THE SAME SPELL AS ITOU-SAN...
ANYWAY, I'M ASKING YOU TO QUIET THE TEAM DOWN FOR ME!
FUME
FUME
FUME
WE CAN'T HAVE PRACTICES LIKE THIS!!
HEY, MIYAMURA-KUN! ARE YOU LISTENING?!
...
YOU'RE NOT!!

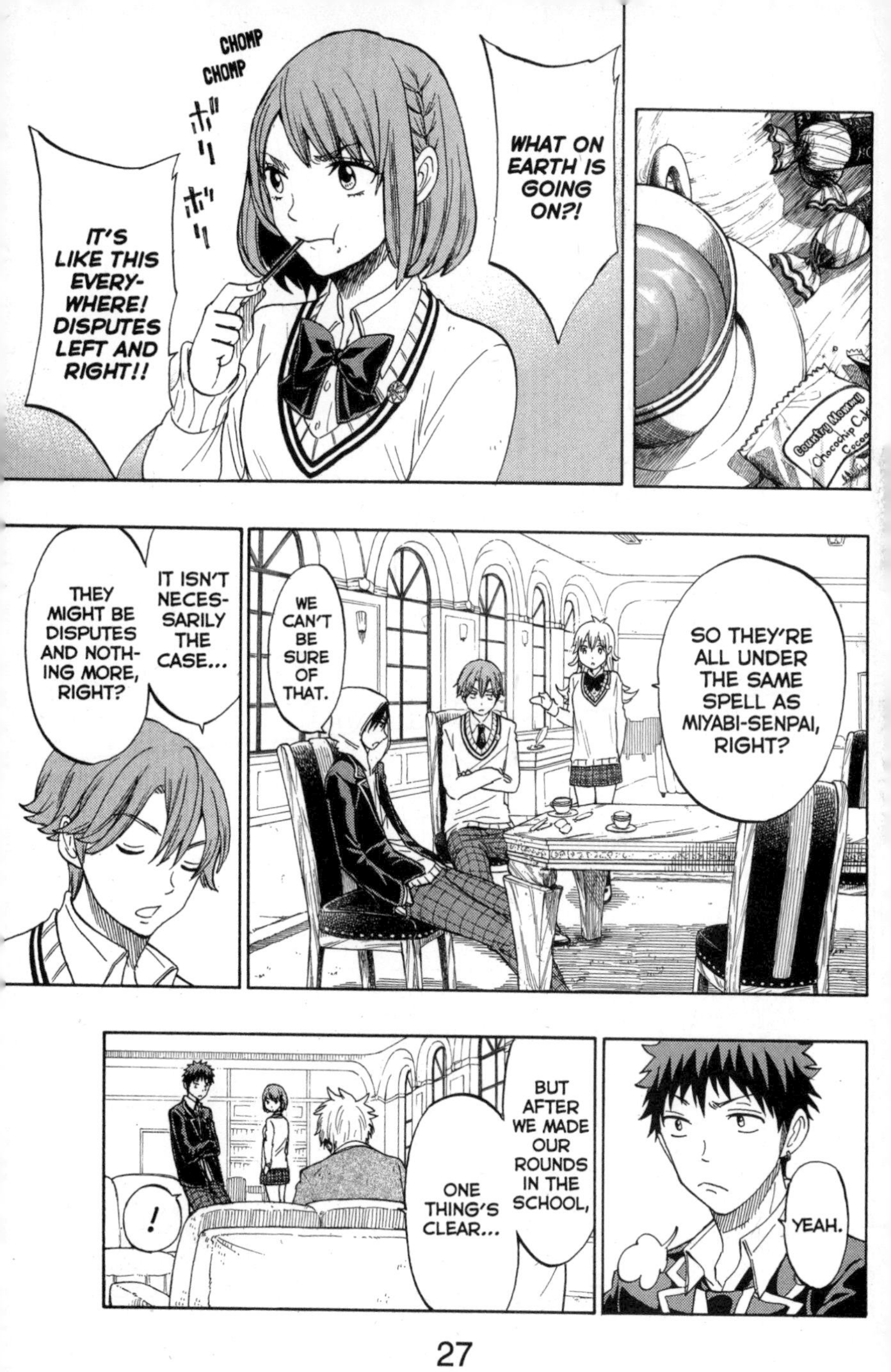
WHAT ON EARTH IS GOING ON?!
CHOMP CHOMP
ボリ ボリ
IT'S LIKE THIS EVERYWHERE! DISPUTES LEFT AND RIGHT!!
SO THEY'RE ALL UNDER THE SAME SPELL AS MIYABI-SENPAI, RIGHT?
WE CAN'T BE SURE OF THAT.
IT ISN'T NECESSARILY THE CASE...
THEY MIGHT BE DISPUTES AND NOTHING MORE, RIGHT?
YEAH.
BUT AFTER WE MADE OUR ROUNDS IN THE SCHOOL,
ONE THING'S CLEAR...
!

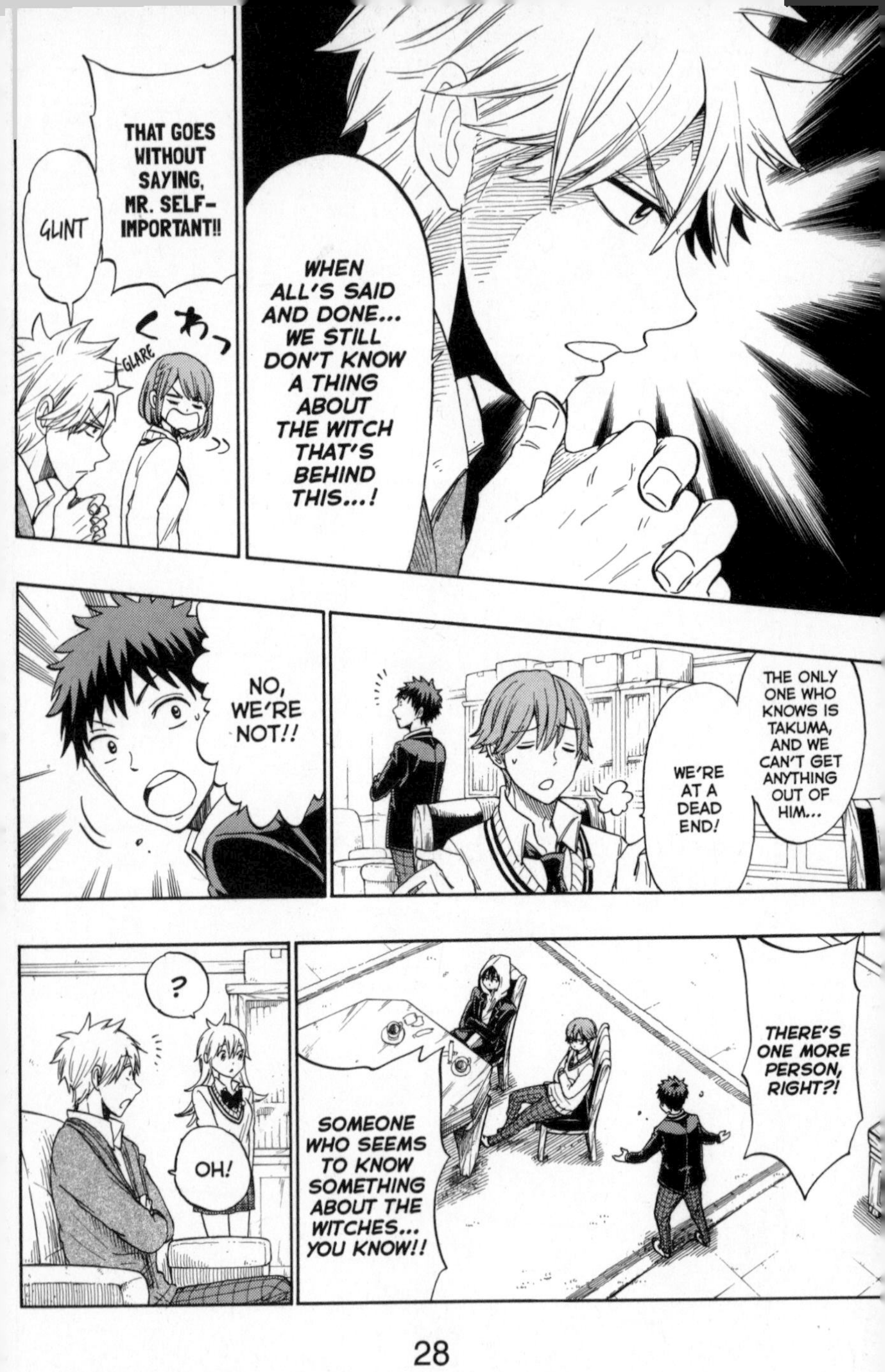
WHEN ALL'S SAID AND DONE... WE STILL DON'T KNOW A THING ABOUT THE WITCH THAT'S BEHIND THIS...!
THAT GOES WITHOUT SAYING, MR. SELF-IMPORTANT!!
GLINT
くわっ
GLARE
THE ONLY ONE WHO KNOWS IS TAKUMA, AND WE CAN'T GET ANYTHING OUT OF HIM...
WE'RE AT A DEAD END!
NO, WE'RE NOT!!
THERE'S ONE MORE PERSON, RIGHT?!
SOMEONE WHO SEEMS TO KNOW SOMETHING ABOUT THE WITCHES... YOU KNOW!!
?
OH!

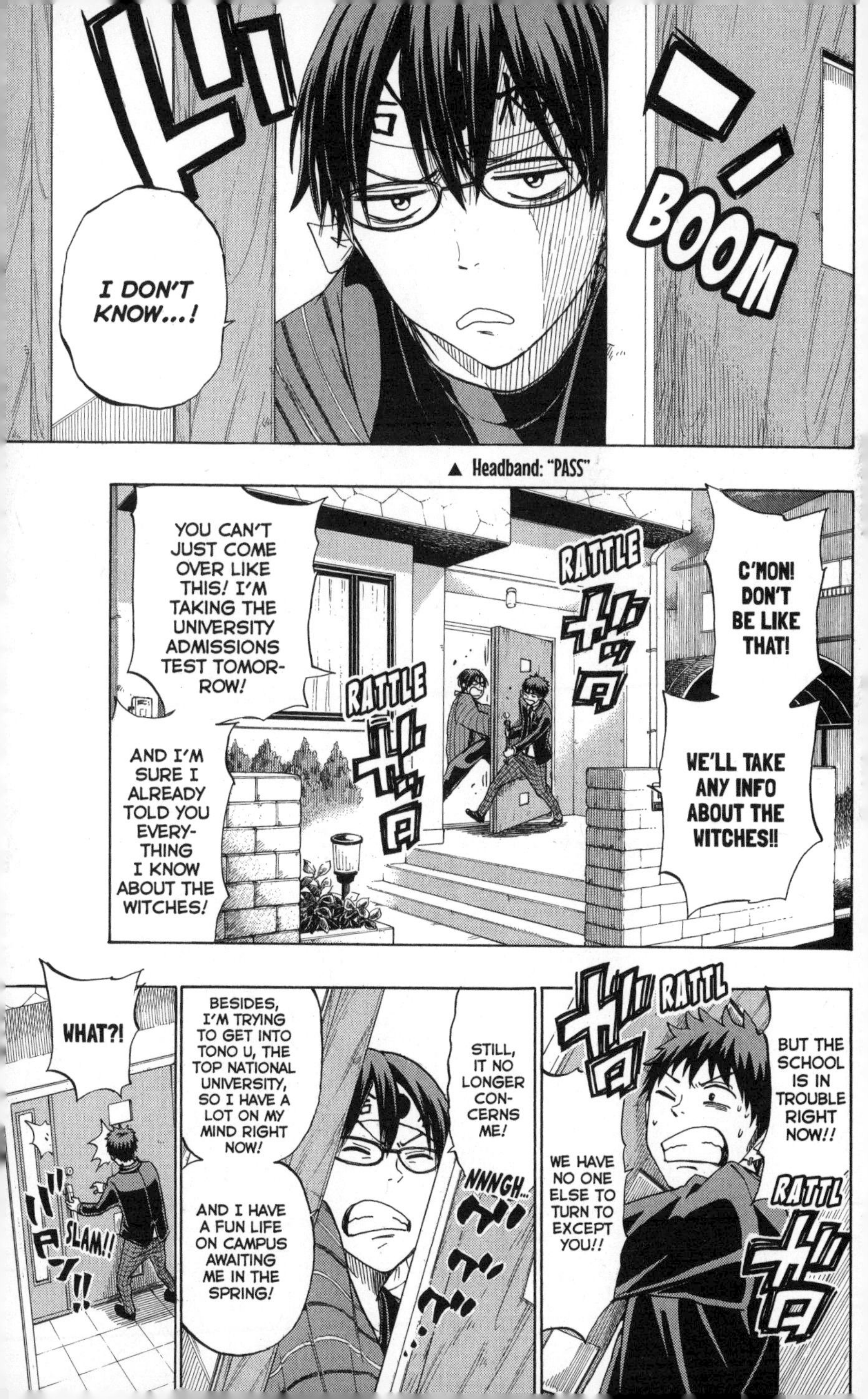
BOOM
I DON'T KNOW...!
▲ Headband: "PASS"
C'MON! DON'T BE LIKE THAT!
RATTLE
YOU CAN'T JUST COME OVER LIKE THIS! I'M TAKING THE UNIVERSITY ADMISSIONS TEST TOMOR-ROW!
RATTLE
WE'LL TAKE ANY INFO ABOUT THE WITCHES!!
AND I'M SURE I ALREADY TOLD YOU EVERY-THING I KNOW ABOUT THE WITCHES!
RATTL
BUT THE SCHOOL IS IN TROUBLE RIGHT NOW!!
RATTL
WE HAVE NO ONE ELSE TO TURN TO EXCEPT YOU!!
STILL, IT NO LONGER CON-CERNS ME!
BESIDES, I'M TRYING TO GET INTO TONO U, THE TOP NATIONAL UNIVERSITY, SO I HAVE A LOT ON MY MIND RIGHT NOW!
NNNGH...
AND I HAVE A FUN LIFE ON CAMPUS AWAITING ME IN THE SPRING!
WHAT?!
SLAM!!

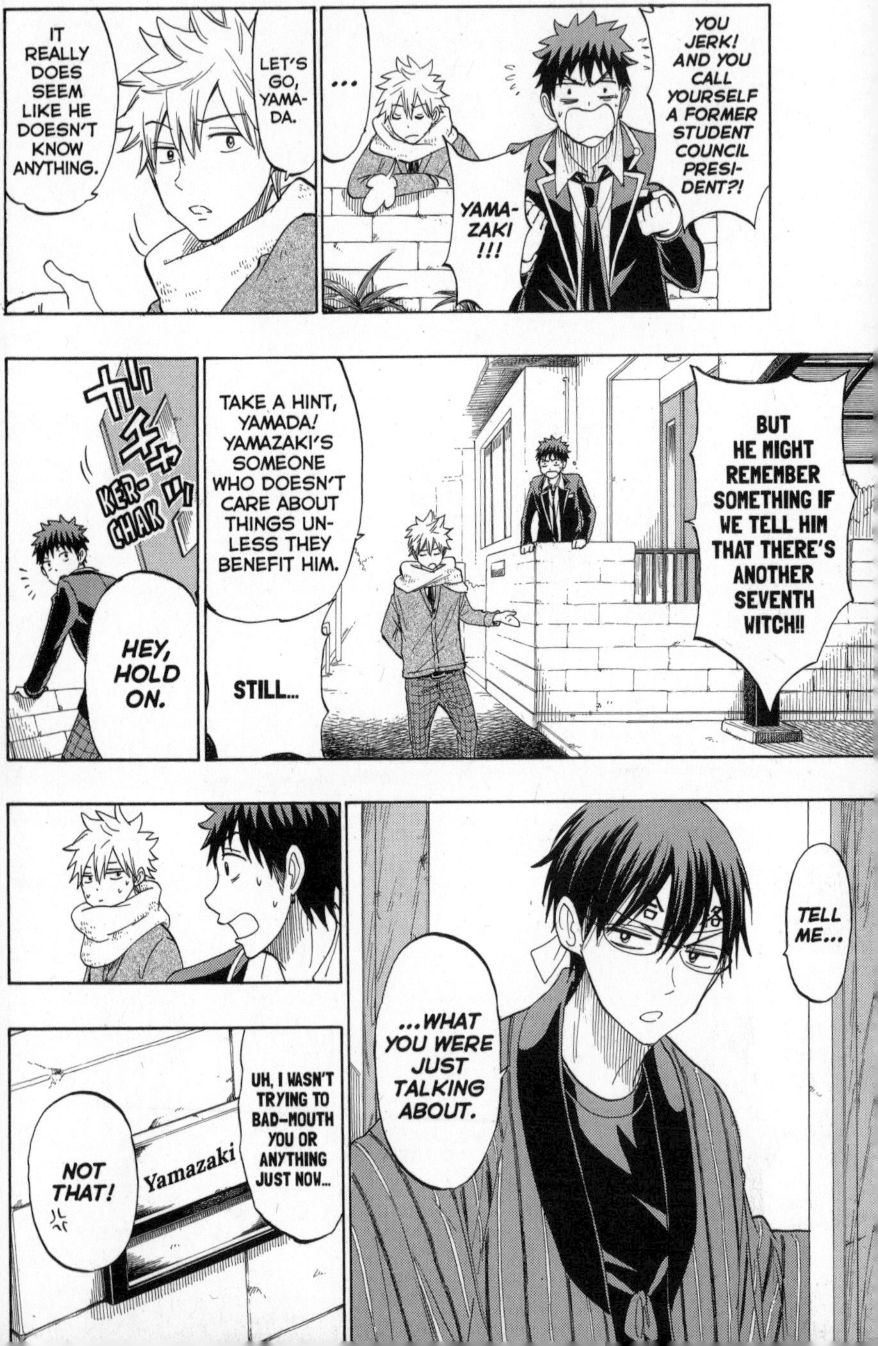
YOU JERK! AND YOU CALL YOURSELF A FORMER STUDENT COUNCIL PRESIDENT?!
YAMAZAKI!!!
...
LET'S GO, YAMADA.
IT REALLY DOES SEEM LIKE HE DOESN'T KNOW ANYTHING.
BUT HE MIGHT REMEMBER SOMETHING IF WE TELL HIM THAT THERE'S ANOTHER SEVENTH WITCH!!
TAKE A HINT, YAMADA! YAMAZAKI'S SOMEONE WHO DOESN'T CARE ABOUT THINGS UNLESS THEY BENEFIT HIM.
STILL...
KER-CHAK
HEY, HOLD ON.
TELL ME...
...WHAT YOU WERE JUST TALKING ABOUT.
UH, I WASN'T TRYING TO BAD-MOUTH YOU OR ANYTHING JUST NOW...
Yamazaki
NOT THAT!

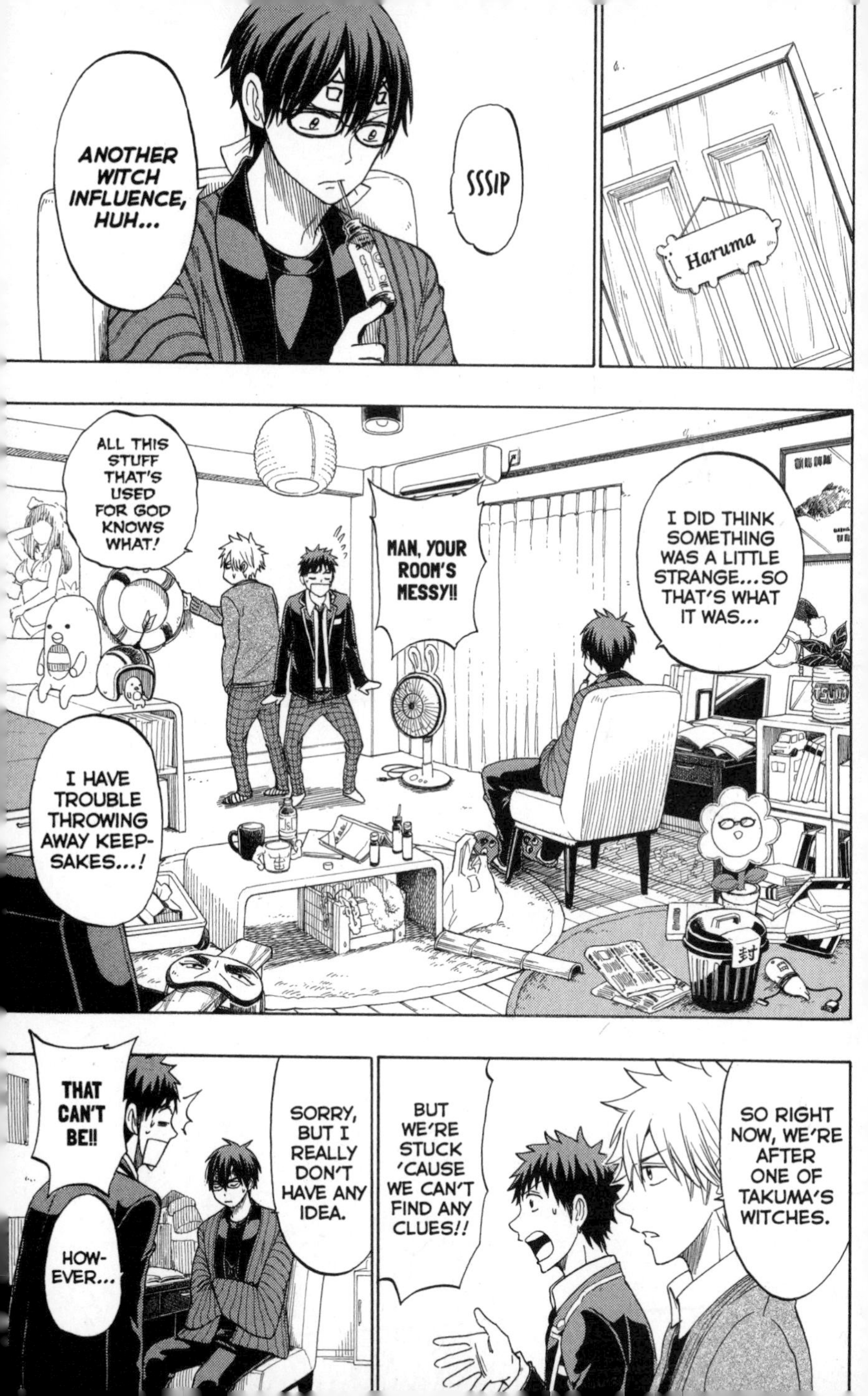
Haruma
SSSIP
ANOTHER WITCH INFLUENCE, HUH...
I DID THINK SOMETHING WAS A LITTLE STRANGE...SO THAT'S WHAT IT WAS...
MAN, YOUR ROOM'S MESSY!!
ALL THIS STUFF THAT'S USED FOR GOD KNOWS WHAT!
I HAVE TROUBLE THROWING AWAY KEEP-SAKES...!
SO RIGHT NOW, WE'RE AFTER ONE OF TAKUMA'S WITCHES.
BUT WE'RE STUCK 'CAUSE WE CAN'T FIND ANY CLUES!!
SORRY, BUT I REALLY DON'T HAVE ANY IDEA.
THAT CAN'T BE!!
HOW-EVER...

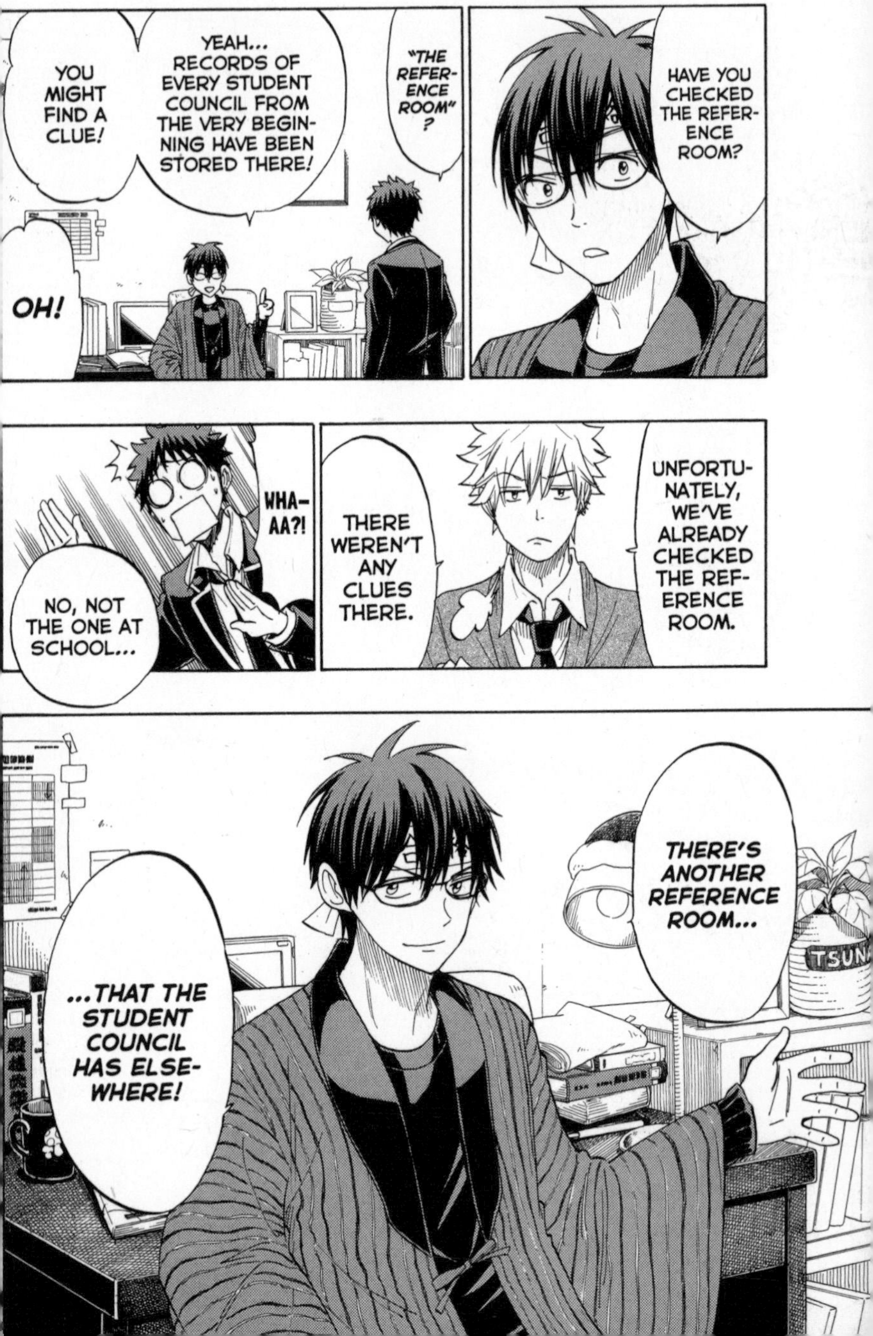
HAVE YOU CHECKED THE REFERENCE ROOM?
"THE REFERENCE ROOM"?
YEAH... RECORDS OF EVERY STUDENT COUNCIL FROM THE VERY BEGINNING HAVE BEEN STORED THERE!
YOU MIGHT FIND A CLUE!
OH!
UNFORTUNATELY, WE'VE ALREADY CHECKED THE REFERENCE ROOM.
THERE WEREN'T ANY CLUES THERE.
WHAAA?!
NO, NOT THE ONE AT SCHOOL...
THERE'S ANOTHER REFERENCE ROOM...
TSUN
...THAT THE STUDENT COUNCIL HAS ELSEWHERE!

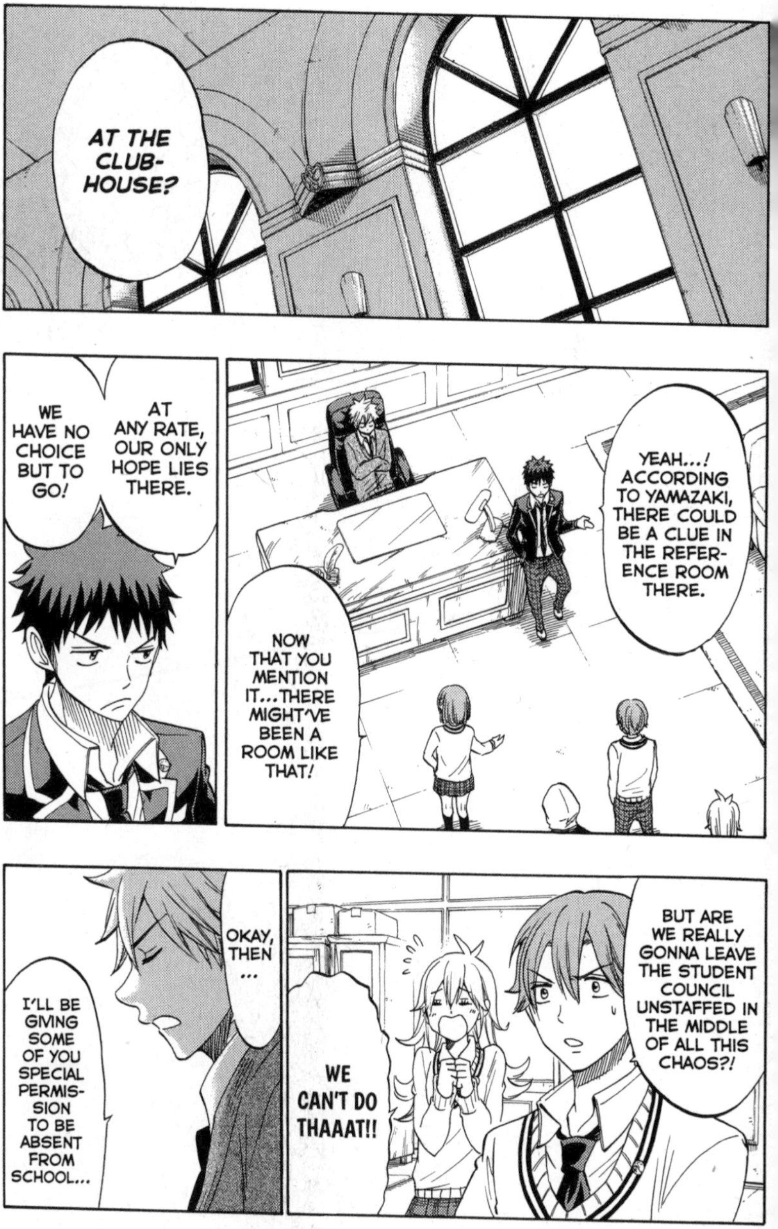
AT THE CLUB-HOUSE?
YEAH...! ACCORDING TO YAMAZAKI, THERE COULD BE A CLUE IN THE REFER-ENCE ROOM THERE.
NOW THAT YOU MENTION IT...THERE MIGHT'VE BEEN A ROOM LIKE THAT!
AT ANY RATE, OUR ONLY HOPE LIES THERE.
WE HAVE NO CHOICE BUT TO GO!
BUT ARE WE REALLY GONNA LEAVE THE STUDENT COUNCIL UNSTAFFED IN THE MIDDLE OF ALL THIS CHAOS?!
WE CAN'T DO THAAAT!!
OKAY, THEN...
I'LL BE GIVING SOME OF YOU SPECIAL PERMIS-SION TO BE ABSENT FROM SCHOOL...

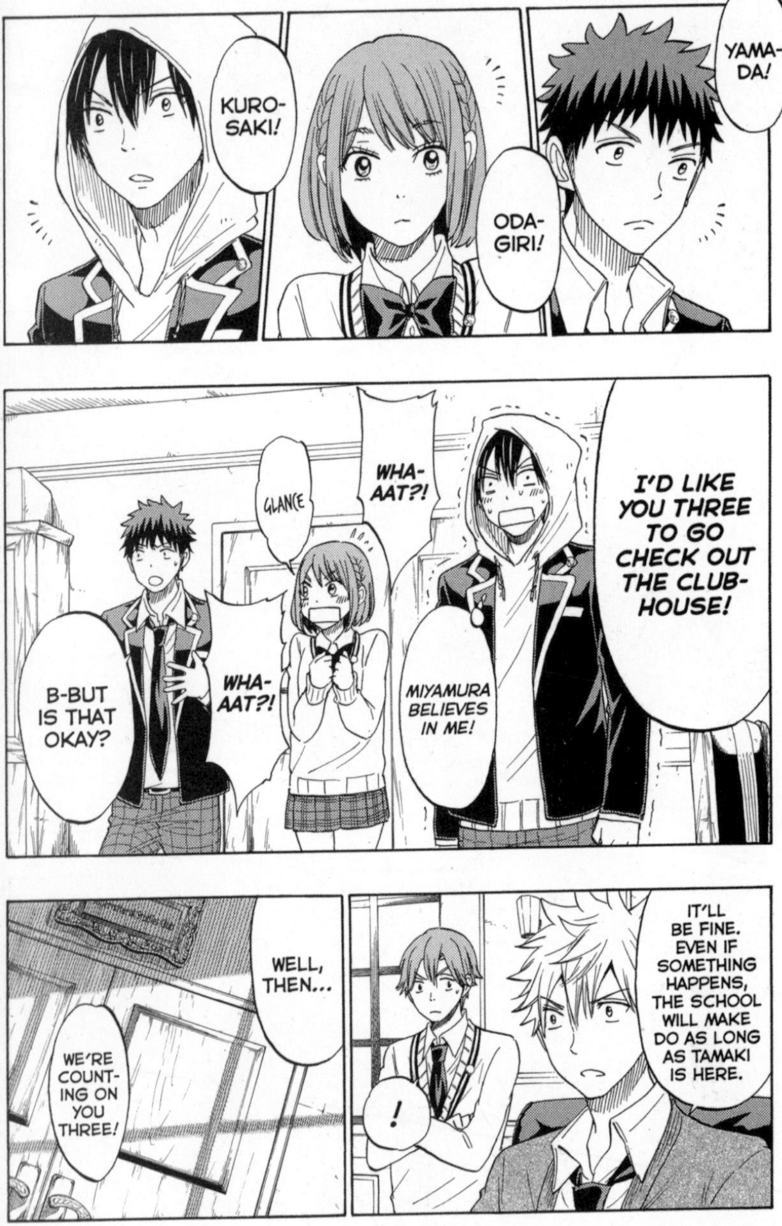
YAMA-
DA!
ODA-
GIRI!
KURO-
SAKI!
I'D LIKE YOU THREE TO GO CHECK OUT THE CLUB-HOUSE!
WHA-
AAT?!
MIYAMURA BELIEVES IN ME!
GLANCE
WHA-
AAT?!
B-BUT IS THAT OKAY?
IT'LL BE FINE. EVEN IF SOMETHING HAPPENS, THE SCHOOL WILL MAKE DO AS LONG AS TAMAKI IS HERE.
!
WELL, THEN...
WE'RE COUNTING ON YOU THREE!

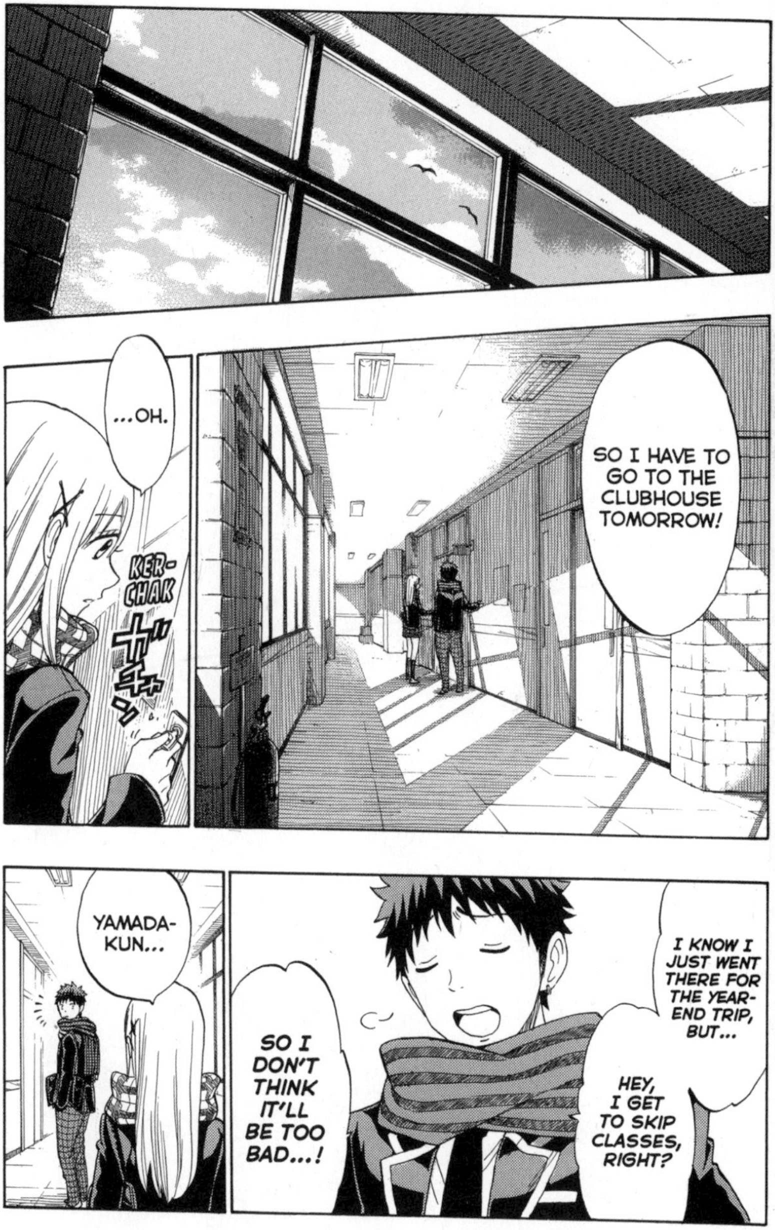
SO I HAVE TO GO TO THE CLUBHOUSE TOMORROW!
...OH.
KER-CHAK
ガチャッ
I KNOW I JUST WENT THERE FOR THE YEAR-END TRIP, BUT...
HEY, I GET TO SKIP CLASSES, RIGHT?
SO I DON'T THINK IT'LL BE TOO BAD...!
YAMADA-KUN...

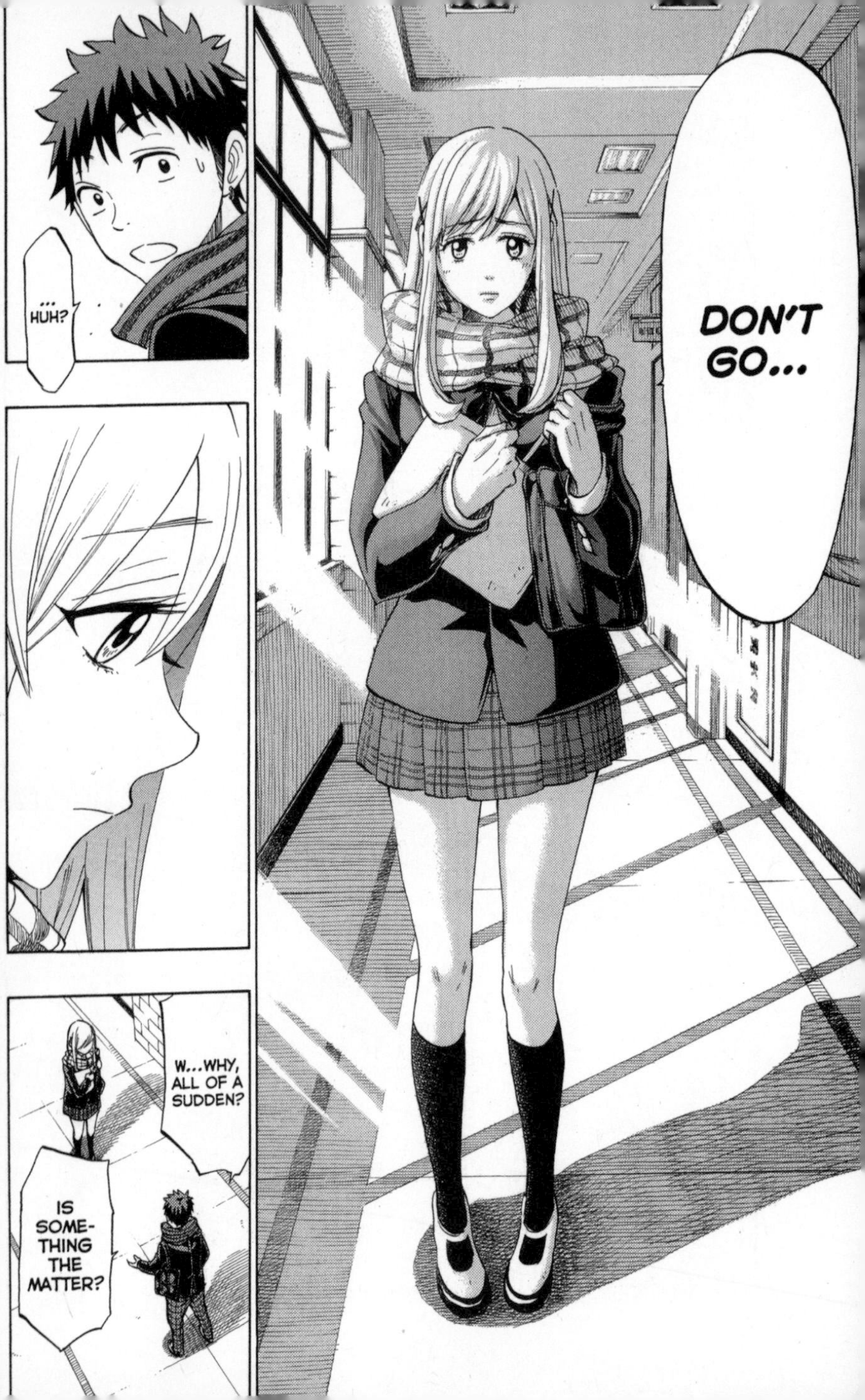
DON'T GO...
... HUH?
W...WHY, ALL OF A SUDDEN?
IS SOME-THING THE MATTER?

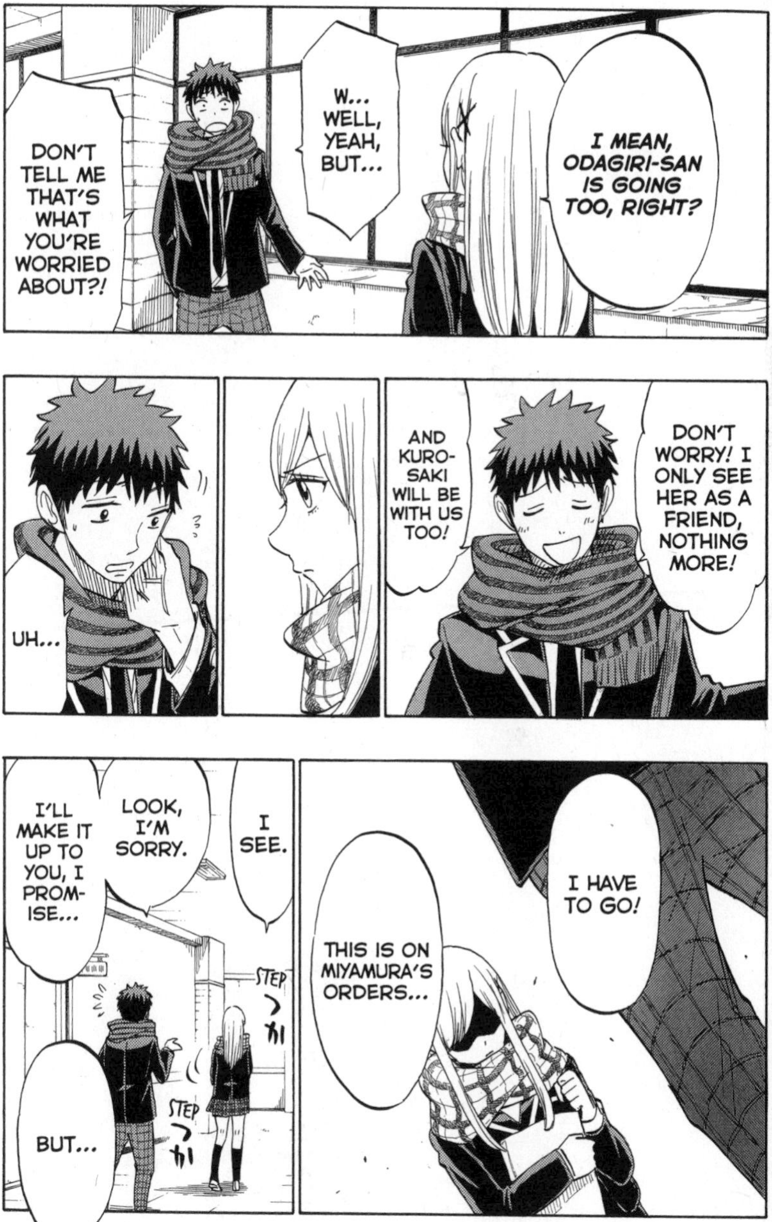
I MEAN, ODAGIRI-SAN IS GOING TOO, RIGHT?
W... WELL, YEAH, BUT...
DON'T TELL ME THAT'S WHAT YOU'RE WORRIED ABOUT?!
DON'T WORRY! I ONLY SEE HER AS A FRIEND, NOTHING MORE!
AND KURO-SAKI WILL BE WITH US TOO!
UH...
I HAVE TO GO!
THIS IS ON MIYAMURA'S ORDERS...
I SEE.
LOOK, I'M SORRY.
I'LL MAKE IT UP TO YOU, I PROMISE...
STEP
STEP
BUT...

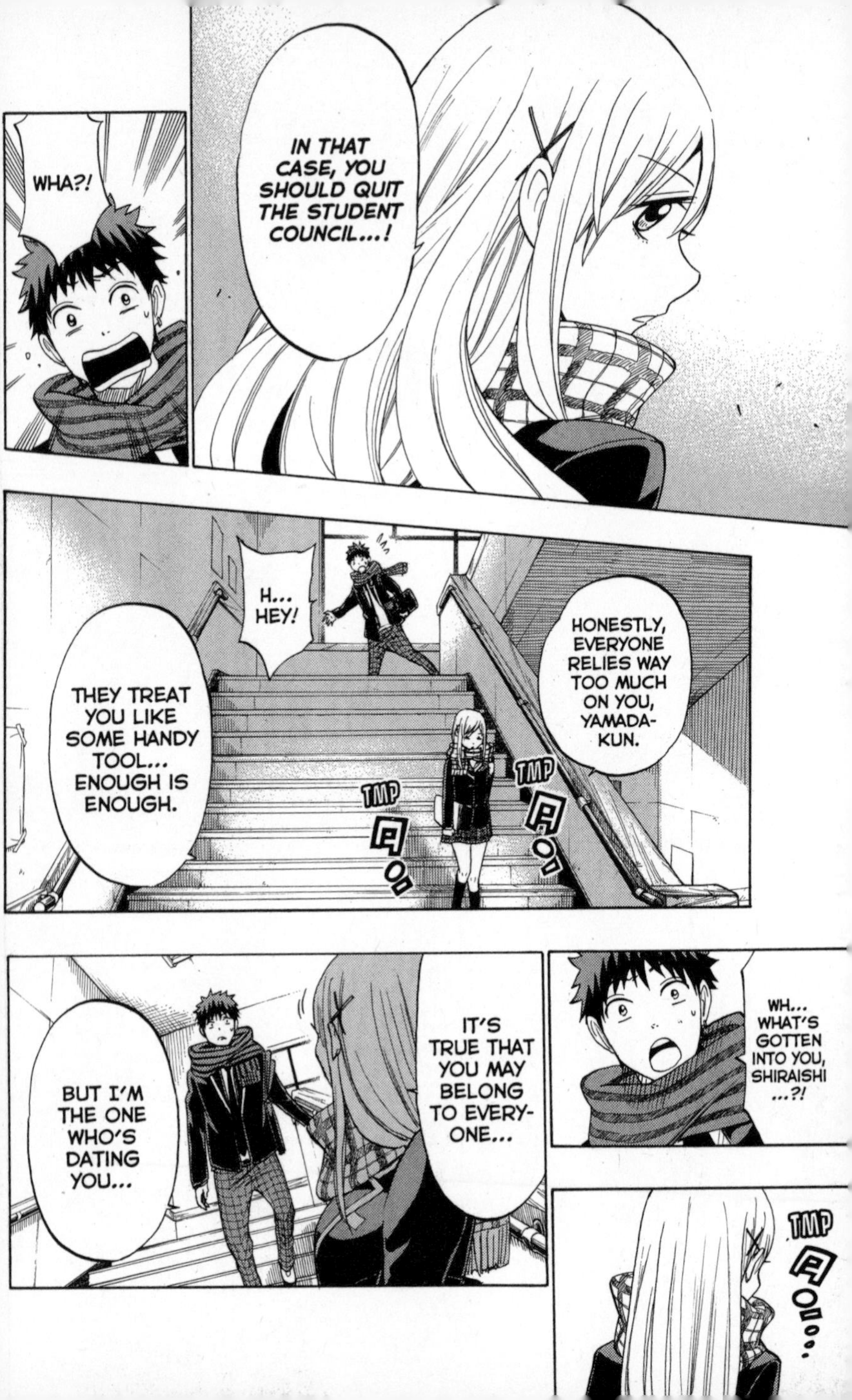
IN THAT CASE, YOU SHOULD QUIT THE STUDENT COUNCIL...!
WHA?!
HONESTLY, EVERYONE RELIES WAY TOO MUCH ON YOU, YAMADA-KUN.
TMP
H... HEY!
TMP
THEY TREAT YOU LIKE SOME HANDY TOOL... ENOUGH IS ENOUGH.
WH... WHAT'S GOTTEN INTO YOU, SHIRAISHI...?!
TMP
IT'S TRUE THAT YOU MAY BELONG TO EVERY-ONE...
BUT I'M THE ONE WHO'S DATING YOU...

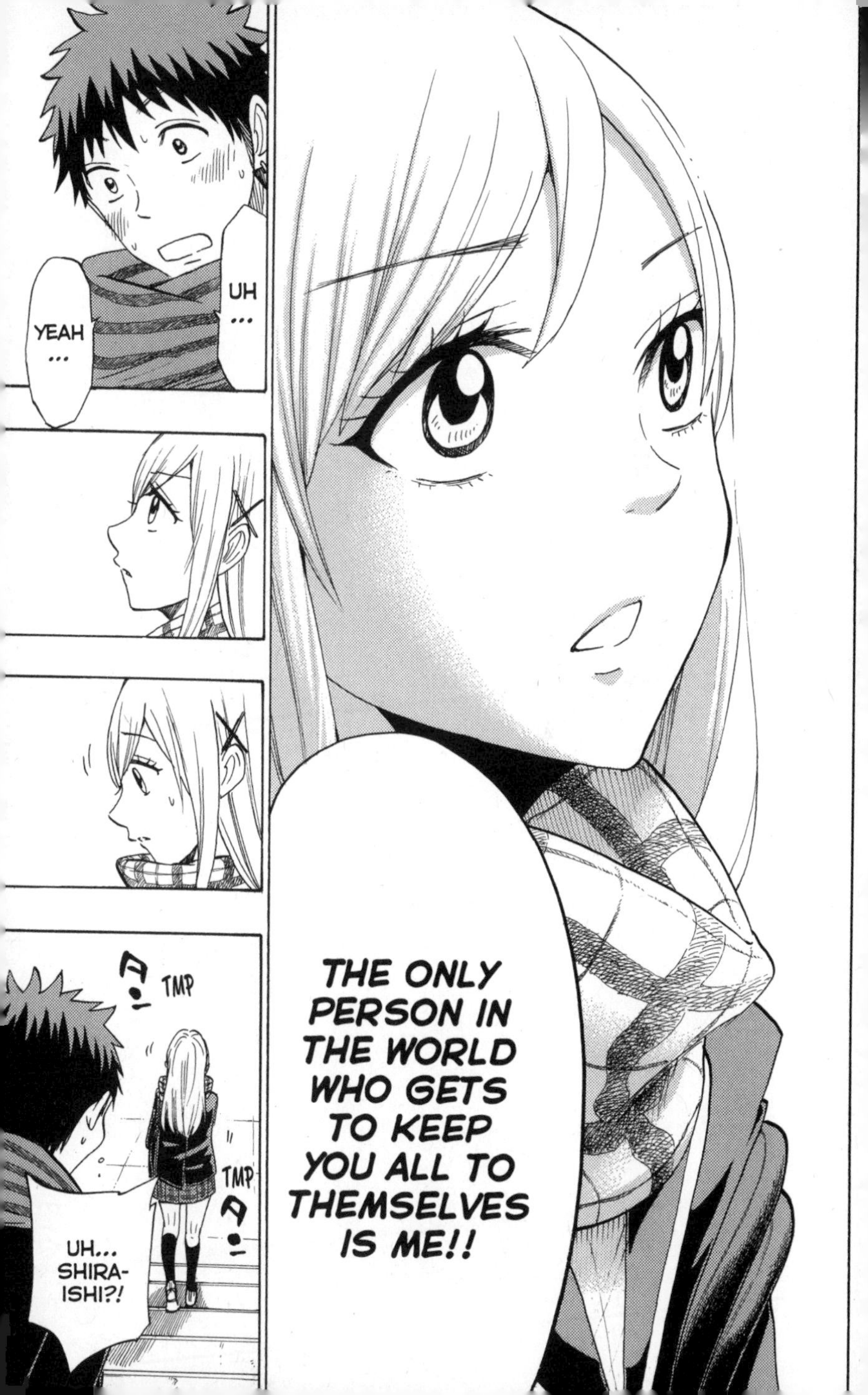
THE ONLY PERSON IN THE WORLD WHO GETS TO KEEP YOU ALL TO THEMSELVES IS ME!!
UH ...
YEAH ...
TMP
TMP
UH... SHIRA-ISHI?!

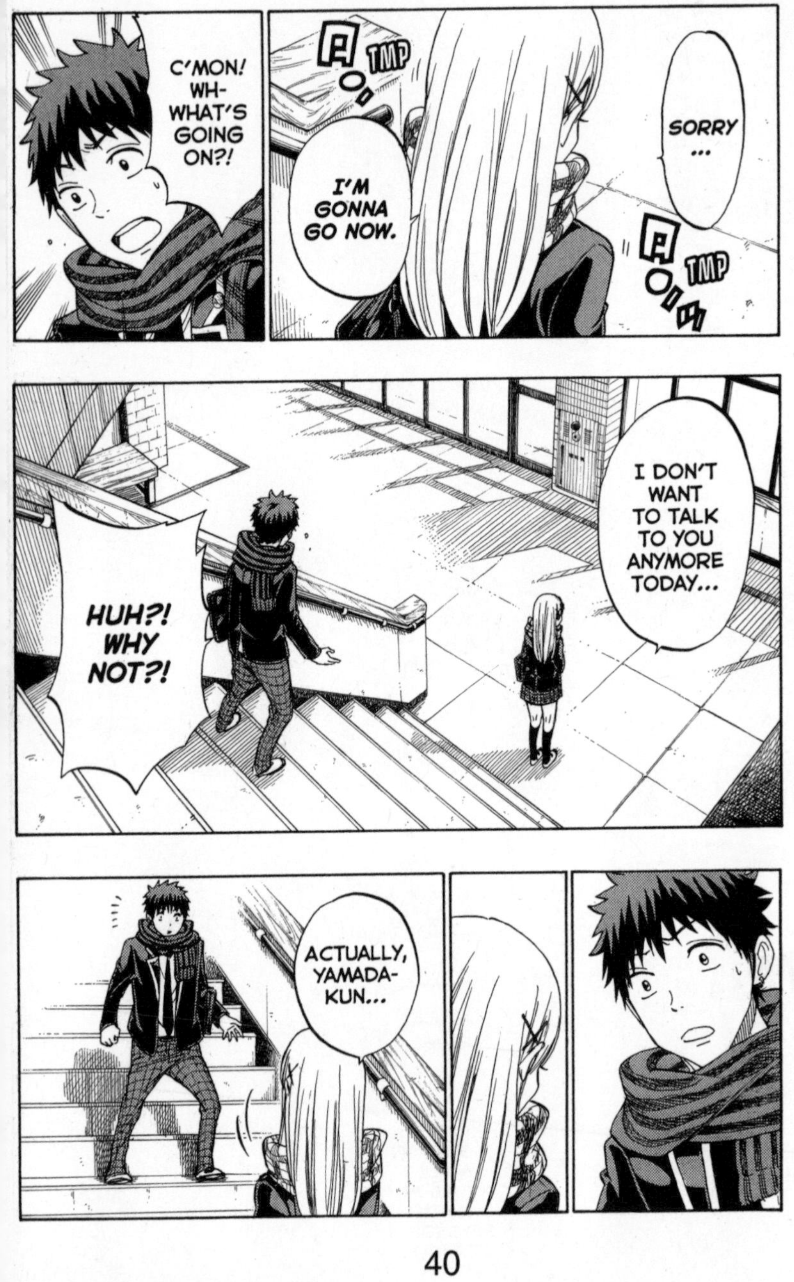
SORRY...
TMP
TMP
I'M GONNA GO NOW.
C'MON! WH-WHAT'S GOING ON?!
I DON'T WANT TO TALK TO YOU ANYMORE TODAY...
HUH?! WHY NOT?!
ACTUALLY, YAMADA-KUN...

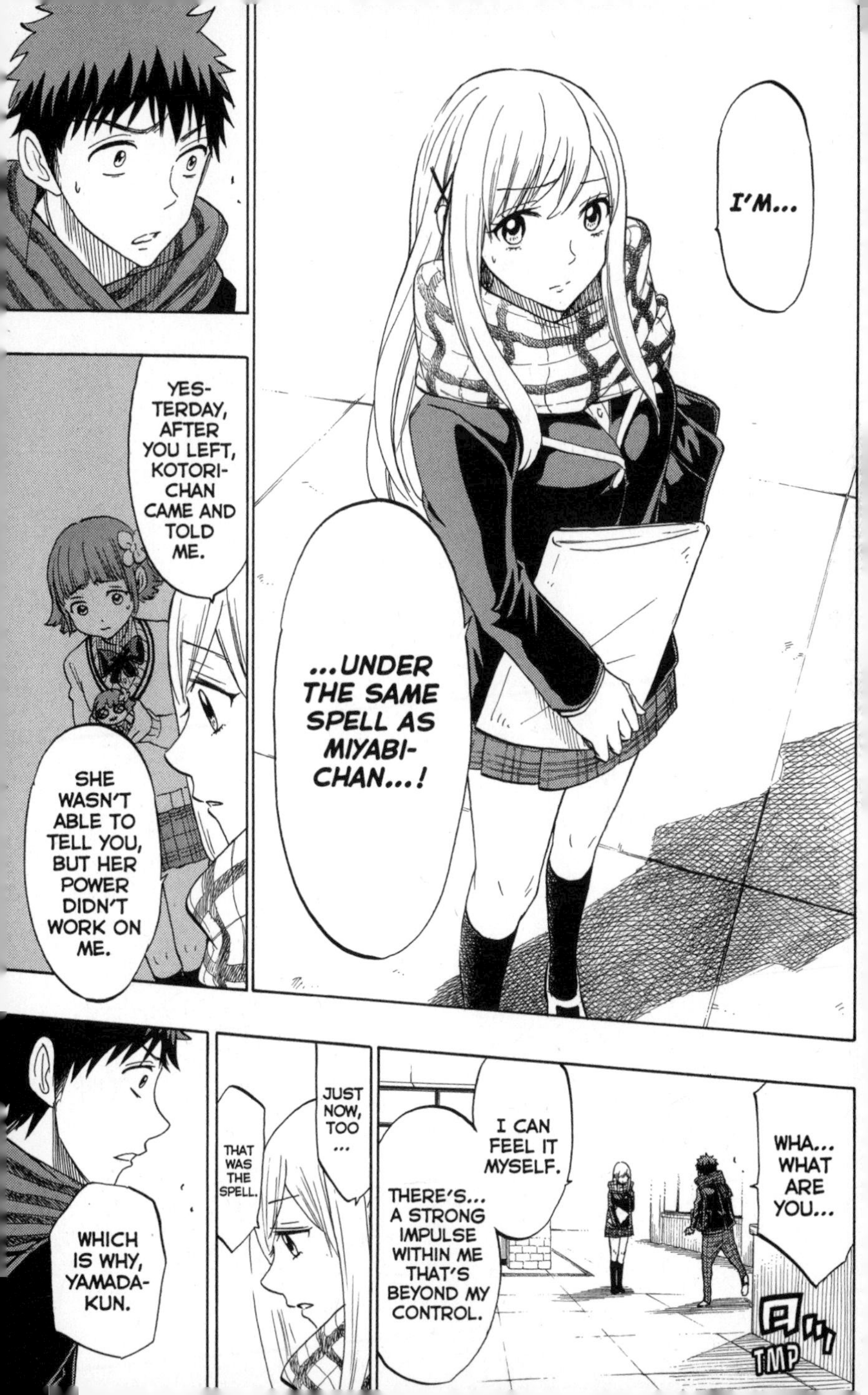
I'M...
...UNDER THE SAME SPELL AS MIYABI-CHAN...!
YESTERDAY, AFTER YOU LEFT, KOTORI-CHAN CAME AND TOLD ME.
SHE WASN'T ABLE TO TELL YOU, BUT HER POWER DIDN'T WORK ON ME.
WHA... WHAT ARE YOU...
TMP
I CAN FEEL IT MYSELF.
THERE'S... A STRONG IMPULSE WITHIN ME THAT'S BEYOND MY CONTROL.
JUST NOW, TOO...
THAT WAS THE SPELL.
WHICH IS WHY, YAMADA-KUN.

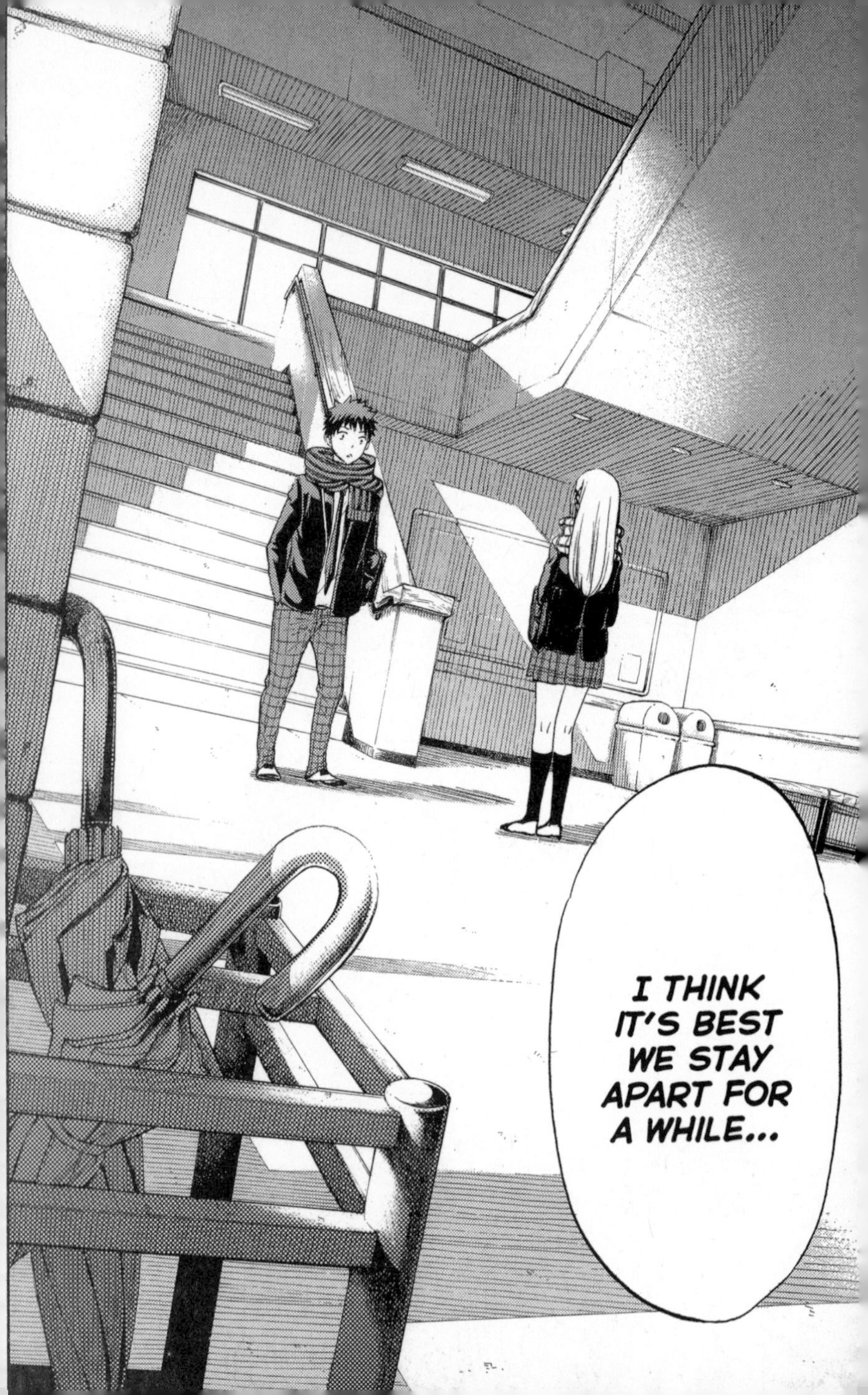
I THINK IT'S BEST WE STAY APART FOR A WHILE...

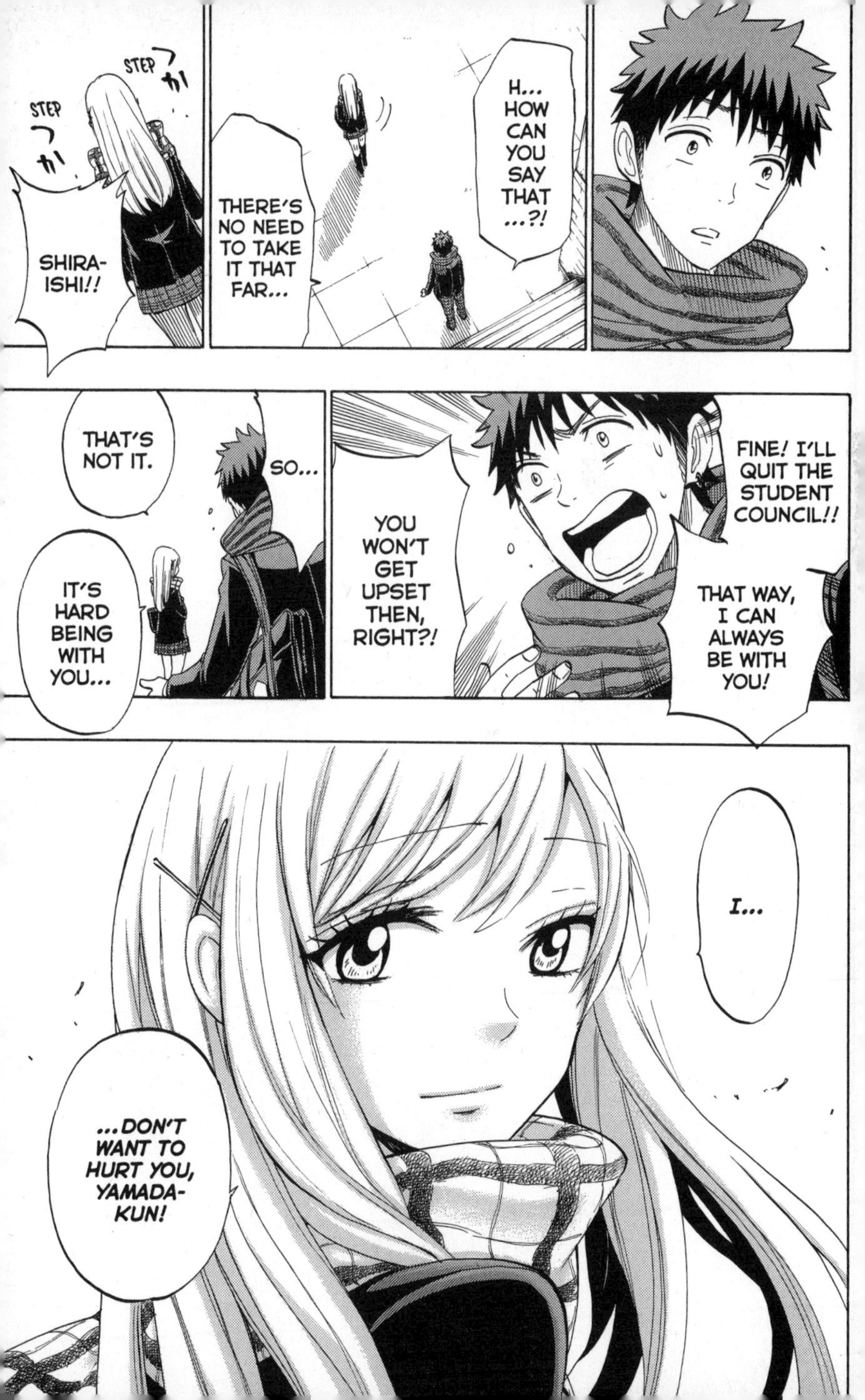
H... HOW CAN YOU SAY THAT ...?!
THERE'S NO NEED TO TAKE IT THAT FAR...
STEP
STEP
SHIRA-ISHI!!
FINE! I'LL QUIT THE STUDENT COUNCIL!!
YOU WON'T GET UPSET THEN, RIGHT?!
THAT WAY, I CAN ALWAYS BE WITH YOU!
SO...
THAT'S NOT IT.
IT'S HARD BEING WITH YOU...
I...
...DON'T WANT TO HURT YOU, YAMADA-KUN!

Yamada-kun
AND THE
Seven Witches

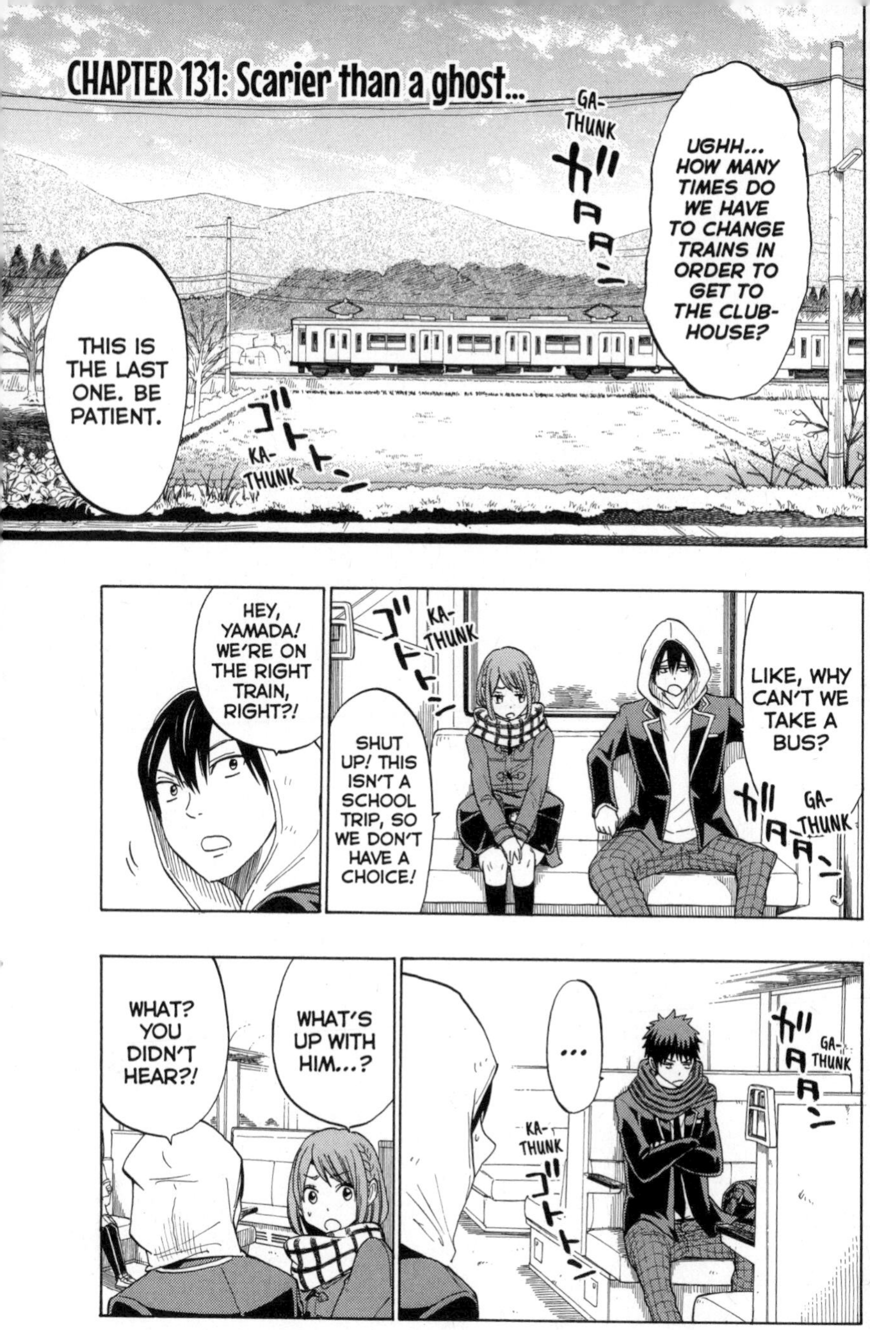
CHAPTER 131: Scarier than a ghost...
GA-THUNK
UGHH... HOW MANY TIMES DO WE HAVE TO CHANGE TRAINS IN ORDER TO GET TO THE CLUB-HOUSE?
THIS IS THE LAST ONE. BE PATIENT.
KA-THUNK
LIKE, WHY CAN'T WE TAKE A BUS?
GA-THUNK
KA-THUNK
SHUT UP! THIS ISN'T A SCHOOL TRIP, SO WE DON'T HAVE A CHOICE!
HEY, YAMADA! WE'RE ON THE RIGHT TRAIN, RIGHT?!
GA-THUNK
...
KA-THUNK
WHAT'S UP WITH HIM...?
WHAT? YOU DIDN'T HEAR?!

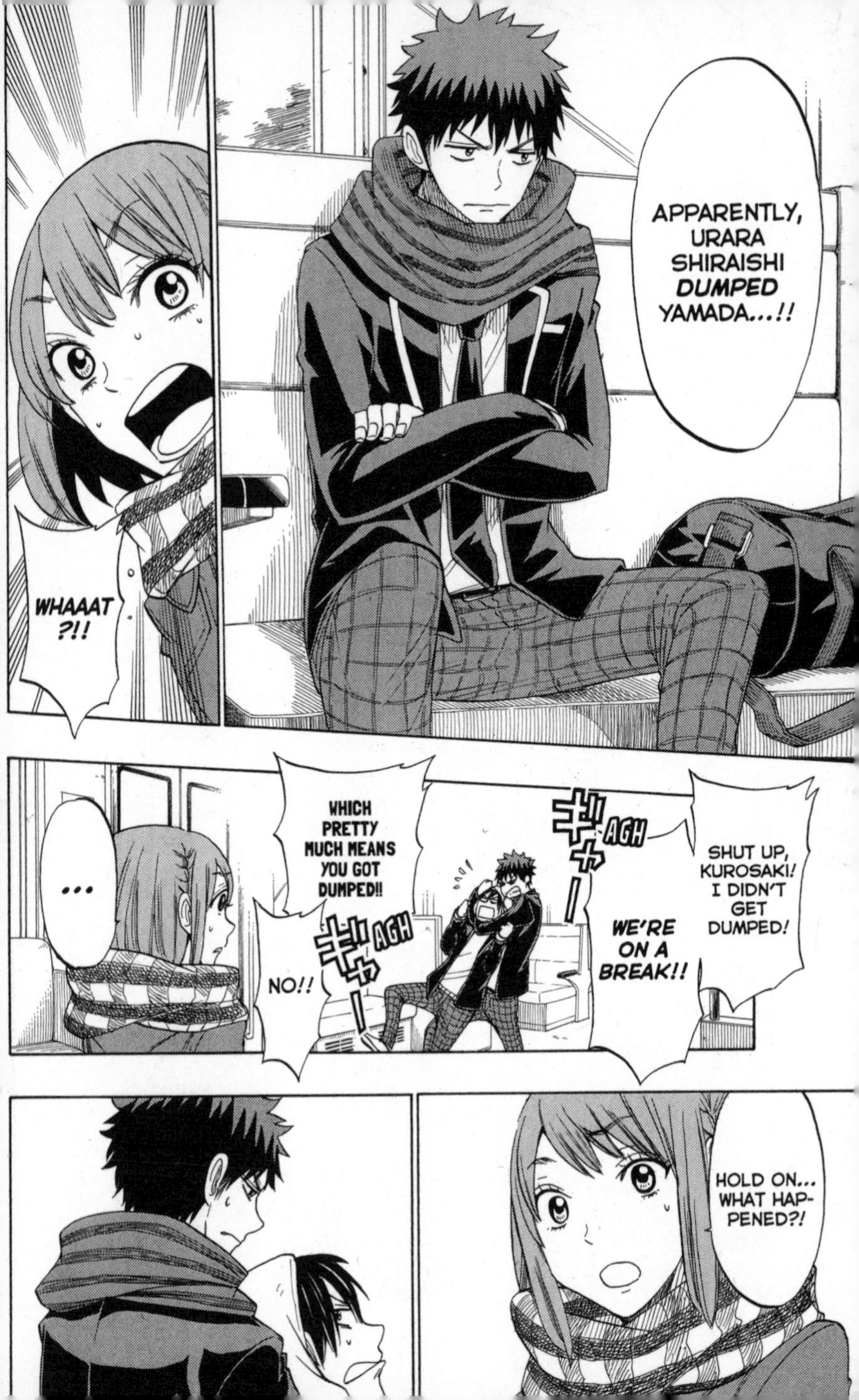
APPARENTLY, URARA SHIRAISHI DUMPED YAMADA...!!
WHAAAT ?!!
SHUT UP, KUROSAKI! I DIDN'T GET DUMPED!
ギャー AGH
WE'RE ON A BREAK!!
WHICH PRETTY MUCH MEANS YOU GOT DUMPED!!
ギャー AGH
NO!!
...
HOLD ON... WHAT HAP-PENED?!

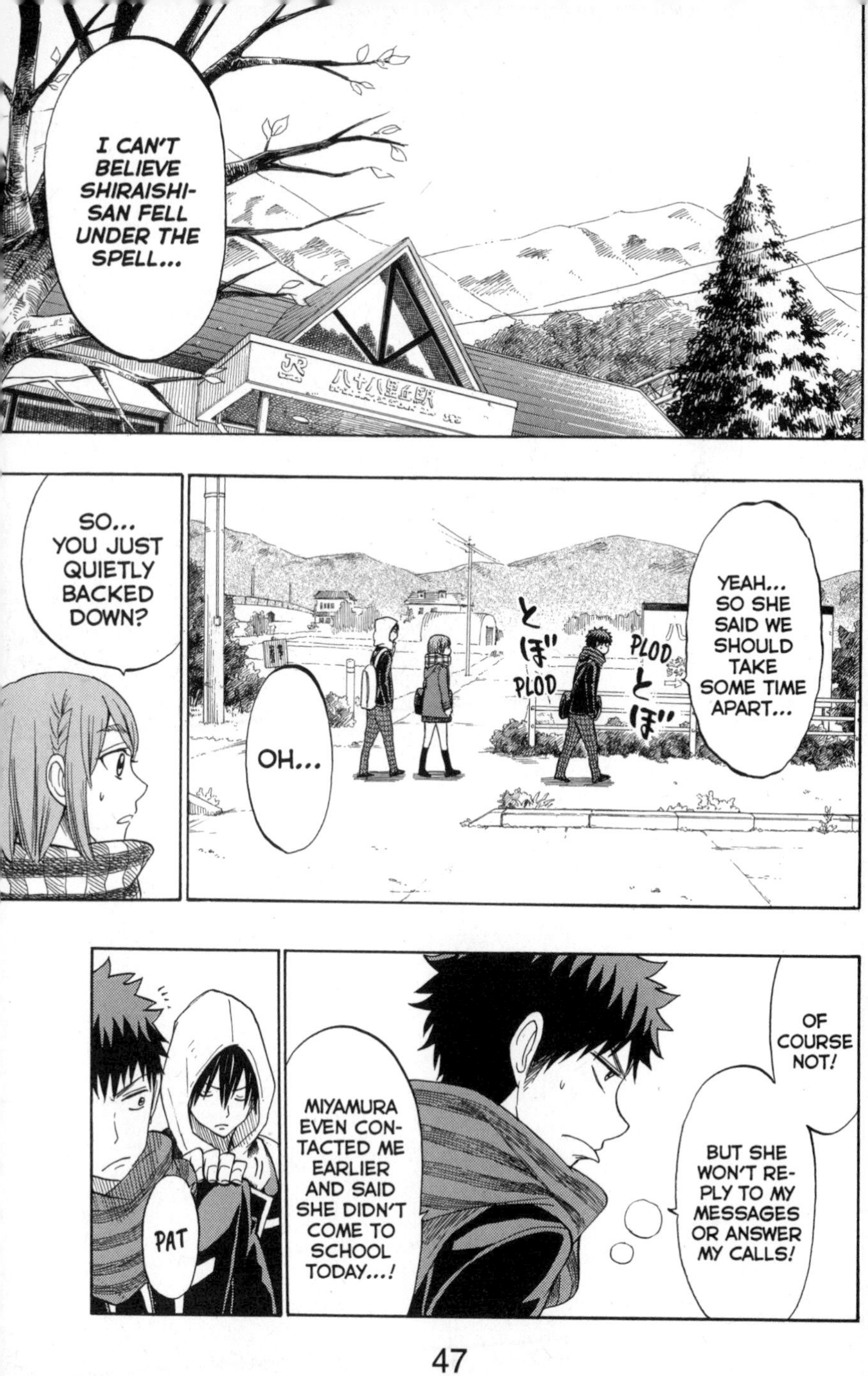
I CAN'T BELIEVE SHIRAISHI-SAN FELL UNDER THE SPELL...
SO... YOU JUST QUIETLY BACKED DOWN?
YEAH... SO SHE SAID WE SHOULD TAKE SOME TIME APART...
とぼ PLOD
とぼ PLOD
OH...
PAT
OF COURSE NOT!
BUT SHE WON'T RE-PLY TO MY MESSAGES OR ANSWER MY CALLS!
MIYAMURA EVEN CON-TACTED ME EARLIER AND SAID SHE DIDN'T COME TO SCHOOL TODAY...!

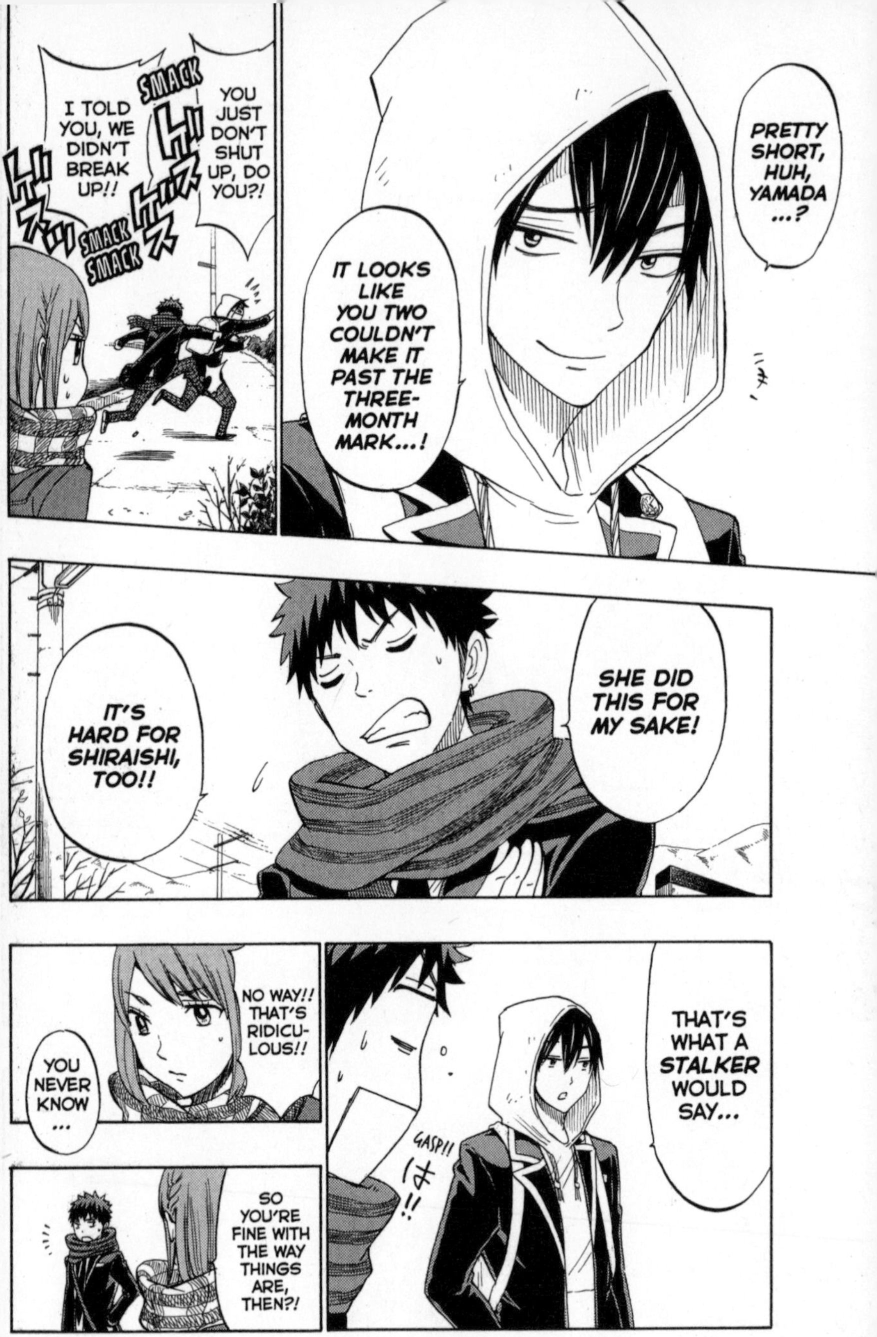
PRETTY SHORT, HUH, YAMADA...?
IT LOOKS LIKE YOU TWO COULDN'T MAKE IT PAST THE THREE-MONTH MARK...!
YOU JUST DON'T SHUT UP, DO YOU?!
SMACK
I TOLD YOU, WE DIDN'T BREAK UP!!
SMACK SMACK
SHE DID THIS FOR MY SAKE!
IT'S HARD FOR SHIRAISHI, TOO!!
THAT'S WHAT A STALKER WOULD SAY...
GASP!!
は!!
NO WAY!! THAT'S RIDICULOUS!!
YOU NEVER KNOW...
SO YOU'RE FINE WITH THE WAY THINGS ARE, THEN?!

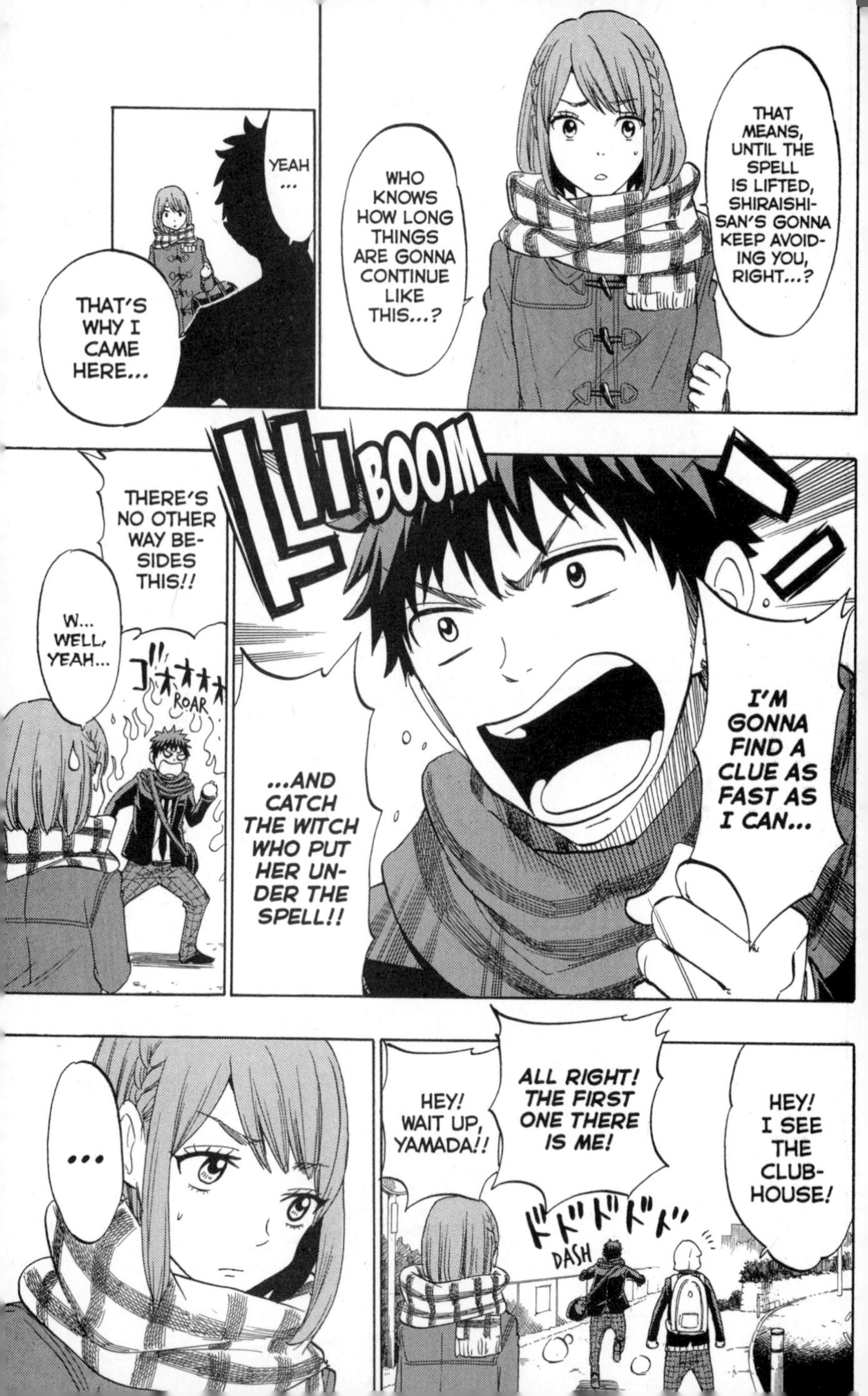
THAT MEANS, UNTIL THE SPELL IS LIFTED, SHIRAISHI-SAN'S GONNA KEEP AVOIDING YOU, RIGHT...?
WHO KNOWS HOW LONG THINGS ARE GONNA CONTINUE LIKE THIS...?
YEAH...
THAT'S WHY I CAME HERE...
BOOM
I'M GONNA FIND A CLUE AS FAST AS I CAN...
...AND CATCH THE WITCH WHO PUT HER UNDER THE SPELL!!
THERE'S NO OTHER WAY BESIDES THIS!!
W... WELL, YEAH...
ROAR
HEY! I SEE THE CLUBHOUSE!
ALL RIGHT! THE FIRST ONE THERE IS ME!
HEY! WAIT UP, YAMADA!!
DASH
...

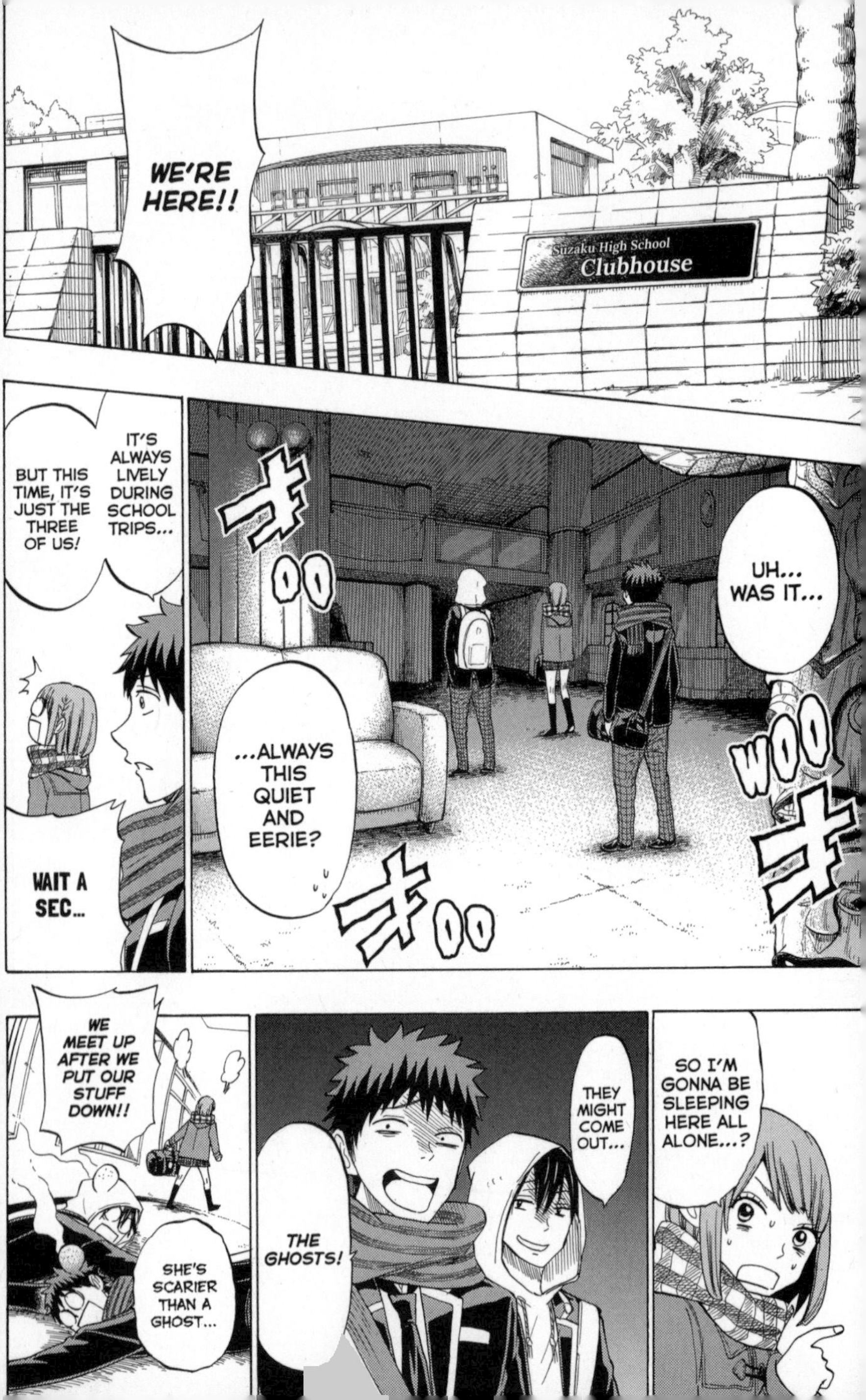
WE'RE HERE!!
Suzaku High School
Clubhouse
UH... WAS IT...
WOO オ
オ OO
...ALWAYS THIS QUIET AND EERIE?
オ OO
IT'S ALWAYS LIVELY DURING SCHOOL TRIPS...
BUT THIS TIME, IT'S JUST THE THREE OF US!
WAIT A SEC...
SO I'M GONNA BE SLEEPING HERE ALL ALONE...?
THEY MIGHT COME OUT...
THE GHOSTS!
WE MEET UP AFTER WE PUT OUR STUFF DOWN!!
SHE'S SCARIER THAN A GHOST...

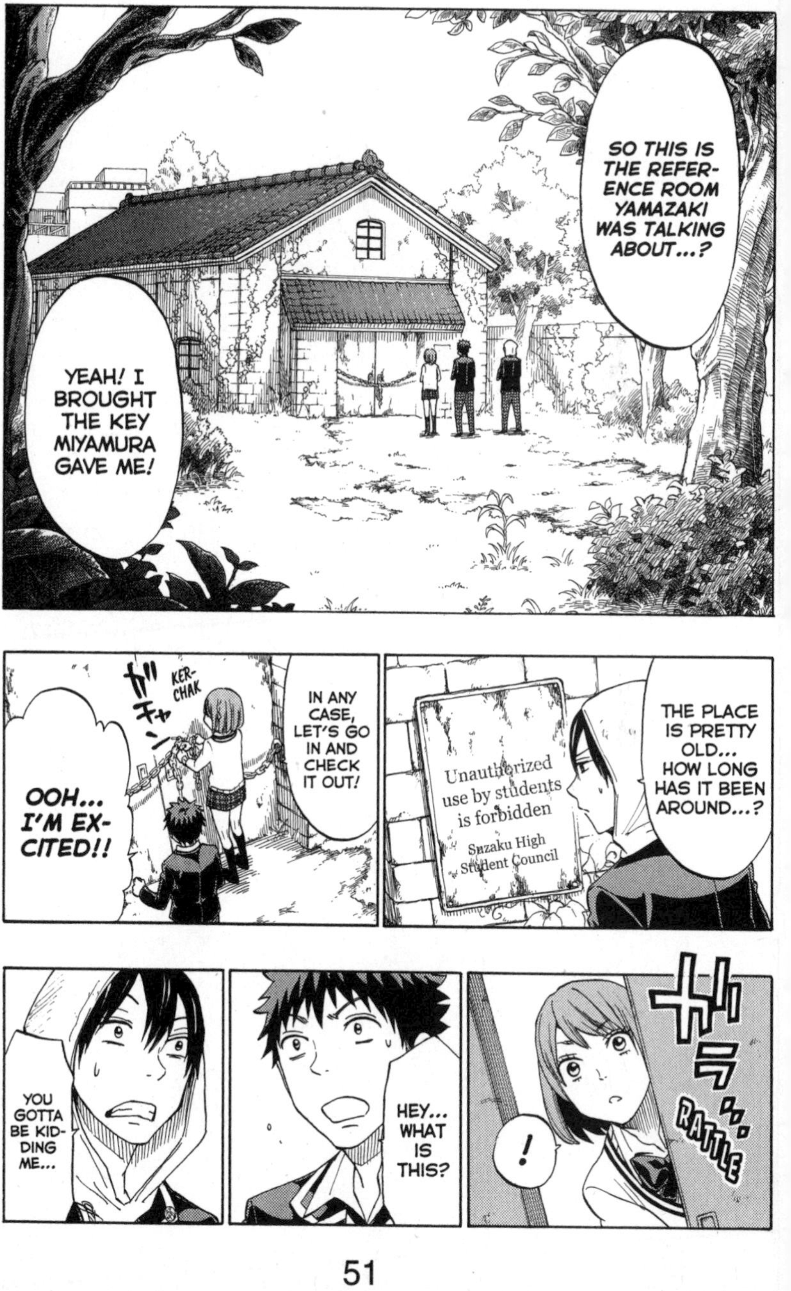
SO THIS IS THE REFERENCE ROOM YAMAZAKI WAS TALKING ABOUT...?
YEAH! I BROUGHT THE KEY MIYAMURA GAVE ME!
THE PLACE IS PRETTY OLD... HOW LONG HAS IT BEEN AROUND...?
Unauthorized use by students is forbidden
Suzaku High Student Council
IN ANY CASE, LET'S GO IN AND CHECK IT OUT!
KER-CHAK
OOH... I'M EXCITED!!
RATTLE
!
HEY... WHAT IS THIS?
YOU GOTTA BE KIDDING ME...

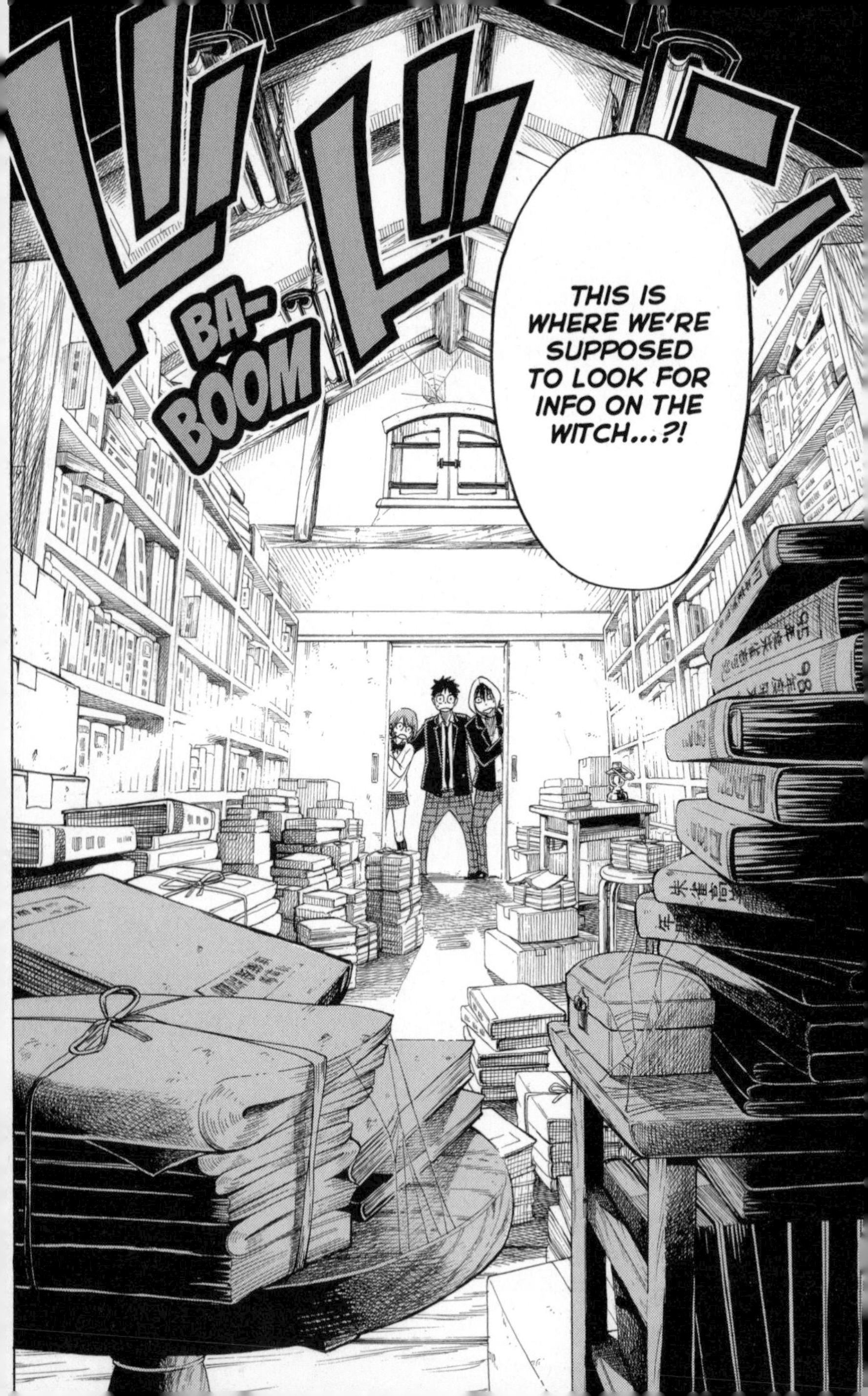
BA-
BOOM
THIS IS WHERE WE'RE SUPPOSED TO LOOK FOR INFO ON THE WITCH...?!

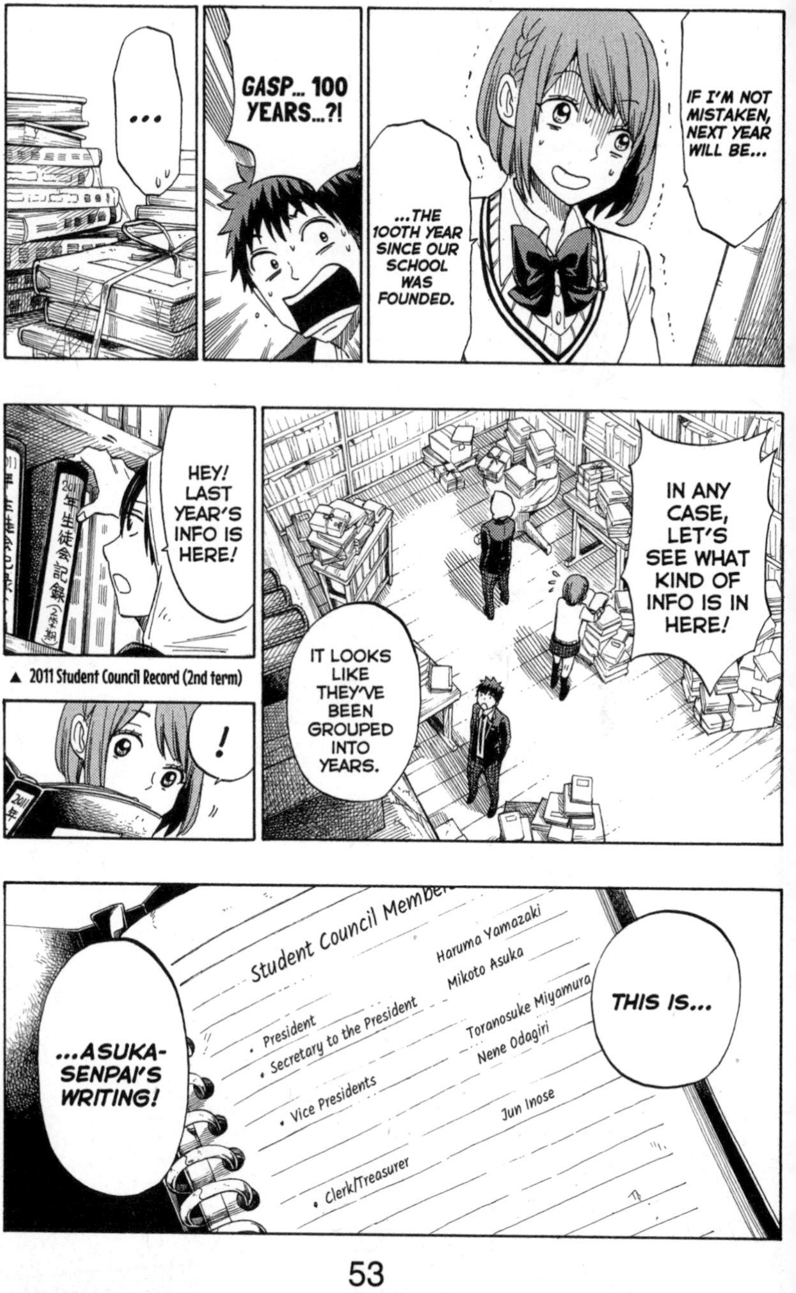
IF I'M NOT MISTAKEN, NEXT YEAR WILL BE...
...THE 100TH YEAR SINCE OUR SCHOOL WAS FOUNDED.
GASP... 100 YEARS...?!
...
IN ANY CASE, LET'S SEE WHAT KIND OF INFO IS IN HERE!
IT LOOKS LIKE THEY'VE BEEN GROUPED INTO YEARS.
HEY! LAST YEAR'S INFO IS HERE!
▲ 2011 Student Council Record (2nd term)
!
THIS IS...
...ASUKA-SENPAI'S WRITING!
Student Council Membe
President
Haruma Yamazaki
Secretary to the President
Mikoto Asuka
Vice Presidents
Toranosuke Miyamura
Nene Odagiri
Clerk/Treasurer
Jun Inose

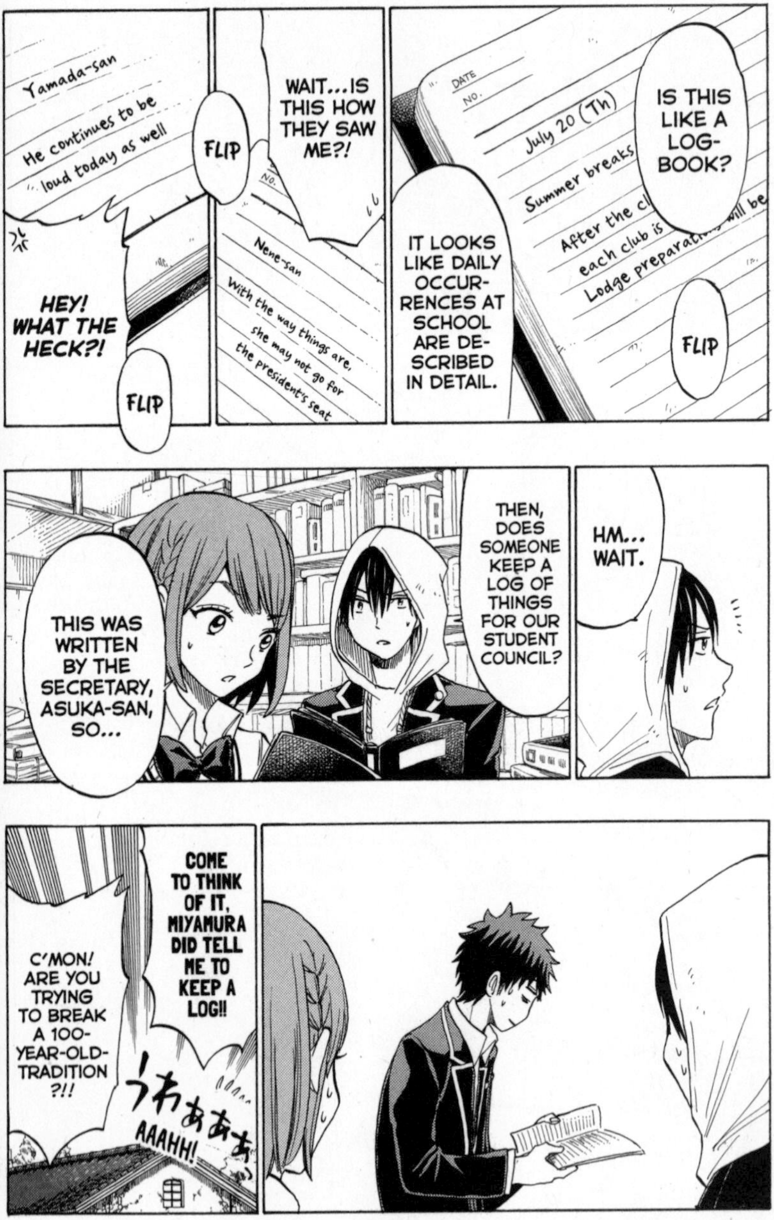
IS THIS LIKE A LOG-BOOK?
DATE
NO.
July 20 (Th)
Summer breaks
After the cl
each club is
Lodge preparations will be
IT LOOKS LIKE DAILY OCCURRENCES AT SCHOOL ARE DESCRIBED IN DETAIL.
FLIP
WAIT...IS THIS HOW THEY SAW ME?!
NO.
Nene-san
With the way things are, she may not go for the president's seat
FLIP
Yamada-san
He continues to be loud today as well
HEY! WHAT THE HECK?!
FLIP
HM... WAIT.
THEN, DOES SOMEONE KEEP A LOG OF THINGS FOR OUR STUDENT COUNCIL?
THIS WAS WRITTEN BY THE SECRETARY, ASUKA-SAN, SO...
COME TO THINK OF IT, MIYAMURA DID TELL ME TO KEEP A LOG!!
C'MON! ARE YOU TRYING TO BREAK A 100-YEAR-OLD-TRADITION ?!!
うわあああ
AAAHH!

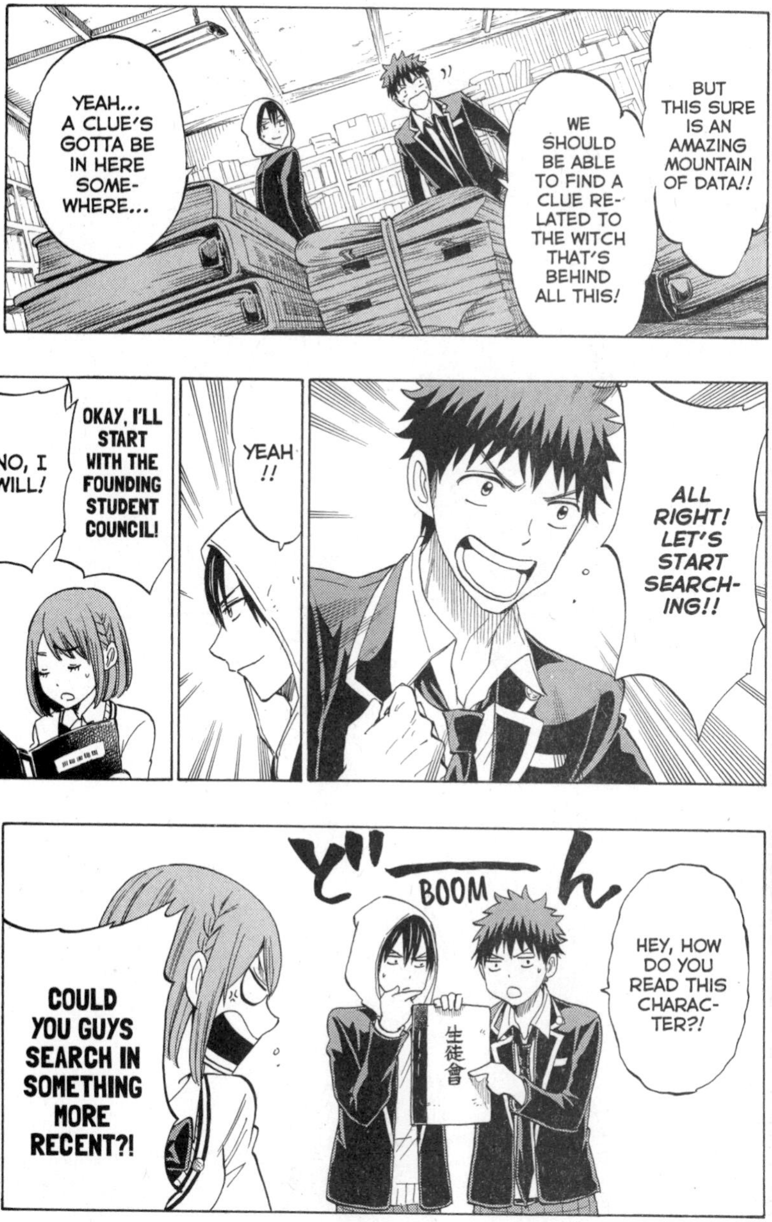
BUT THIS SURE IS AN AMAZING MOUNTAIN OF DATA!!
WE SHOULD BE ABLE TO FIND A CLUE RE-LATED TO THE WITCH THAT'S BEHIND ALL THIS!
YEAH... A CLUE'S GOTTA BE IN HERE SOME-WHERE...
ALL RIGHT! LET'S START SEARCH-ING!!
YEAH!!
OKAY, I'LL START WITH THE FOUNDING STUDENT COUNCIL!
NO, I WILL!
NO, I WILL...
SIGH...
HEY, HOW DO YOU READ THIS CHARAC-TER?!
どーーん
BOOM
生徒會
COULD YOU GUYS SEARCH IN SOMETHING MORE RECENT?!

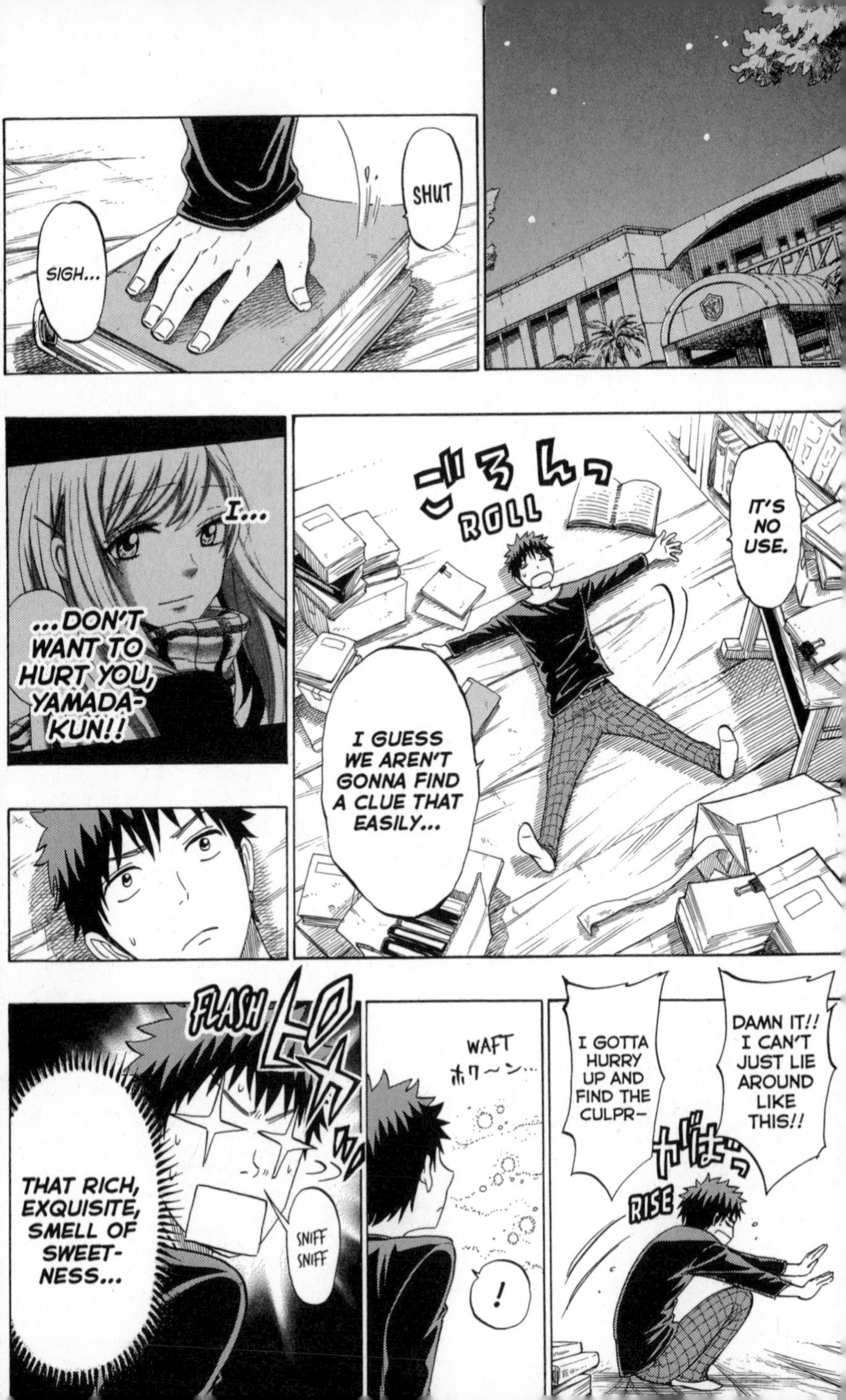
SHUT
SIGH...
ごろんっ
ROLL
IT'S NO USE.
I GUESS WE AREN'T GONNA FIND A CLUE THAT EASILY...
I...
...DON'T WANT TO HURT YOU, YAMADA-KUN!!
DAMN IT!! I CAN'T JUST LIE AROUND LIKE THIS!!
I GOTTA HURRY UP AND FIND THE CULPR–
がばっ
RISE
WAFT
ホワ〜ン…
!
FLASH
ピカッ
SNIFF SNIFF
THAT RICH, EXQUISITE, SMELL OF SWEET-NESS...

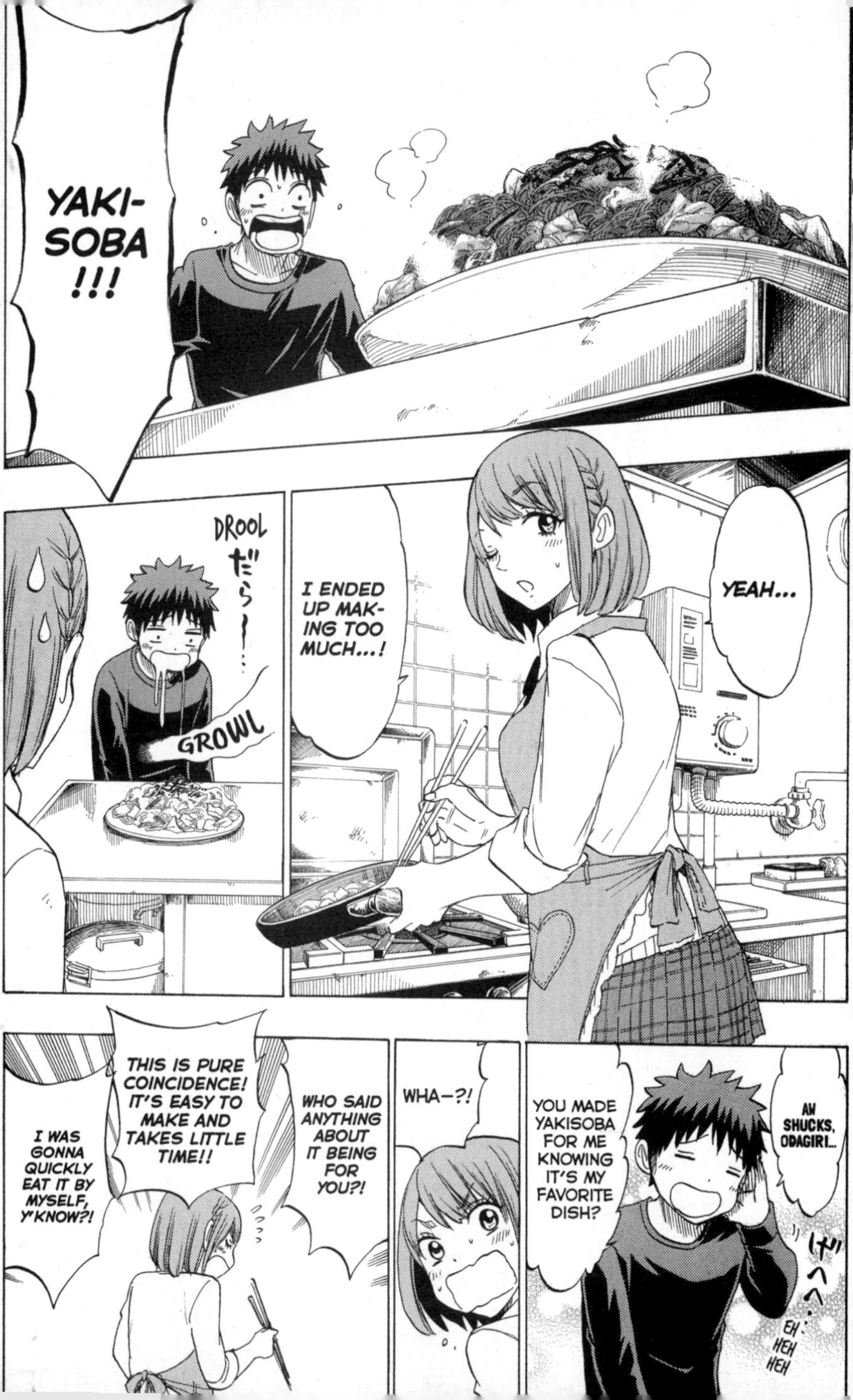
YAKI-SOBA !!!
YEAH...
I ENDED UP MAKING TOO MUCH...!
DROOL
だら～…
GROWL
AW SHUCKS, ODAGIRI...
YOU MADE YAKISOBA FOR ME KNOWING IT'S MY FAVORITE DISH?
げへへ…
EH HEH HEH
WHA-?!
WHO SAID ANYTHING ABOUT IT BEING FOR YOU?!
THIS IS PURE COINCIDENCE! IT'S EASY TO MAKE AND TAKES LITTLE TIME!!
I WAS GONNA QUICKLY EAT IT BY MYSELF, Y'KNOW?!

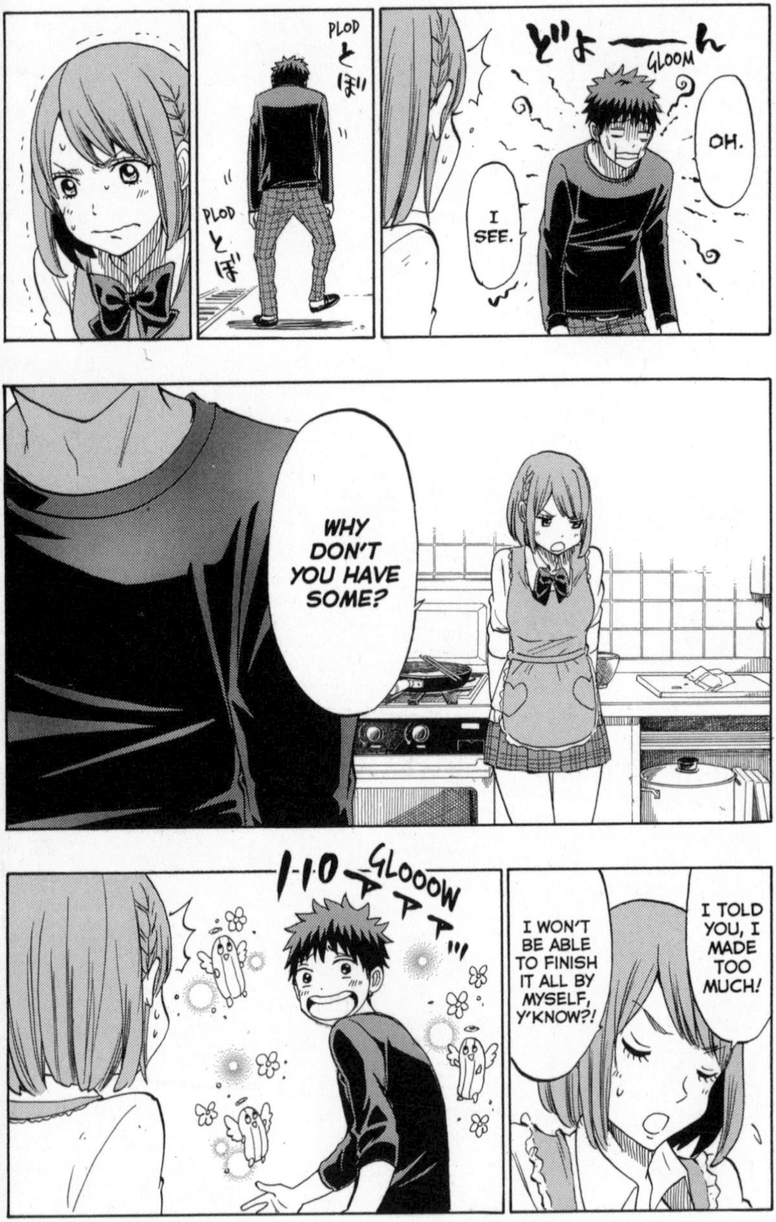
どよーーん
GLOOM
OH.
I SEE.
PLOD
とぼ
PLOD
とぼ
WHY DON'T YOU HAVE SOME?
I TOLD YOU, I MADE TOO MUCH!
I WON'T BE ABLE TO FINISH IT ALL BY MYSELF, Y'KNOW?!
GLOOOW

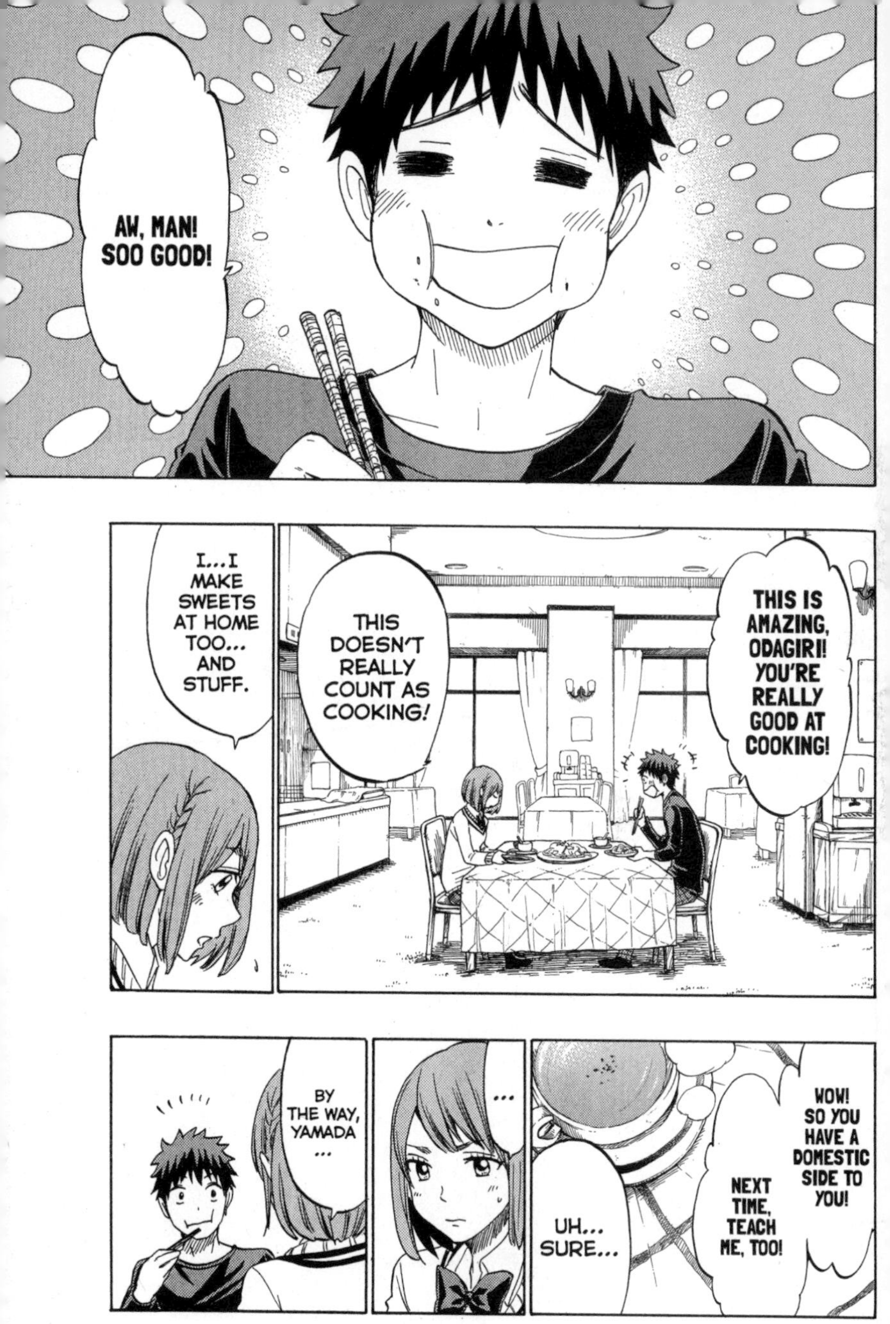
AW, MAN! SOO GOOD!
THIS IS AMAZING, ODAGIRI! YOU'RE REALLY GOOD AT COOKING!
THIS DOESN'T REALLY COUNT AS COOKING!
I...I MAKE SWEETS AT HOME TOO... AND STUFF.
WOW! SO YOU HAVE A DOMESTIC SIDE TO YOU!
NEXT TIME, TEACH ME, TOO!
UH... SURE...
...
BY THE WAY, YAMADA...

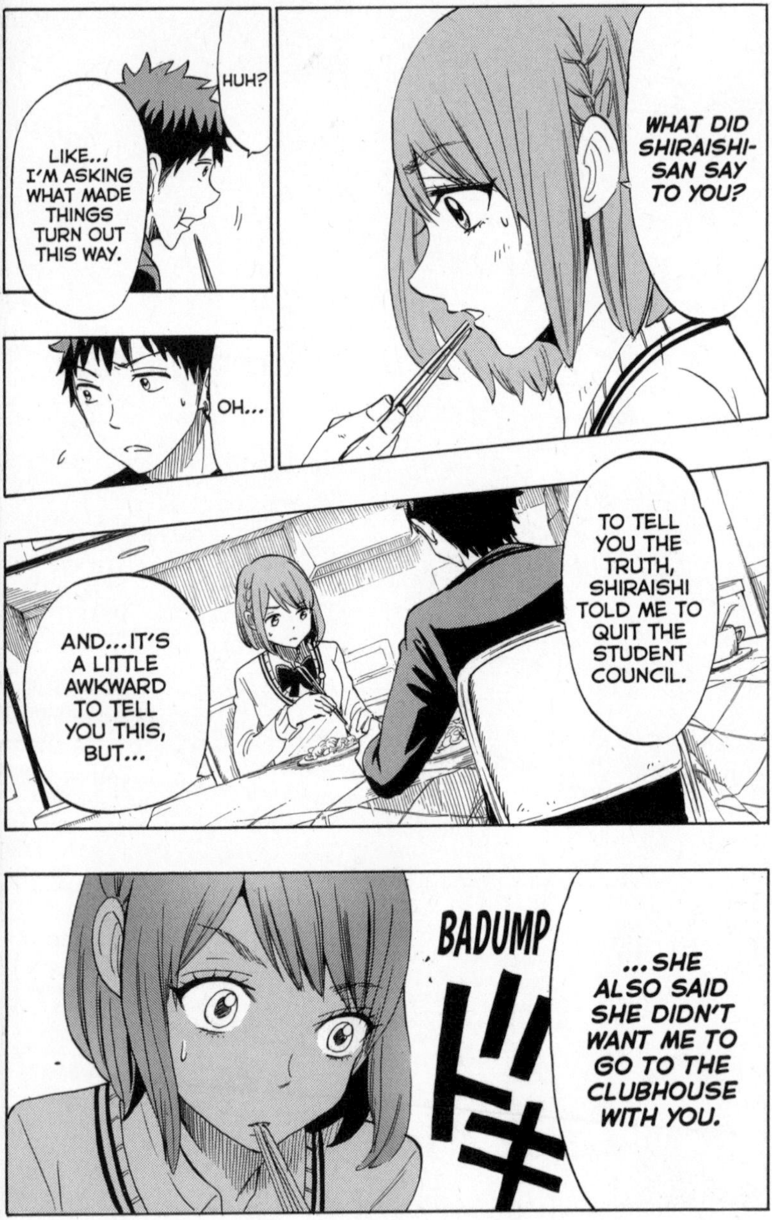
WHAT DID SHIRAISHI-SAN SAY TO YOU?
HUH?
LIKE... I'M ASKING WHAT MADE THINGS TURN OUT THIS WAY.
OH...
TO TELL YOU THE TRUTH, SHIRAISHI TOLD ME TO QUIT THE STUDENT COUNCIL.
AND...IT'S A LITTLE AWKWARD TO TELL YOU THIS, BUT...
...SHE ALSO SAID SHE DIDN'T WANT ME TO GO TO THE CLUBHOUSE WITH YOU.
BADUMP
ドキ

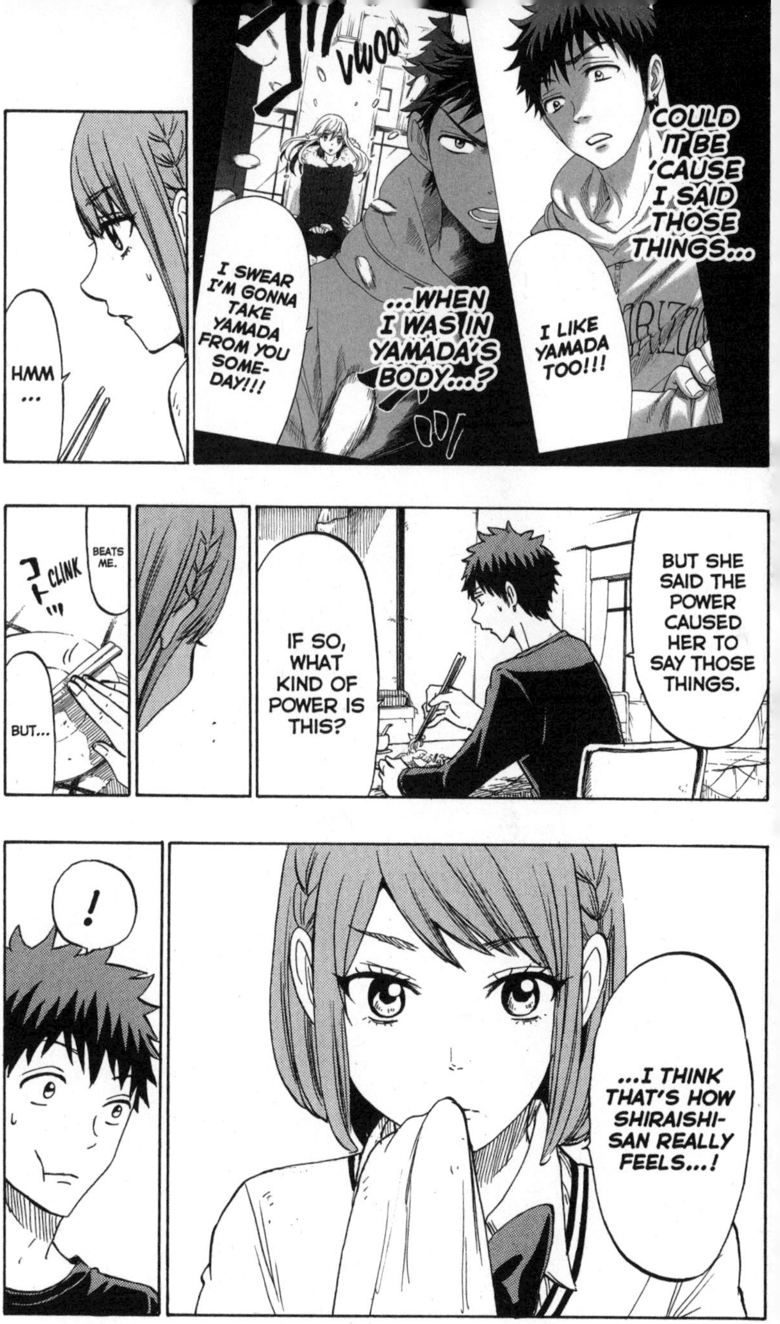
COULD IT BE 'CAUSE I SAID THOSE THINGS...
I LIKE YAMADA TOO!!!
VWOO
...WHEN I WAS IN YAMADA'S BODY...?
I SWEAR I'M GONNA TAKE YAMADA FROM YOU SOME-DAY!!!
HMM...
BUT SHE SAID THE POWER CAUSED HER TO SAY THOSE THINGS.
IF SO, WHAT KIND OF POWER IS THIS?
BEATS ME.
CLINK
BUT...
...I THINK THAT'S HOW SHIRAISHI-SAN REALLY FEELS...!
!

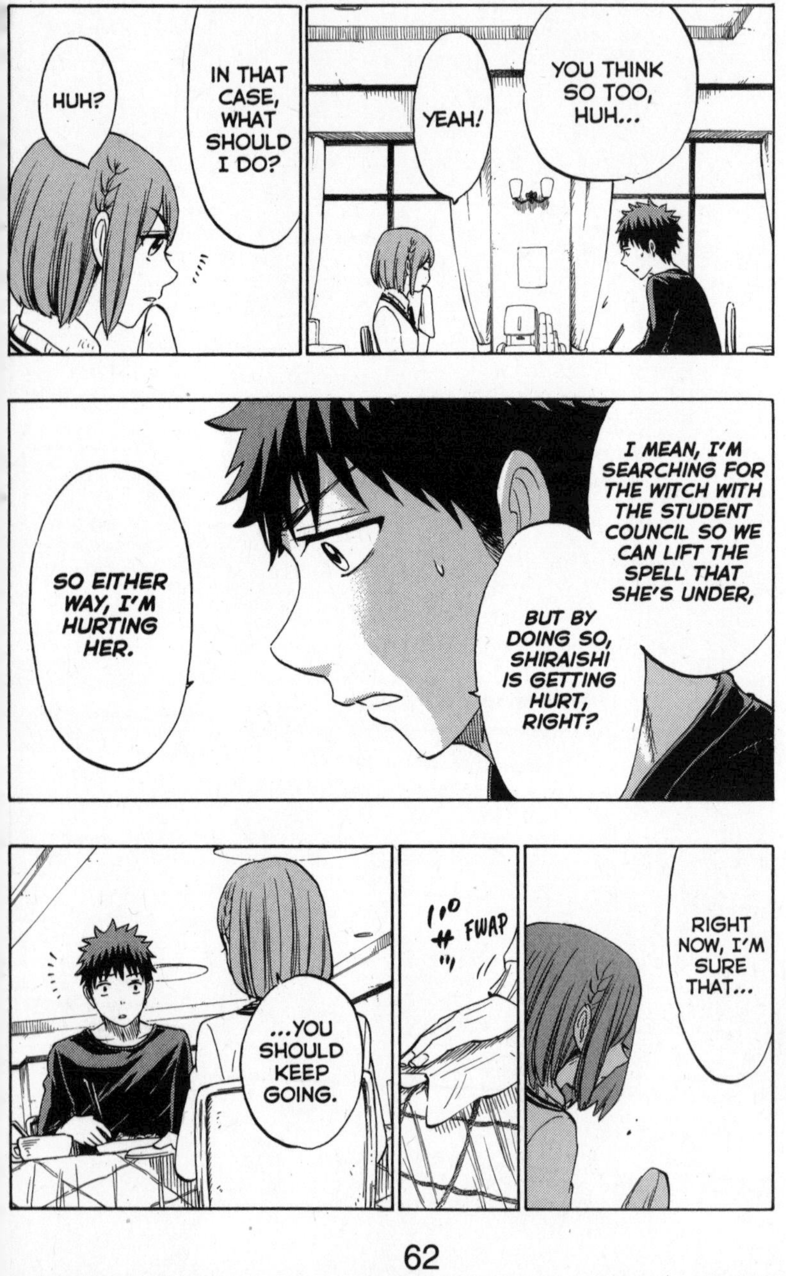
YOU THINK SO TOO, HUH...
YEAH!
IN THAT CASE, WHAT SHOULD I DO?
HUH?
I MEAN, I'M SEARCHING FOR THE WITCH WITH THE STUDENT COUNCIL SO WE CAN LIFT THE SPELL THAT SHE'S UNDER,
BUT BY DOING SO, SHIRAISHI IS GETTING HURT, RIGHT?
SO EITHER WAY, I'M HURTING HER.
RIGHT NOW, I'M SURE THAT...
FWAP
...YOU SHOULD KEEP GOING.

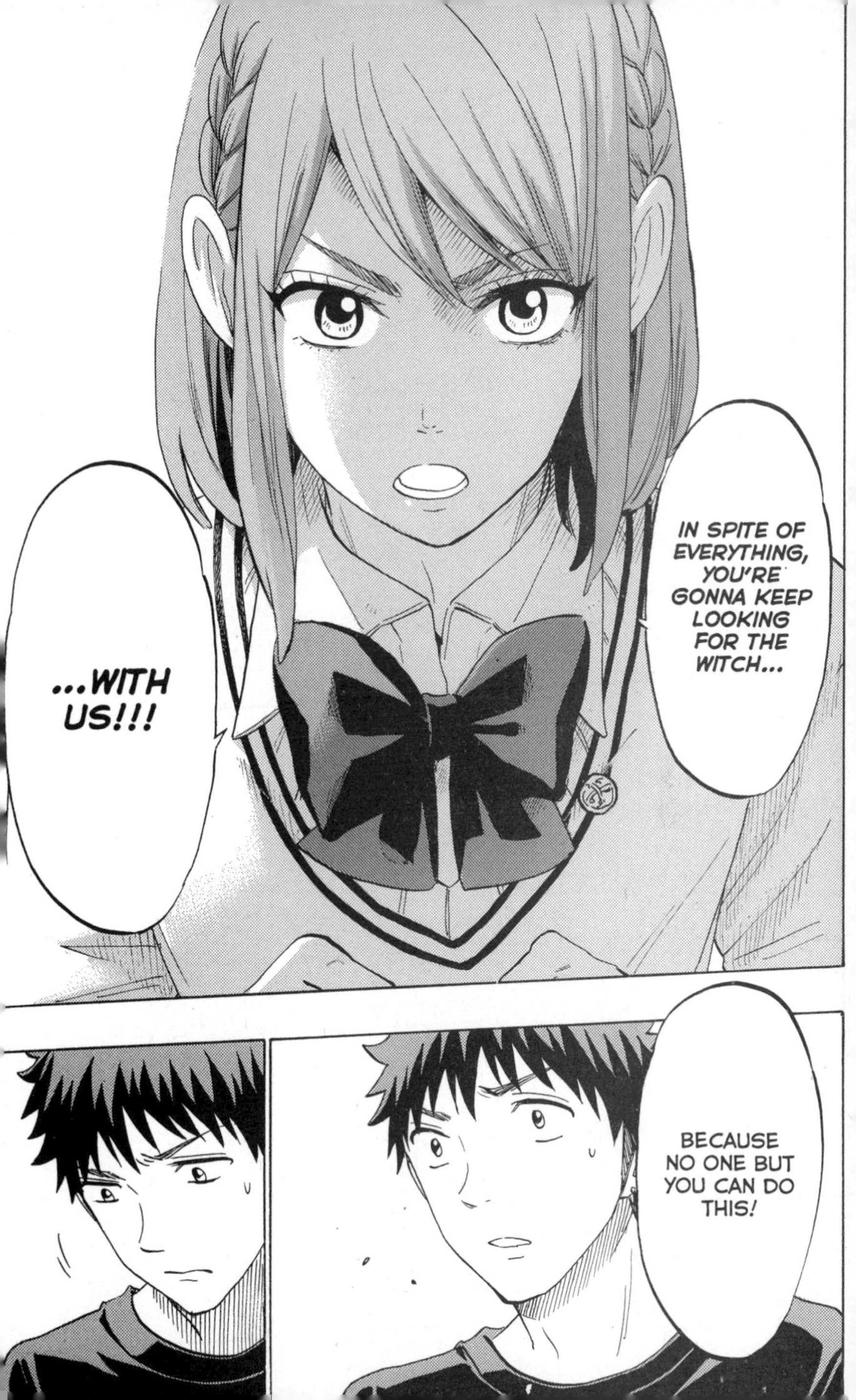
IN SPITE OF EVERYTHING, YOU'RE GONNA KEEP LOOKING FOR THE WITCH...
...WITH US!!!
BECAUSE NO ONE BUT YOU CAN DO THIS!

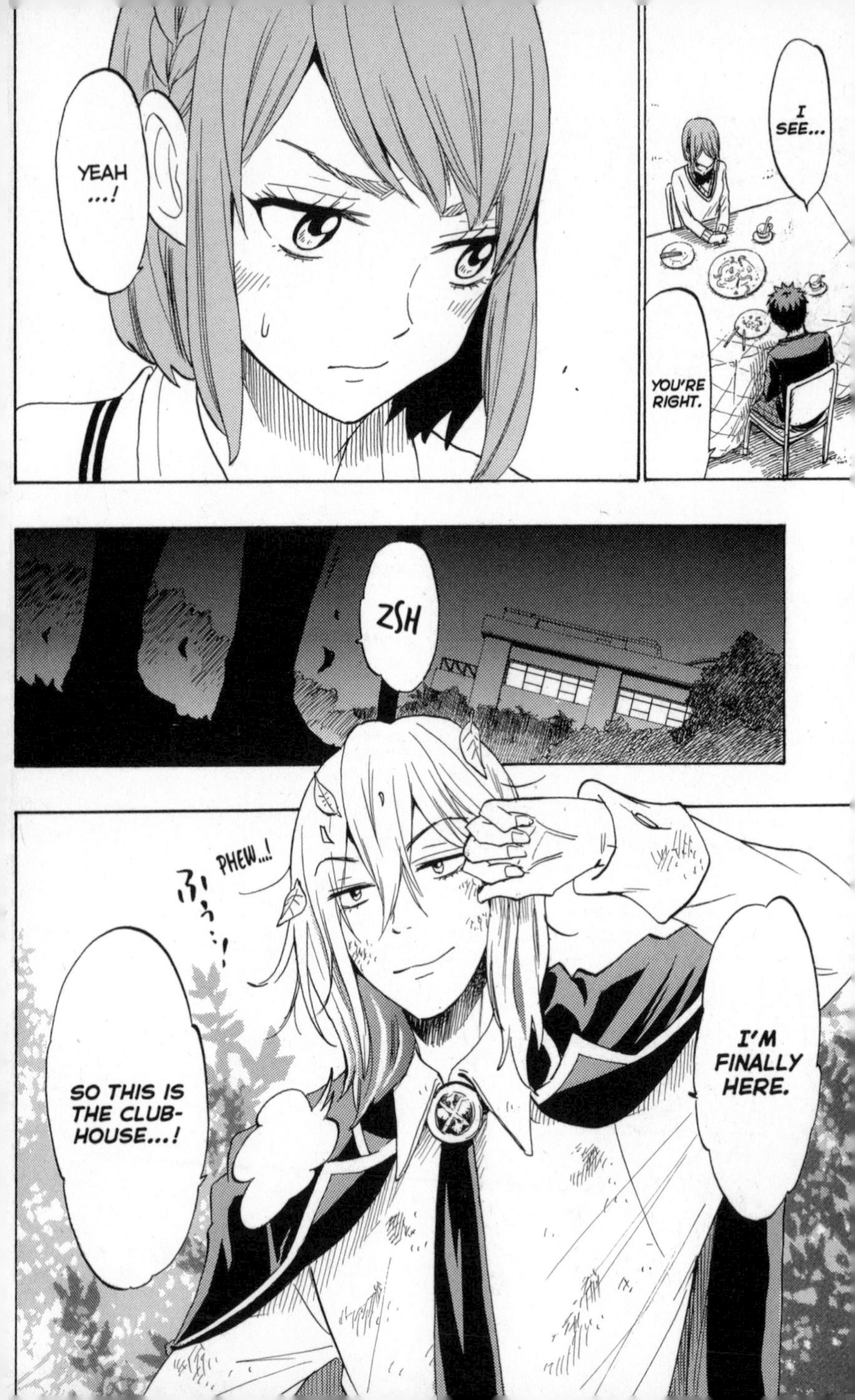
I SEE...
YOU'RE RIGHT.
YEAH ...!
ZSH
PHEW...!
ふぅ…!
I'M FINALLY HERE.
SO THIS IS THE CLUB-HOUSE...!

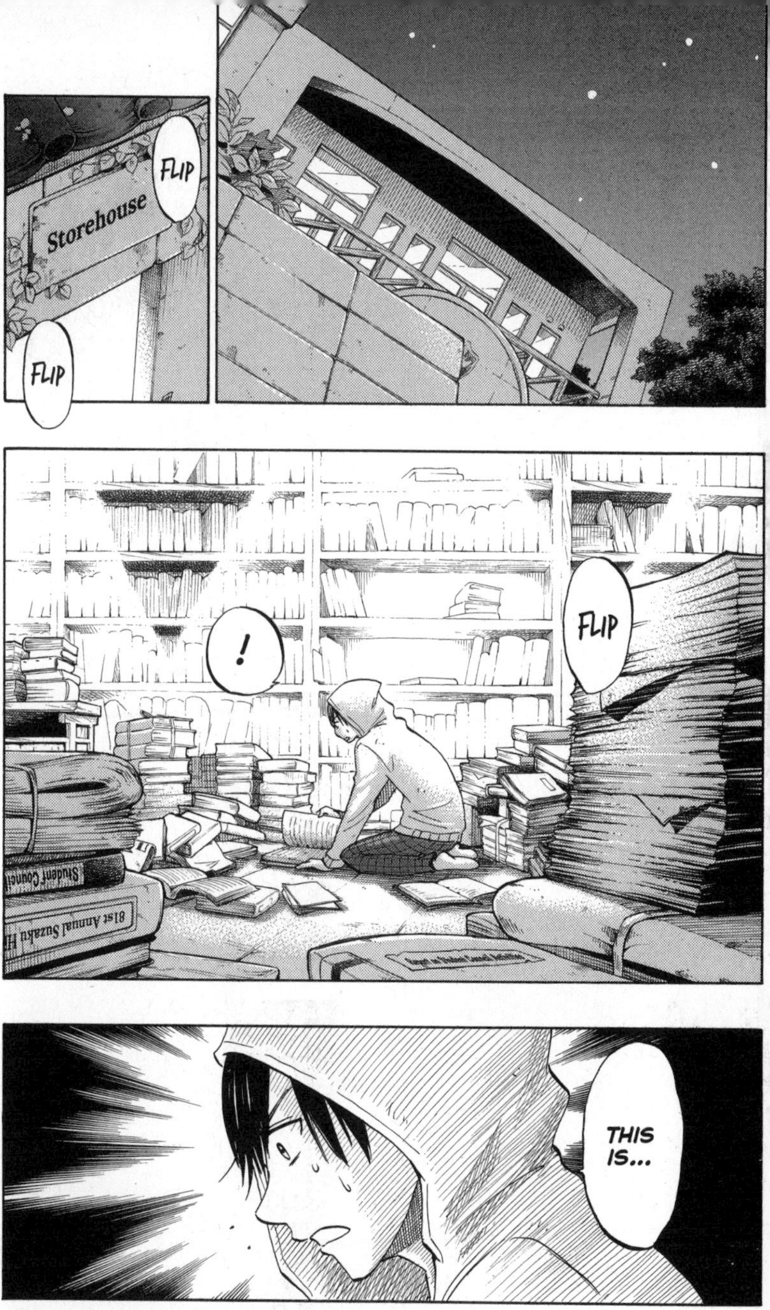
FLIP
Storehouse
FLIP
FLIP
!
THIS IS...

CHAPTER 132: Can't you tell?

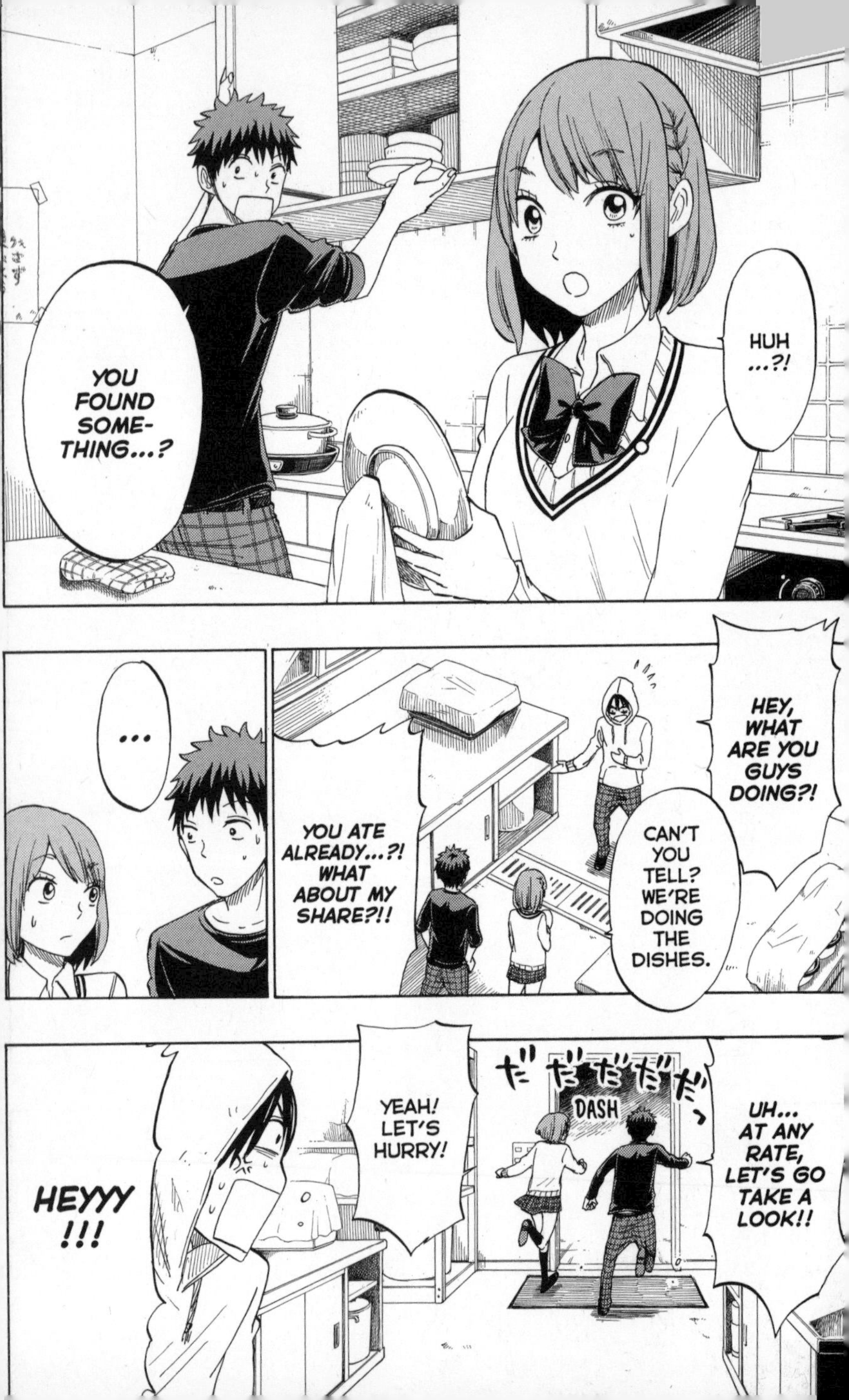
HUH ...?!
YOU FOUND SOME-THING...?
HEY, WHAT ARE YOU GUYS DOING?!
CAN'T YOU TELL? WE'RE DOING THE DISHES.
YOU ATE ALREADY...?! WHAT ABOUT MY SHARE?!!
...
UH... AT ANY RATE, LET'S GO TAKE A LOOK!!
だだだだだ
DASH
YEAH! LET'S HURRY!
HEYYY !!!

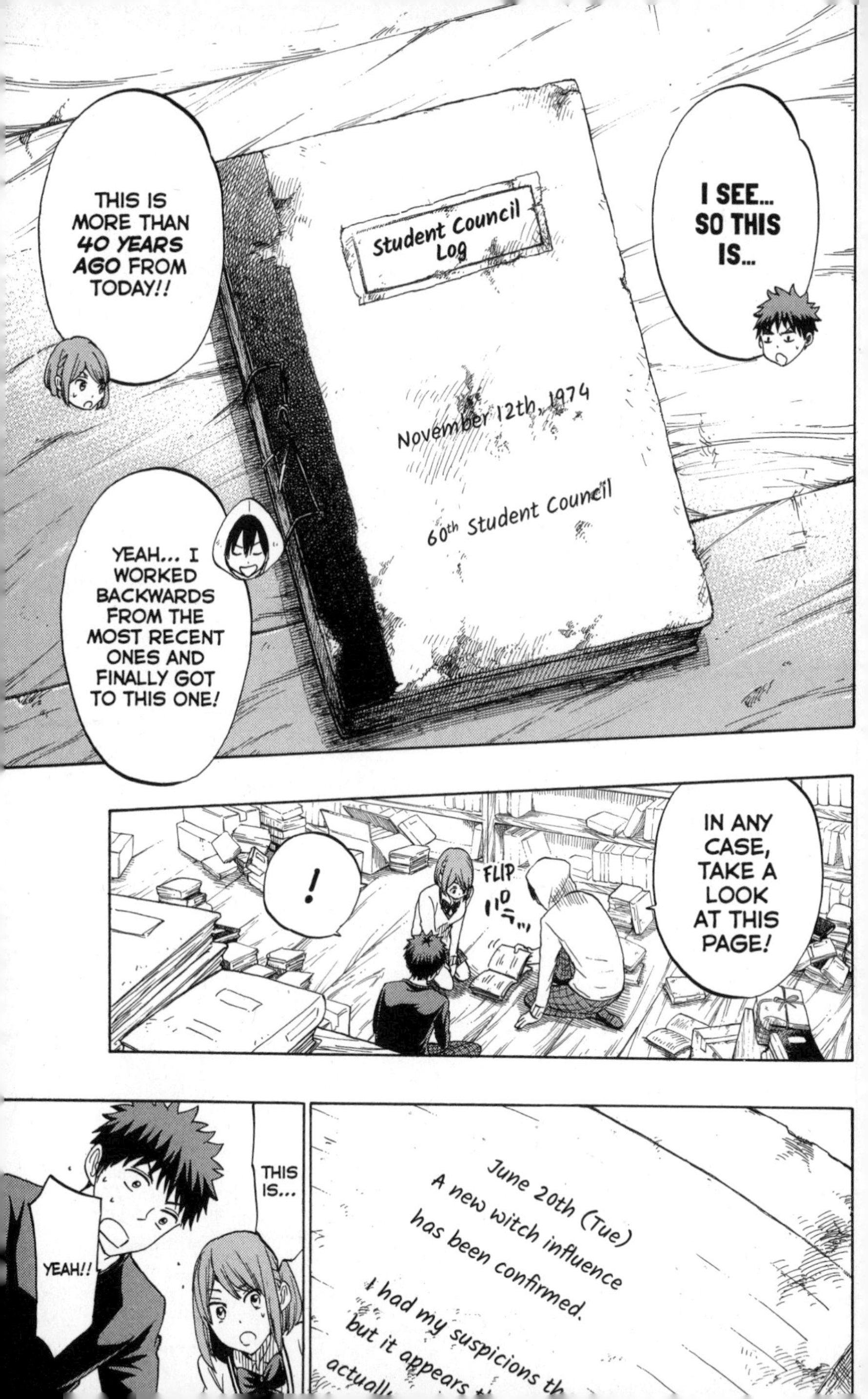
I SEE... SO THIS IS...
THIS IS MORE THAN 40 YEARS AGO FROM TODAY!!
Student Council Log
November 12th, 1974
60th Student Council
YEAH... I WORKED BACKWARDS FROM THE MOST RECENT ONES AND FINALLY GOT TO THIS ONE!
IN ANY CASE, TAKE A LOOK AT THIS PAGE!
FLIP
!
June 20th (Tue)
A new witch influence
has been confirmed.
I had my suspicions
but it appears
THIS IS...
YEAH!!

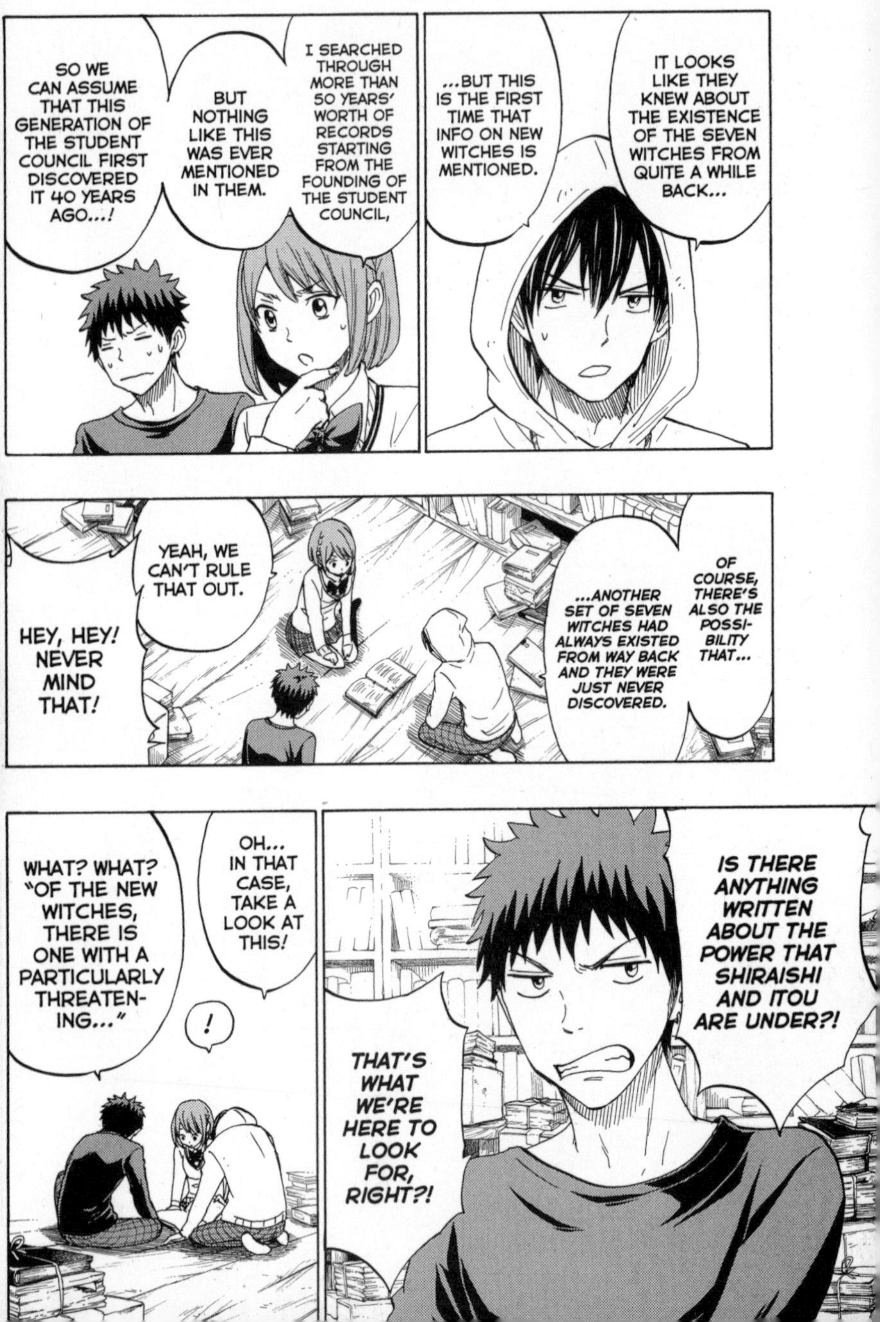
IT LOOKS LIKE THEY KNEW ABOUT THE EXISTENCE OF THE SEVEN WITCHES FROM QUITE A WHILE BACK...
...BUT THIS IS THE FIRST TIME THAT INFO ON NEW WITCHES IS MENTIONED.
I SEARCHED THROUGH MORE THAN 50 YEARS' WORTH OF RECORDS STARTING FROM THE FOUNDING OF THE STUDENT COUNCIL,
BUT NOTHING LIKE THIS WAS EVER MENTIONED IN THEM.
SO WE CAN ASSUME THAT THIS GENERATION OF THE STUDENT COUNCIL FIRST DISCOVERED IT 40 YEARS AGO...!
OF COURSE, THERE'S ALSO THE POSSI-BILITY THAT...
...ANOTHER SET OF SEVEN WITCHES HAD ALWAYS EXISTED FROM WAY BACK AND THEY WERE JUST NEVER DISCOVERED.
YEAH, WE CAN'T RULE THAT OUT.
HEY, HEY! NEVER MIND THAT!
IS THERE ANYTHING WRITTEN ABOUT THE POWER THAT SHIRAISHI AND ITOU ARE UNDER?!
THAT'S WHAT WE'RE HERE TO LOOK FOR, RIGHT?!
OH... IN THAT CASE, TAKE A LOOK AT THIS!
!
WHAT? WHAT? "OF THE NEW WITCHES, THERE IS ONE WITH A PARTICULARLY THREATEN-ING..."

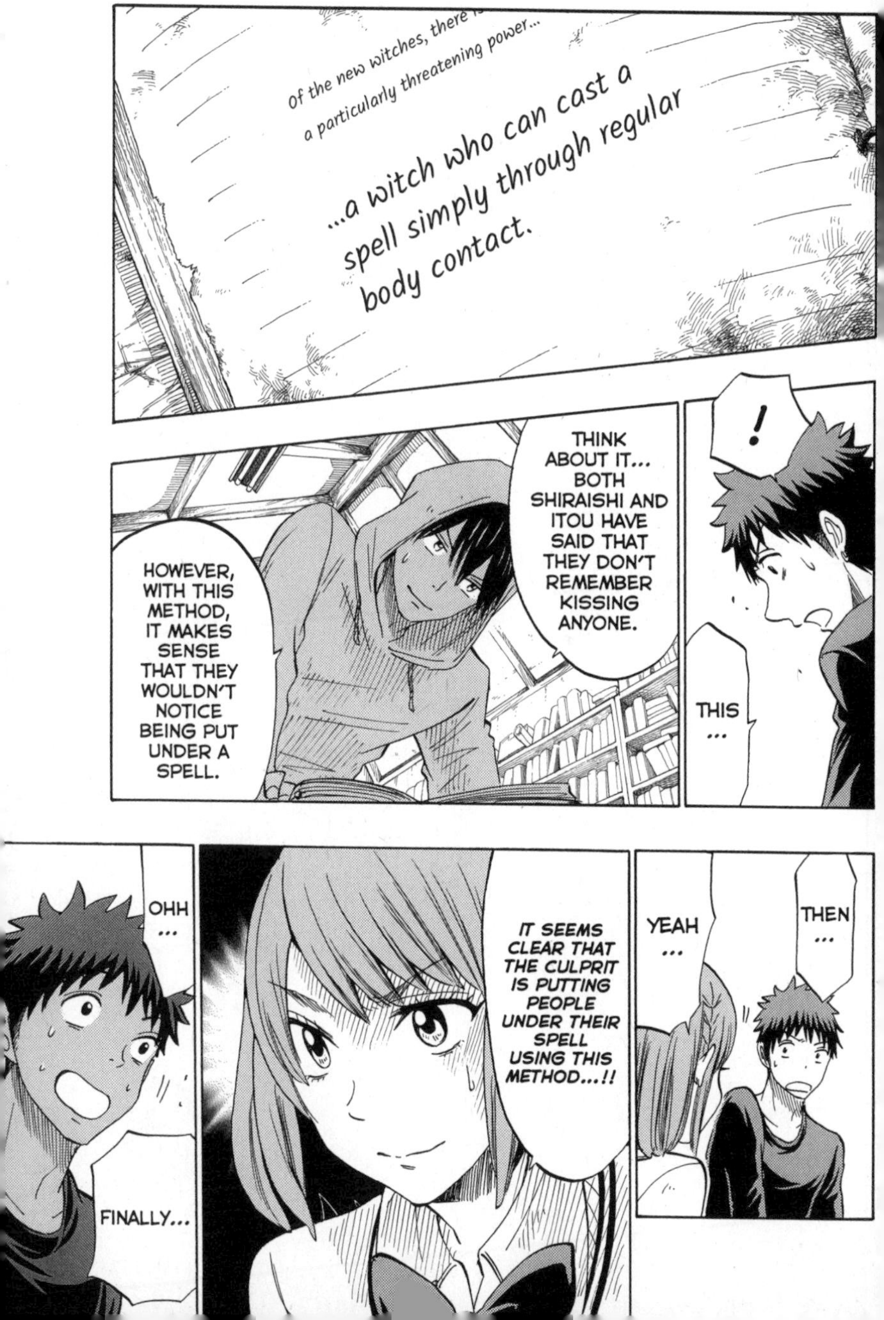

Of the new witches, there
a particularly threatening power...
...a witch who can cast a spell simply through regular body contact.
!
THIS...
THINK ABOUT IT... BOTH SHIRAISHI AND ITOU HAVE SAID THAT THEY DON'T REMEMBER KISSING ANYONE.
HOWEVER, WITH THIS METHOD, IT MAKES SENSE THAT THEY WOULDN'T NOTICE BEING PUT UNDER A SPELL.
THEN...
YEAH...
IT SEEMS CLEAR THAT THE CULPRIT IS PUTTING PEOPLE UNDER THEIR SPELL USING THIS METHOD...!!
OHH...
FINALLY...

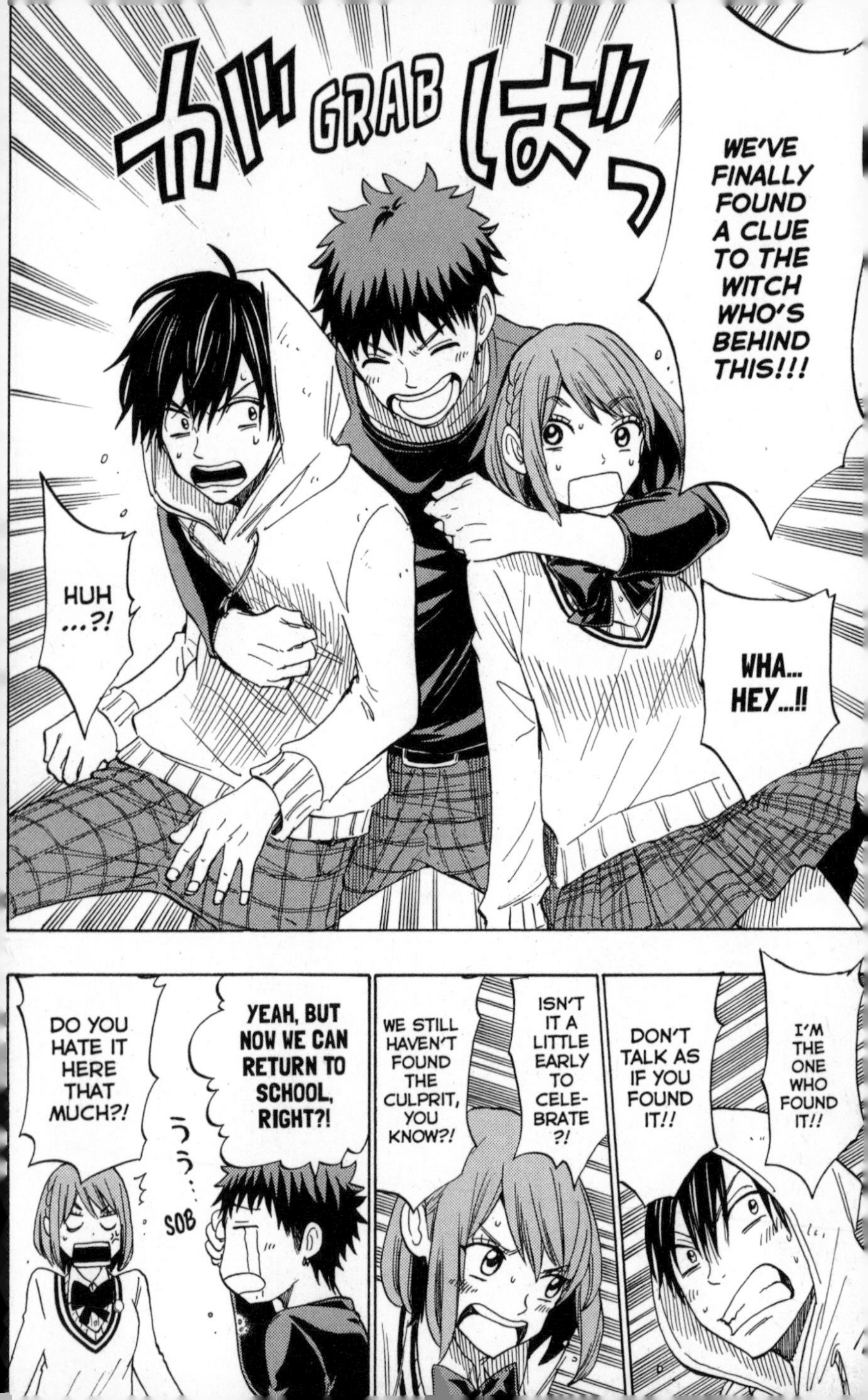
GRAB
WE'VE FINALLY FOUND A CLUE TO THE WITCH WHO'S BEHIND THIS!!!
WHA... HEY...!!
HUH ...?!
I'M THE ONE WHO FOUND IT!!
DON'T TALK AS IF YOU FOUND IT!!
ISN'T IT A LITTLE EARLY TO CELE-BRATE ?!
WE STILL HAVEN'T FOUND THE CULPRIT, YOU KNOW?!
YEAH, BUT NOW WE CAN RETURN TO SCHOOL, RIGHT?!
うう…
SOB
DO YOU HATE IT HERE THAT MUCH?!

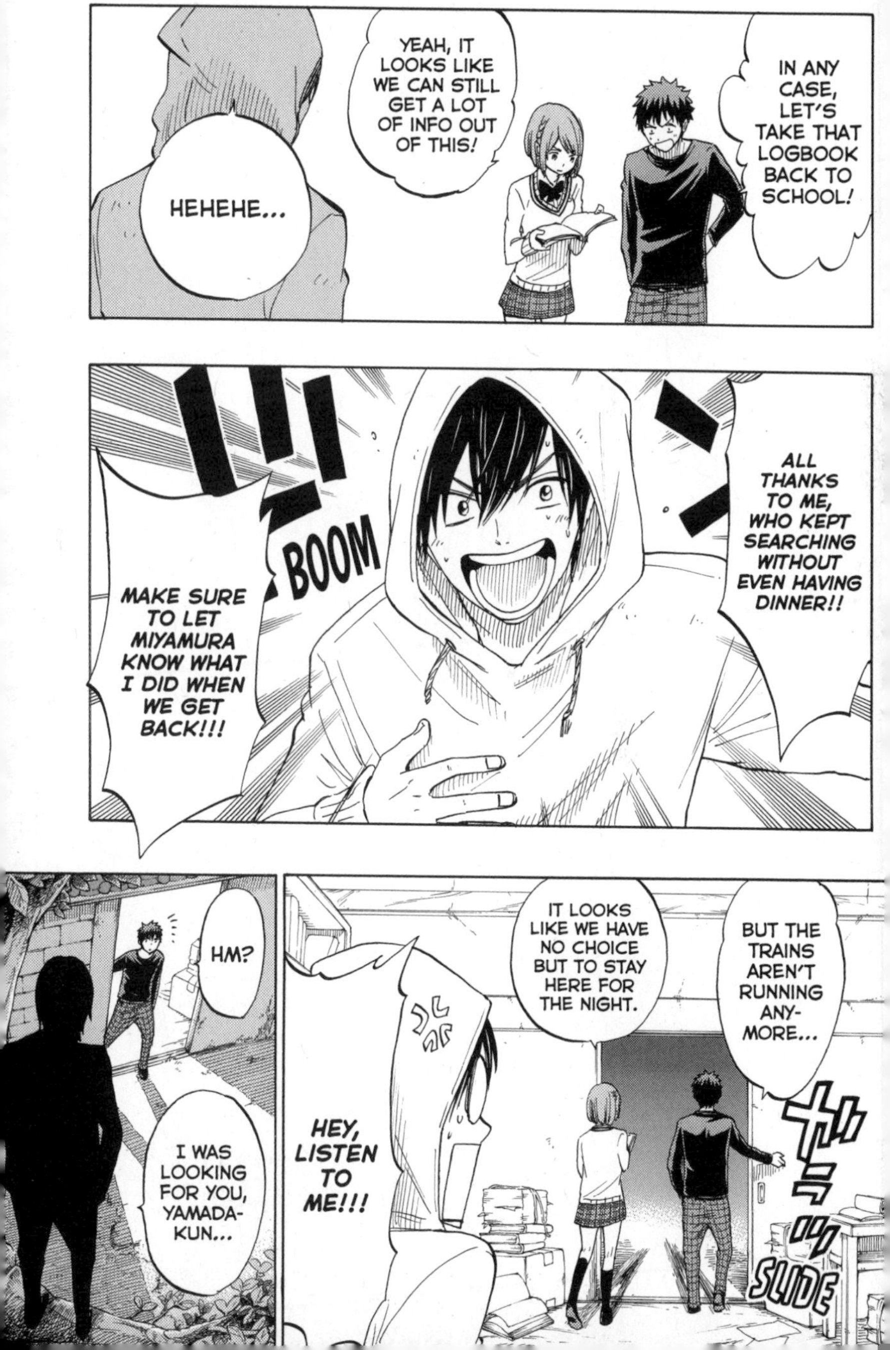
IN ANY CASE, LET'S TAKE THAT LOGBOOK BACK TO SCHOOL!
YEAH, IT LOOKS LIKE WE CAN STILL GET A LOT OF INFO OUT OF THIS!
HEHEHE...
ALL THANKS TO ME, WHO KEPT SEARCHING WITHOUT EVEN HAVING DINNER!!
BOOM
MAKE SURE TO LET MIYAMURA KNOW WHAT I DID WHEN WE GET BACK!!!
BUT THE TRAINS AREN'T RUNNING ANY-MORE...
IT LOOKS LIKE WE HAVE NO CHOICE BUT TO STAY HERE FOR THE NIGHT.
SLIDE
HEY, LISTEN TO ME!!!
HM?
I WAS LOOKING FOR YOU, YAMADA-KUN...

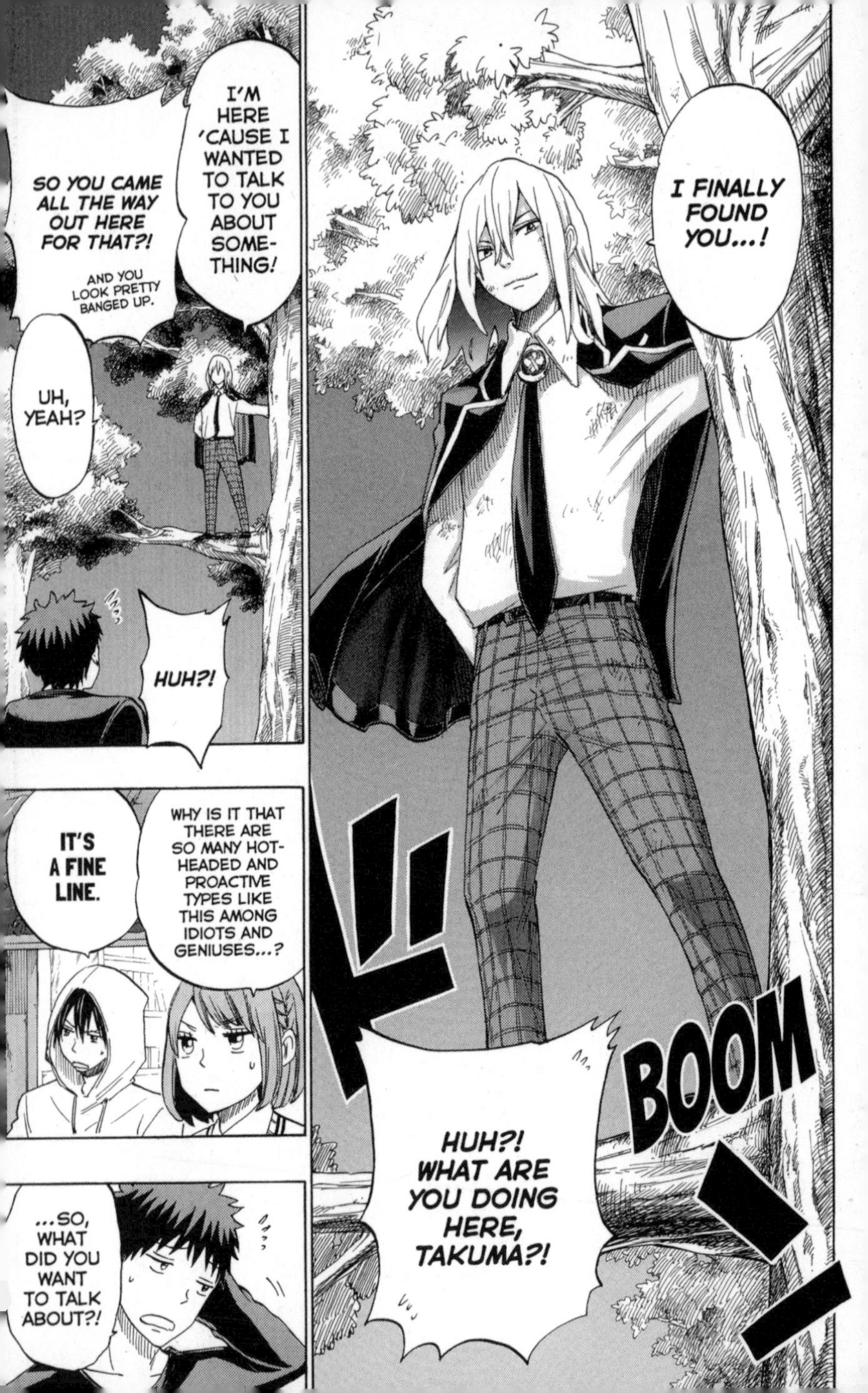

I FINALLY FOUND YOU...!
BOOM
HUH?! WHAT ARE YOU DOING HERE, TAKUMA?!
I'M HERE 'CAUSE I WANTED TO TALK TO YOU ABOUT SOME-THING!
SO YOU CAME ALL THE WAY OUT HERE FOR THAT?!
AND YOU LOOK PRETTY BANGED UP.
UH, YEAH?
HUH?!
WHY IS IT THAT THERE ARE SO MANY HOT-HEADED AND PROACTIVE TYPES LIKE THIS AMONG IDIOTS AND GENIUSES...?
IT'S A FINE LINE.
...SO, WHAT DID YOU WANT TO TALK ABOUT?!

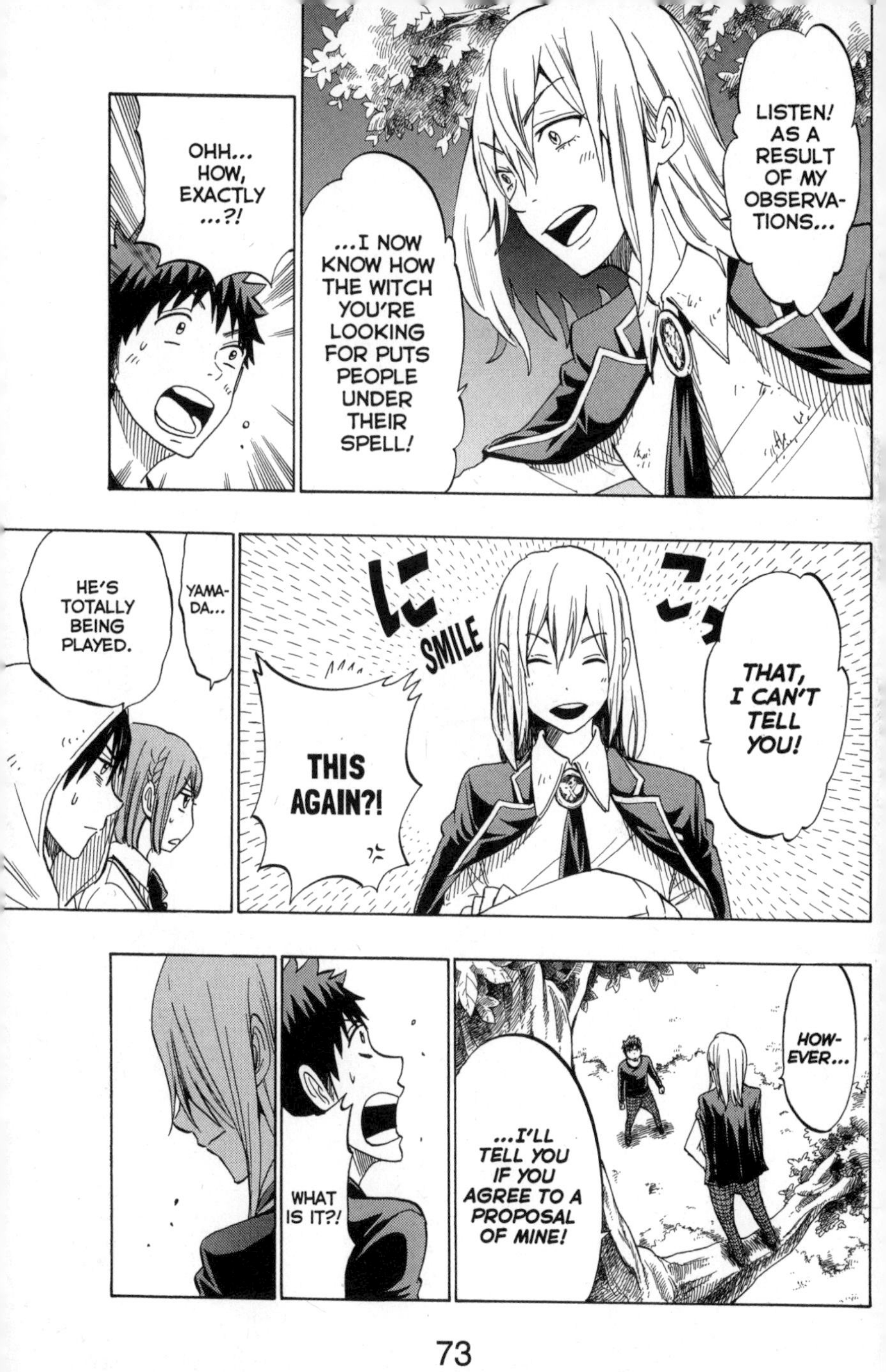
LISTEN! AS A RESULT OF MY OBSERVATIONS...
...I NOW KNOW HOW THE WITCH YOU'RE LOOKING FOR PUTS PEOPLE UNDER THEIR SPELL!
OHH... HOW, EXACTLY ...?!
にこっ
SMILE
THAT, I CAN'T TELL YOU!
THIS AGAIN?!
YAMADA...
HE'S TOTALLY BEING PLAYED.
HOWEVER...
...I'LL TELL YOU IF YOU AGREE TO A PROPOSAL OF MINE!
WHAT IS IT?!

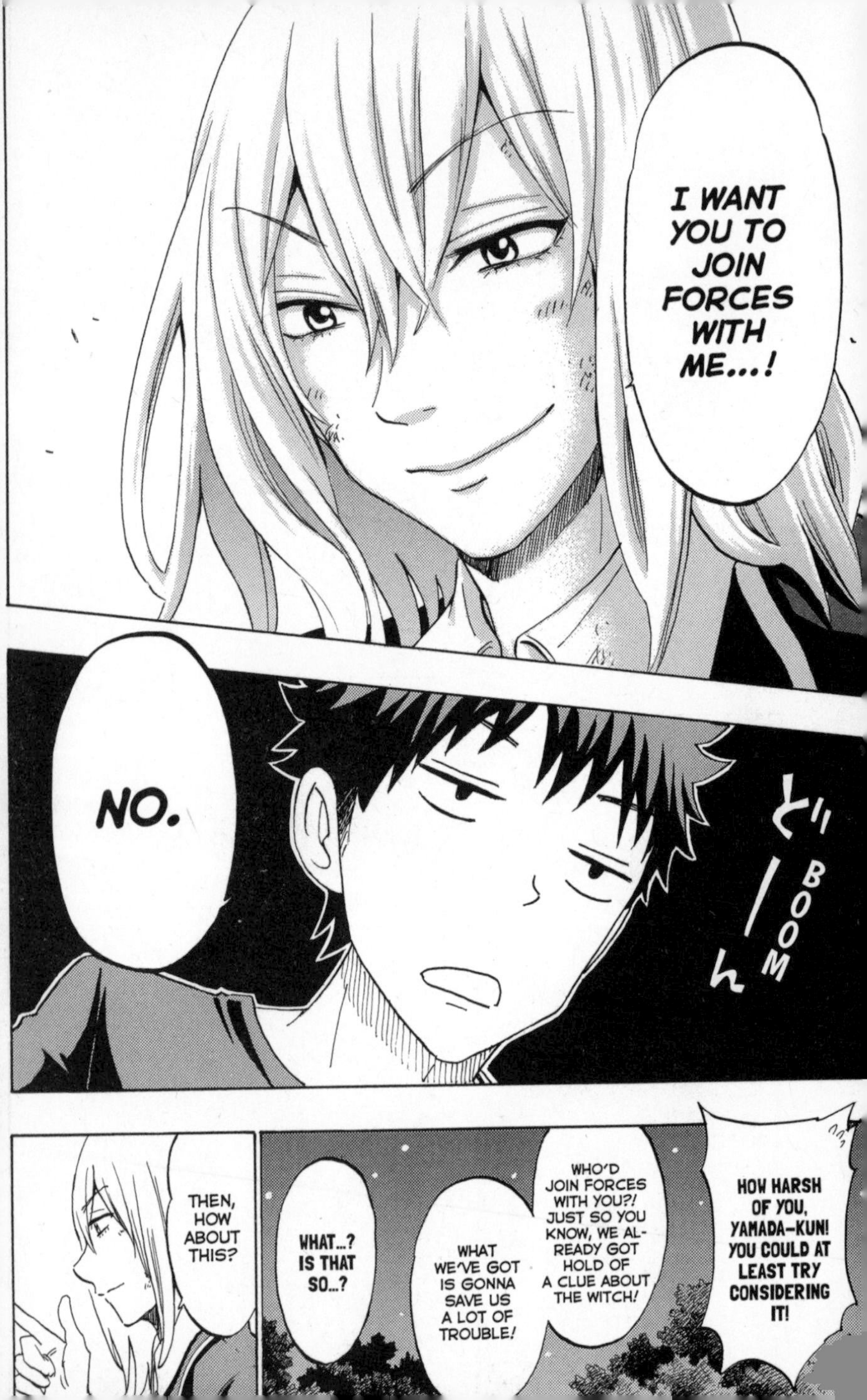

I WANT YOU TO JOIN FORCES WITH ME...!
NO.
どーん
BOOM
HOW HARSH OF YOU, YAMADA-KUN! YOU COULD AT LEAST TRY CONSIDERING IT!
WHO'D JOIN FORCES WITH YOU?! JUST SO YOU KNOW, WE AL-READY GOT HOLD OF A CLUE ABOUT THE WITCH!
WHAT WE'VE GOT IS GONNA SAVE US A LOT OF TROUBLE!
WHAT...? IS THAT SO...?
THEN, HOW ABOUT THIS?

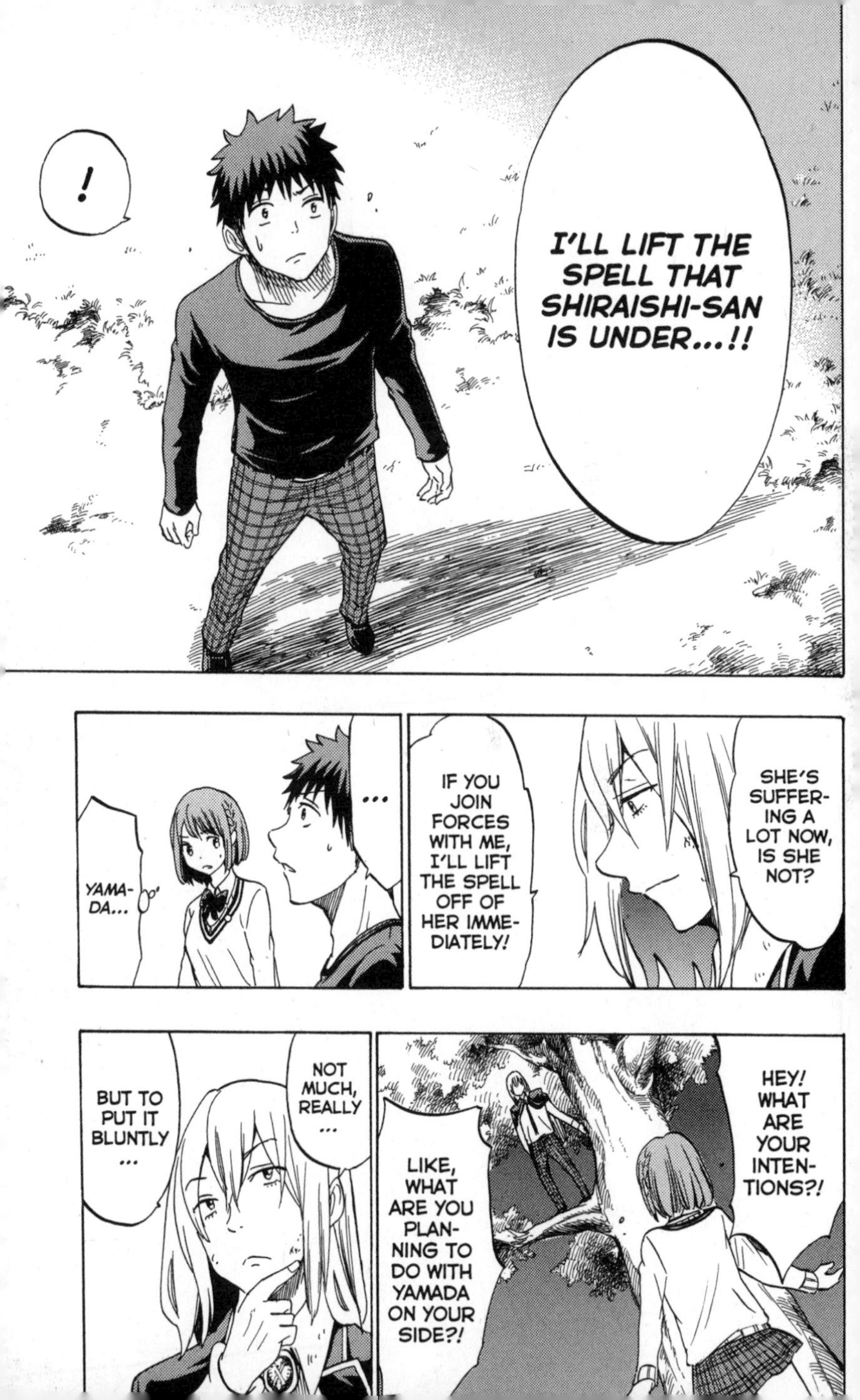
I'LL LIFT THE SPELL THAT SHIRAISHI-SAN IS UNDER...!!
!
SHE'S SUFFERING A LOT NOW, IS SHE NOT?
IF YOU JOIN FORCES WITH ME, I'LL LIFT THE SPELL OFF OF HER IMMEDIATELY!
...
YAMADA...
HEY! WHAT ARE YOUR INTENTIONS?!
LIKE, WHAT ARE YOU PLANNING TO DO WITH YAMADA ON YOUR SIDE?!
NOT MUCH, REALLY...
BUT TO PUT IT BLUNTLY...

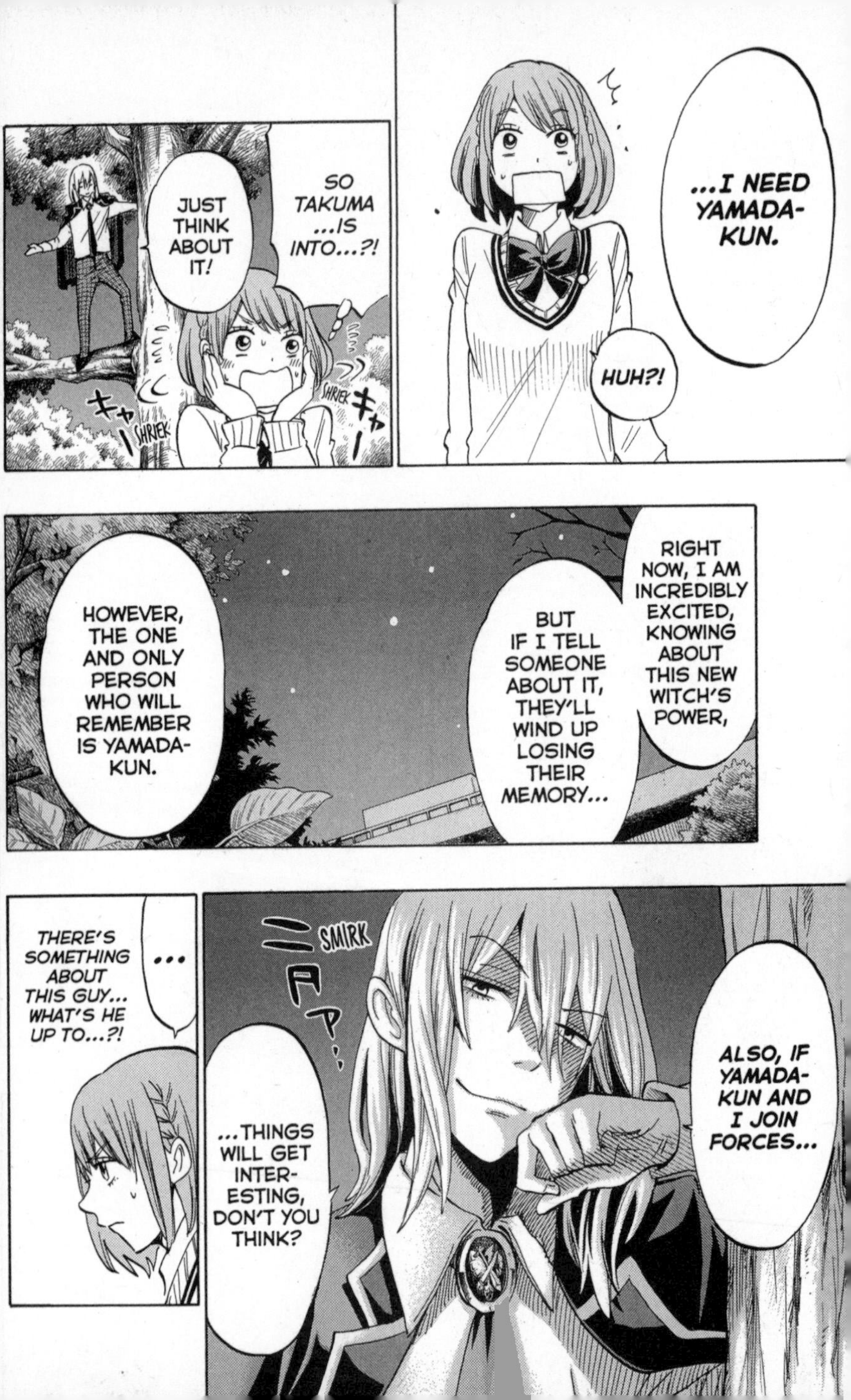
...I NEED YAMADA-KUN.
HUH?!
SO TAKUMA ...IS INTO...?!
JUST THINK ABOUT IT!
SHRIEK
SHRIEK
RIGHT NOW, I AM INCREDIBLY EXCITED, KNOWING ABOUT THIS NEW WITCH'S POWER,
BUT IF I TELL SOMEONE ABOUT IT, THEY'LL WIND UP LOSING THEIR MEMORY...
HOWEVER, THE ONE AND ONLY PERSON WHO WILL REMEMBER IS YAMADA-KUN.
ALSO, IF YAMADA-KUN AND I JOIN FORCES...
SMIRK
...THINGS WILL GET INTER-ESTING, DON'T YOU THINK?
...
THERE'S SOMETHING ABOUT THIS GUY... WHAT'S HE UP TO...?!

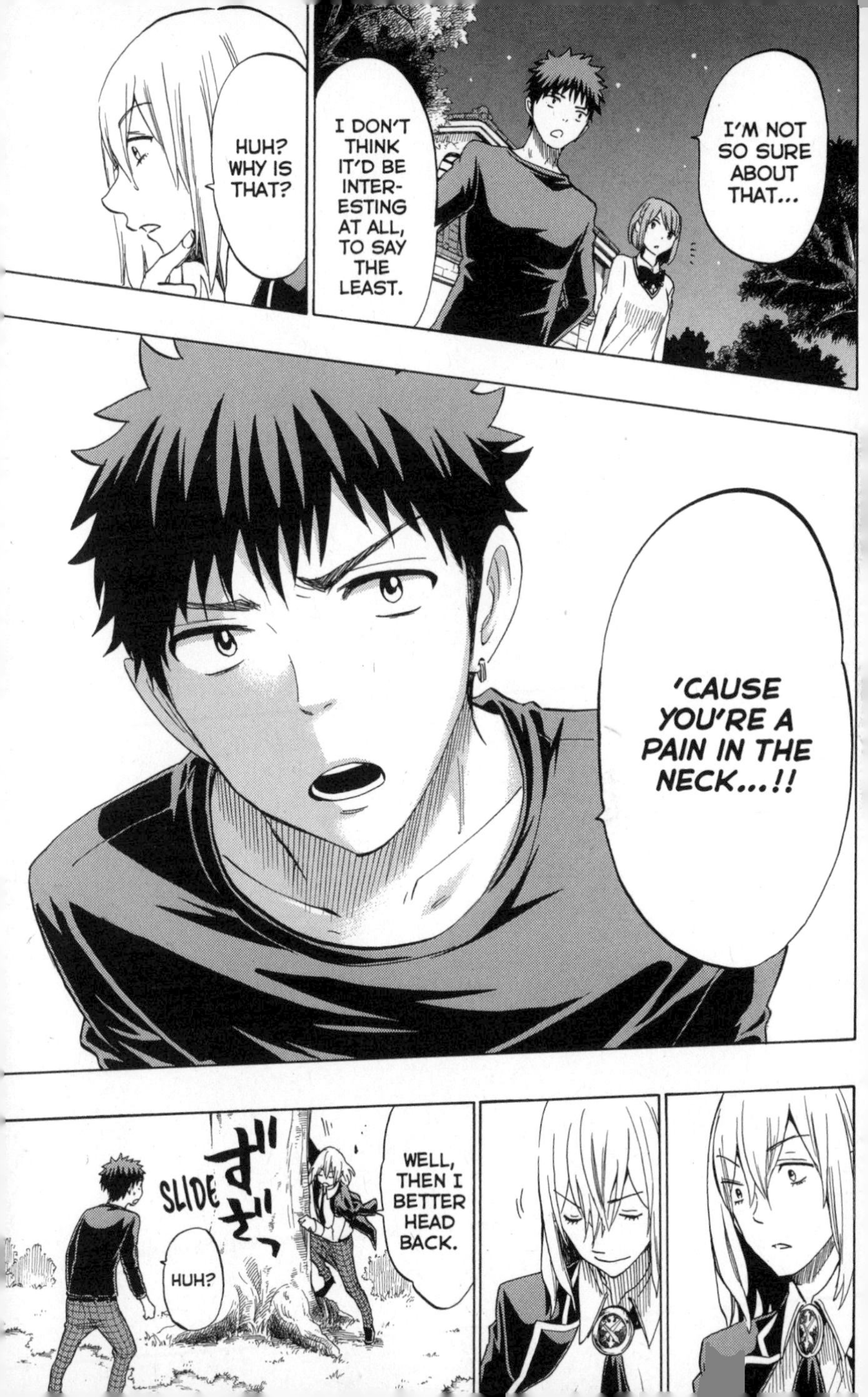
I'M NOT SO SURE ABOUT THAT...
I DON'T THINK IT'D BE INTER-ESTING AT ALL, TO SAY THE LEAST.
HUH? WHY IS THAT?
'CAUSE YOU'RE A PAIN IN THE NECK...!!
WELL, THEN I BETTER HEAD BACK.
ずざっ
SLIDE
HUH?

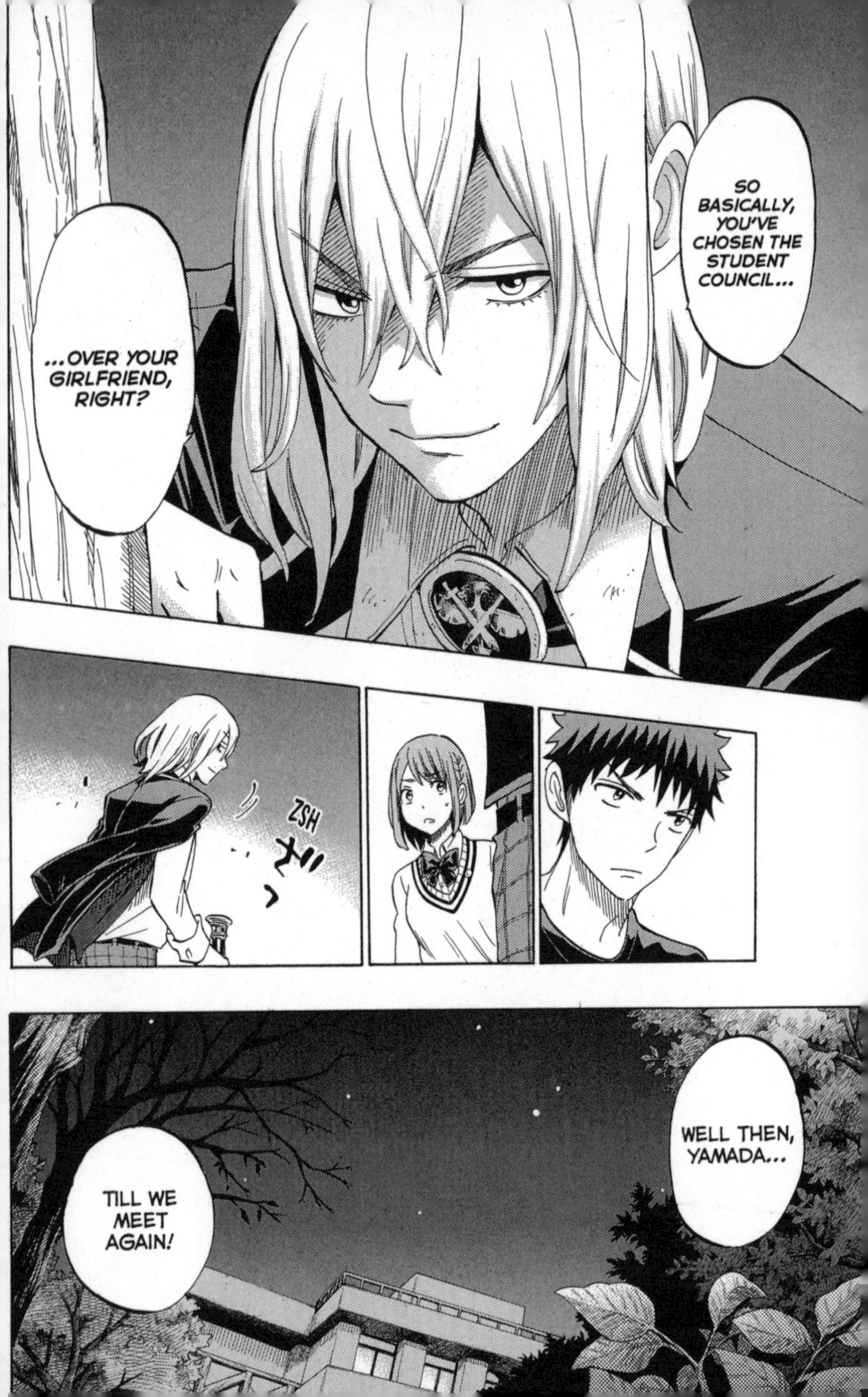
SO BASICALLY, YOU'VE CHOSEN THE STUDENT COUNCIL...
...OVER YOUR GIRLFRIEND, RIGHT?
ZSH
WELL THEN, YAMADA...
TILL WE MEET AGAIN!

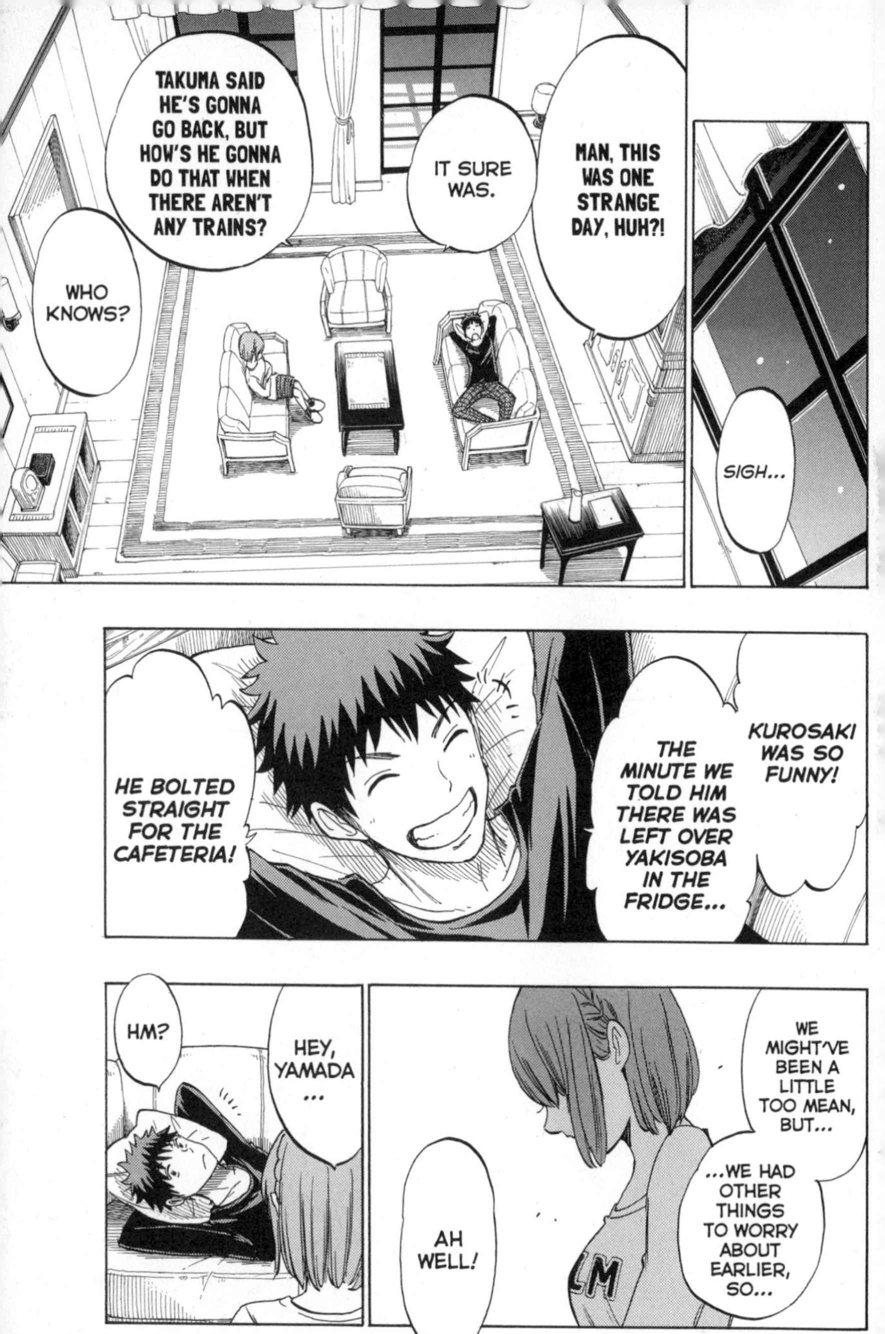
SIGH...
MAN, THIS WAS ONE STRANGE DAY, HUH?!
IT SURE WAS.
TAKUMA SAID HE'S GONNA GO BACK, BUT HOW'S HE GONNA DO THAT WHEN THERE AREN'T ANY TRAINS?
WHO KNOWS?
KUROSAKI WAS SO FUNNY!
THE MINUTE WE TOLD HIM THERE WAS LEFT OVER YAKISOBA IN THE FRIDGE...
HE BOLTED STRAIGHT FOR THE CAFETERIA!
WE MIGHT'VE BEEN A LITTLE TOO MEAN, BUT...
...WE HAD OTHER THINGS TO WORRY ABOUT EARLIER, SO...
AH WELL!
HEY, YAMADA...
HM?

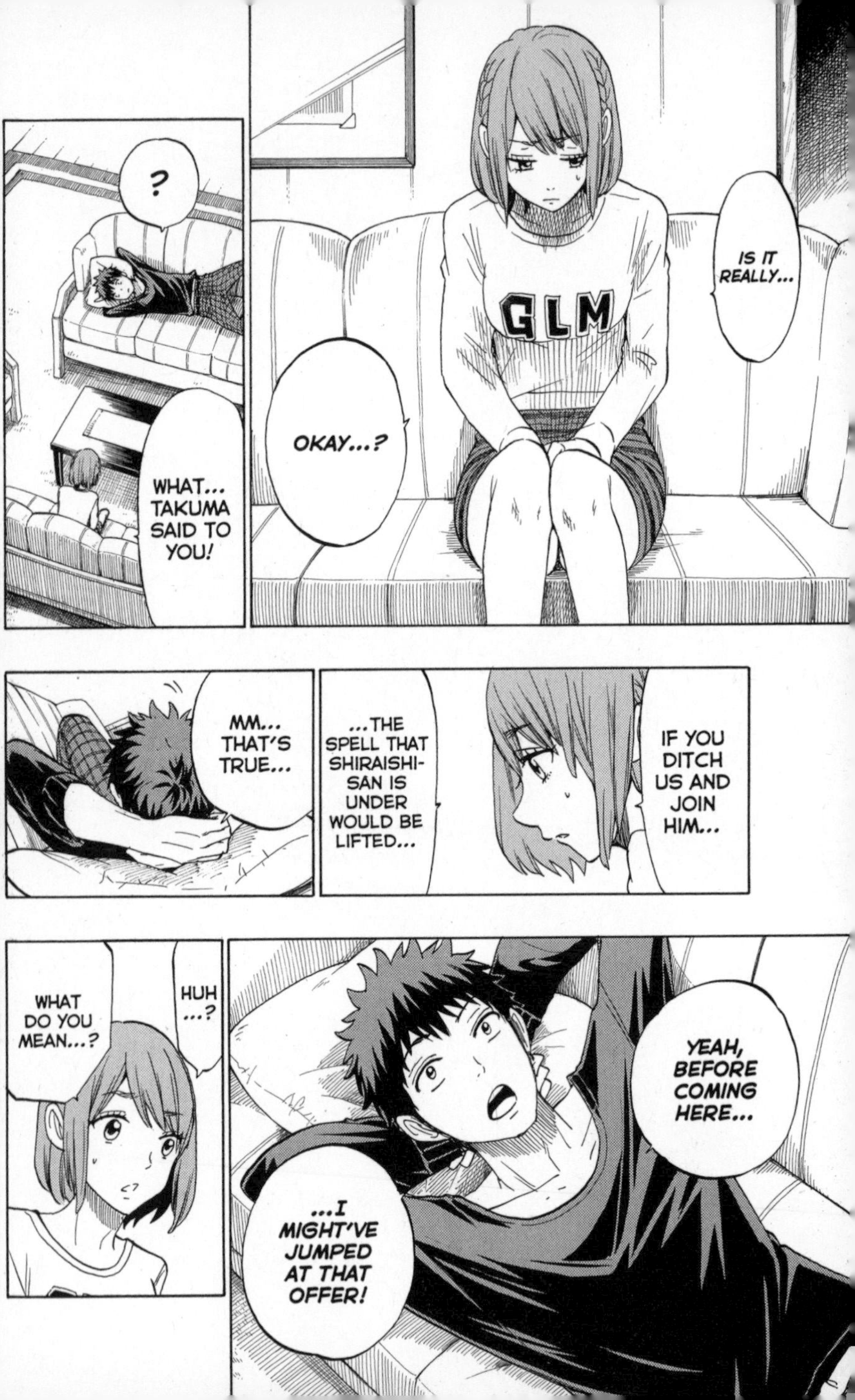
IS IT REALLY...
OKAY...?
WHAT... TAKUMA SAID TO YOU!
?
IF YOU DITCH US AND JOIN HIM...
...THE SPELL THAT SHIRAISHI-SAN IS UNDER WOULD BE LIFTED...
MM... THAT'S TRUE...
YEAH, BEFORE COMING HERE...
...I MIGHT'VE JUMPED AT THAT OFFER!
HUH...?
WHAT DO YOU MEAN...?

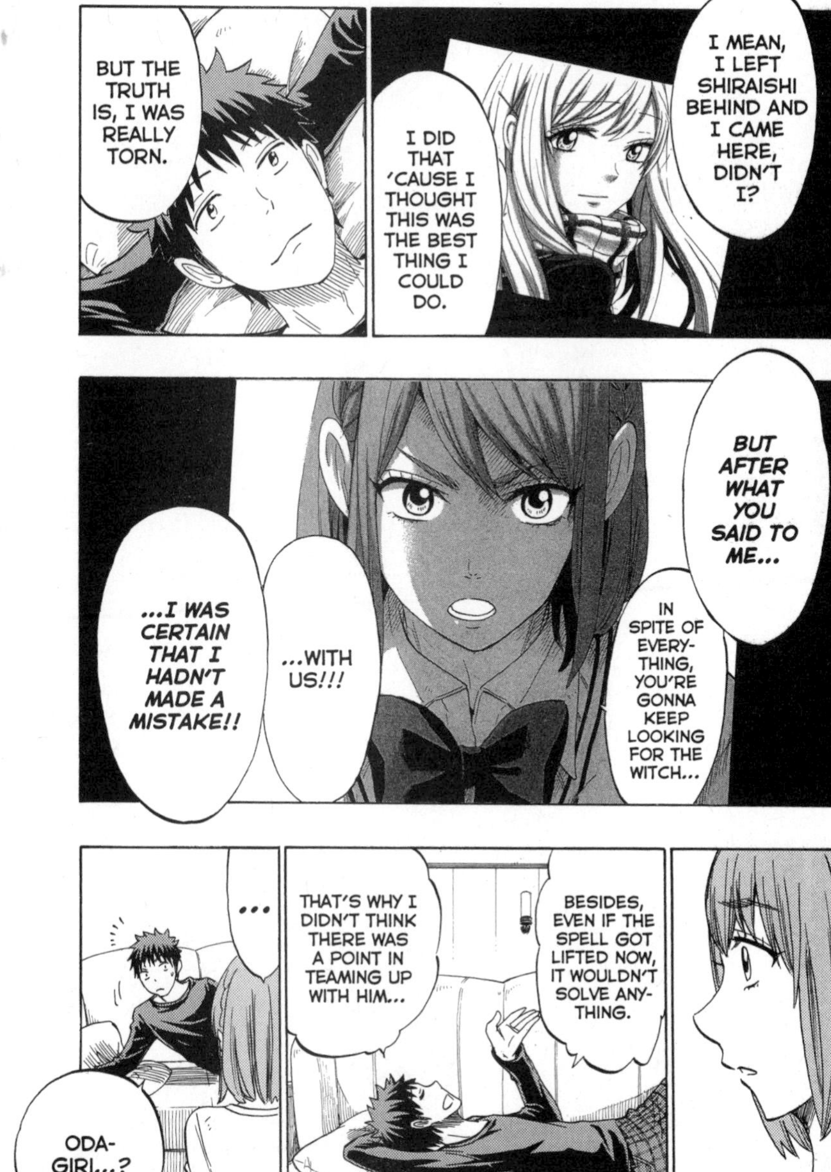
I MEAN, I LEFT SHIRAISHI BEHIND AND I CAME HERE, DIDN'T I?
I DID THAT 'CAUSE I THOUGHT THIS WAS THE BEST THING I COULD DO.
BUT THE TRUTH IS, I WAS REALLY TORN.
BUT AFTER WHAT YOU SAID TO ME...
IN SPITE OF EVERY-THING, YOU'RE GONNA KEEP LOOKING FOR THE WITCH...
...WITH US!!!
...I WAS CERTAIN THAT I HADN'T MADE A MISTAKE!!
BESIDES, EVEN IF THE SPELL GOT LIFTED NOW, IT WOULDN'T SOLVE ANY-THING.
THAT'S WHY I DIDN'T THINK THERE WAS A POINT IN TEAMING UP WITH HIM...
...
ODA-GIRI...?

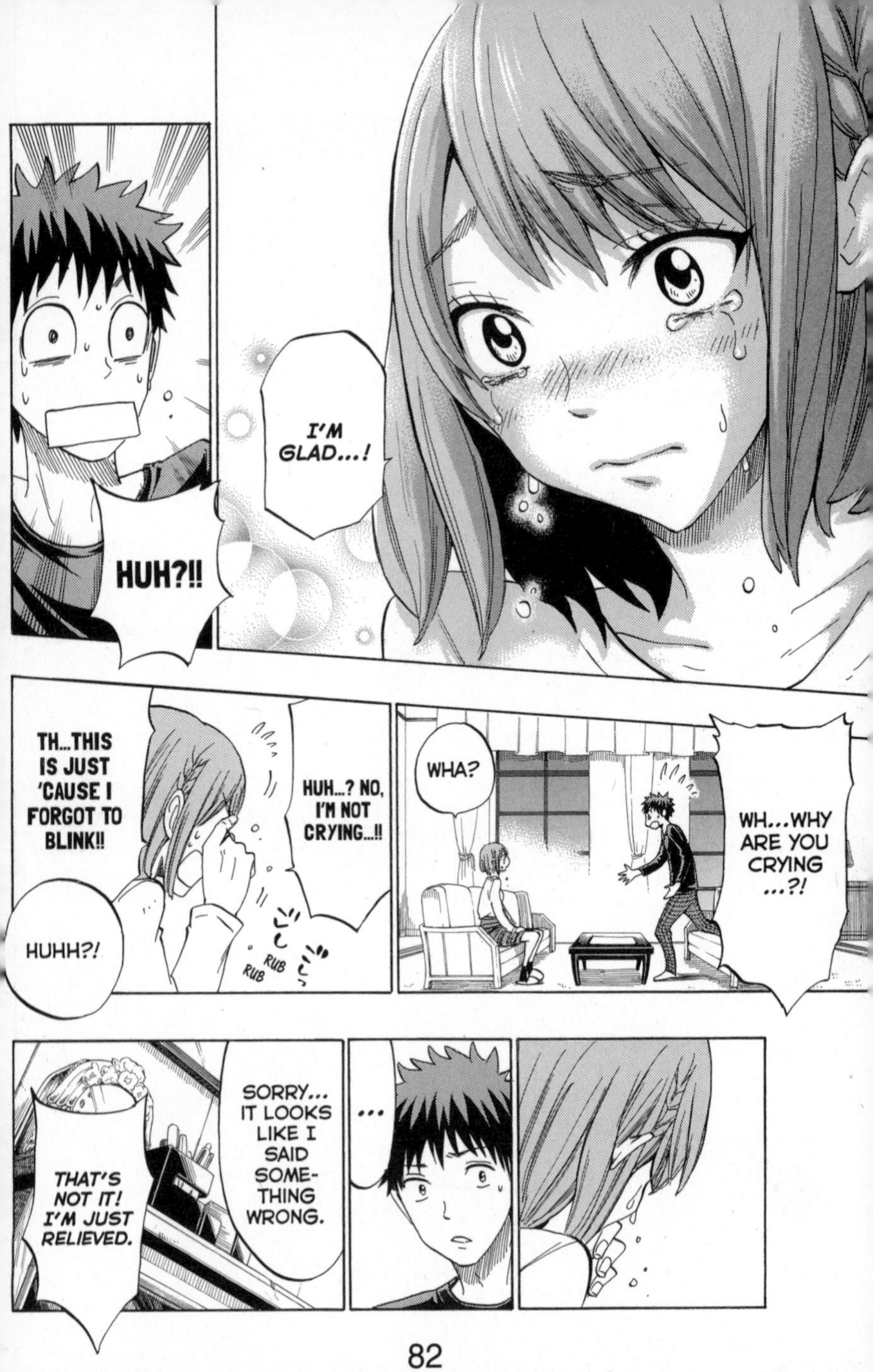
I'M GLAD...!
HUH?!!
WH...WHY ARE YOU CRYING ...?!
WHA?
HUH...? NO, I'M NOT CRYING...!!
TH...THIS IS JUST 'CAUSE I FORGOT TO BLINK!!
HUHH?!
RUB RUB
...
SORRY... IT LOOKS LIKE I SAID SOME-THING WRONG.
THAT'S NOT IT! I'M JUST RELIEVED.

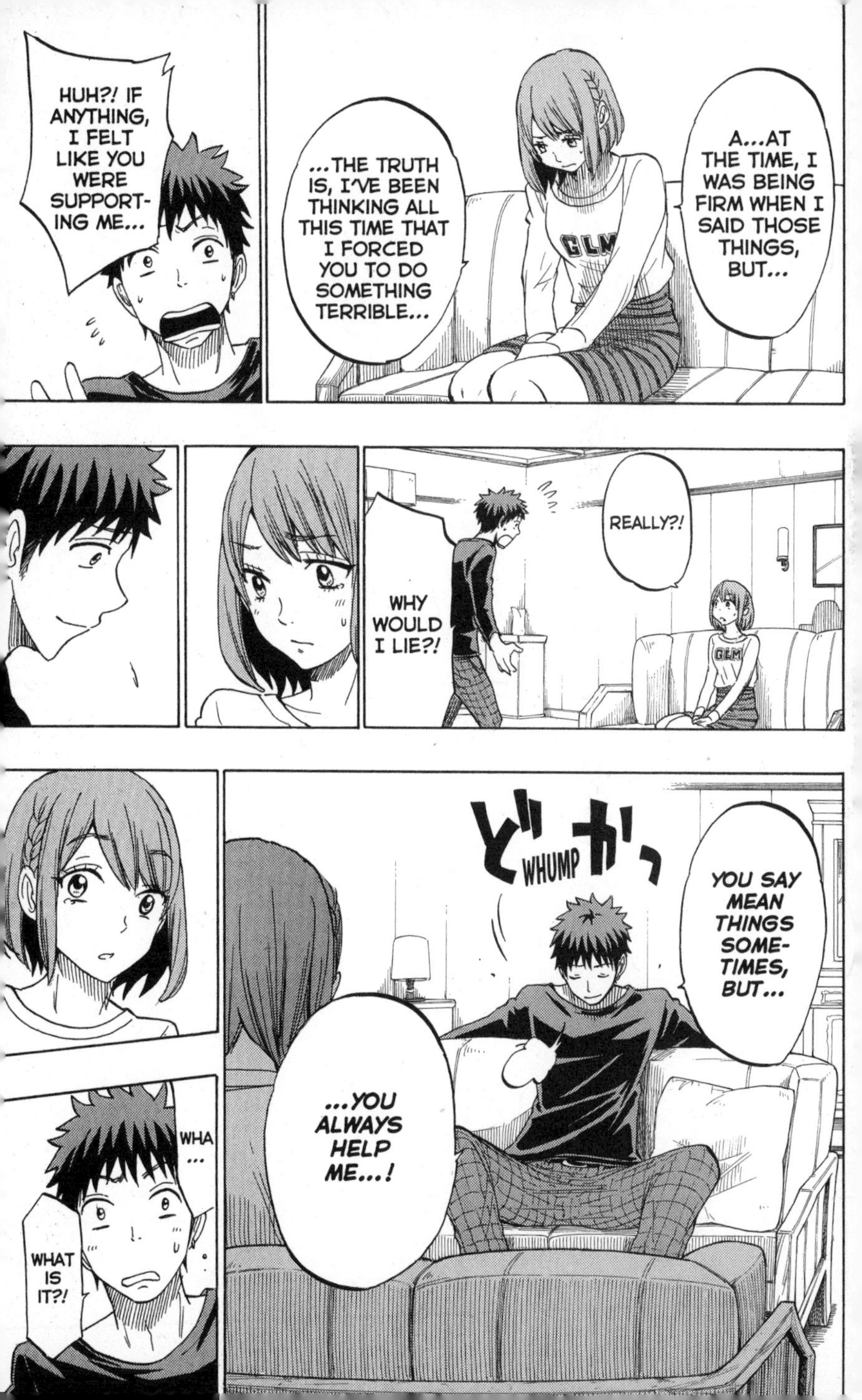
A...AT THE TIME, I WAS BEING FIRM WHEN I SAID THOSE THINGS, BUT...
...THE TRUTH IS, I'VE BEEN THINKING ALL THIS TIME THAT I FORCED YOU TO DO SOMETHING TERRIBLE...
HUH?! IF ANYTHING, I FELT LIKE YOU WERE SUPPORT-ING ME...
REALLY?!
WHY WOULD I LIE?!
どかっ WHUMP
YOU SAY MEAN THINGS SOME-TIMES, BUT...
...YOU ALWAYS HELP ME...!
WHA...
WHAT IS IT?!

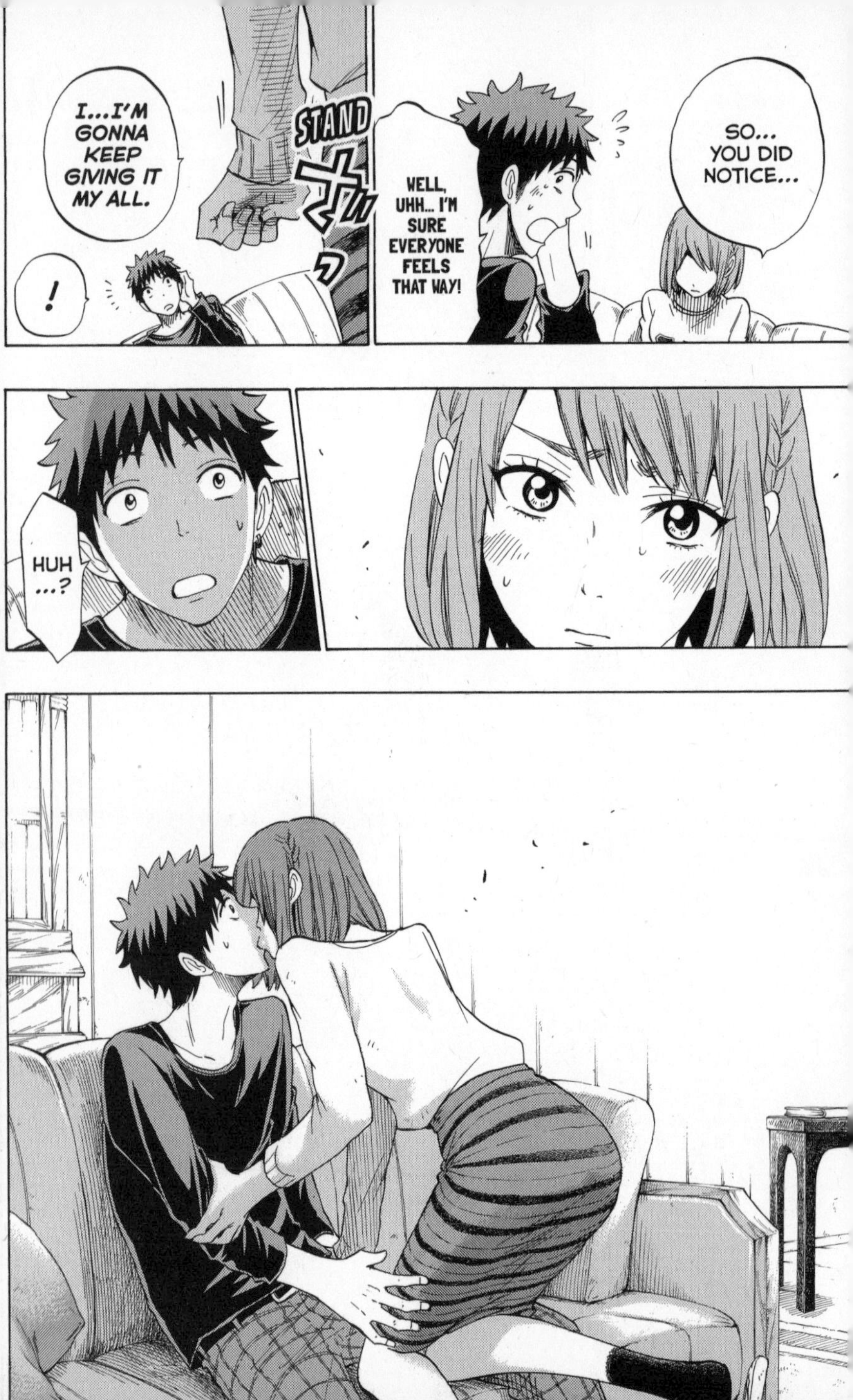
SO... YOU DID NOTICE...
WELL, UHH... I'M SURE EVERYONE FEELS THAT WAY!
STAND
I...I'M GONNA KEEP GIVING IT MY ALL.
!
HUH ...?

CHAPTER 133: Come at me!!

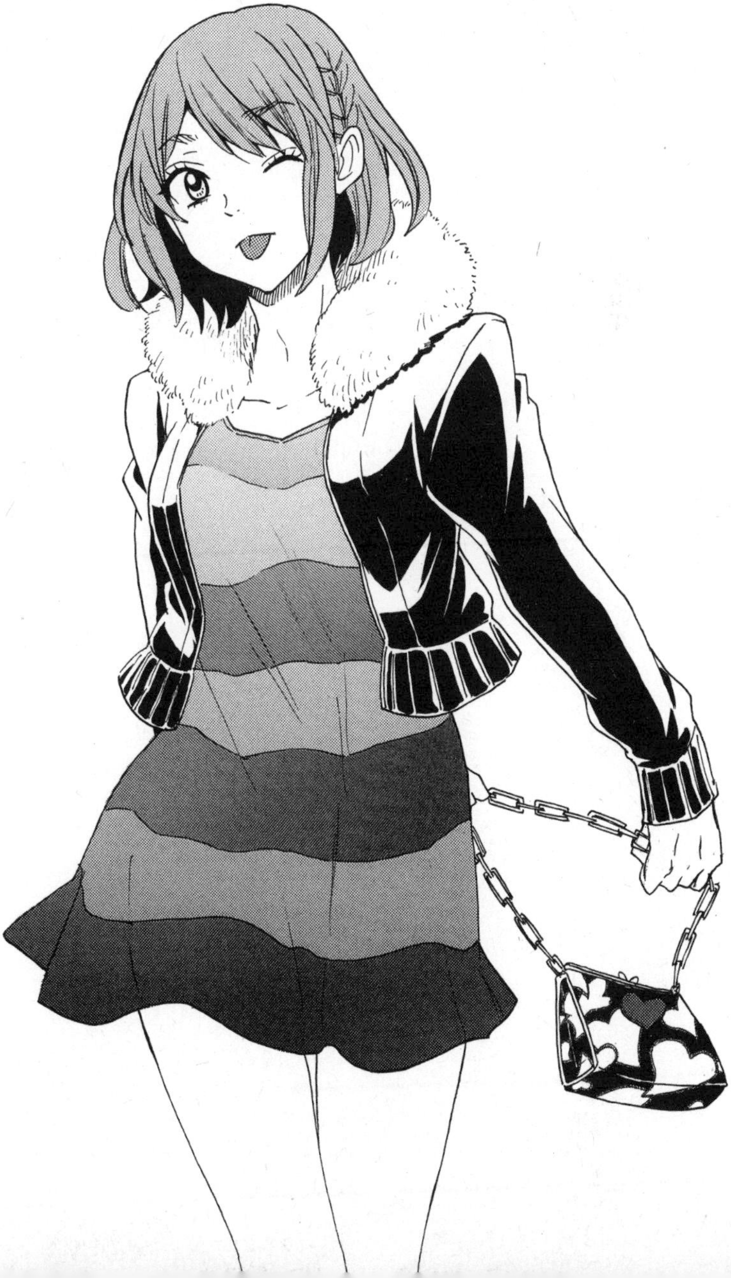

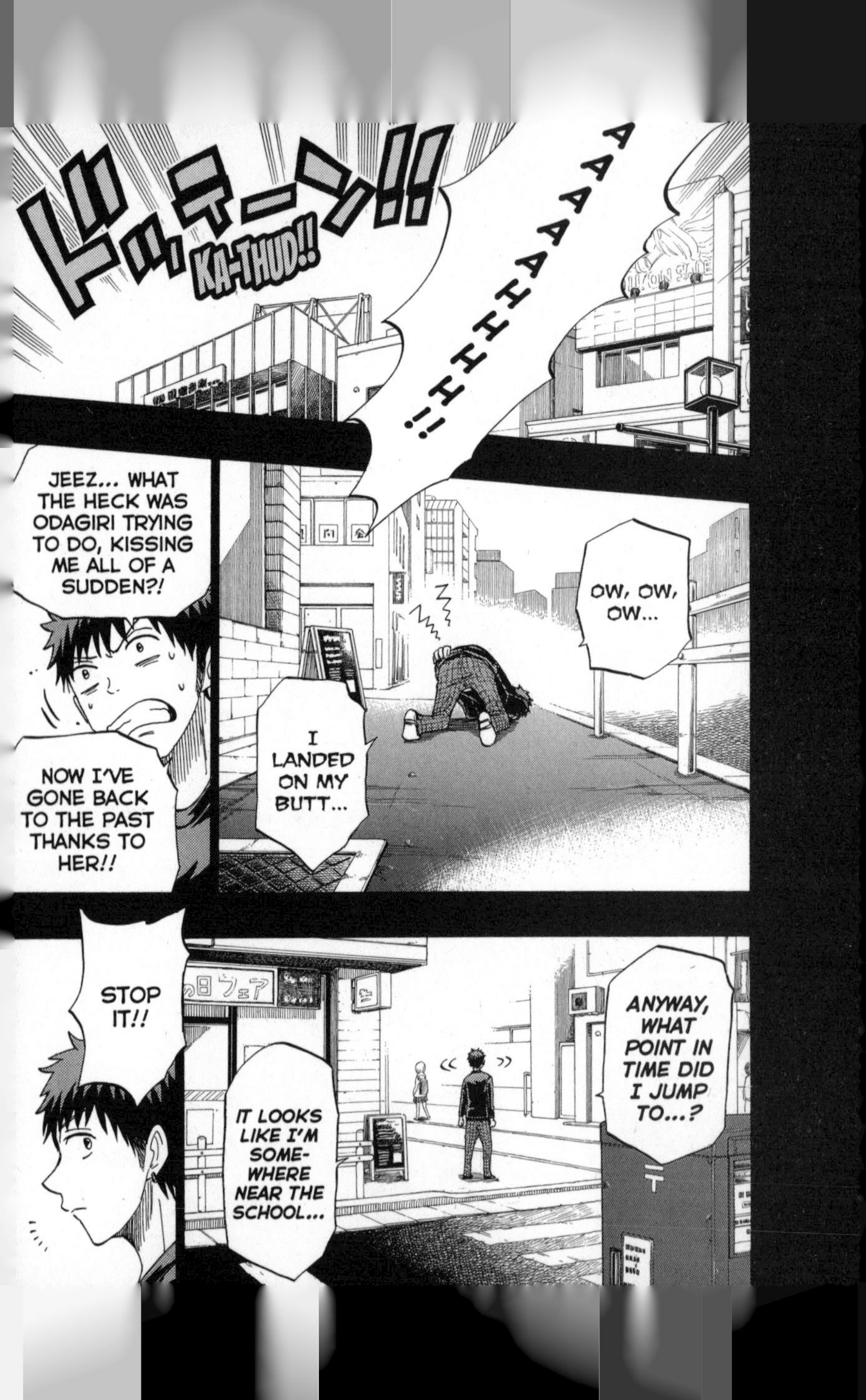
AAAAAHHHH!!
ドッテーン!!
KA-THUD!!
OW, OW, OW...
I LANDED ON MY BUTT...
JEEZ... WHAT THE HECK WAS ODAGIRI TRYING TO DO, KISSING ME ALL OF A SUDDEN?!
NOW I'VE GONE BACK TO THE PAST THANKS TO HER!!
ANYWAY, WHAT POINT IN TIME DID I JUMP TO...?
IT LOOKS LIKE I'M SOME-WHERE NEAR THE SCHOOL...
STOP IT!!

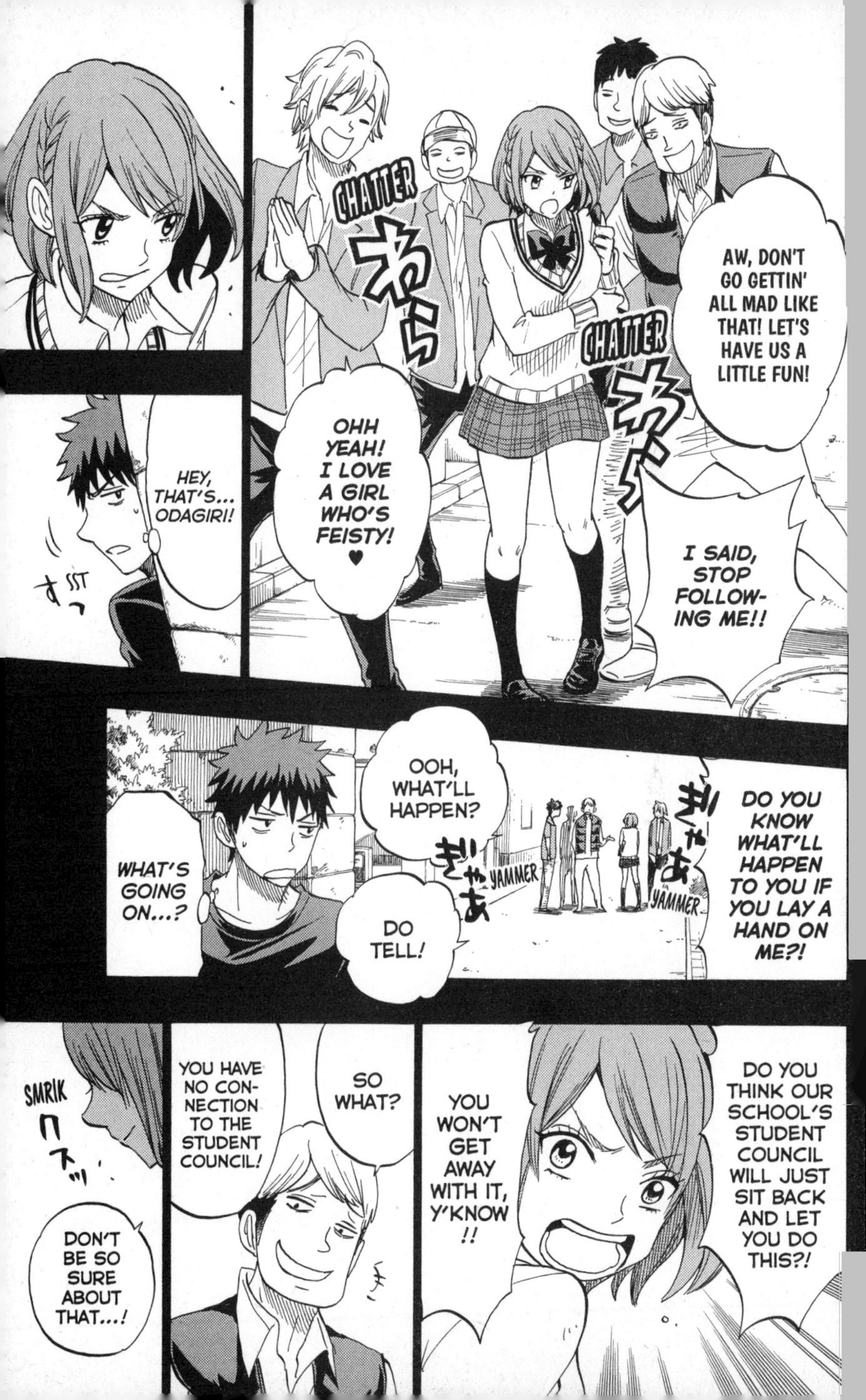
AW, DON'T GO GETTIN' ALL MAD LIKE THAT! LET'S HAVE US A LITTLE FUN!
CHATTER
わら
CHATTER
わら
I SAID, STOP FOLLOW-ING ME!!
OHH YEAH! I LOVE A GIRL WHO'S FEISTY! ♥
HEY, THAT'S... ODAGIRI!
SST
DO YOU KNOW WHAT'LL HAPPEN TO YOU IF YOU LAY A HAND ON ME?!
ぎゃあ
YAMMER
OOH, WHAT'LL HAPPEN?
ぎゃあ
YAMMER
DO TELL!
WHAT'S GOING ON...?
DO YOU THINK OUR SCHOOL'S STUDENT COUNCIL WILL JUST SIT BACK AND LET YOU DO THIS?!
YOU WON'T GET AWAY WITH IT, Y'KNOW!!
SO WHAT?
YOU HAVE NO CON-NECTION TO THE STUDENT COUNCIL!
DON'T BE SO SURE ABOUT THAT...!
SMRIK

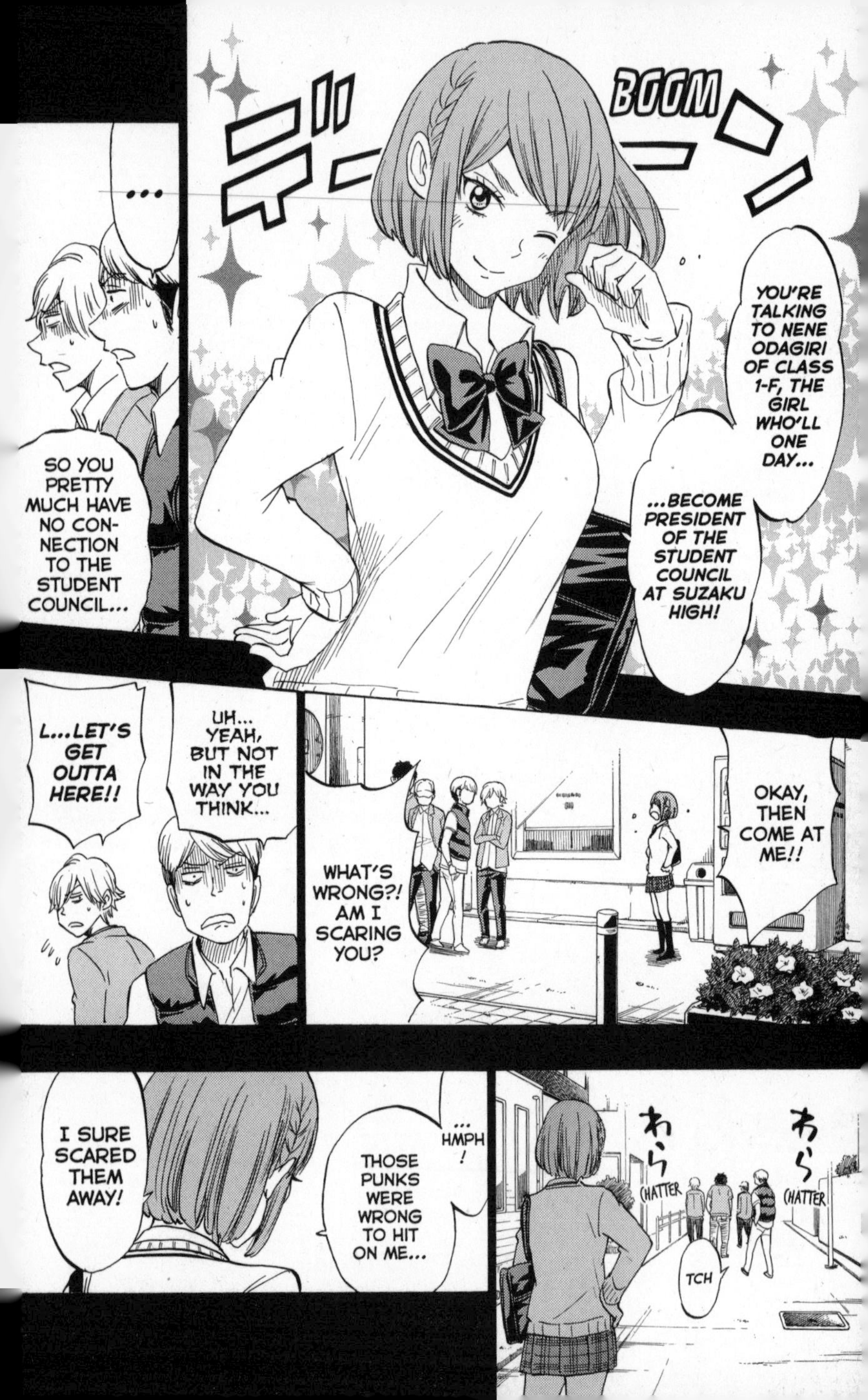
BOOM
YOU'RE TALKING TO NENE ODAGIRI OF CLASS 1-F, THE GIRL WHO'LL ONE DAY...
...BECOME PRESIDENT OF THE STUDENT COUNCIL AT SUZAKU HIGH!
...
SO YOU PRETTY MUCH HAVE NO CON-NECTION TO THE STUDENT COUNCIL...
OKAY, THEN COME AT ME!!
WHAT'S WRONG?! AM I SCARING YOU?
UH... YEAH, BUT NOT IN THE WAY YOU THINK...
L...LET'S GET OUTTA HERE!!
わら CHATTER
わら CHATTER
TCH
...HMPH!
THOSE PUNKS WERE WRONG TO HIT ON ME...
I SURE SCARED THEM AWAY!

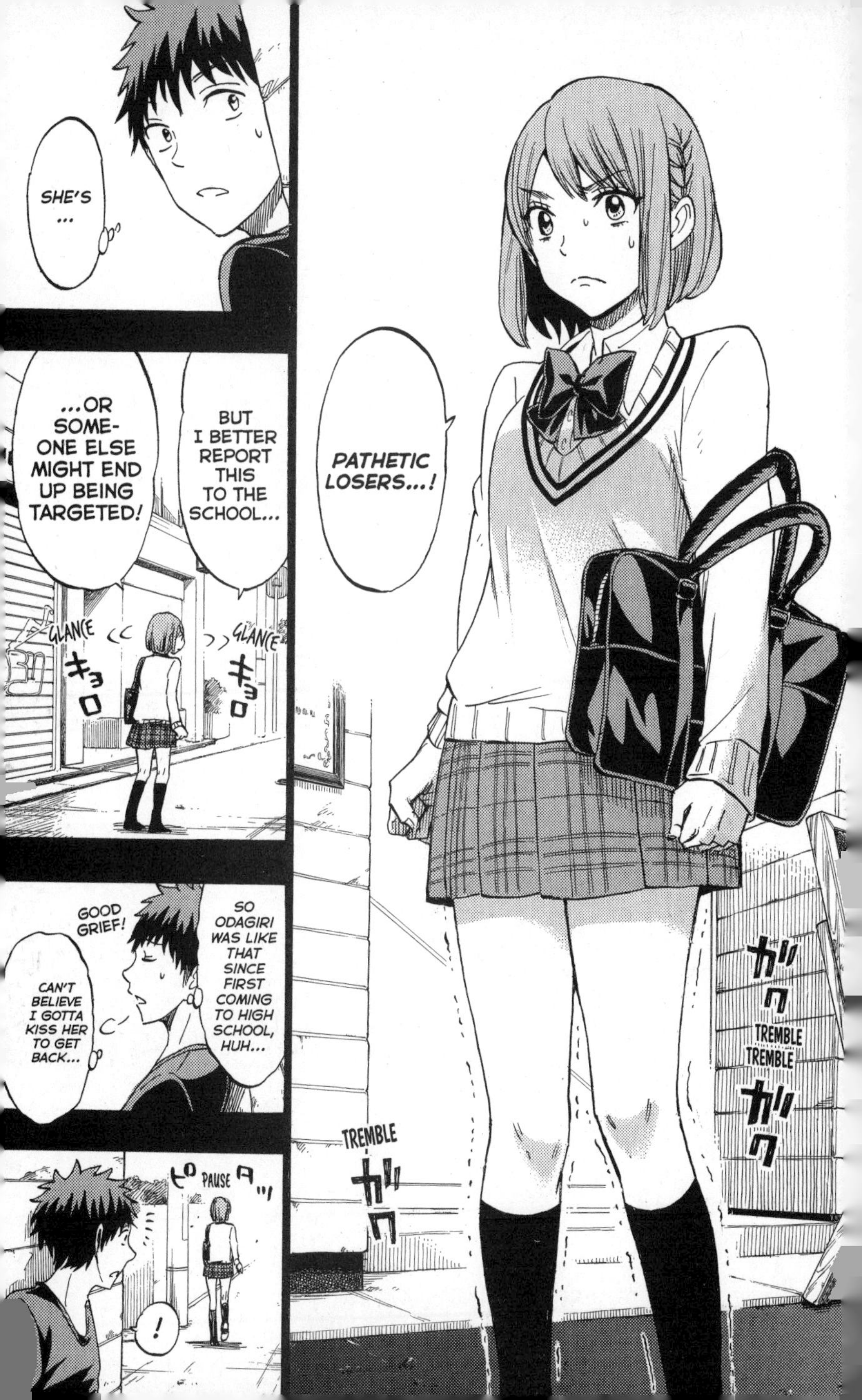
PATHETIC LOSERS...!
ガクガク
TREMBLE TREMBLE
ガク
TREMBLE
SHE'S ...
BUT I BETTER REPORT THIS TO THE SCHOOL...
...OR SOME-ONE ELSE MIGHT END UP BEING TARGETED!
キョロ
GLANCE
キョロ
GLANCE
SO ODAGIRI WAS LIKE THAT SINCE FIRST COMING TO HIGH SCHOOL, HUH...
GOOD GRIEF!
CAN'T BELIEVE I GOTTA KISS HER TO GET BACK...
ピタッ
PAUSE
!

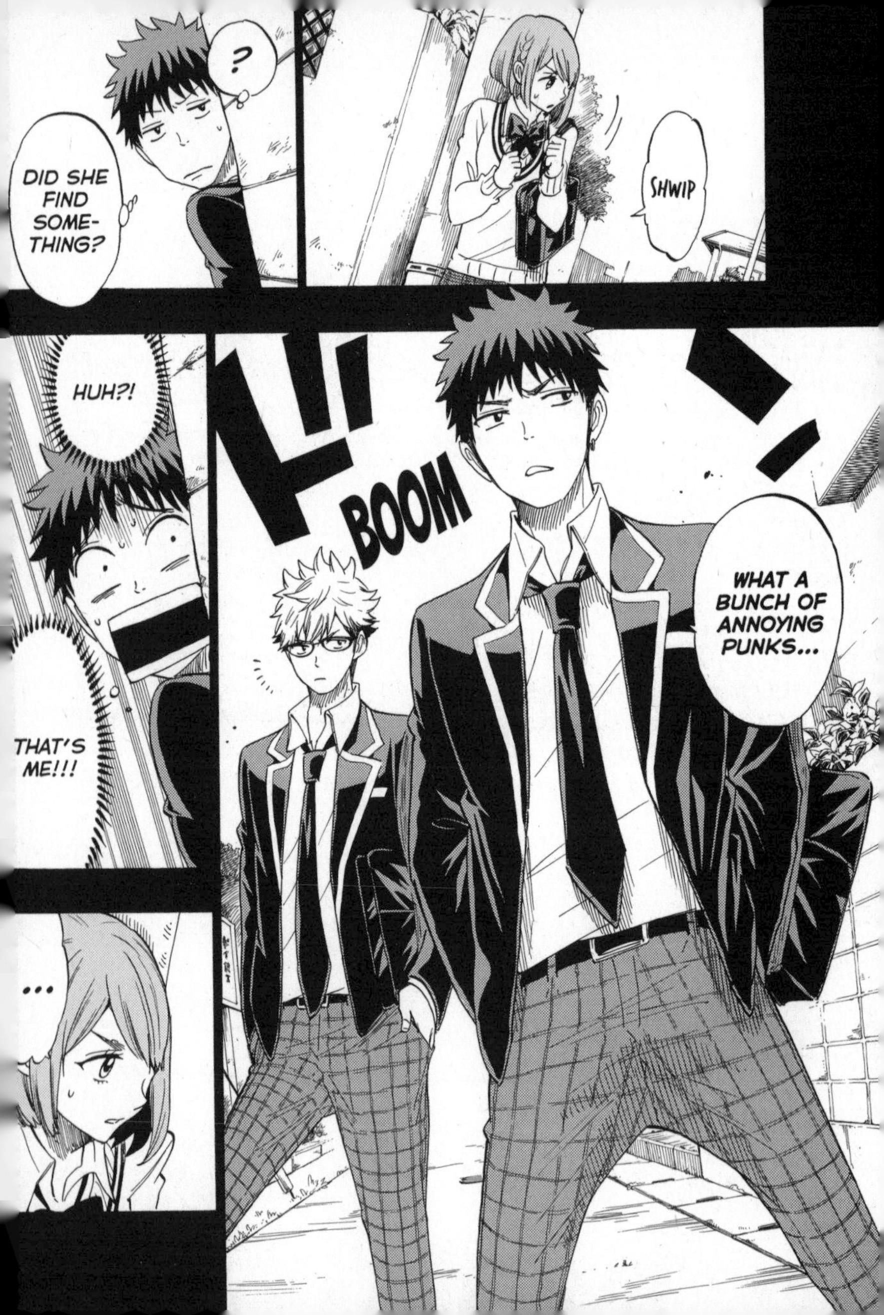
SHWIP
?
DID SHE FIND SOME-THING?
BOOM
WHAT A BUNCH OF ANNOYING PUNKS...
HUH?!
THAT'S ME!!!
...

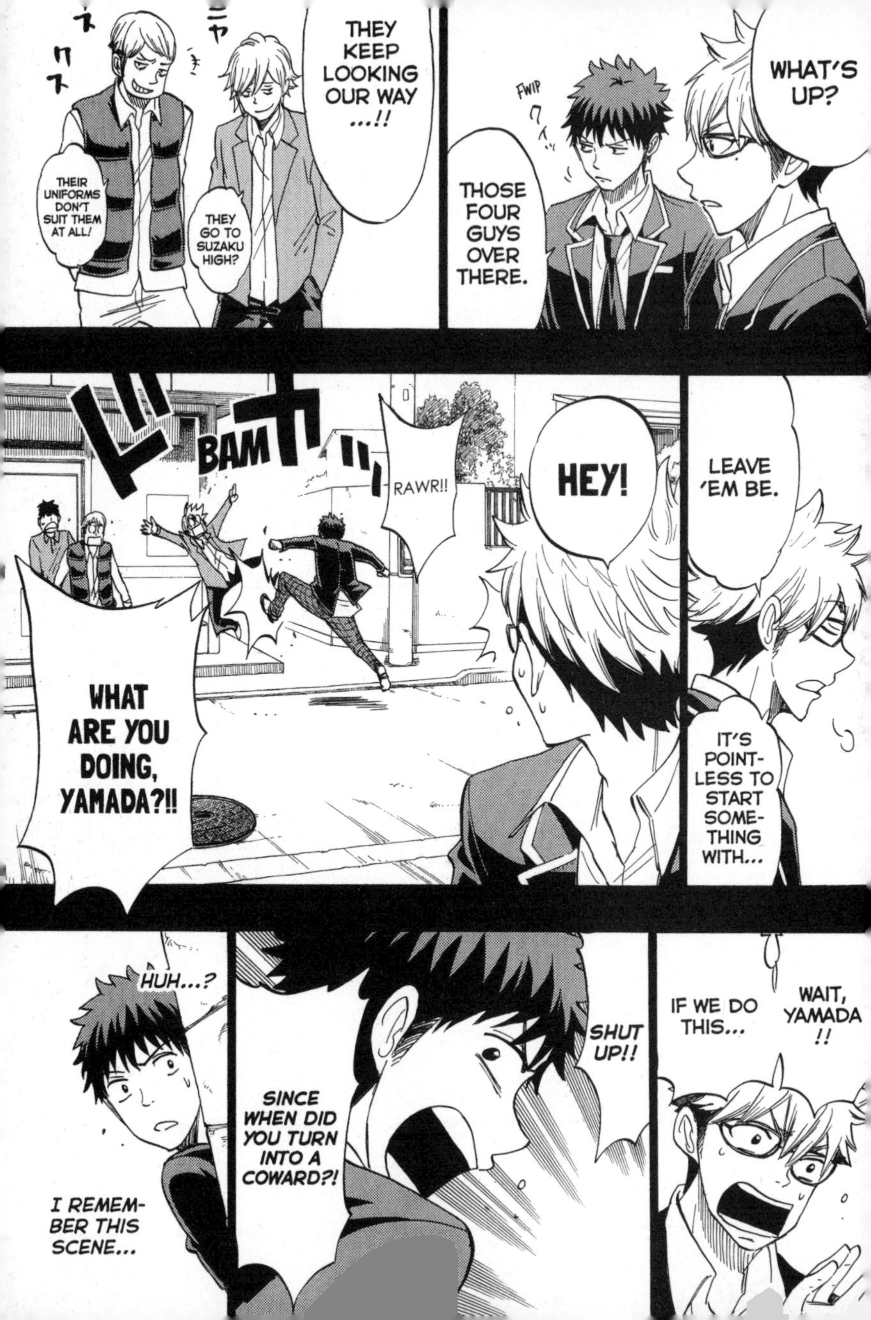
WHAT'S UP?
FWIP
THOSE FOUR GUYS OVER THERE.
THEY KEEP LOOKING OUR WAY ...!!
THEY GO TO SUZAKU HIGH?
THEIR UNIFORMS DON'T SUIT THEM AT ALL!
LEAVE 'EM BE.
IT'S POINTLESS TO START SOMETHING WITH...
HEY!
RAWR!!
BAM
WHAT ARE YOU DOING, YAMADA?!!
WAIT, YAMADA !!
IF WE DO THIS...
SHUT UP!!
SINCE WHEN DID YOU TURN INTO A COWARD?!
HUH...?
I REMEMBER THIS SCENE...

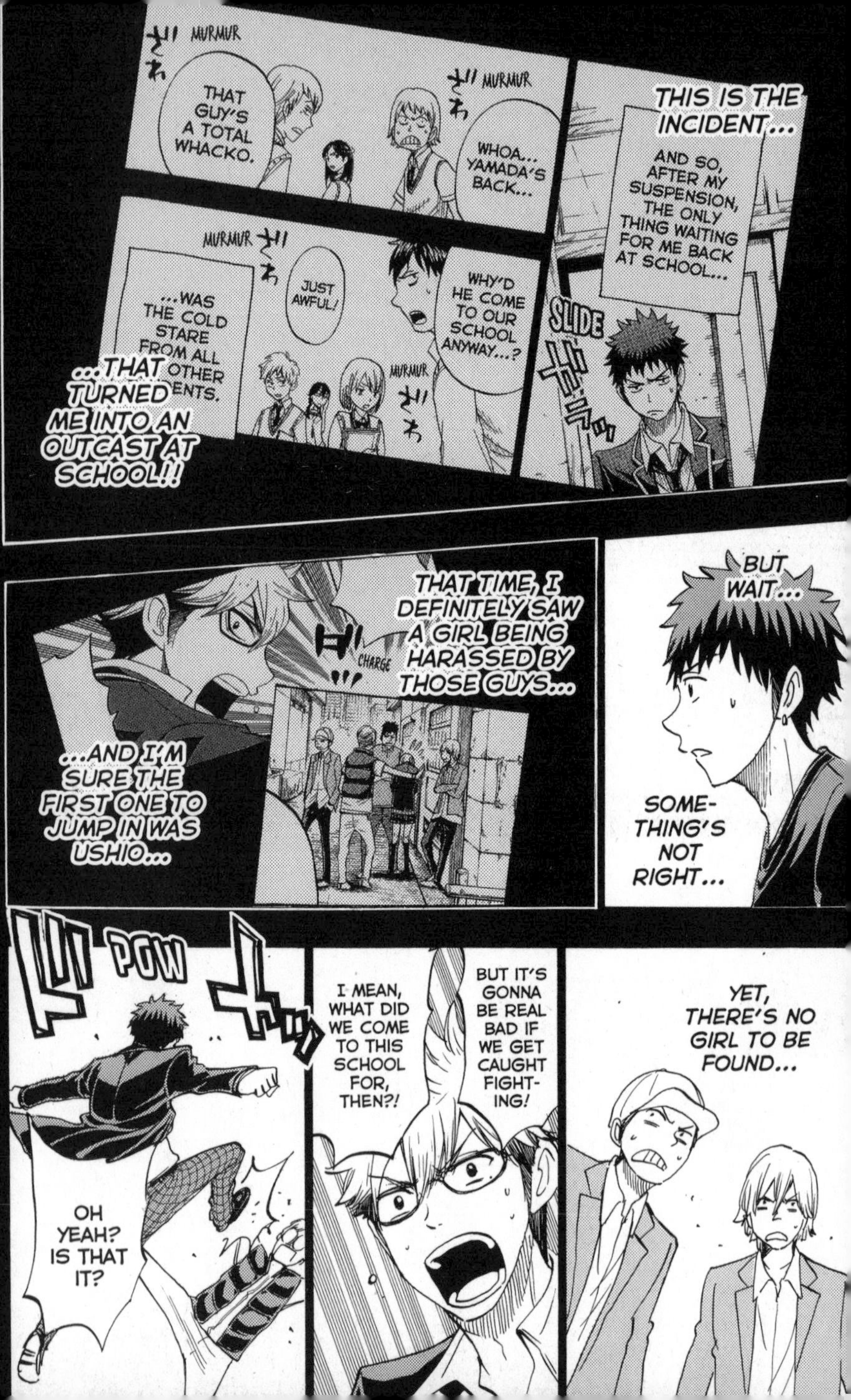
THIS IS THE INCIDENT...
AND SO, AFTER MY SUSPENSION, THE ONLY THING WAITING FOR ME BACK AT SCHOOL...
SLIDE
MURMUR
WHOA... YAMADA'S BACK...
MURMUR
THAT GUY'S A TOTAL WHACKO.
WHY'D HE COME TO OUR SCHOOL ANYWAY...?
JUST AWFUL!
MURMUR
...WAS THE COLD STARE FROM ALL OTHER
ENTS.
MURMUR
...THAT TURNED ME INTO AN OUTCAST AT SCHOOL!!
BUT WAIT...
SOMETHING'S NOT RIGHT...
THAT TIME, I DEFINITELY SAW A GIRL BEING HARASSED BY THOSE GUYS...
CHARGE
...AND I'M SURE THE FIRST ONE TO JUMP IN WAS USHIO...
YET, THERE'S NO GIRL TO BE FOUND...
BUT IT'S GONNA BE REAL BAD IF WE GET CAUGHT FIGHTING!
I MEAN, WHAT DID WE COME TO THIS SCHOOL FOR, THEN?!
POW
OH YEAH? IS THAT IT?

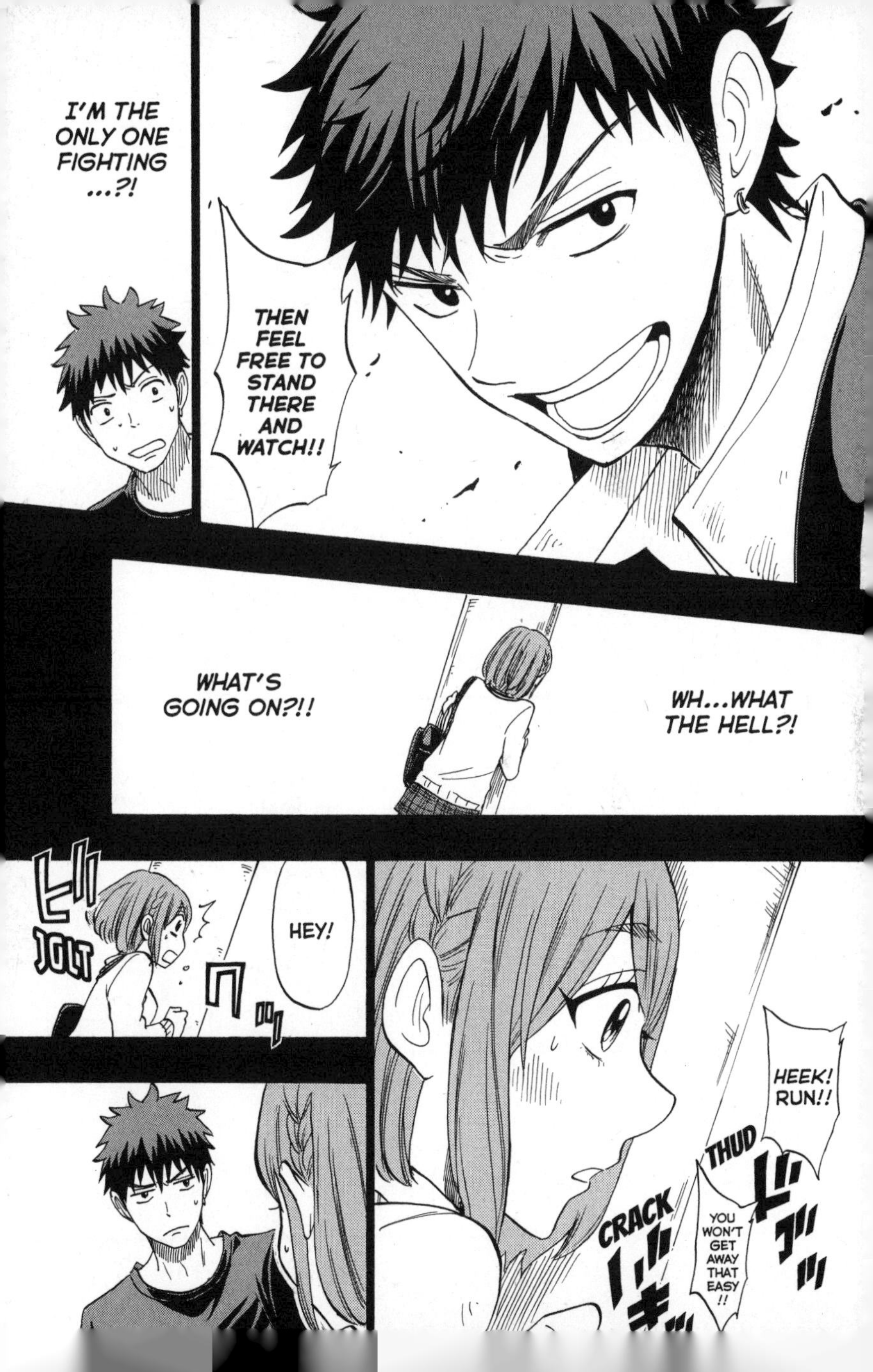
THEN FEEL FREE TO STAND THERE AND WATCH!!
I'M THE ONLY ONE FIGHTING ...?!
WH...WHAT THE HELL?!
WHAT'S GOING ON?!!
HEEK! RUN!!
THUD
YOU WON'T GET AWAY THAT EASY!!
CRACK
HEY!
JOLT

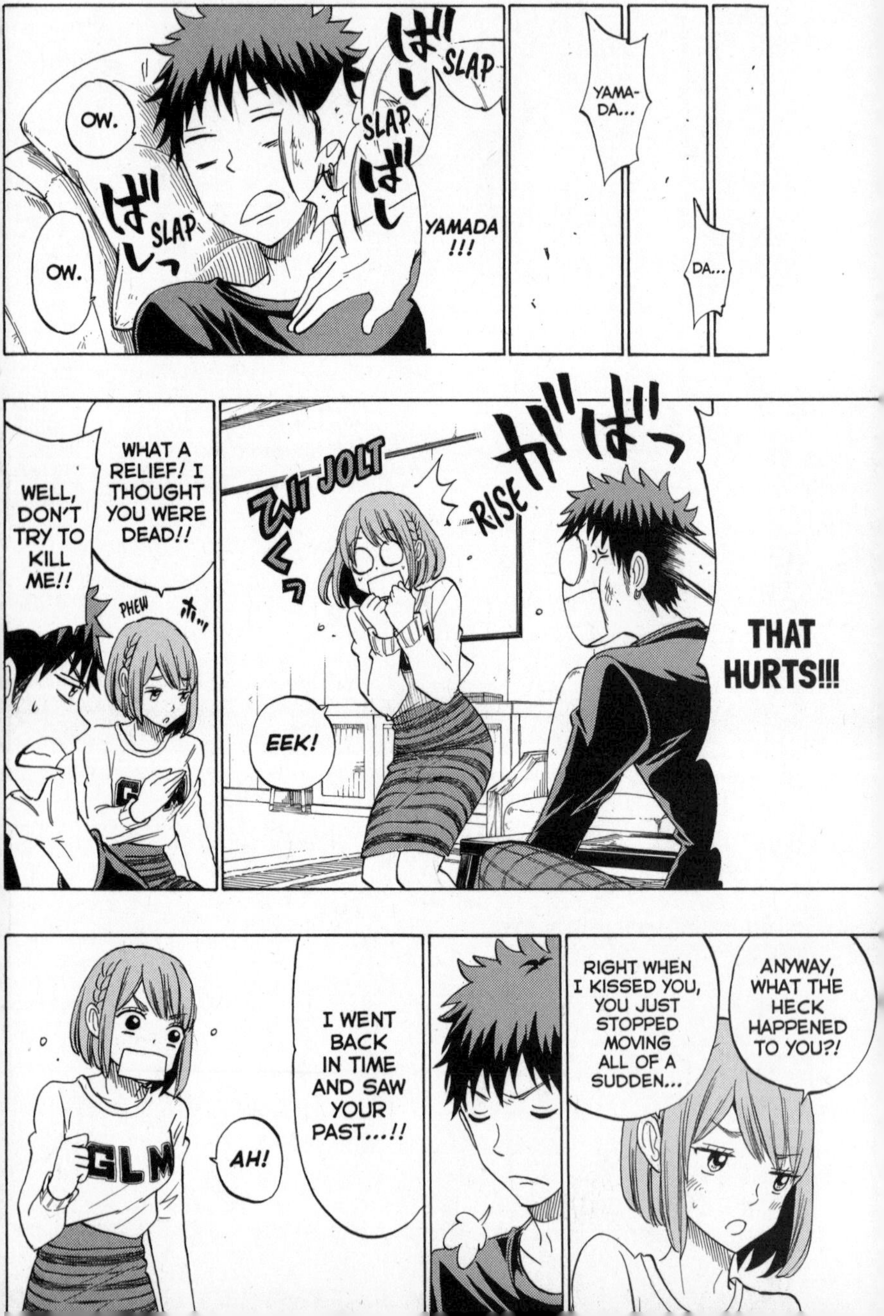
DA...
YAMA-DA...
ばし SLAP
SLAP ばし
YAMADA!!!
OW.
ばしっ SLAP
OW.
THAT HURTS!!!
がばっ RISE
びくっ JOLT
EEK!
WHAT A RELIEF! I THOUGHT YOU WERE DEAD!!
WELL, DON'T TRY TO KILL ME!!
ほ… PHEW
ANYWAY, WHAT THE HECK HAPPENED TO YOU?!
RIGHT WHEN I KISSED YOU, YOU JUST STOPPED MOVING ALL OF A SUDDEN...
I WENT BACK IN TIME AND SAW YOUR PAST...!!
AH!

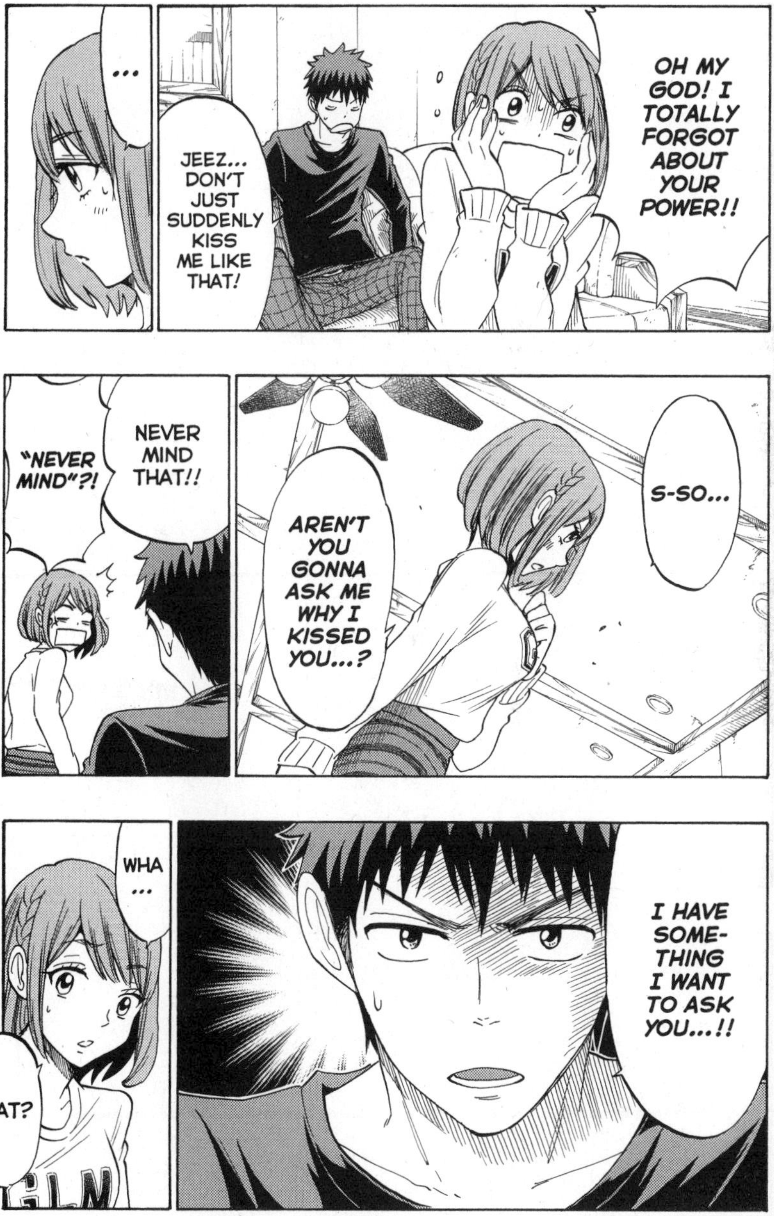
OH MY GOD! I TOTALLY FORGOT ABOUT YOUR POWER!!
JEEZ... DON'T JUST SUDDENLY KISS ME LIKE THAT!
...
S-SO...
AREN'T YOU GONNA ASK ME WHY I KISSED YOU...?
NEVER MIND THAT!!
"NEVER MIND"?!
I HAVE SOME-THING I WANT TO ASK YOU...!!
WHA...
WHAT?

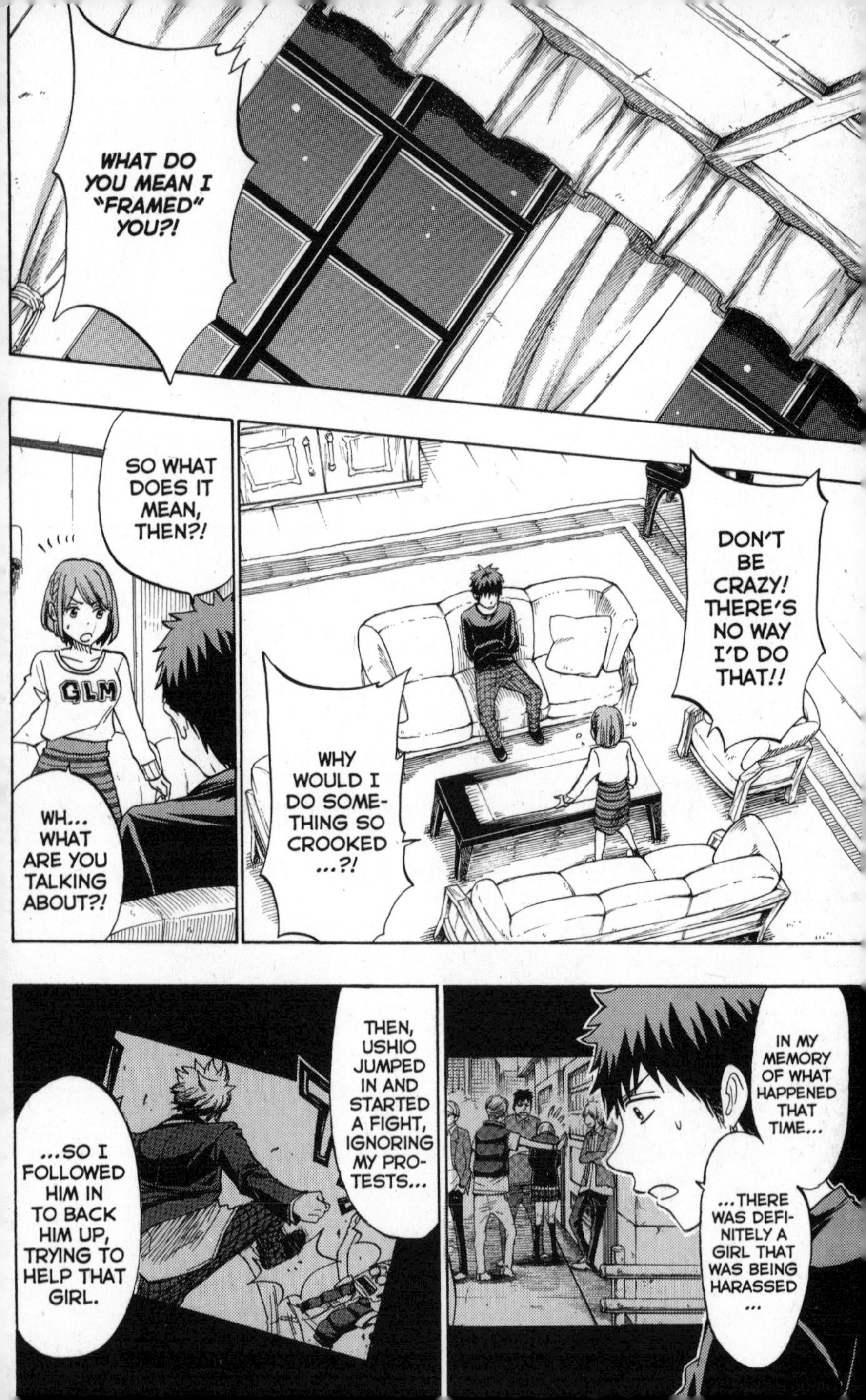
WHAT DO YOU MEAN I "FRAMED" YOU?!
DON'T BE CRAZY! THERE'S NO WAY I'D DO THAT!!
WHY WOULD I DO SOMETHING SO CROOKED ...?!
SO WHAT DOES IT MEAN, THEN?!
WH... WHAT ARE YOU TALKING ABOUT?!
IN MY MEMORY OF WHAT HAPPENED THAT TIME...
...THERE WAS DEFINITELY A GIRL THAT WAS BEING HARASSED ...
THEN, USHIO JUMPED IN AND STARTED A FIGHT, IGNORING MY PROTESTS...
...SO I FOLLOWED HIM IN TO BACK HIM UP, TRYING TO HELP THAT GIRL.

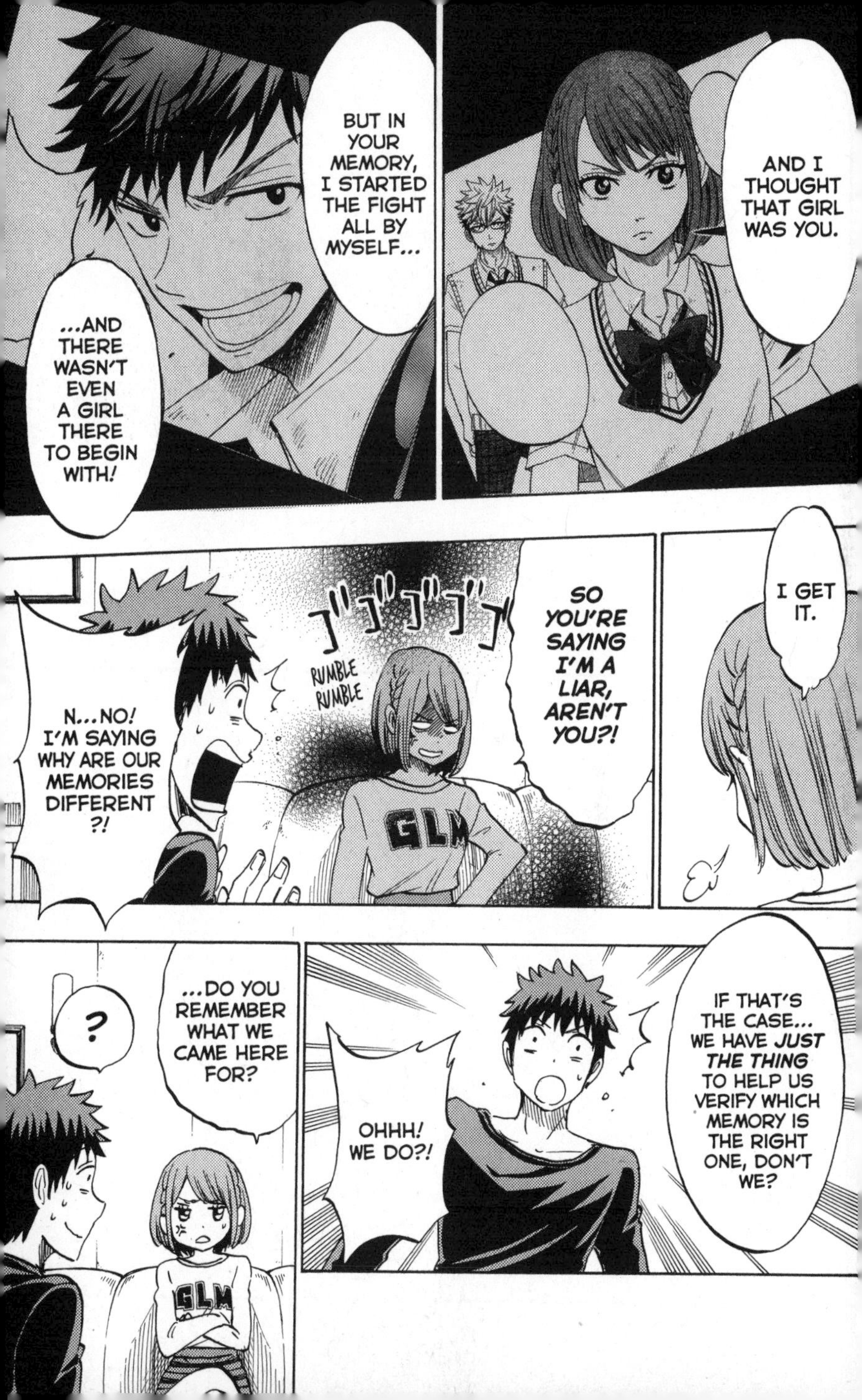
AND I THOUGHT THAT GIRL WAS YOU.
BUT IN YOUR MEMORY, I STARTED THE FIGHT ALL BY MYSELF...
...AND THERE WASN'T EVEN A GIRL THERE TO BEGIN WITH!
I GET IT.
SO YOU'RE SAYING I'M A LIAR, AREN'T YOU?!
RUMBLE RUMBLE
N...NO! I'M SAYING WHY ARE OUR MEMORIES DIFFERENT ?!
IF THAT'S THE CASE... WE HAVE *JUST THE THING* TO HELP US VERIFY WHICH MEMORY IS THE RIGHT ONE, DON'T WE?
OHHH! WE DO?!
...DO YOU REMEMBER WHAT WE CAME HERE FOR?
?

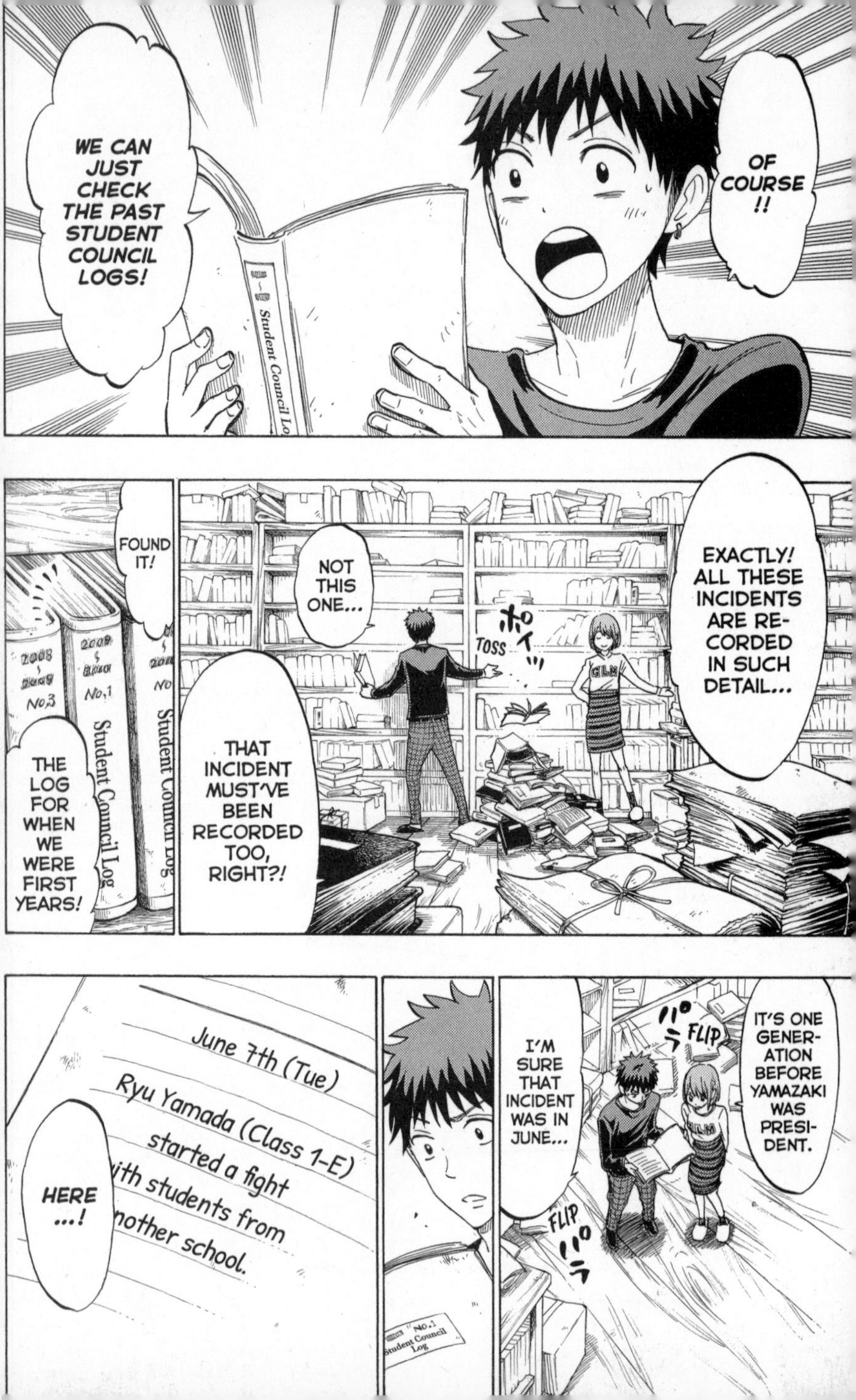
OF COURSE !!
WE CAN JUST CHECK THE PAST STUDENT COUNCIL LOGS!
Student Council Log
EXACTLY! ALL THESE INCIDENTS ARE RE-CORDED IN SUCH DETAIL...
NOT THIS ONE...
TOSS
THAT INCIDENT MUST'VE BEEN RECORDED TOO, RIGHT?!
FOUND IT!
No.3
No.1
Student Council Log
Student Council Log
THE LOG FOR WHEN WE WERE FIRST YEARS!
IT'S ONE GENER-ATION BEFORE YAMAZAKI WAS PRESI-DENT.
FLIP
I'M SURE THAT INCIDENT WAS IN JUNE...
FLIP
No.1 Student Council Log
June 7th (Tue)
Ryu Yamada (Class 1-E)
started a fight
ith students from
nother school.
HERE ...!

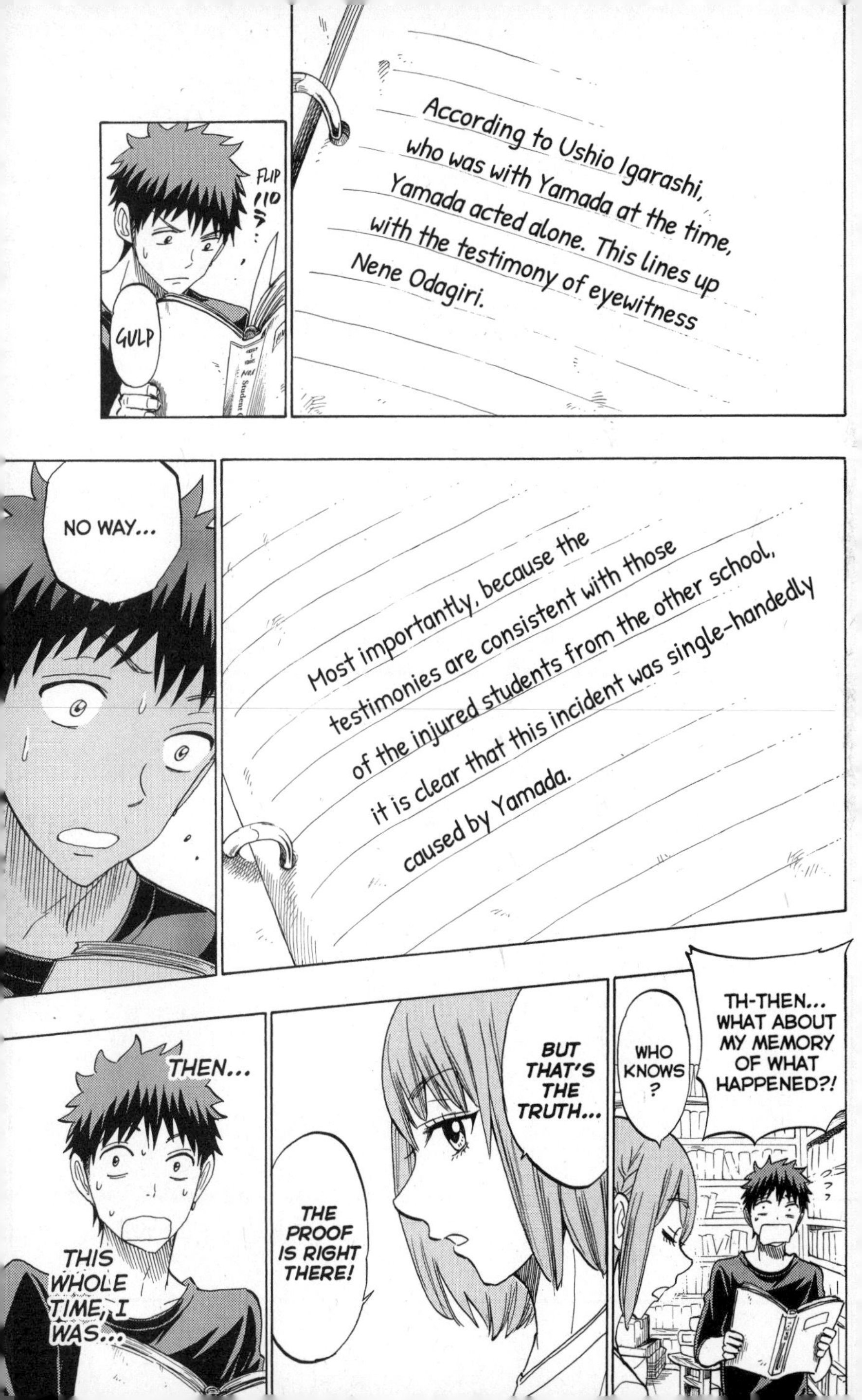
According to Ushio Igarashi, who was with Yamada at the time, Yamada acted alone. This lines up with the testimony of eyewitness Nene Odagiri.
FLIP
GULP
Student
Most importantly, because the testimonies are consistent with those of the injured students from the other school, it is clear that this incident was single-handedly caused by Yamada.
NO WAY...
TH-THEN... WHAT ABOUT MY MEMORY OF WHAT HAPPENED?!
WHO KNOWS?
BUT THAT'S THE TRUTH...
THE PROOF IS RIGHT THERE!
THEN...
THIS WHOLE TIME, I WAS...

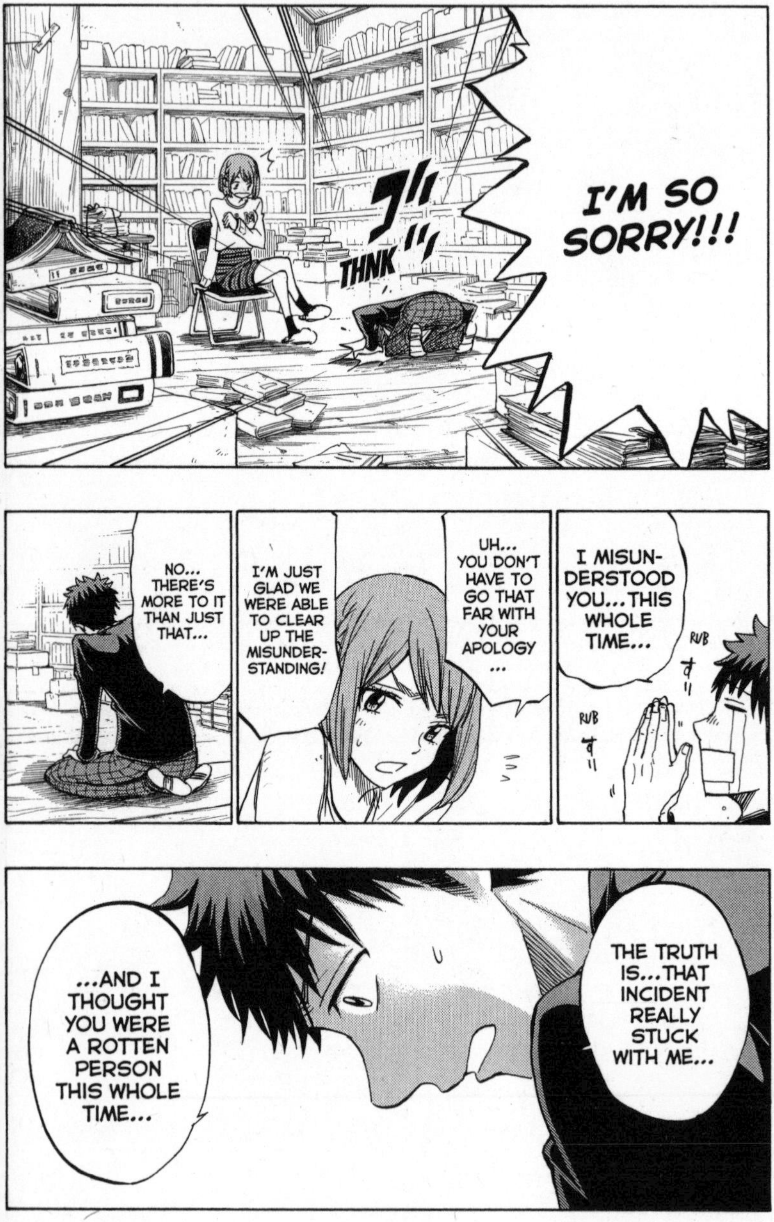
I'M SO SORRY!!!
ゴッ
THNK
I MISUNDERSTOOD YOU... THIS WHOLE TIME...
RUB
すり
RUB
すり
UH... YOU DON'T HAVE TO GO THAT FAR WITH YOUR APOLOGY ...
I'M JUST GLAD WE WERE ABLE TO CLEAR UP THE MISUNDERSTANDING!
NO... THERE'S MORE TO IT THAN JUST THAT...
THE TRUTH IS... THAT INCIDENT REALLY STUCK WITH ME...
...AND I THOUGHT YOU WERE A ROTTEN PERSON THIS WHOLE TIME...

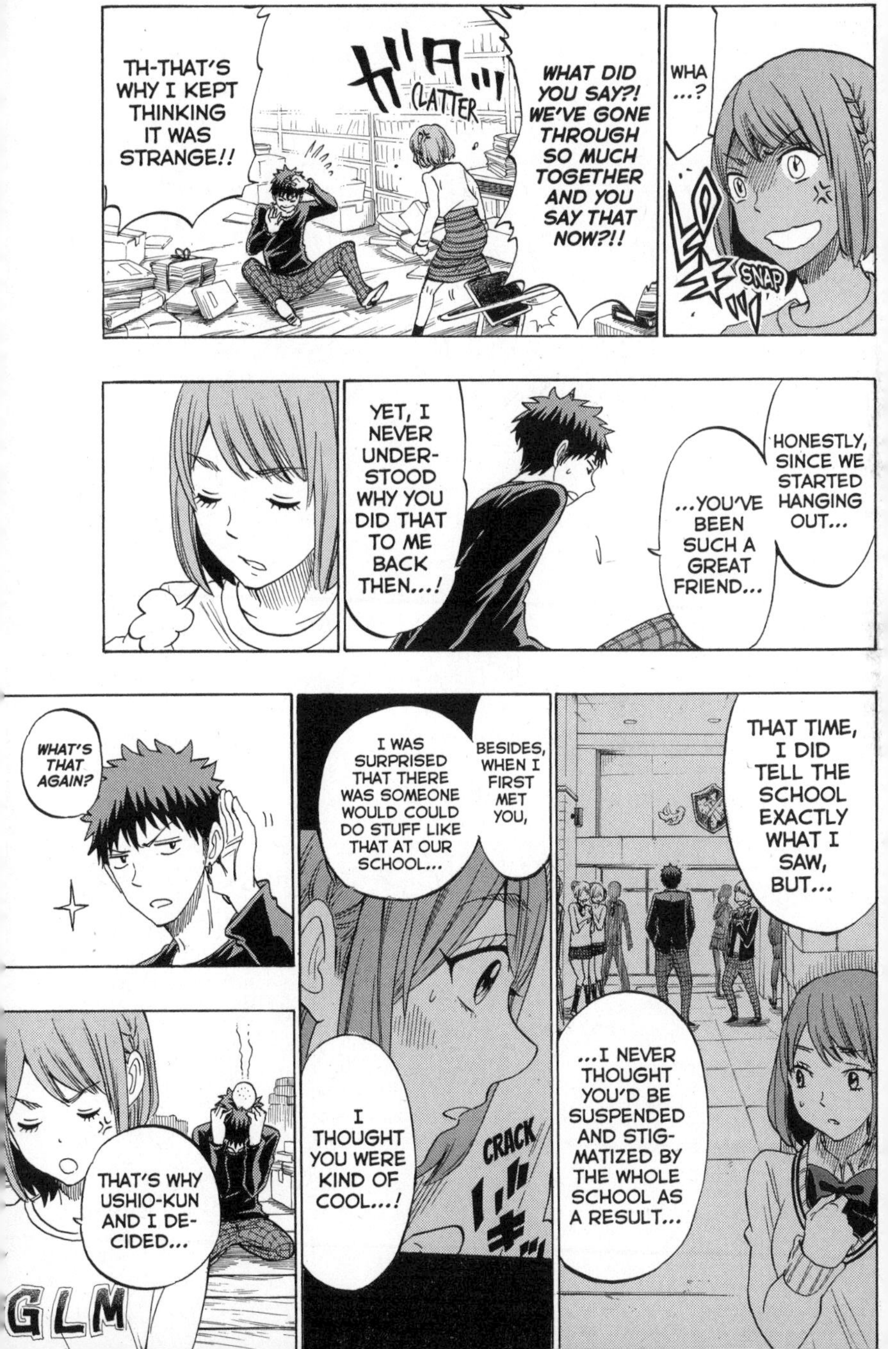
WHA ...?
SNAP
WHAT DID YOU SAY?! WE'VE GONE THROUGH SO MUCH TOGETHER AND YOU SAY THAT NOW?!!
CLATTER
TH-THAT'S WHY I KEPT THINKING IT WAS STRANGE!!
HONESTLY, SINCE WE STARTED HANGING OUT...
...YOU'VE BEEN SUCH A GREAT FRIEND...
YET, I NEVER UNDER-STOOD WHY YOU DID THAT TO ME BACK THEN...!
THAT TIME, I DID TELL THE SCHOOL EXACTLY WHAT I SAW, BUT...
...I NEVER THOUGHT YOU'D BE SUSPENDED AND STIG-MATIZED BY THE WHOLE SCHOOL AS A RESULT...
BESIDES, WHEN I FIRST MET YOU,
I WAS SURPRISED THAT THERE WAS SOMEONE WOULD COULD DO STUFF LIKE THAT AT OUR SCHOOL...
CRACK
I THOUGHT YOU WERE KIND OF COOL...!
WHAT'S THAT AGAIN?
THAT'S WHY USHIO-KUN AND I DE-CIDED...
GLM

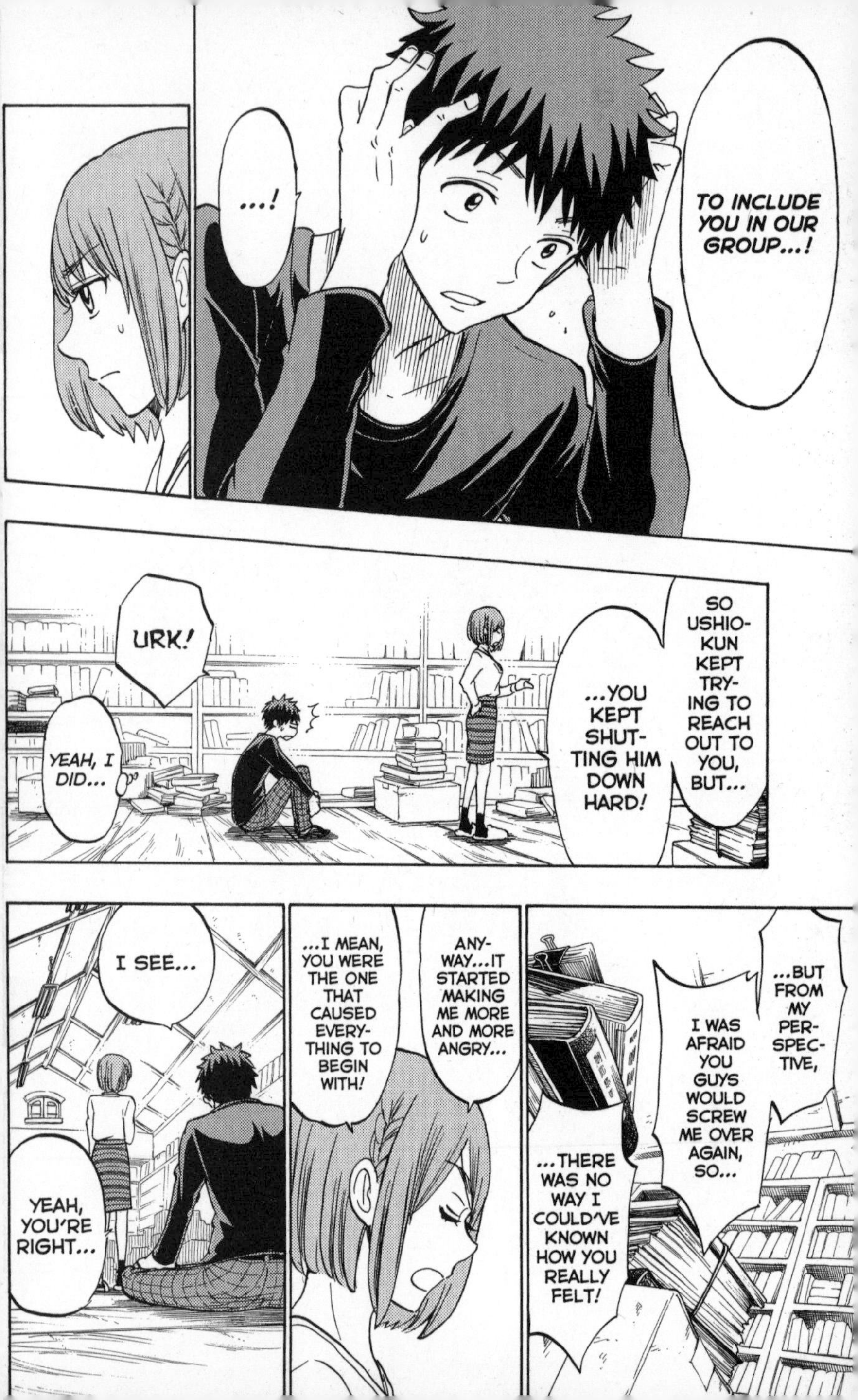
TO INCLUDE YOU IN OUR GROUP...!
...!
SO USHIO-KUN KEPT TRYING TO REACH OUT TO YOU, BUT...
...YOU KEPT SHUTTING HIM DOWN HARD!
URK!
YEAH, I DID...
...BUT FROM MY PERSPECTIVE,
I WAS AFRAID YOU GUYS WOULD SCREW ME OVER AGAIN, SO...
...THERE WAS NO WAY I COULD'VE KNOWN HOW YOU REALLY FELT!
ANYWAY...IT STARTED MAKING ME MORE AND MORE ANGRY...
...I MEAN, YOU WERE THE ONE THAT CAUSED EVERYTHING TO BEGIN WITH!
I SEE...
YEAH, YOU'RE RIGHT...

I REALLY WAS...

...YOU WERE LOOKING OUT FOR ME THAT MUCH!

I HAD NO IDEA...

WHEN YOU WERE HAVING A HARD TIME, SHIRAISHI WASN'T THE ONE WHO REACHED OUT TO YOU...

...I WAS!!

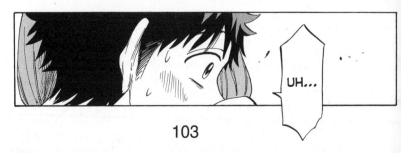

UH...

103

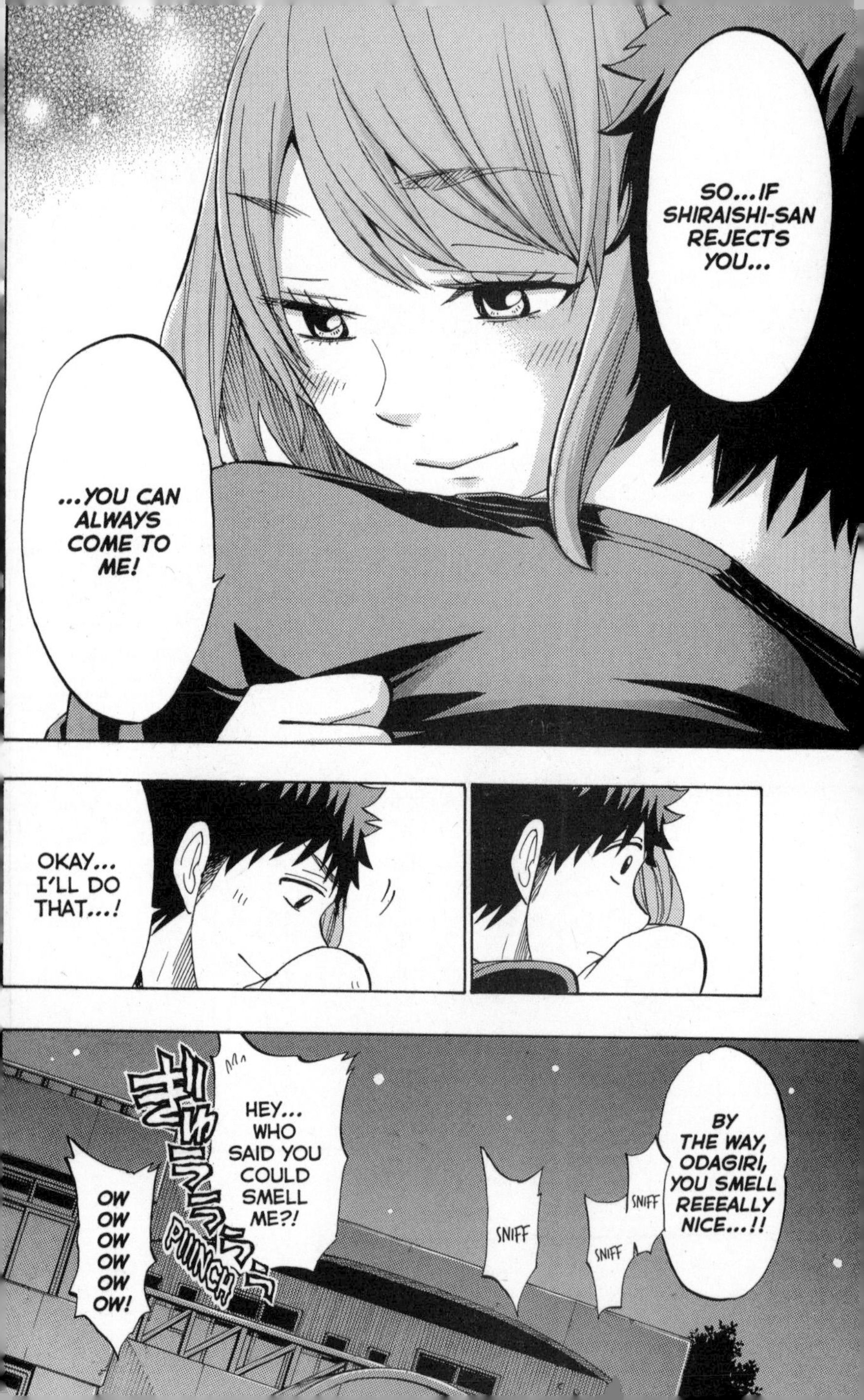
SO...IF SHIRAISHI-SAN REJECTS YOU...
...YOU CAN ALWAYS COME TO ME!
OKAY... I'LL DO THAT...!
BY THE WAY, ODAGIRI, YOU SMELL REEEALLY NICE...!!
SNIFF
SNIFF
SNIFF
HEY... WHO SAID YOU COULD SMELL ME?!
PIIINCH
OW OW OW OW OW OW!

CHAPTER 134: Too hot to handle!

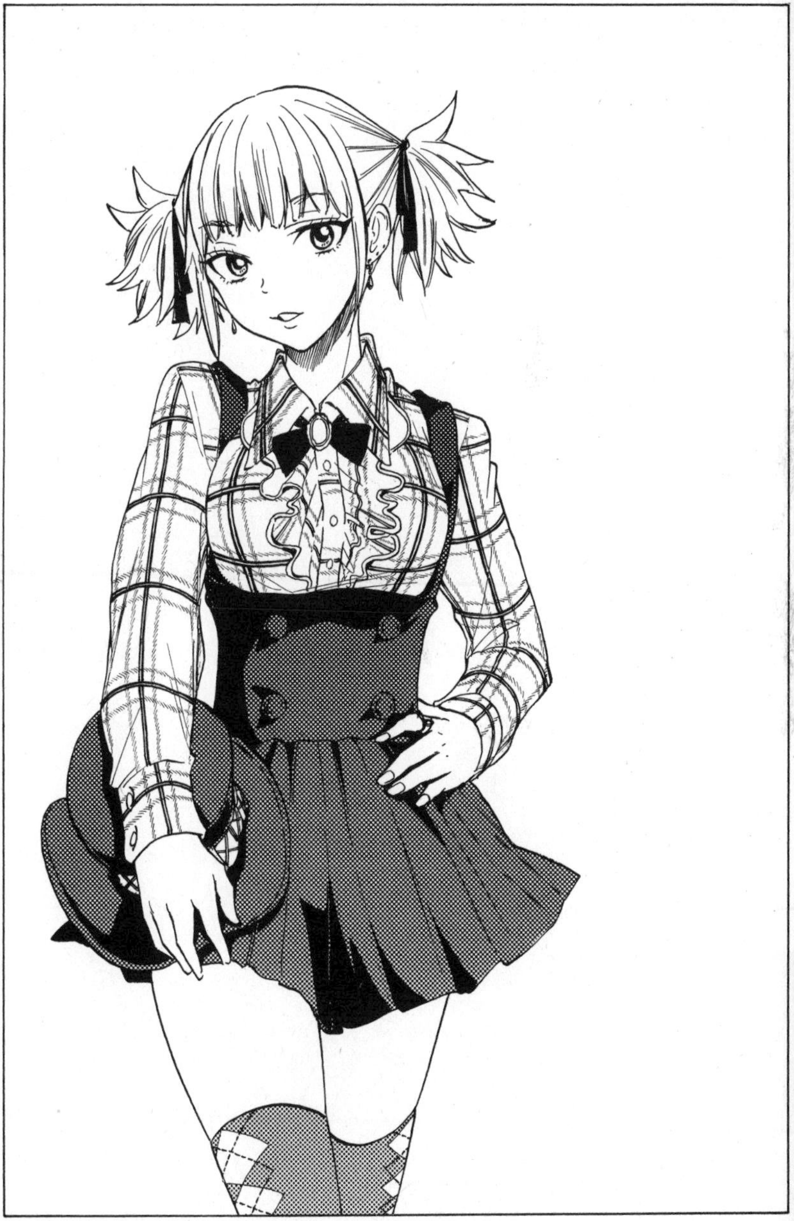

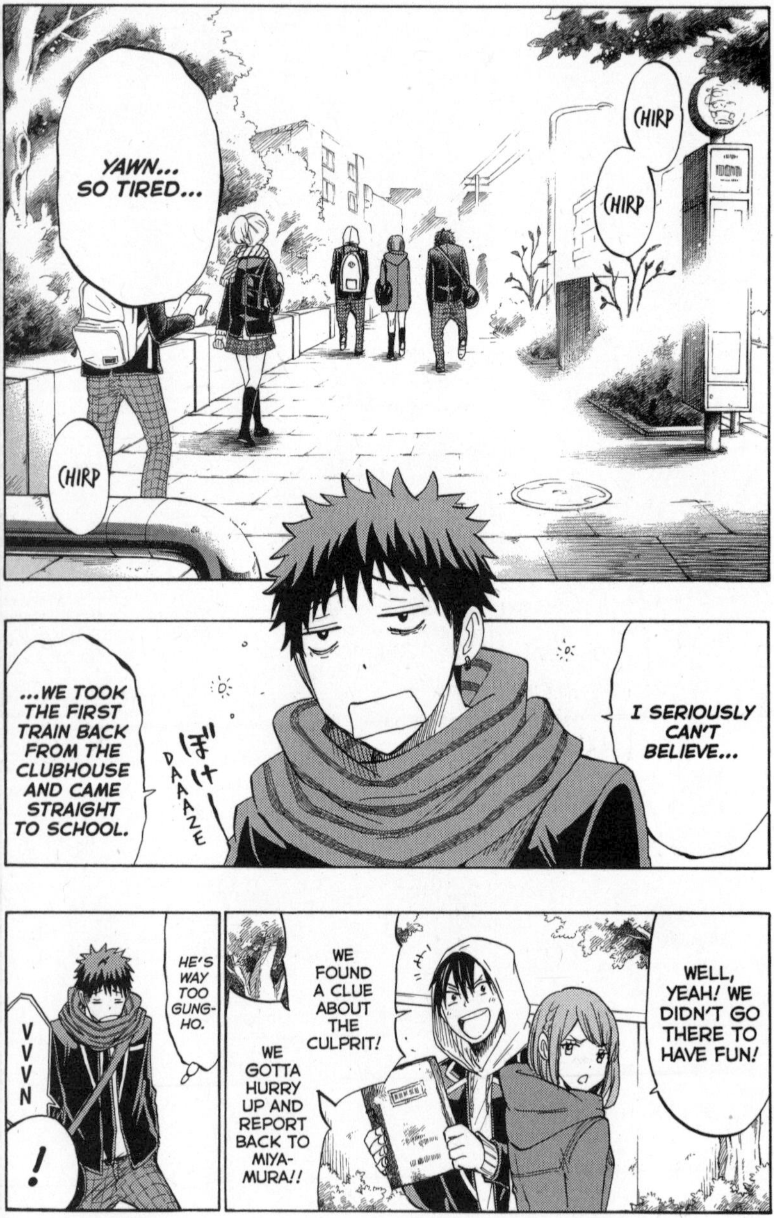
CHIRP
CHIRP
YAWN... SO TIRED...
CHIRP
I SERIOUSLY CAN'T BELIEVE...
...WE TOOK THE FIRST TRAIN BACK FROM THE CLUBHOUSE AND CAME STRAIGHT TO SCHOOL.
ぼけ
DAAAAZE
WELL, YEAH! WE DIDN'T GO THERE TO HAVE FUN!
WE FOUND A CLUE ABOUT THE CULPRIT!
WE GOTTA HURRY UP AND REPORT BACK TO MIYA-MURA!!
HE'S WAY TOO GUNG-HO.
VVVN
!

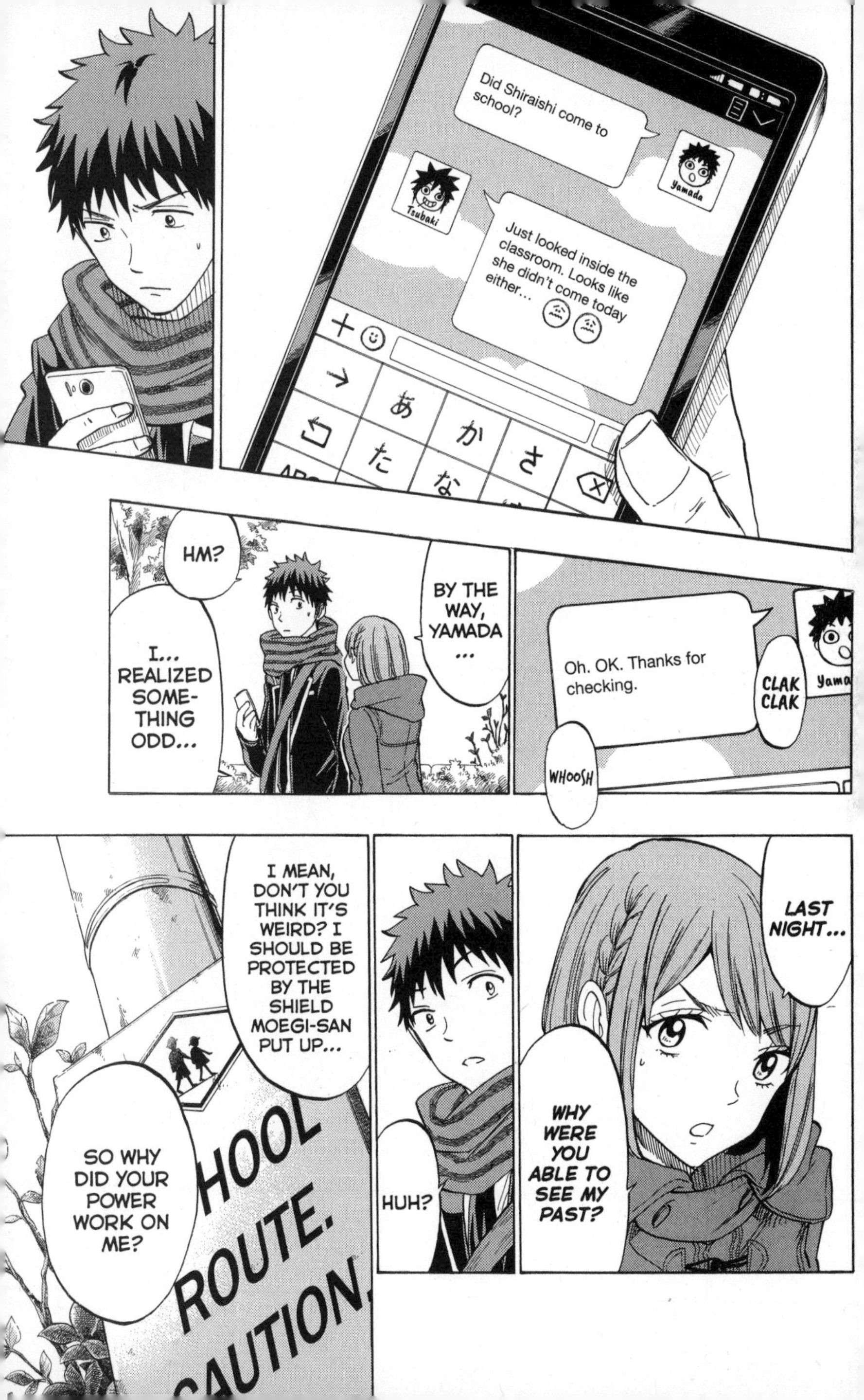
Did Shiraishi come to school?
Yamada
Tsubaki
Just looked inside the classroom. Looks like she didn't come today either...
Oh. OK. Thanks for checking.
Yama
CLAK CLAK
WHOOSH
BY THE WAY, YAMADA...
HM?
I... REALIZED SOME-THING ODD...
LAST NIGHT...
WHY WERE YOU ABLE TO SEE MY PAST?
HUH?
I MEAN, DON'T YOU THINK IT'S WEIRD? I SHOULD BE PROTECTED BY THE SHIELD MOEGI-SAN PUT UP...
SO WHY DID YOUR POWER WORK ON ME?
HOOL ROUTE. CAUTION.

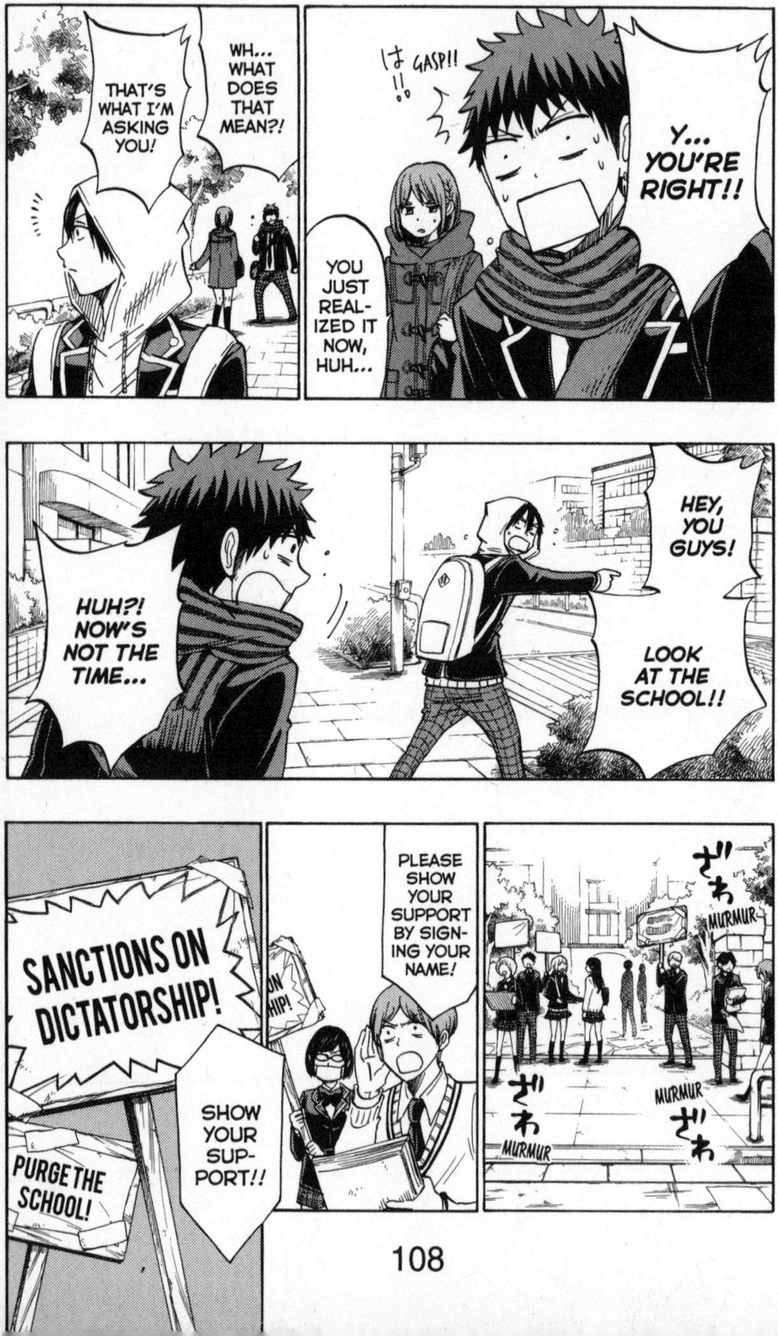
Y... YOU'RE RIGHT!!
は!! GASP!!
YOU JUST REALIZED IT NOW, HUH...
WH... WHAT DOES THAT MEAN?!
THAT'S WHAT I'M ASKING YOU!
HEY, YOU GUYS!
LOOK AT THE SCHOOL!!
HUH?! NOW'S NOT THE TIME...
ざわ MURMUR
ざわ MURMUR
ざわ MURMUR
PLEASE SHOW YOUR SUPPORT BY SIGNING YOUR NAME!
SHOW YOUR SUP-PORT!!
SANCTIONS ON DICTATORSHIP!
PURGE THE SCHOOL!

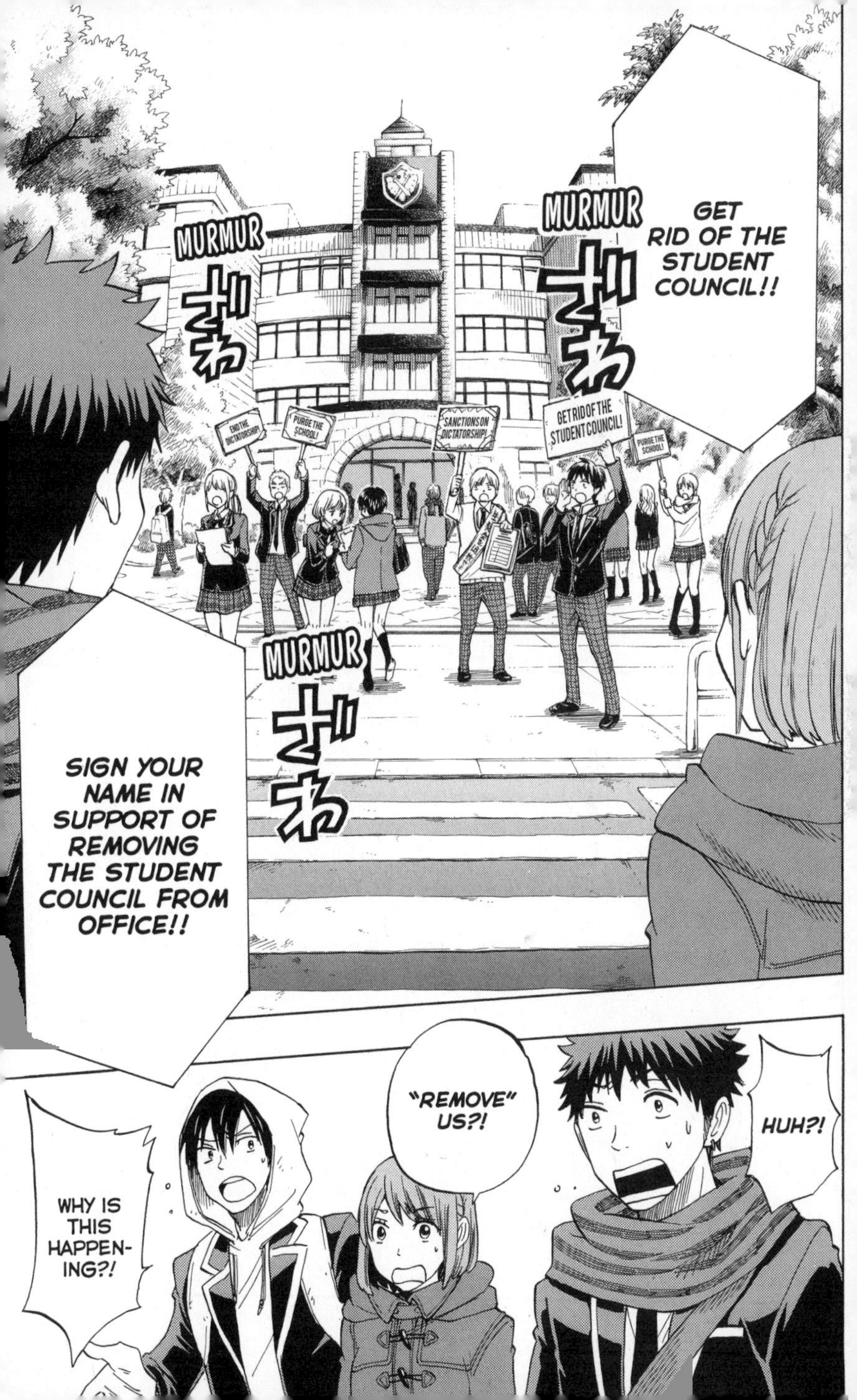
GET RID OF THE STUDENT COUNCIL!!
MURMUR ざわ
PURGE THE SCHOOL!
GET RID OF THE STUDENT COUNCIL!
SANCTIONS ON DICTATORSHIP!
PURGE THE SCHOOL!
END THE DICTATORSHIP!
MURMUR ざわ
MURMUR ざわ
SIGN YOUR NAME IN SUPPORT OF REMOVING THE STUDENT COUNCIL FROM OFFICE!!
HUH?!
"REMOVE" US?!
WHY IS THIS HAPPEN-ING?!

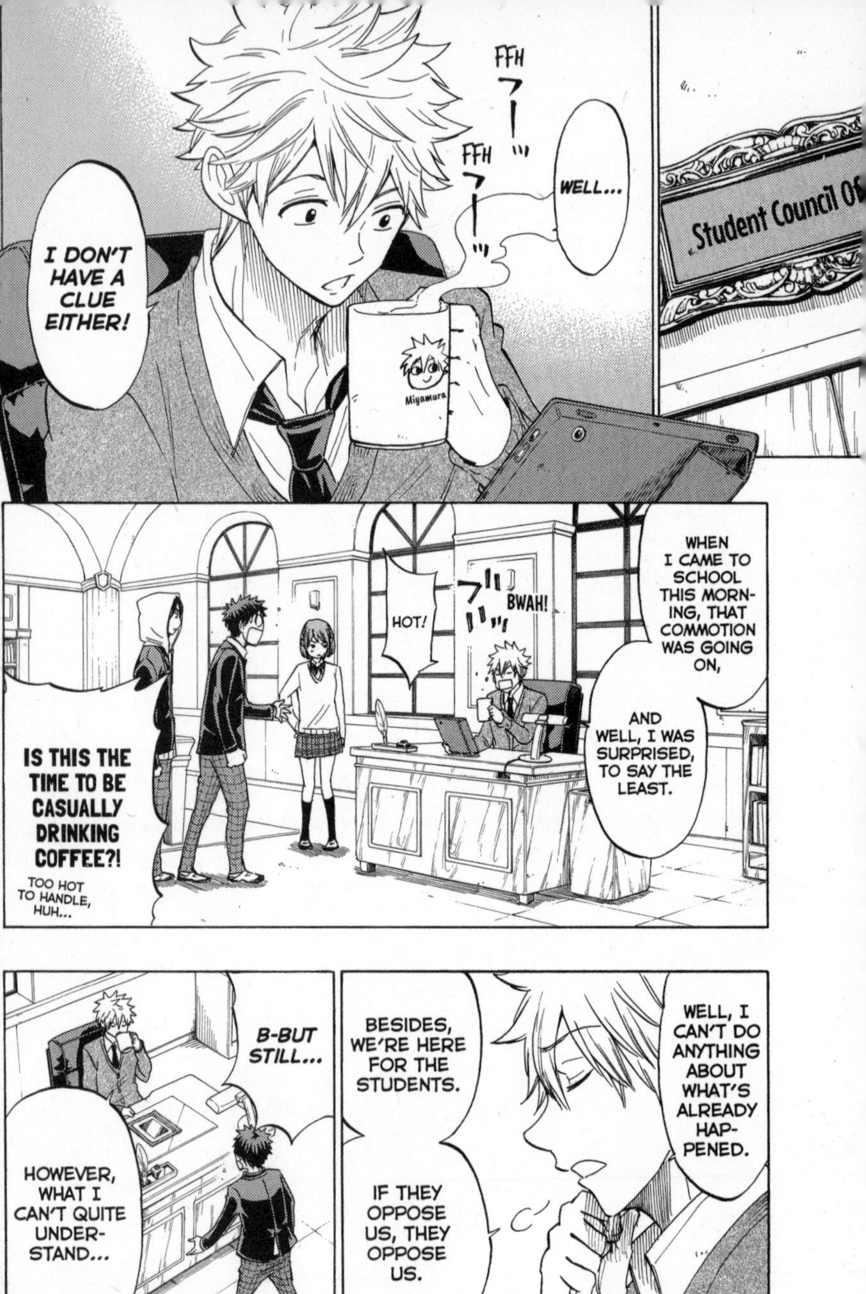
Student Council Of
WELL...
FFH
FFH
Miyamura
I DON'T HAVE A CLUE EITHER!
WHEN I CAME TO SCHOOL THIS MORN-ING, THAT COMMOTION WAS GOING ON,
AND WELL, I WAS SURPRISED, TO SAY THE LEAST.
BWAH!
HOT!
IS THIS THE TIME TO BE CASUALLY DRINKING COFFEE?!
TOO HOT TO HANDLE, HUH...
WELL, I CAN'T DO ANYTHING ABOUT WHAT'S ALREADY HAP-PENED.
BESIDES, WE'RE HERE FOR THE STUDENTS.
IF THEY OPPOSE US, THEY OPPOSE US.
B-BUT STILL...
HOWEVER, WHAT I CAN'T QUITE UNDER-STAND...

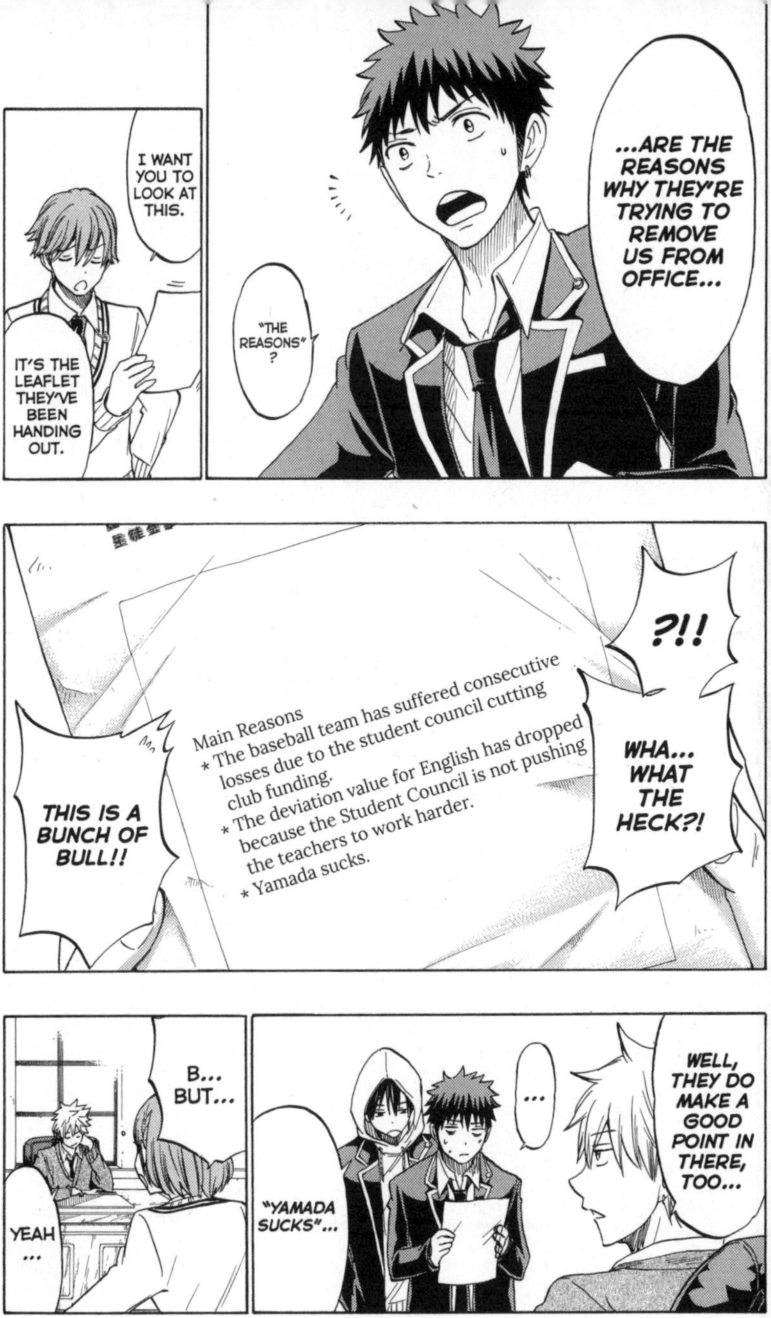
...ARE THE REASONS WHY THEY'RE TRYING TO REMOVE US FROM OFFICE...
"THE REASONS"?
I WANT YOU TO LOOK AT THIS.
IT'S THE LEAFLET THEY'VE BEEN HANDING OUT.
?!!
WHA... WHAT THE HECK?!
Main Reasons
* The baseball team has suffered consecutive losses due to the student council cutting club funding.
* The deviation value for English has dropped because the Student Council is not pushing the teachers to work harder.
* Yamada sucks.
THIS IS A BUNCH OF BULL!!
WELL, THEY DO MAKE A GOOD POINT IN THERE, TOO...
...
"YAMADA SUCKS"...
B... BUT...
YEAH...

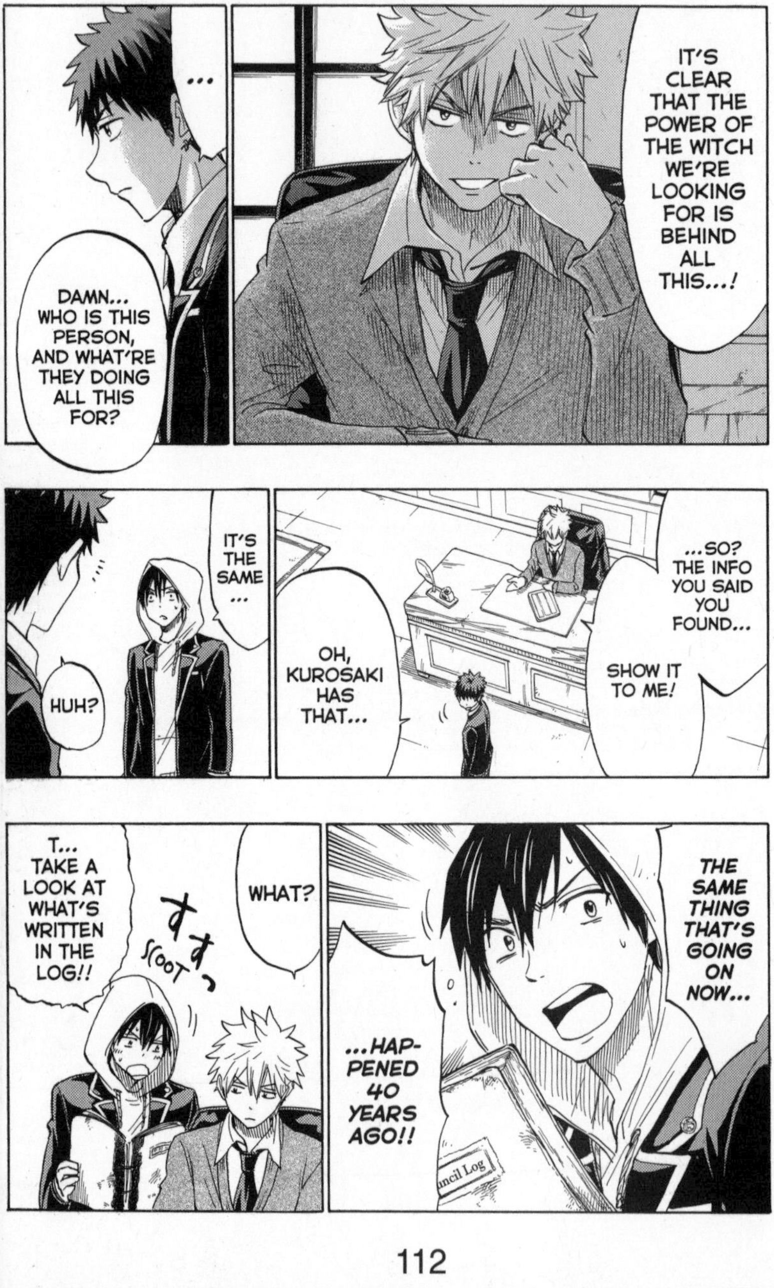
IT'S CLEAR THAT THE POWER OF THE WITCH WE'RE LOOKING FOR IS BEHIND ALL THIS...!
...
DAMN... WHO IS THIS PERSON, AND WHAT'RE THEY DOING ALL THIS FOR?
...SO? THE INFO YOU SAID YOU FOUND...
SHOW IT TO ME!
OH, KUROSAKI HAS THAT...
IT'S THE SAME...
HUH?
THE SAME THING THAT'S GOING ON NOW...
...HAP-PENED 40 YEARS AGO!!
WHAT?
T... TAKE A LOOK AT WHAT'S WRITTEN IN THE LOG!!
すす
SCOOT

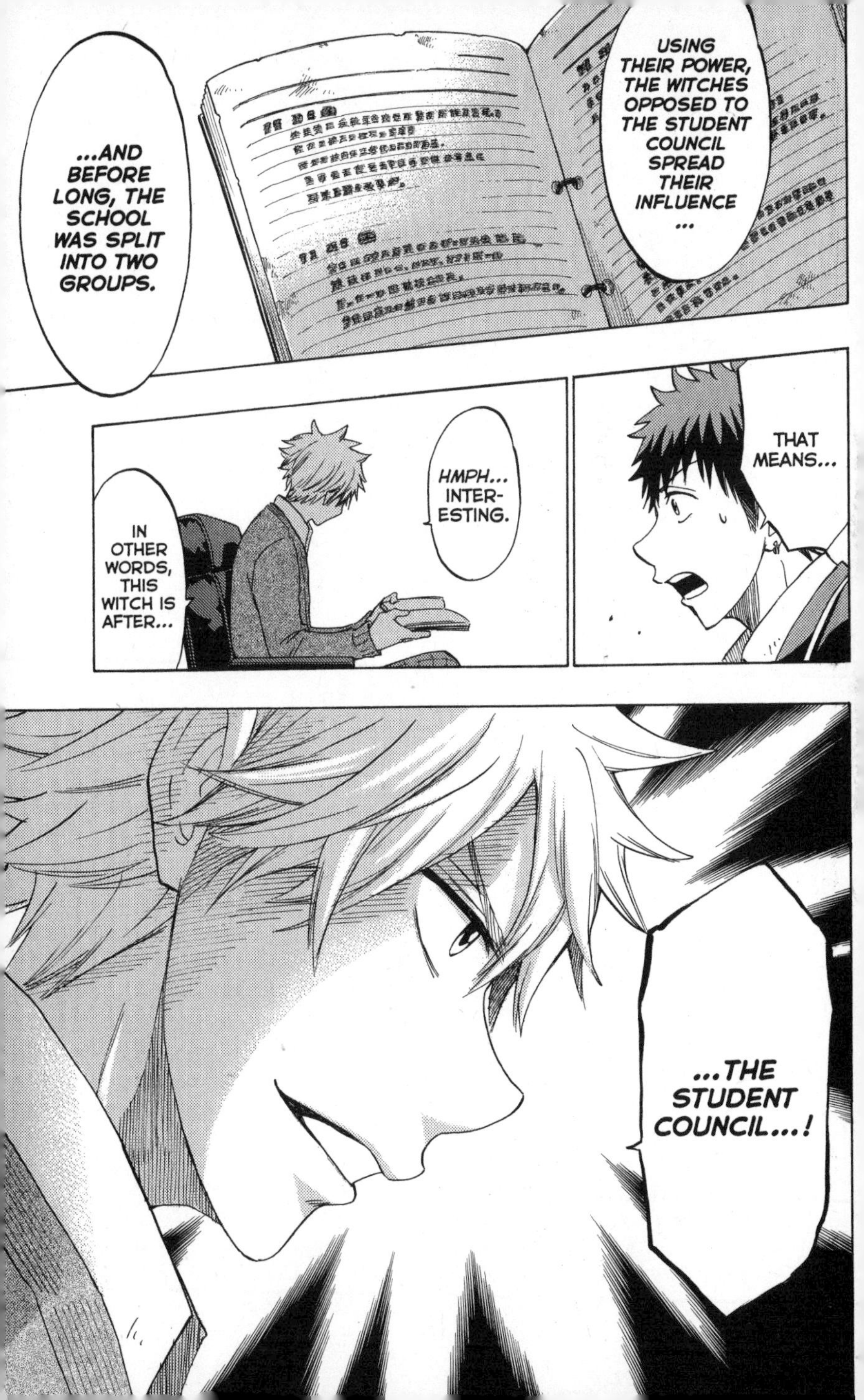
USING THEIR POWER, THE WITCHES OPPOSED TO THE STUDENT COUNCIL SPREAD THEIR INFLUENCE ...
...AND BEFORE LONG, THE SCHOOL WAS SPLIT INTO TWO GROUPS.
THAT MEANS...
HMPH... INTER-ESTING.
IN OTHER WORDS, THIS WITCH IS AFTER...
...THE STUDENT COUNCIL...!

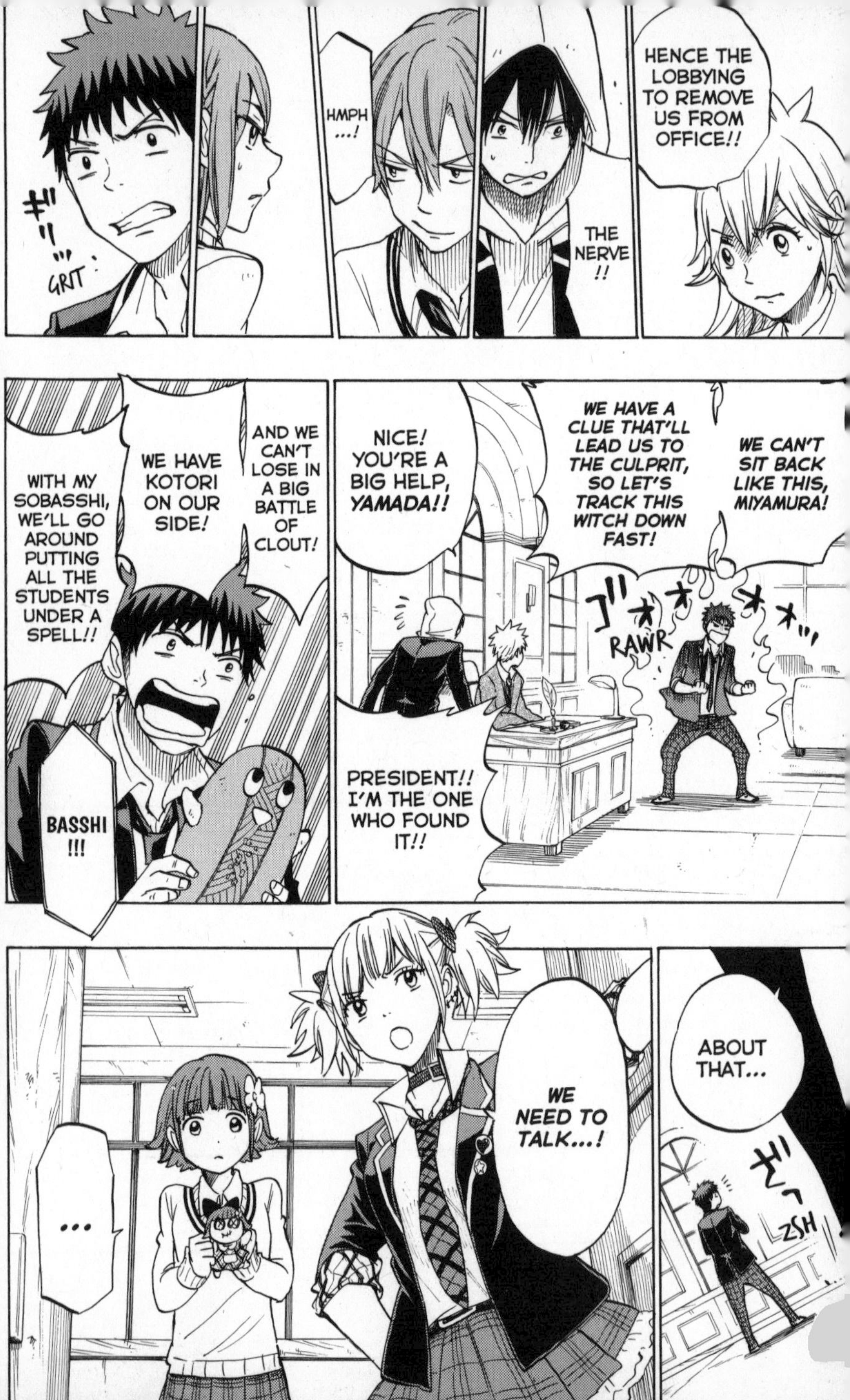
HENCE THE LOBBYING TO REMOVE US FROM OFFICE!!
HMPH ...!
THE NERVE !!
GRIT
WE CAN'T SIT BACK LIKE THIS, MIYAMURA!
WE HAVE A CLUE THAT'LL LEAD US TO THE CULPRIT, SO LET'S TRACK THIS WITCH DOWN FAST!
RAWR
NICE! YOU'RE A BIG HELP, YAMADA!!
PRESIDENT!! I'M THE ONE WHO FOUND IT!!
AND WE CAN'T LOSE IN A BIG BATTLE OF CLOUT!
WE HAVE KOTORI ON OUR SIDE!
WITH MY SOBASSHI, WE'LL GO AROUND PUTTING ALL THE STUDENTS UNDER A SPELL!!
BASSHI !!!
ABOUT THAT...
ZSH
WE NEED TO TALK...!
...

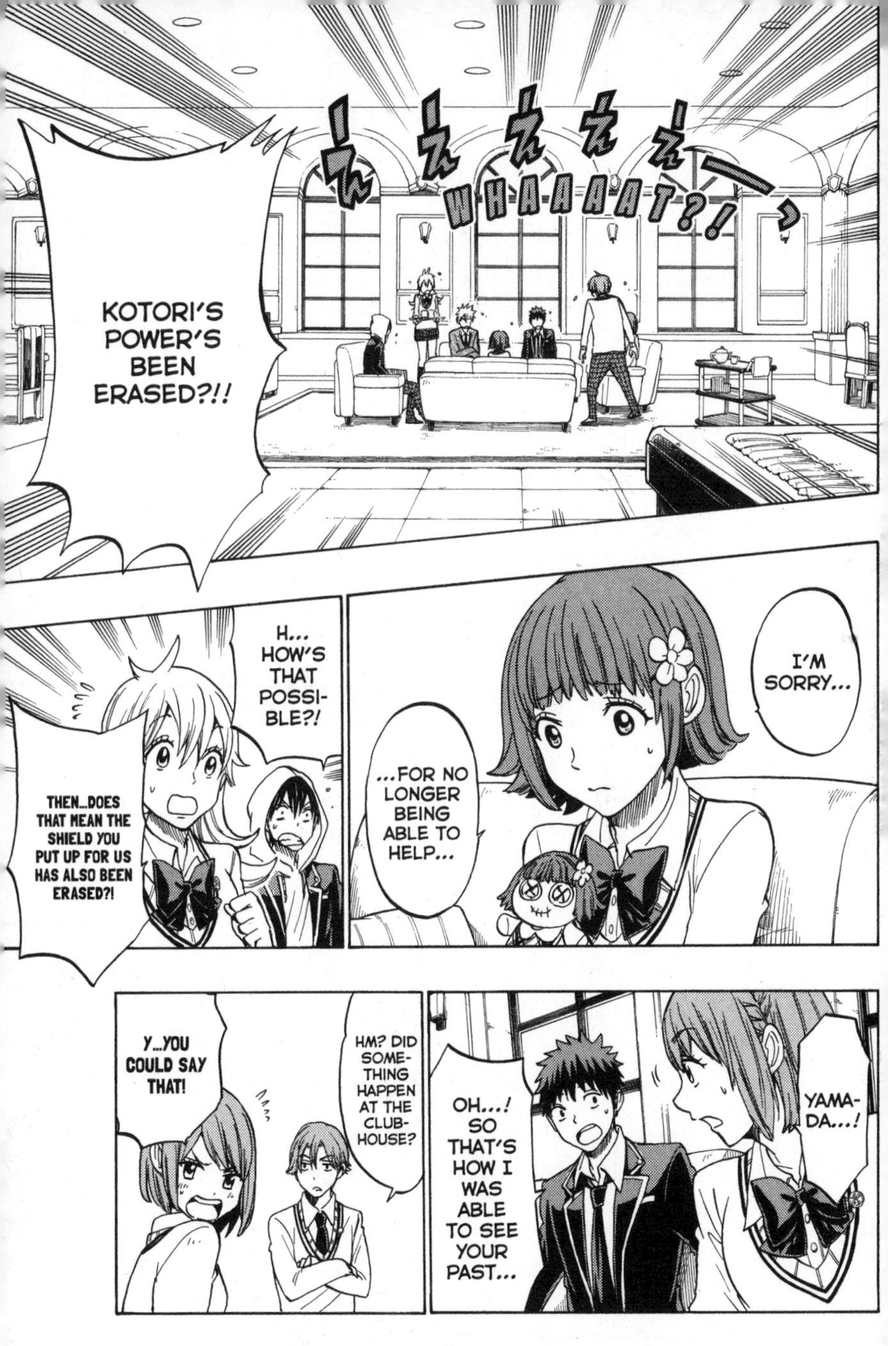
えええええー
WHAAAAAT?!
KOTORI'S POWER'S BEEN ERASED?!!
I'M SORRY...
...FOR NO LONGER BEING ABLE TO HELP...
H... HOW'S THAT POSSIBLE?!
THEN...DOES THAT MEAN THE SHIELD YOU PUT UP FOR US HAS ALSO BEEN ERASED?!
YAMADA...!
OH...! SO THAT'S HOW I WAS ABLE TO SEE YOUR PAST...
HM? DID SOMETHING HAPPEN AT THE CLUBHOUSE?
Y...YOU COULD SAY THAT!

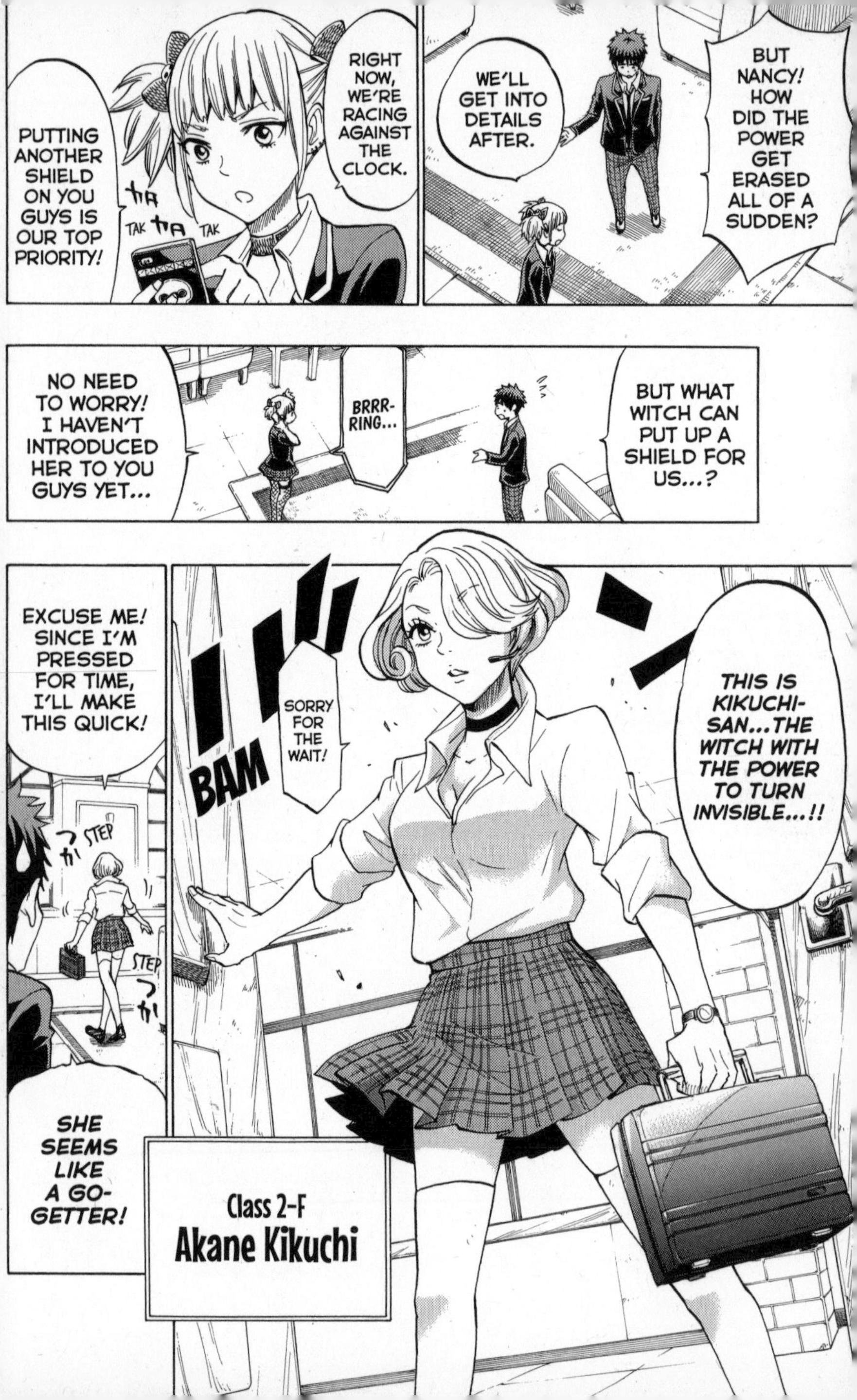
BUT NANCY! HOW DID THE POWER GET ERASED ALL OF A SUDDEN?
WE'LL GET INTO DETAILS AFTER.
RIGHT NOW, WE'RE RACING AGAINST THE CLOCK.
TAK TAK
PUTTING ANOTHER SHIELD ON YOU GUYS IS OUR TOP PRIORITY!
BUT WHAT WITCH CAN PUT UP A SHIELD FOR US...?
BRRR-RING...
NO NEED TO WORRY! I HAVEN'T INTRODUCED HER TO YOU GUYS YET...
THIS IS KIKUCHI-SAN...THE WITCH WITH THE POWER TO TURN INVISIBLE...!!
SORRY FOR THE WAIT!
BAM
Class 2-F
Akane Kikuchi
EXCUSE ME! SINCE I'M PRESSED FOR TIME, I'LL MAKE THIS QUICK!
STEP
STEP
SHE SEEMS LIKE A GO-GETTER!

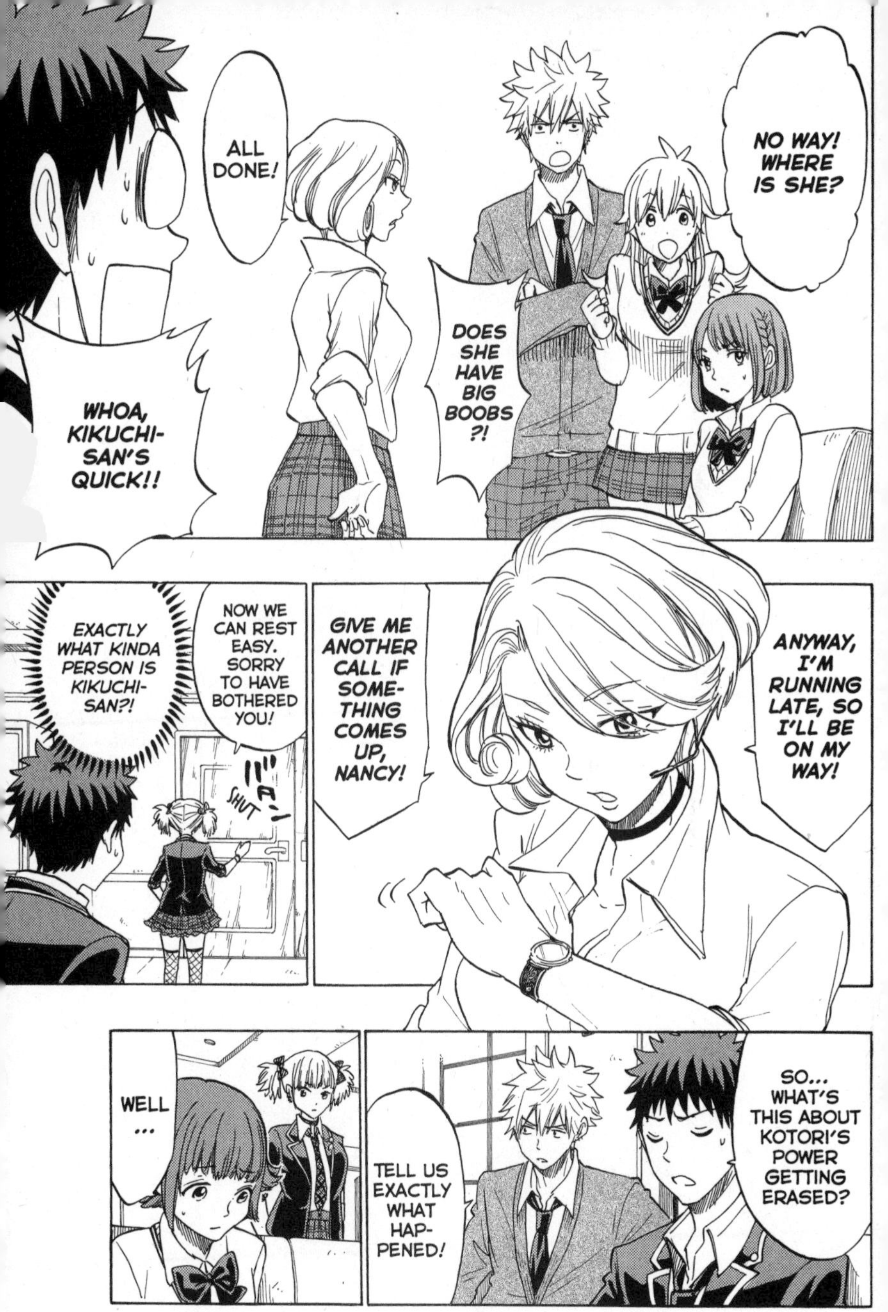

NO WAY! WHERE IS SHE?
ALL DONE!
DOES SHE HAVE BIG BOOBS?!
WHOA, KIKUCHI-SAN'S QUICK!!
ANYWAY, I'M RUNNING LATE, SO I'LL BE ON MY WAY!
GIVE ME ANOTHER CALL IF SOMETHING COMES UP, NANCY!
NOW WE CAN REST EASY. SORRY TO HAVE BOTHERED YOU!
SHUT
EXACTLY WHAT KINDA PERSON IS KIKUCHI-SAN?!
SO... WHAT'S THIS ABOUT KOTORI'S POWER GETTING ERASED?
TELL US EXACTLY WHAT HAPPENED!
WELL ...

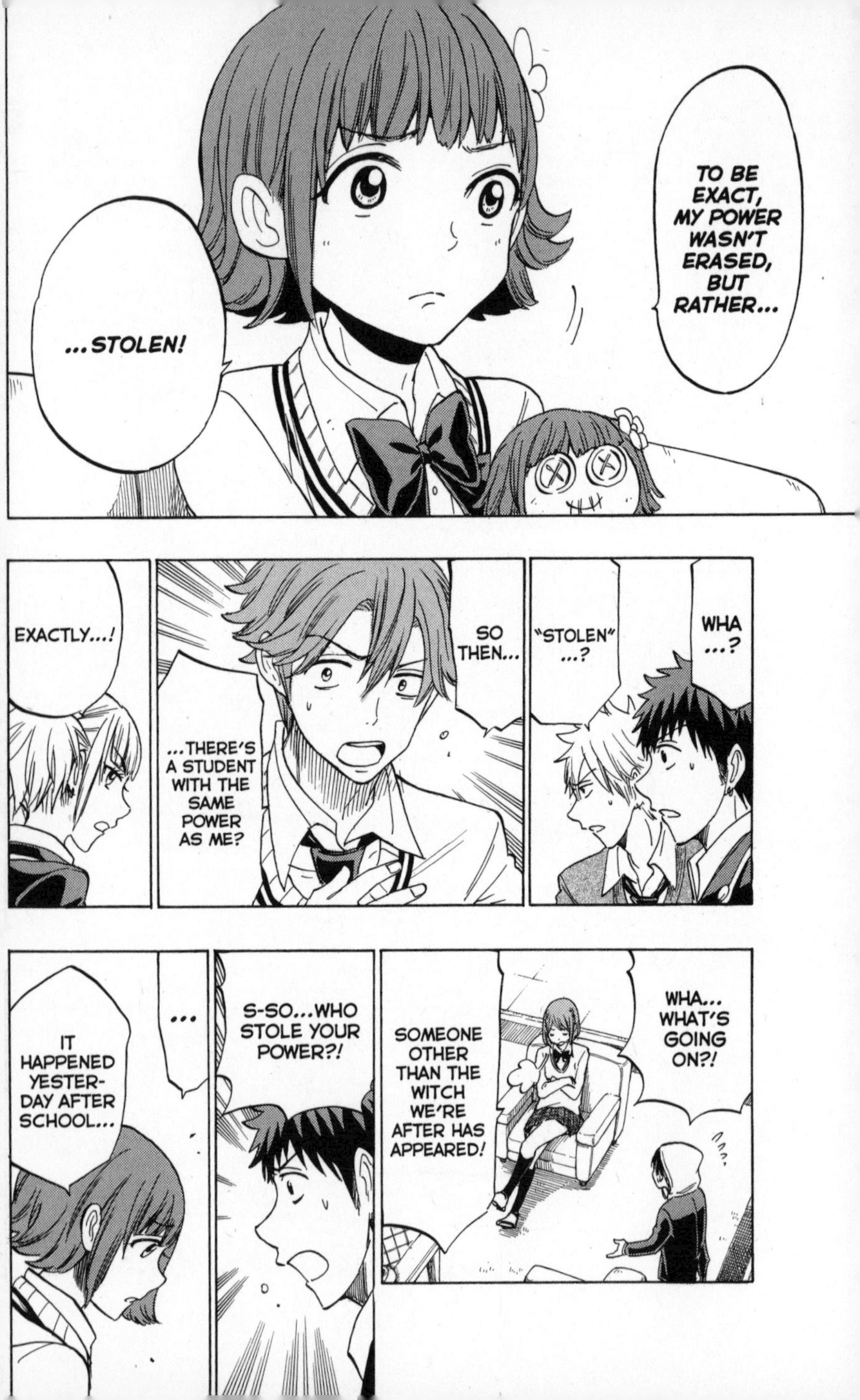
TO BE EXACT, MY POWER WASN'T ERASED, BUT RATHER...
...STOLEN!
WHA ...?
"STOLEN" ...?
SO THEN...
...THERE'S A STUDENT WITH THE SAME POWER AS ME?
EXACTLY...!
WHA... WHAT'S GOING ON?!
SOMEONE OTHER THAN THE WITCH WE'RE AFTER HAS APPEARED!
S-SO...WHO STOLE YOUR POWER?!
...
IT HAPPENED YESTER-DAY AFTER SCHOOL...

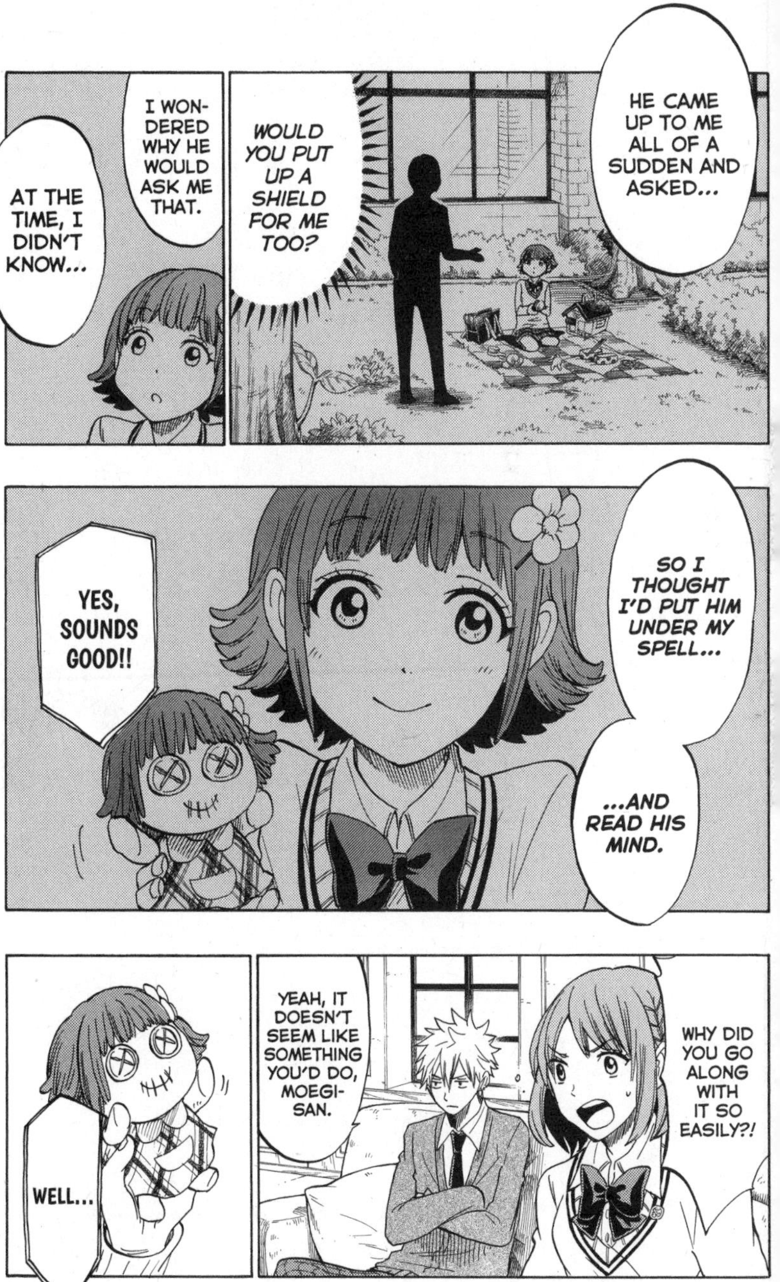
HE CAME UP TO ME ALL OF A SUDDEN AND ASKED...
WOULD YOU PUT UP A SHIELD FOR ME TOO?
I WON-DERED WHY HE WOULD ASK ME THAT.
AT THE TIME, I DIDN'T KNOW...
SO I THOUGHT I'D PUT HIM UNDER MY SPELL...
...AND READ HIS MIND.
YES, SOUNDS GOOD!!
WHY DID YOU GO ALONG WITH IT SO EASILY?!
YEAH, IT DOESN'T SEEM LIKE SOMETHING YOU'D DO, MOEGI-SAN.
WELL...

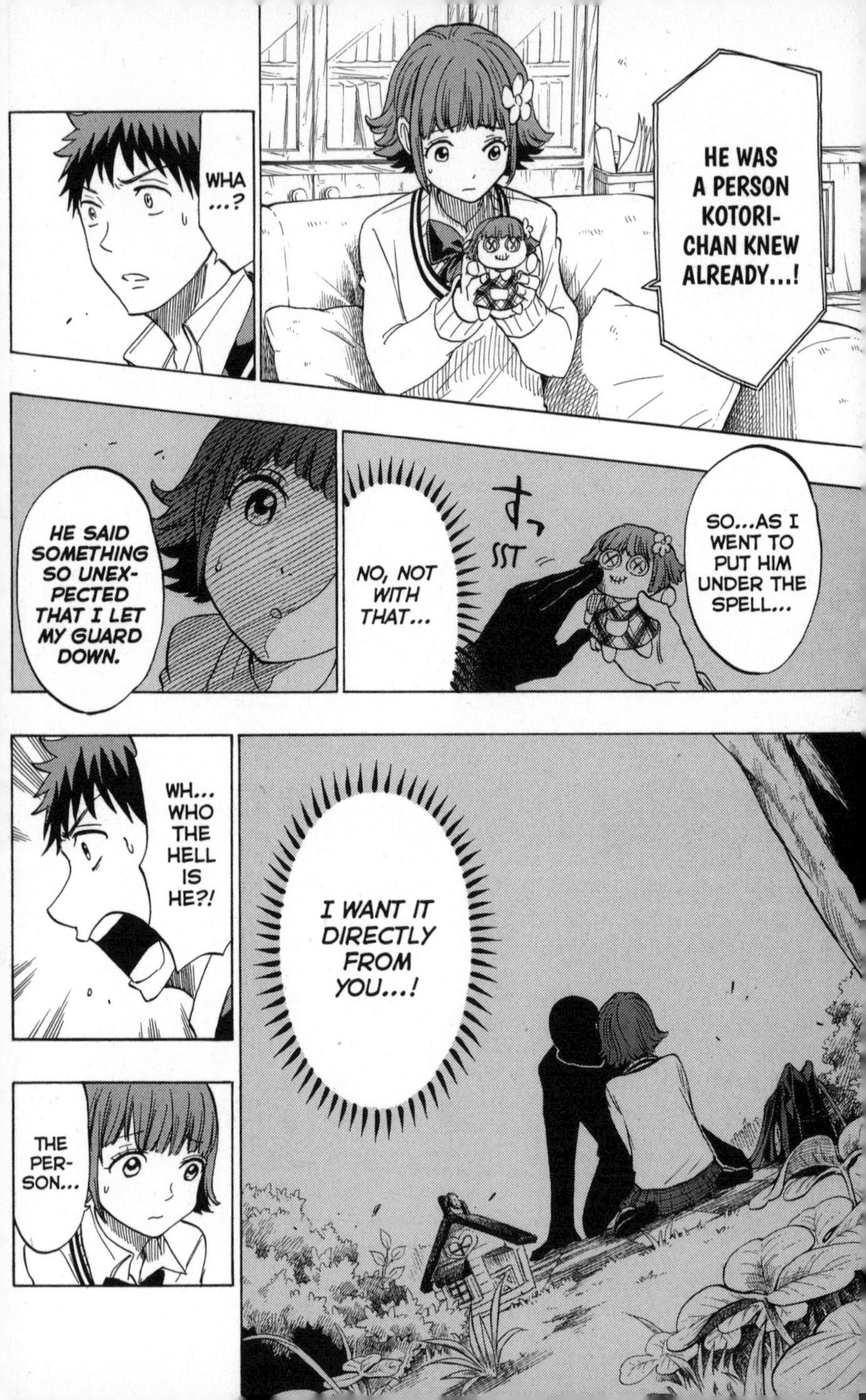
HE WAS A PERSON KOTORI-CHAN KNEW ALREADY...!
WHA ...?
SO...AS I WENT TO PUT HIM UNDER THE SPELL...
すっ
SST
NO, NOT WITH THAT...
HE SAID SOMETHING SO UNEXPECTED THAT I LET MY GUARD DOWN.
I WANT IT DIRECTLY FROM YOU...!
WH... WHO THE HELL IS HE?!
THE PERSON...

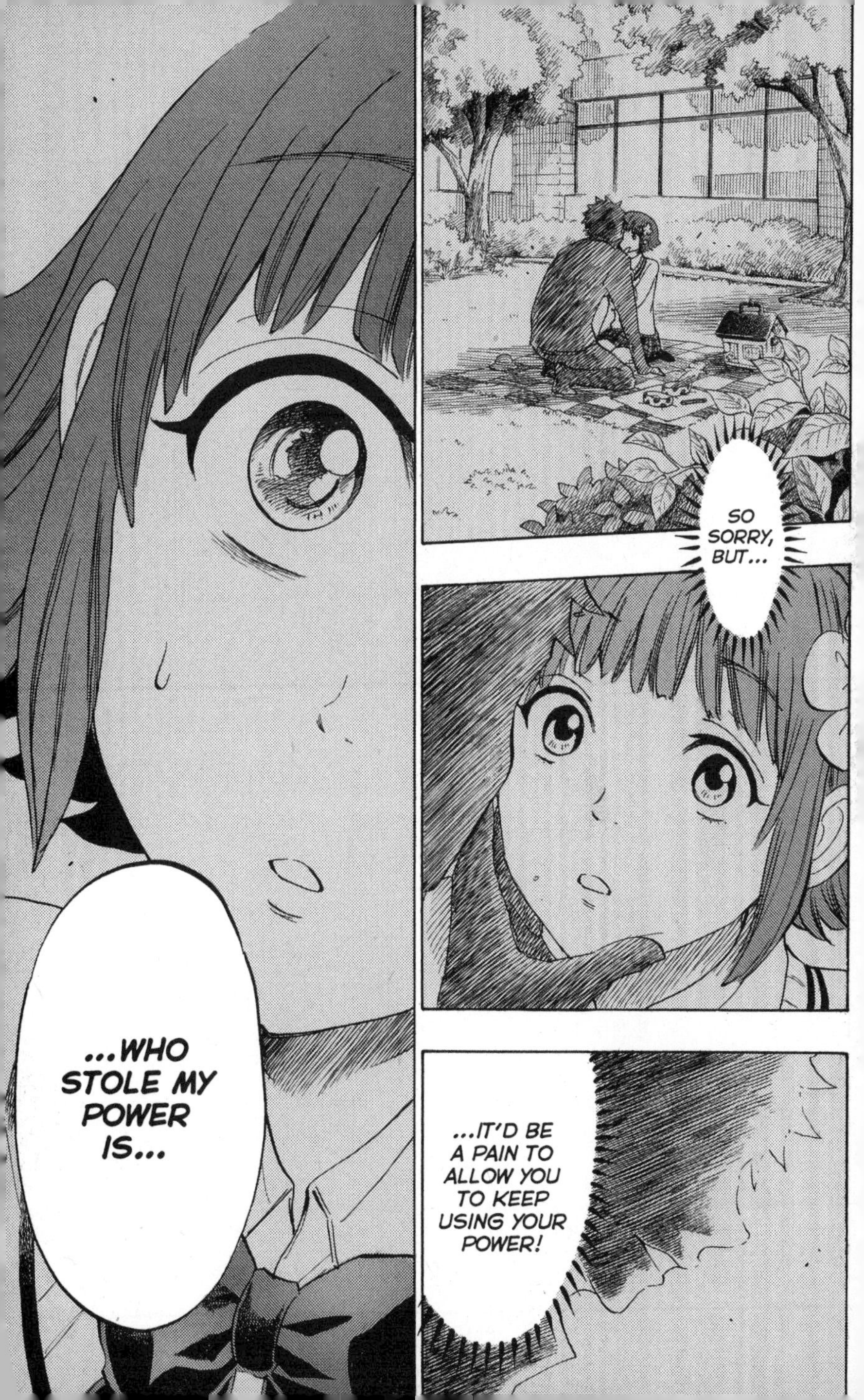
SO SORRY, BUT...
...IT'D BE A PAIN TO ALLOW YOU TO KEEP USING YOUR POWER!
...WHO STOLE MY POWER IS...

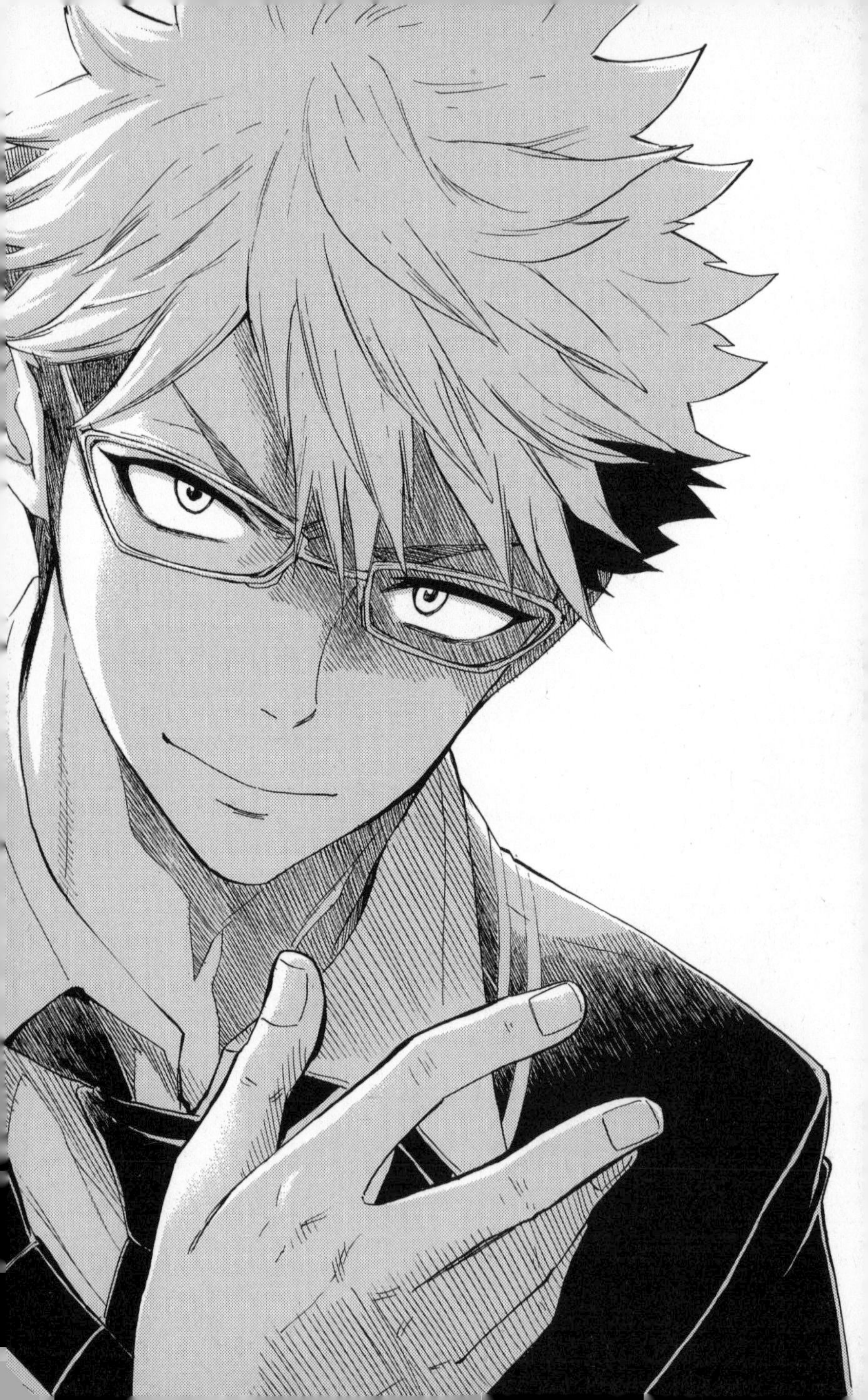

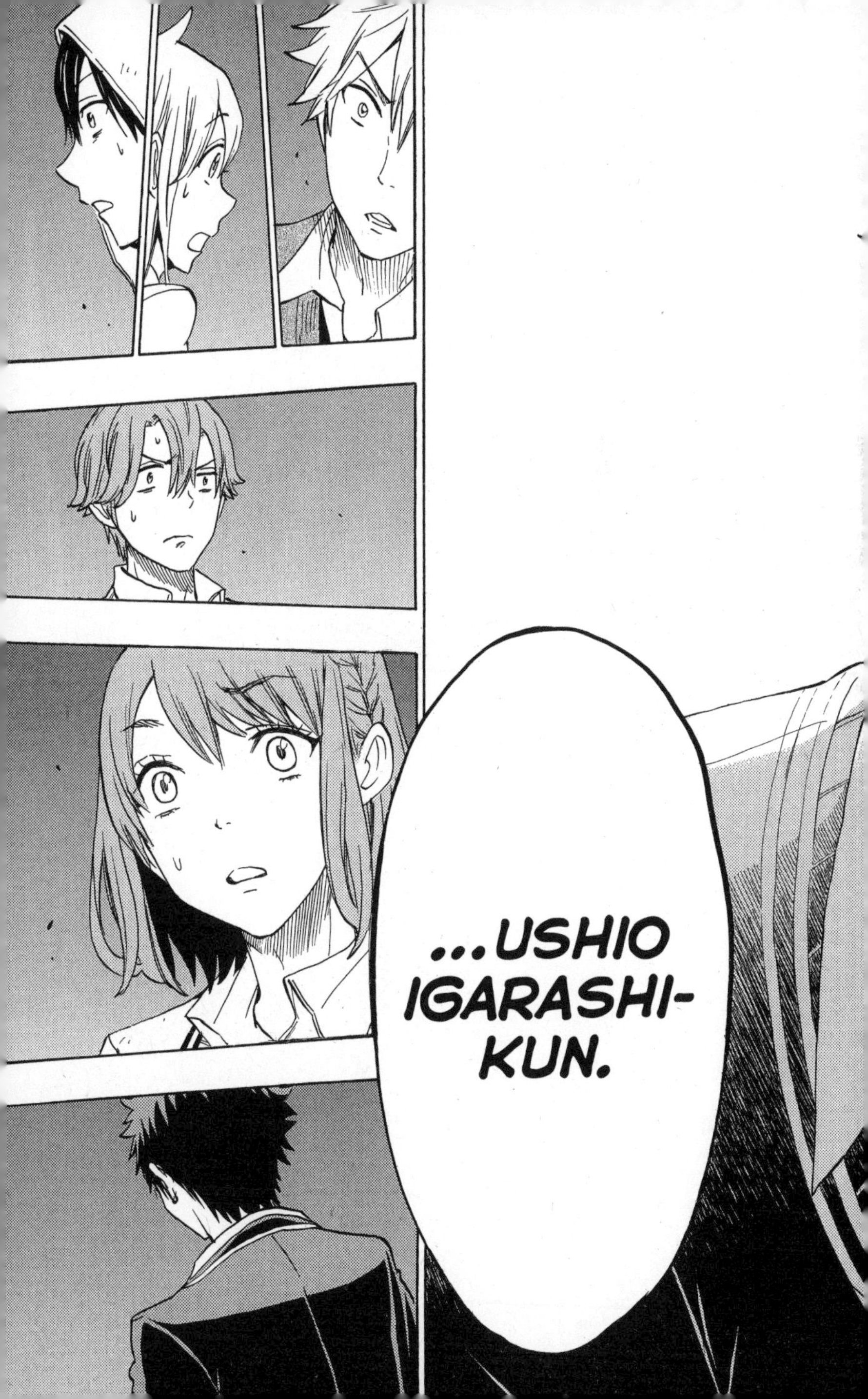
...USHIO IGARASHI-KUN.

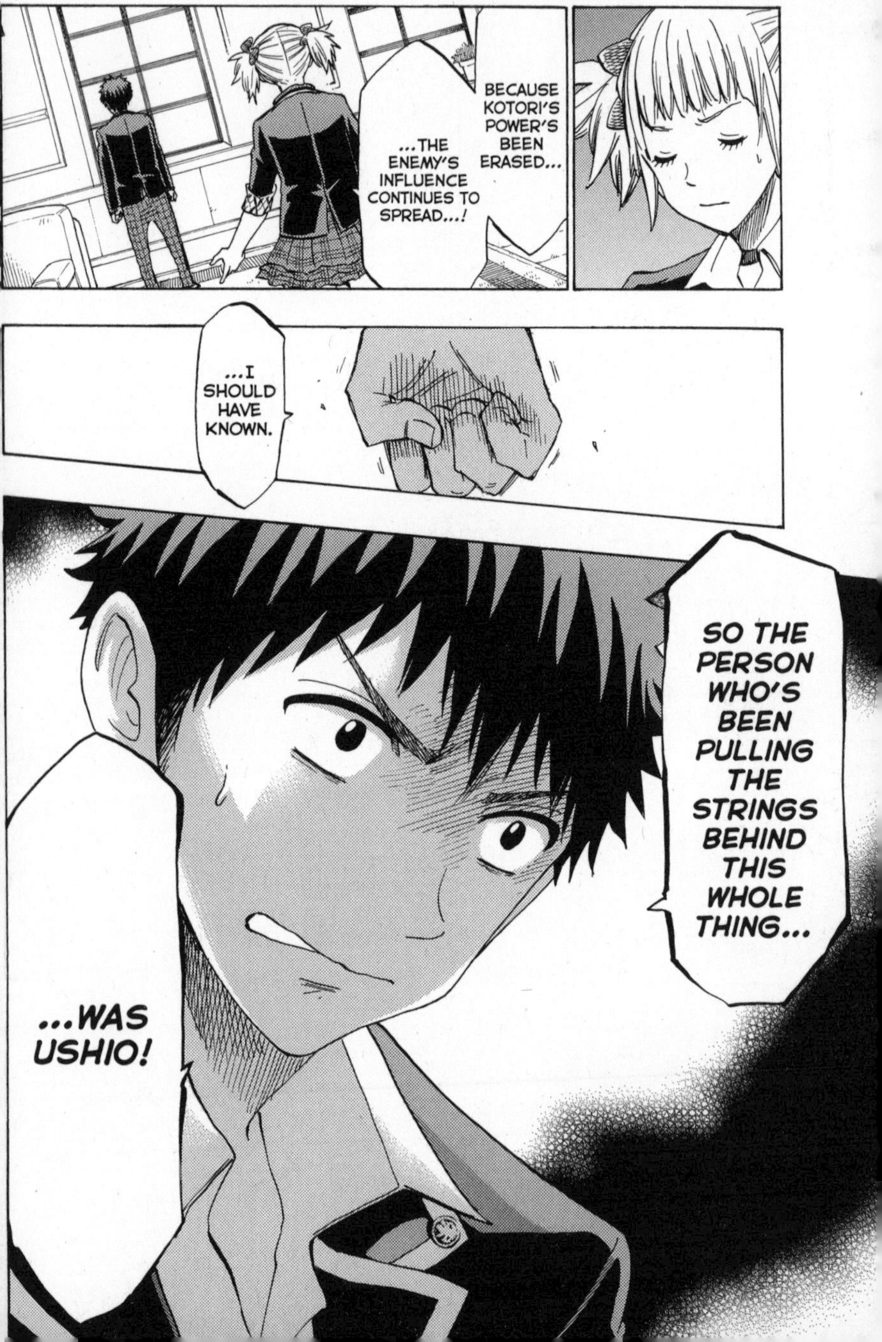
BECAUSE KOTORI'S POWER'S BEEN ERASED...
...THE ENEMY'S INFLUENCE CONTINUES TO SPREAD...!
...I SHOULD HAVE KNOWN.
SO THE PERSON WHO'S BEEN PULLING THE STRINGS BEHIND THIS WHOLE THING...
...WAS USHIO!

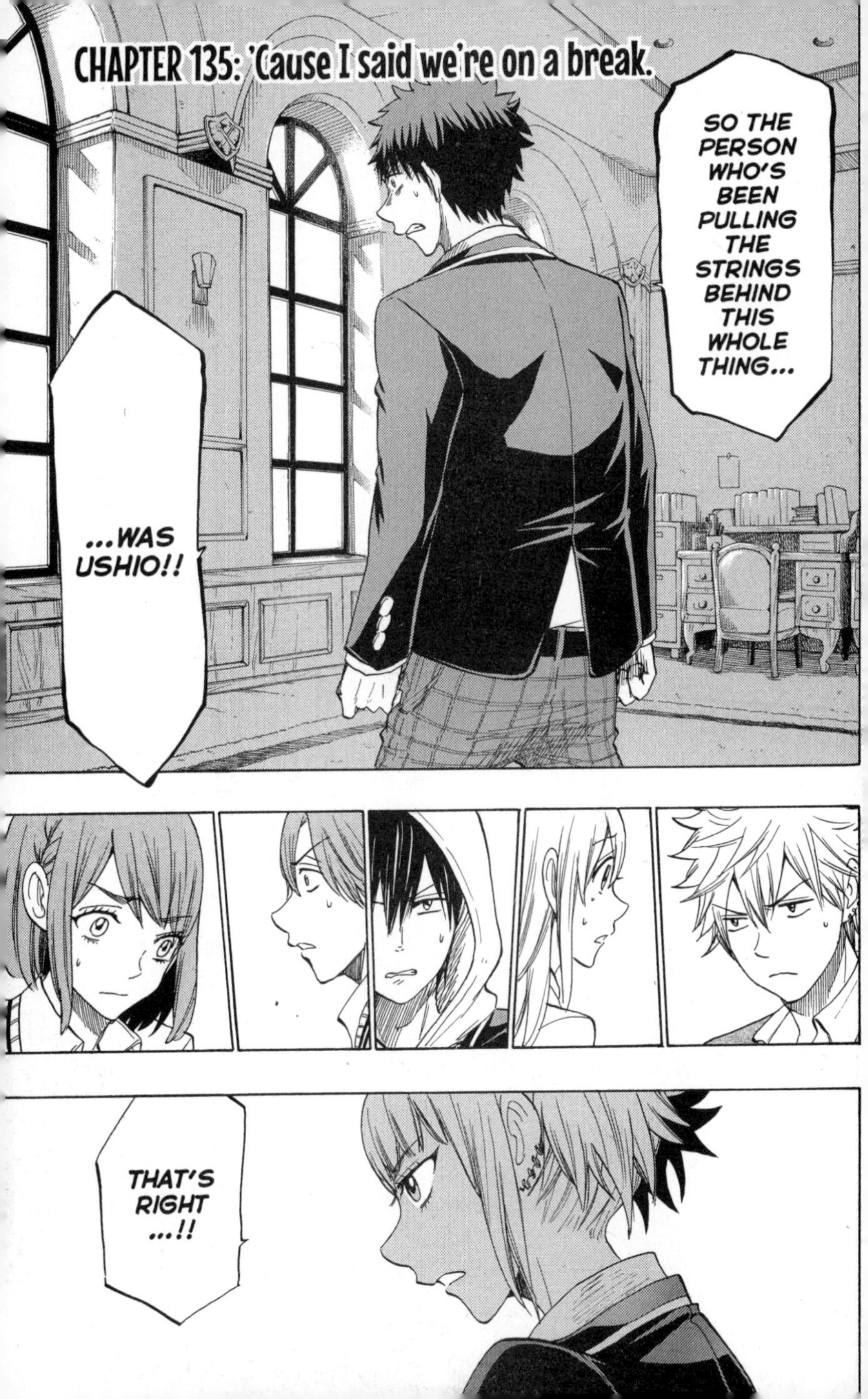
CHAPTER 135: 'Cause I said we're on a break.
SO THE PERSON WHO'S BEEN PULLING THE STRINGS BEHIND THIS WHOLE THING...
...WAS USHIO!!
THAT'S RIGHT ...!!

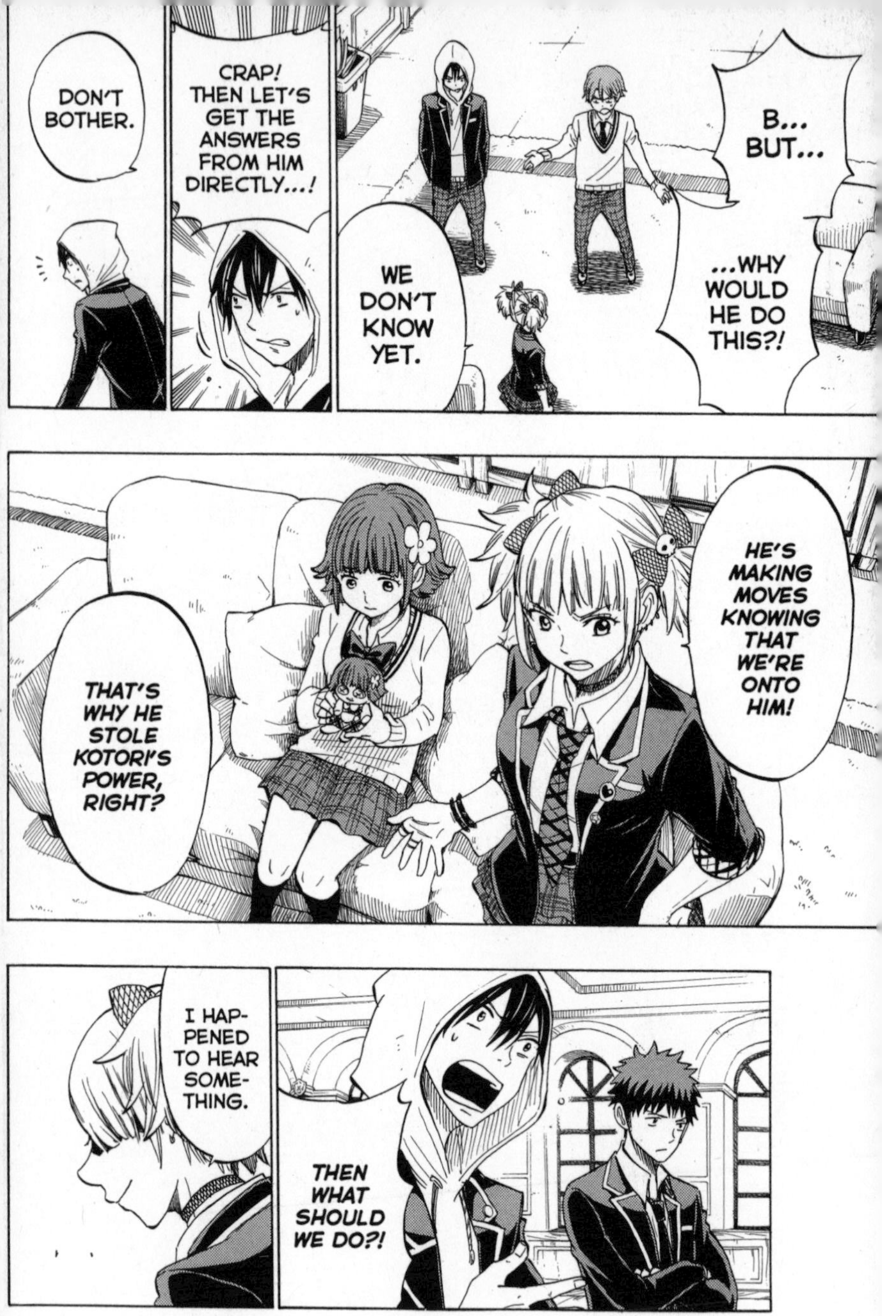
B... BUT...
...WHY WOULD HE DO THIS?!
WE DON'T KNOW YET.
CRAP! THEN LET'S GET THE ANSWERS FROM HIM DIRECTLY...!
DON'T BOTHER.
HE'S MAKING MOVES KNOWING THAT WE'RE ONTO HIM!
THAT'S WHY HE STOLE KOTORI'S POWER, RIGHT?
THEN WHAT SHOULD WE DO?!
I HAP-PENED TO HEAR SOME-THING.

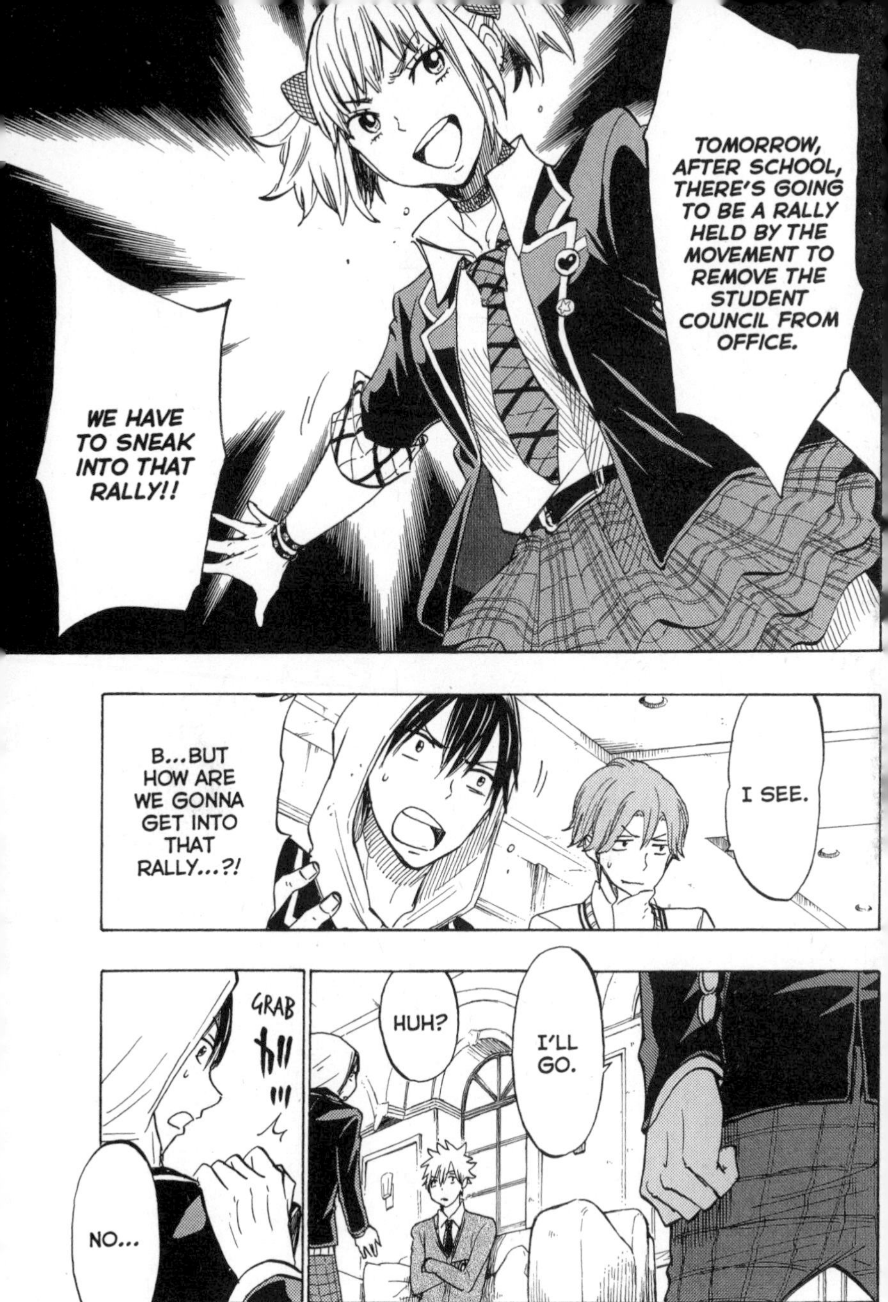
TOMORROW, AFTER SCHOOL, THERE'S GOING TO BE A RALLY HELD BY THE MOVEMENT TO REMOVE THE STUDENT COUNCIL FROM OFFICE.
WE HAVE TO SNEAK INTO THAT RALLY!!
I SEE.
B...BUT HOW ARE WE GONNA GET INTO THAT RALLY...?!
I'LL GO.
HUH?
GRAB
NO...

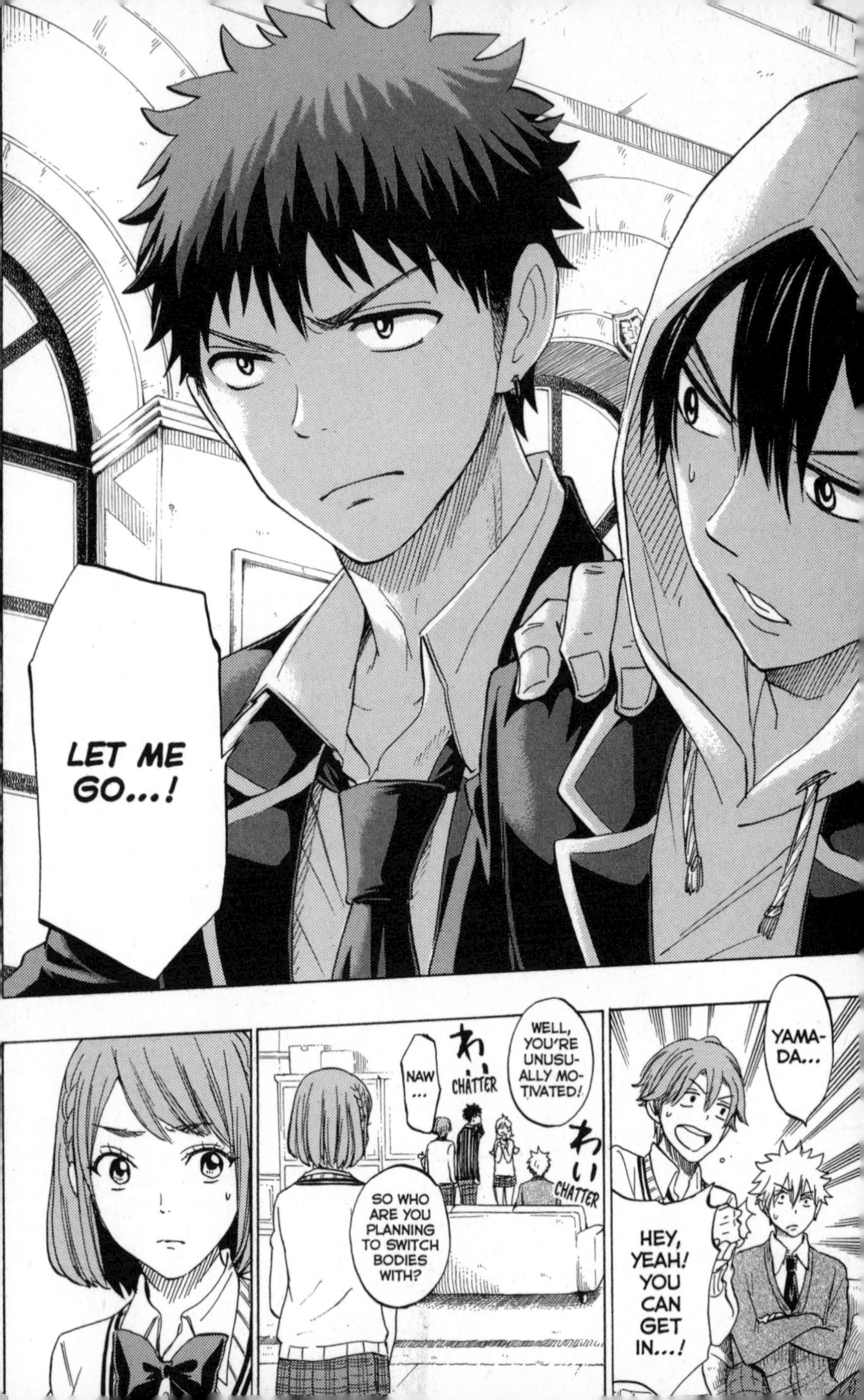
LET ME GO...!
YAMA-DA...
HEY, YEAH! YOU CAN GET IN...!
WELL, YOU'RE UNUSUALLY MOTIVATED!
わい CHATTER
わ CHATTER
NAW...
SO WHO ARE YOU PLANNING TO SWITCH BODIES WITH?

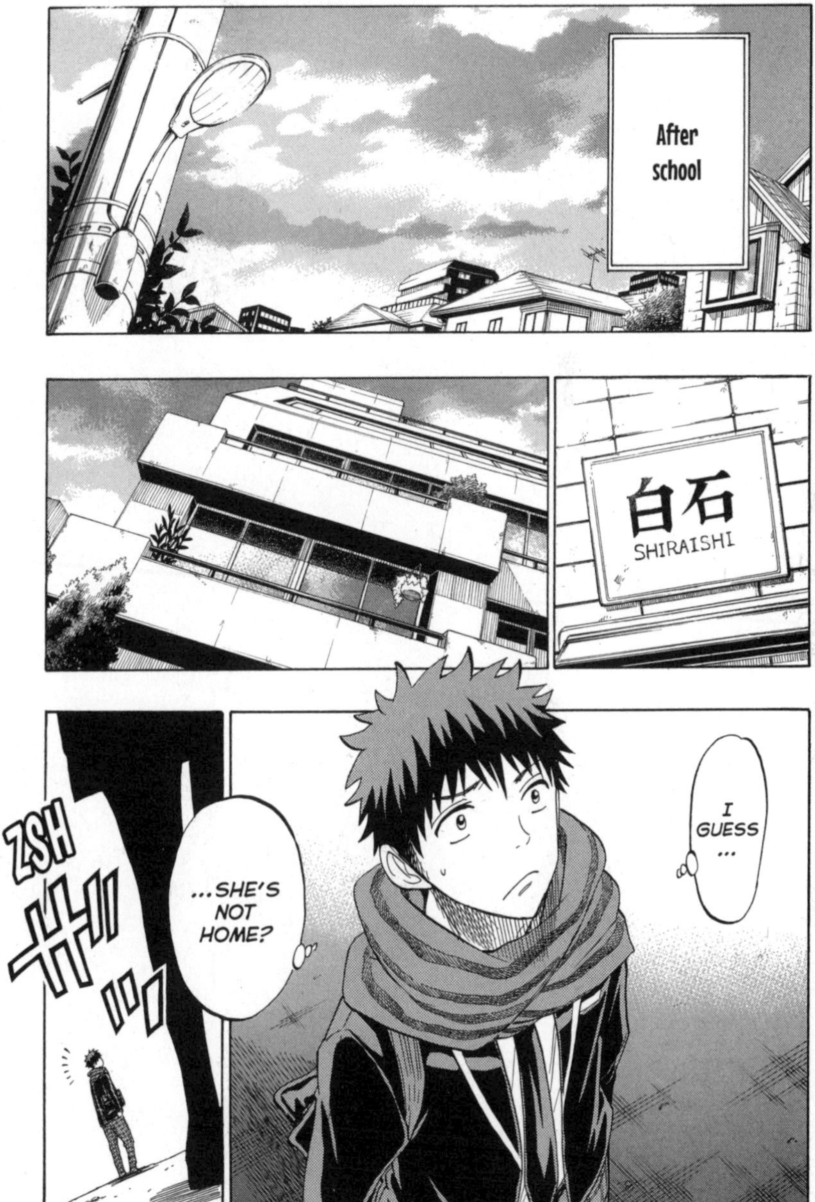
After school
白石
SHIRAISHI
I GUESS ...
...SHE'S NOT HOME?
ZSH

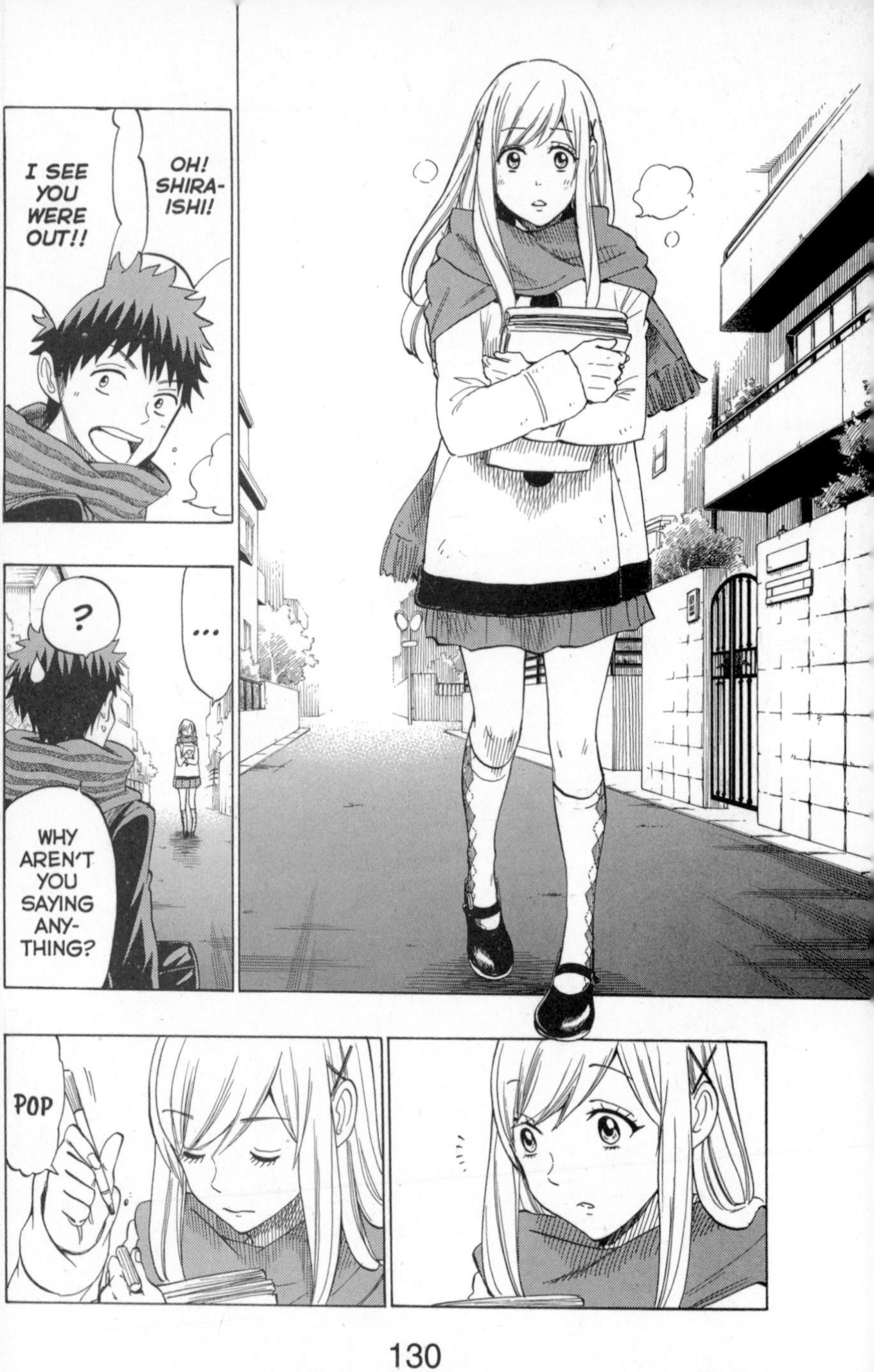
OH! SHIRA-ISHI!
I SEE YOU WERE OUT!!
...
?
WHY AREN'T YOU SAYING ANY-THING?
POP

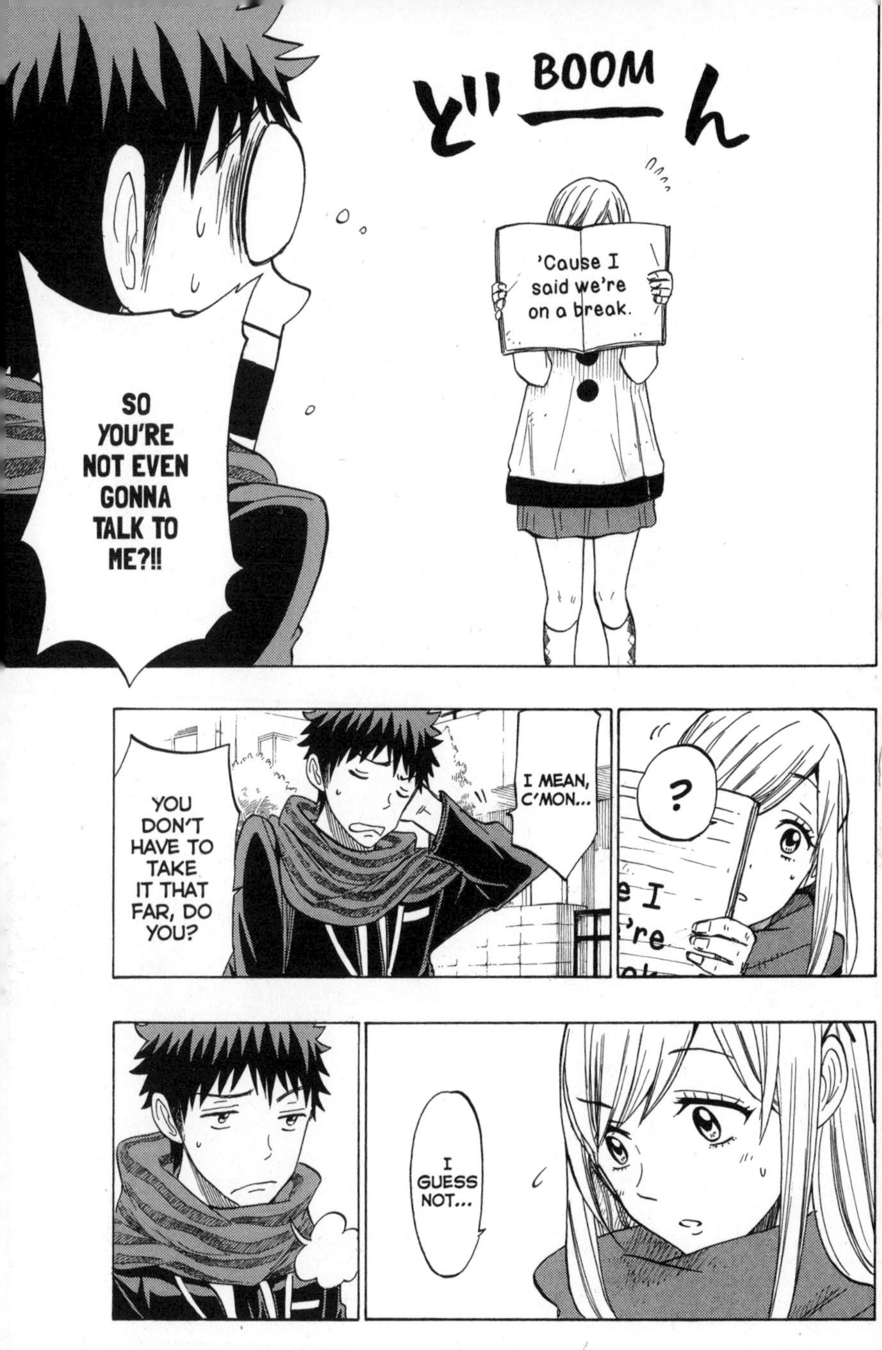
どBOOMーん
'Cause I said we're on a break.
SO YOU'RE NOT EVEN GONNA TALK TO ME?!!
?
I MEAN, C'MON...
YOU DON'T HAVE TO TAKE IT THAT FAR, DO YOU?
I GUESS NOT...

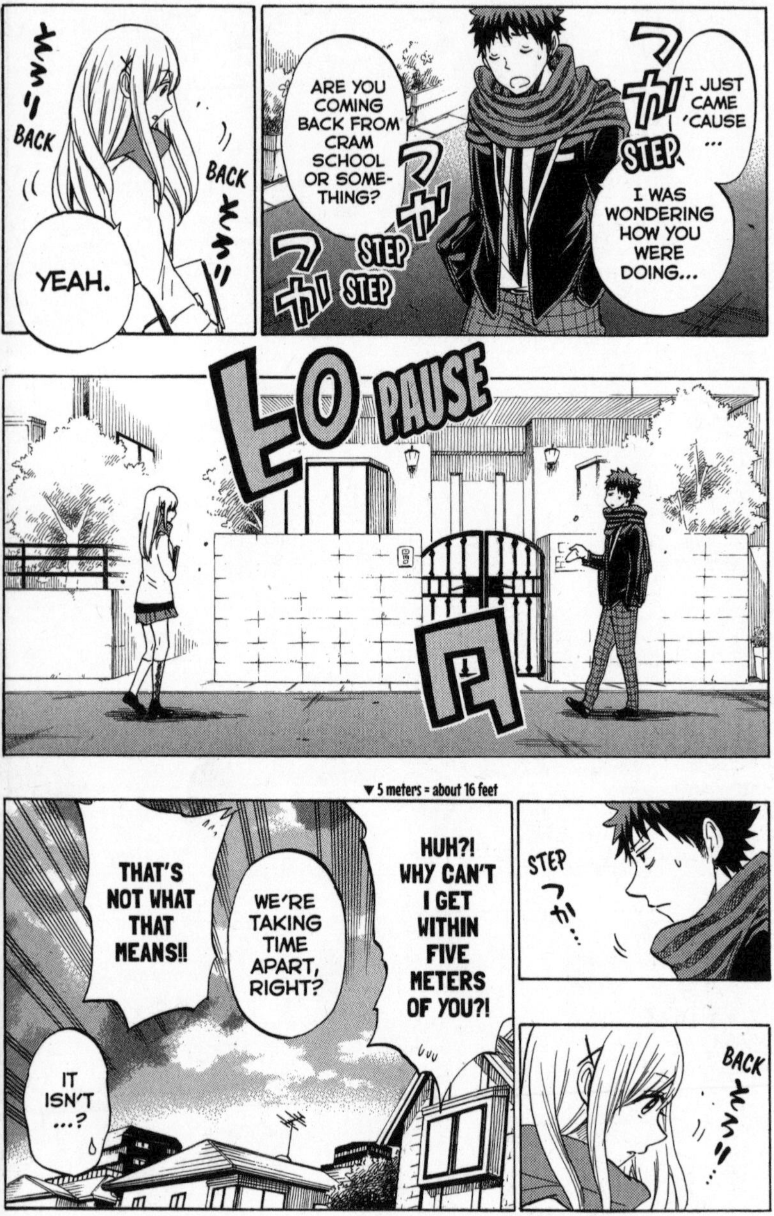
I JUST CAME 'CAUSE ...
STEP
I WAS WONDERING HOW YOU WERE DOING...
ARE YOU COMING BACK FROM CRAM SCHOOL OR SOME-THING?
STEP
STEP
BACK
BACK
YEAH.
PAUSE
▼5 meters = about 16 feet
STEP
BACK
HUH?! WHY CAN'T I GET WITHIN FIVE METERS OF YOU?!
WE'RE TAKING TIME APART, RIGHT?
THAT'S NOT WHAT THAT MEANS!!
IT ISN'T ...?

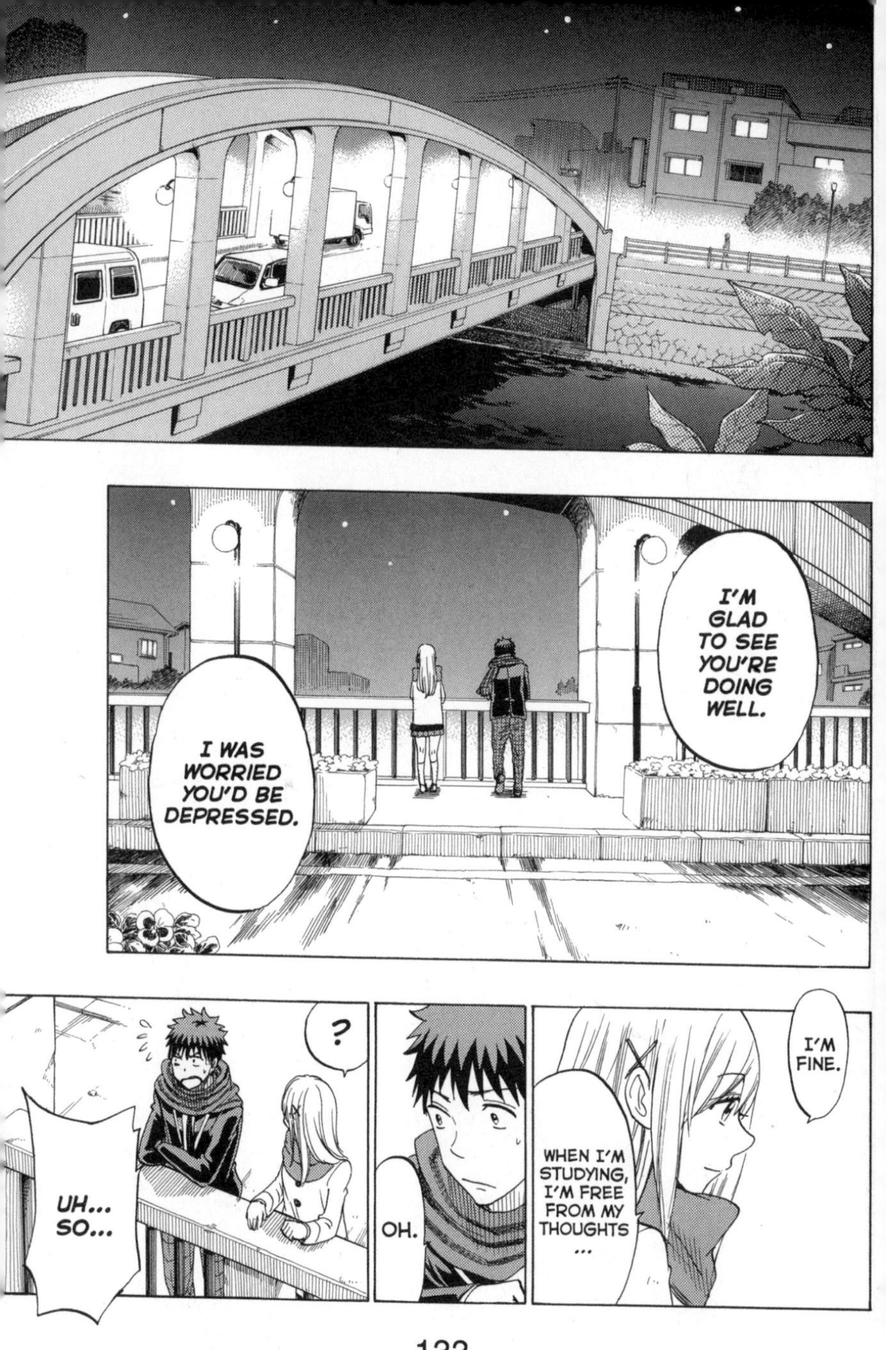
I'M GLAD TO SEE YOU'RE DOING WELL.
I WAS WORRIED YOU'D BE DEPRESSED.
I'M FINE.
WHEN I'M STUDYING, I'M FREE FROM MY THOUGHTS ...
OH.
?
UH... SO...

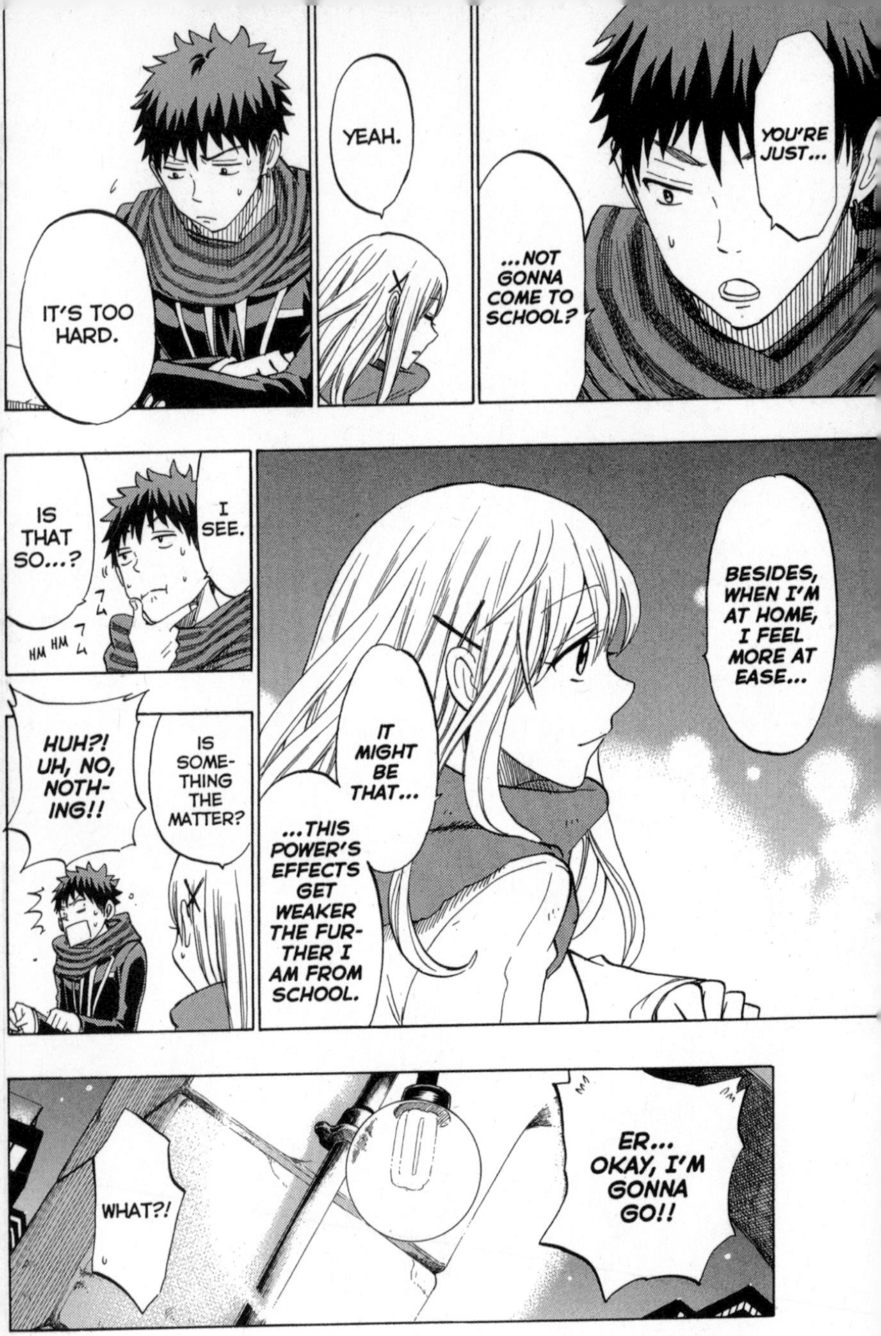
YOU'RE JUST...
...NOT GONNA COME TO SCHOOL?
YEAH.
IT'S TOO HARD.
BESIDES, WHEN I'M AT HOME, I FEEL MORE AT EASE...
IT MIGHT BE THAT...
...THIS POWER'S EFFECTS GET WEAKER THE FUR-THER I AM FROM SCHOOL.
I SEE.
IS THAT SO...?
HM HM
IS SOME-THING THE MATTER?
HUH?! UH, NO, NOTH-ING!!
ER... OKAY, I'M GONNA GO!!
WHAT?!

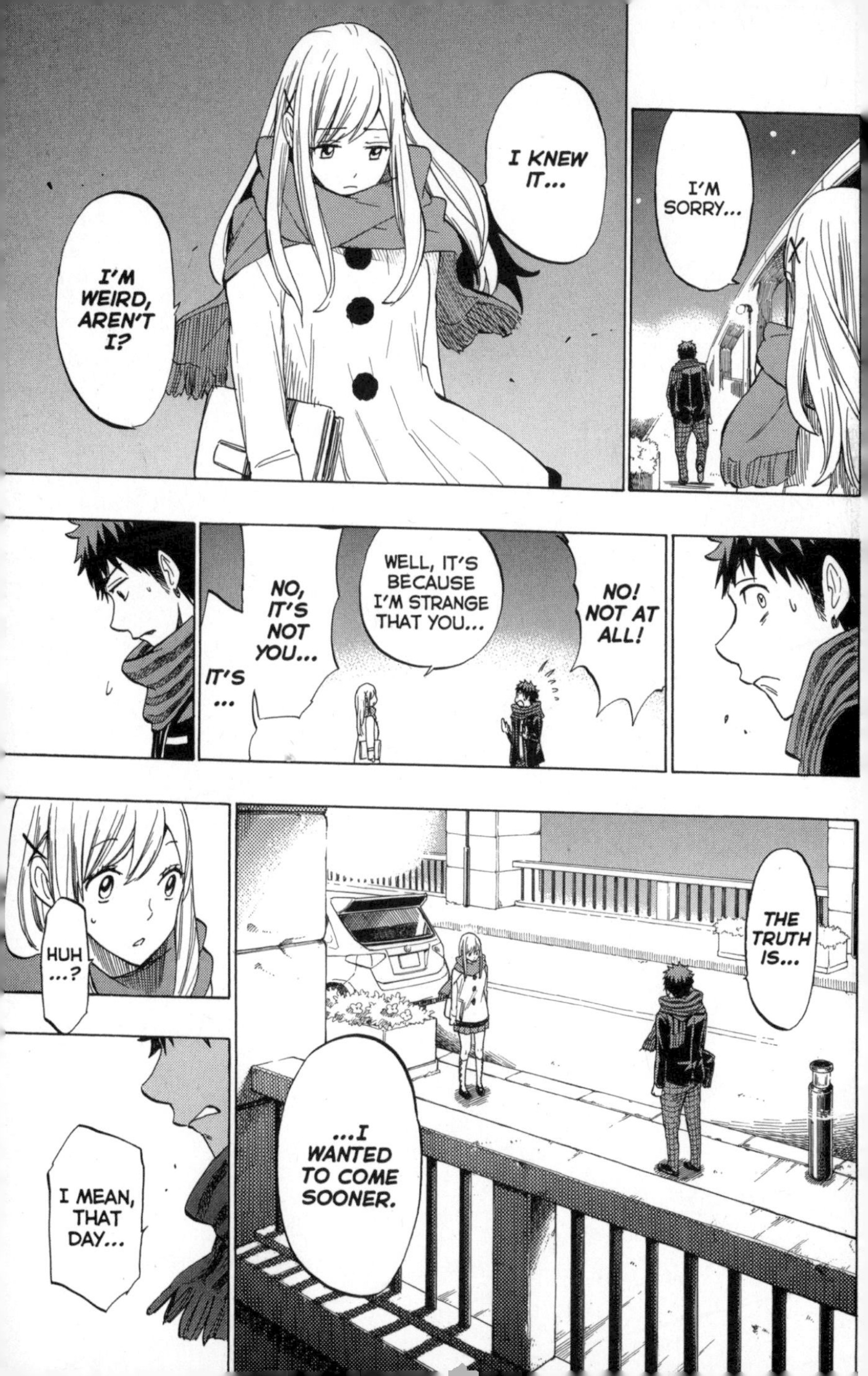
I'M SORRY...
I KNEW IT...
I'M WEIRD, AREN'T I?
NO! NOT AT ALL!
WELL, IT'S BECAUSE I'M STRANGE THAT YOU...
NO, IT'S NOT YOU...
IT'S ...
THE TRUTH IS...
...I WANTED TO COME SOONER.
HUH ...?
I MEAN, THAT DAY...

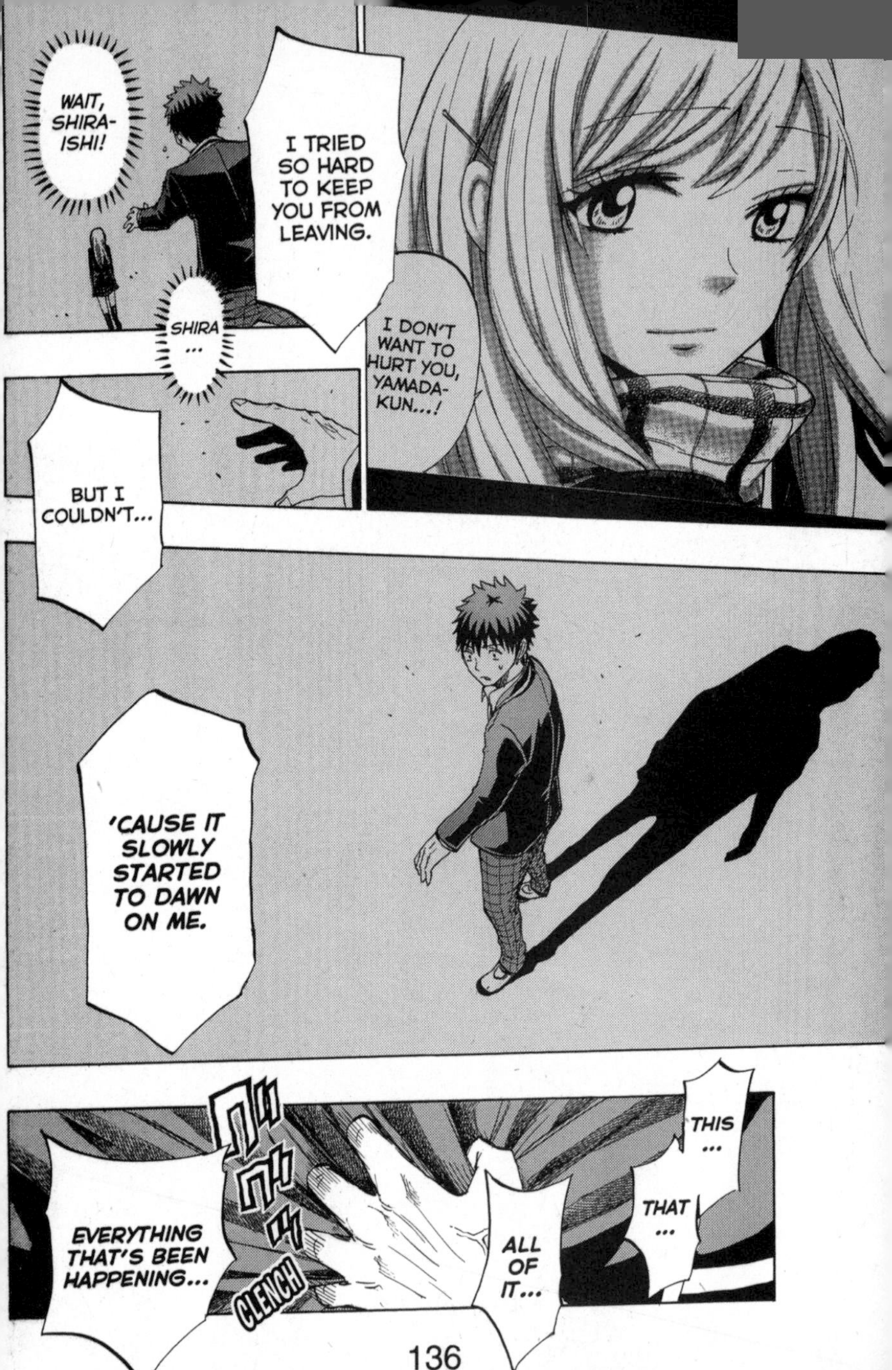
I DON'T WANT TO HURT YOU, YAMADA-KUN...!
I TRIED SO HARD TO KEEP YOU FROM LEAVING.
WAIT, SHIRA-ISHI!
SHIRA ...
BUT I COULDN'T...
'CAUSE IT SLOWLY STARTED TO DAWN ON ME.
THIS ...
THAT ...
ALL OF IT...
CLENCH
EVERYTHING THAT'S BEEN HAPPENING...

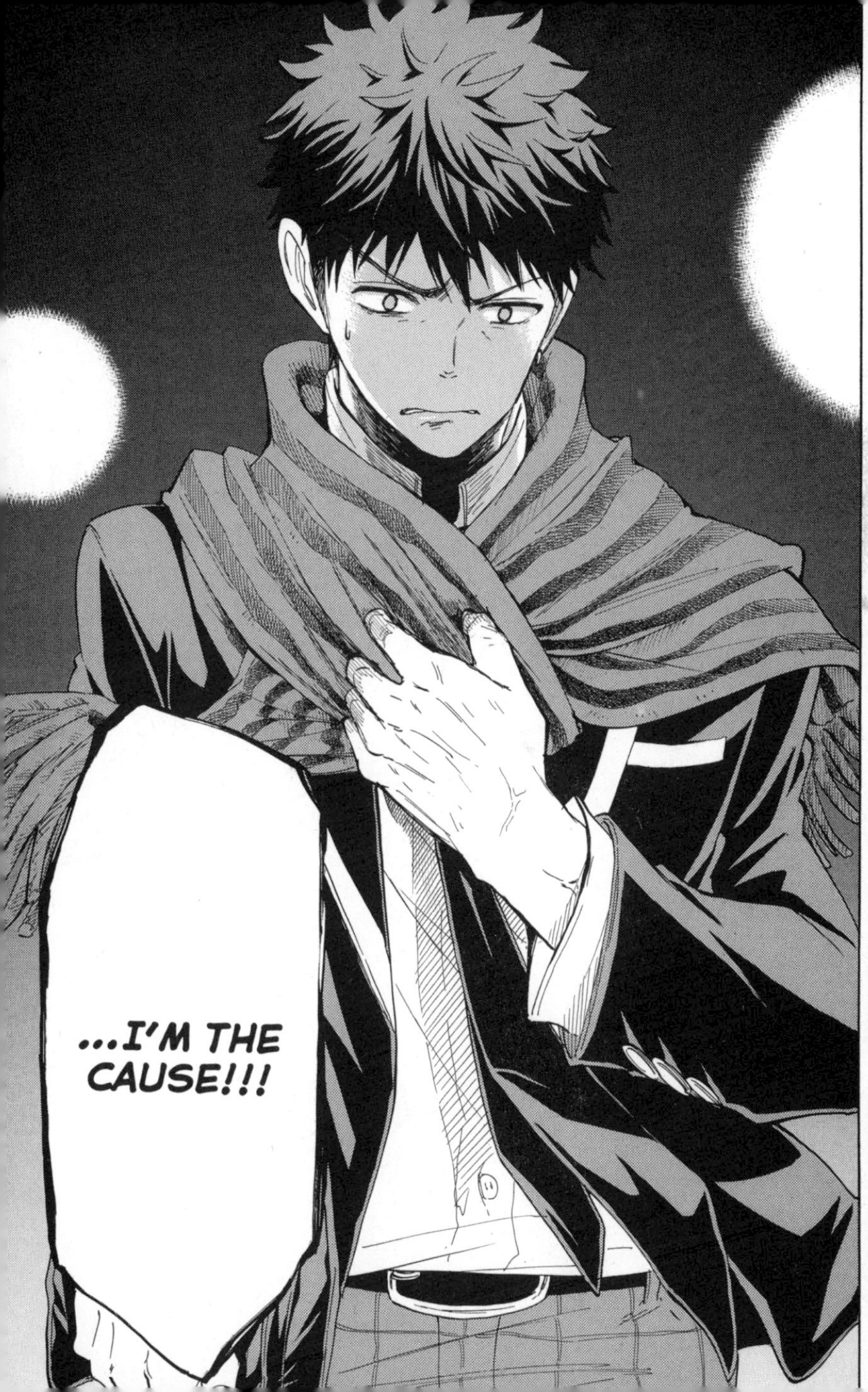
...I'M THE CAUSE!!!

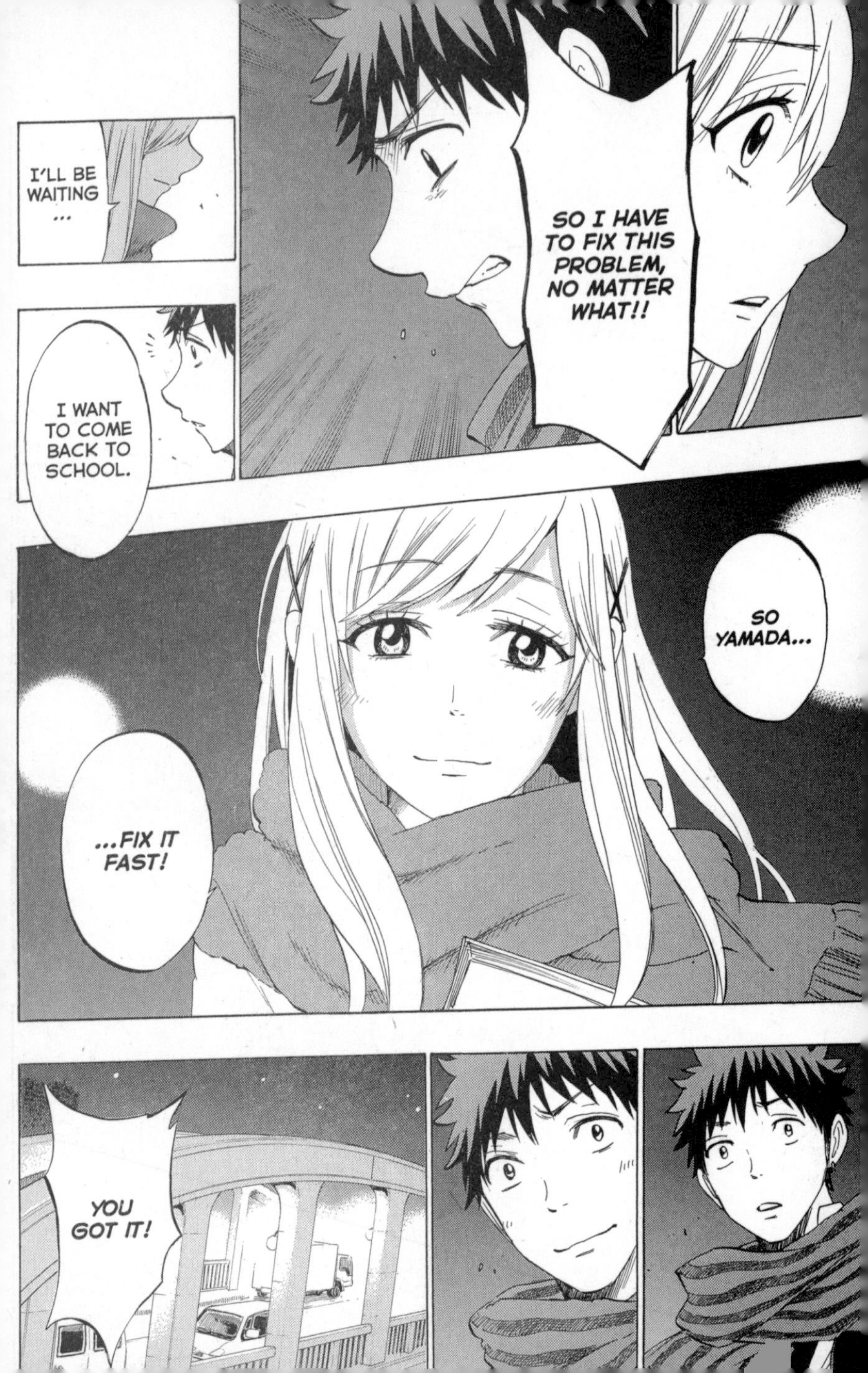
SO I HAVE TO FIX THIS PROBLEM, NO MATTER WHAT!!
I'LL BE WAITING ...
I WANT TO COME BACK TO SCHOOL.
SO YAMADA...
...FIX IT FAST!
YOU GOT IT!

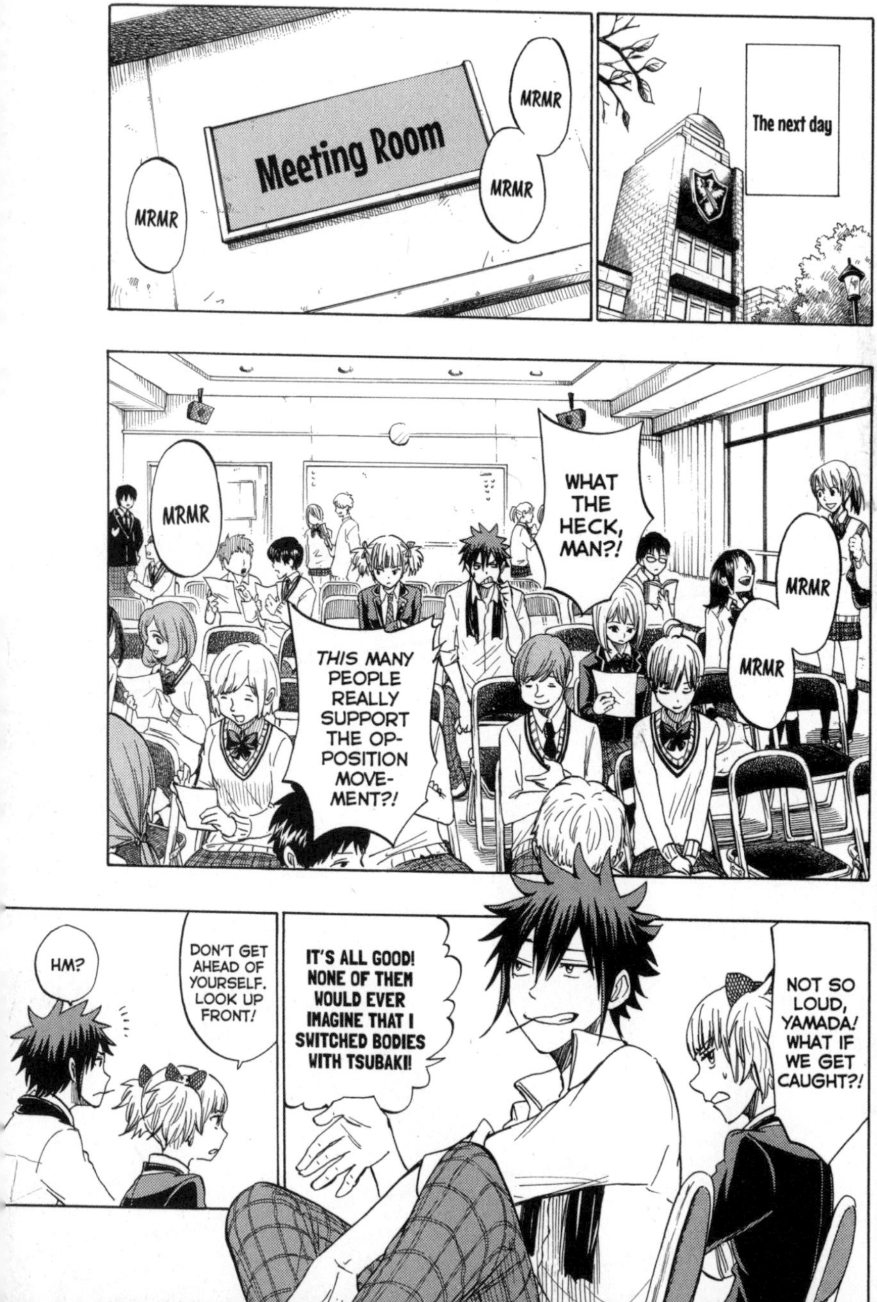
The next day
MRMR
MRMR
Meeting Room
MRMR
MRMR
MRMR
WHAT THE HECK, MAN?!
THIS MANY PEOPLE REALLY SUPPORT THE OP-POSITION MOVE-MENT?!
MRMR
NOT SO LOUD, YAMADA! WHAT IF WE GET CAUGHT?!
IT'S ALL GOOD! NONE OF THEM WOULD EVER IMAGINE THAT I SWITCHED BODIES WITH TSUBAKI!
DON'T GET AHEAD OF YOURSELF. LOOK UP FRONT!
HM?

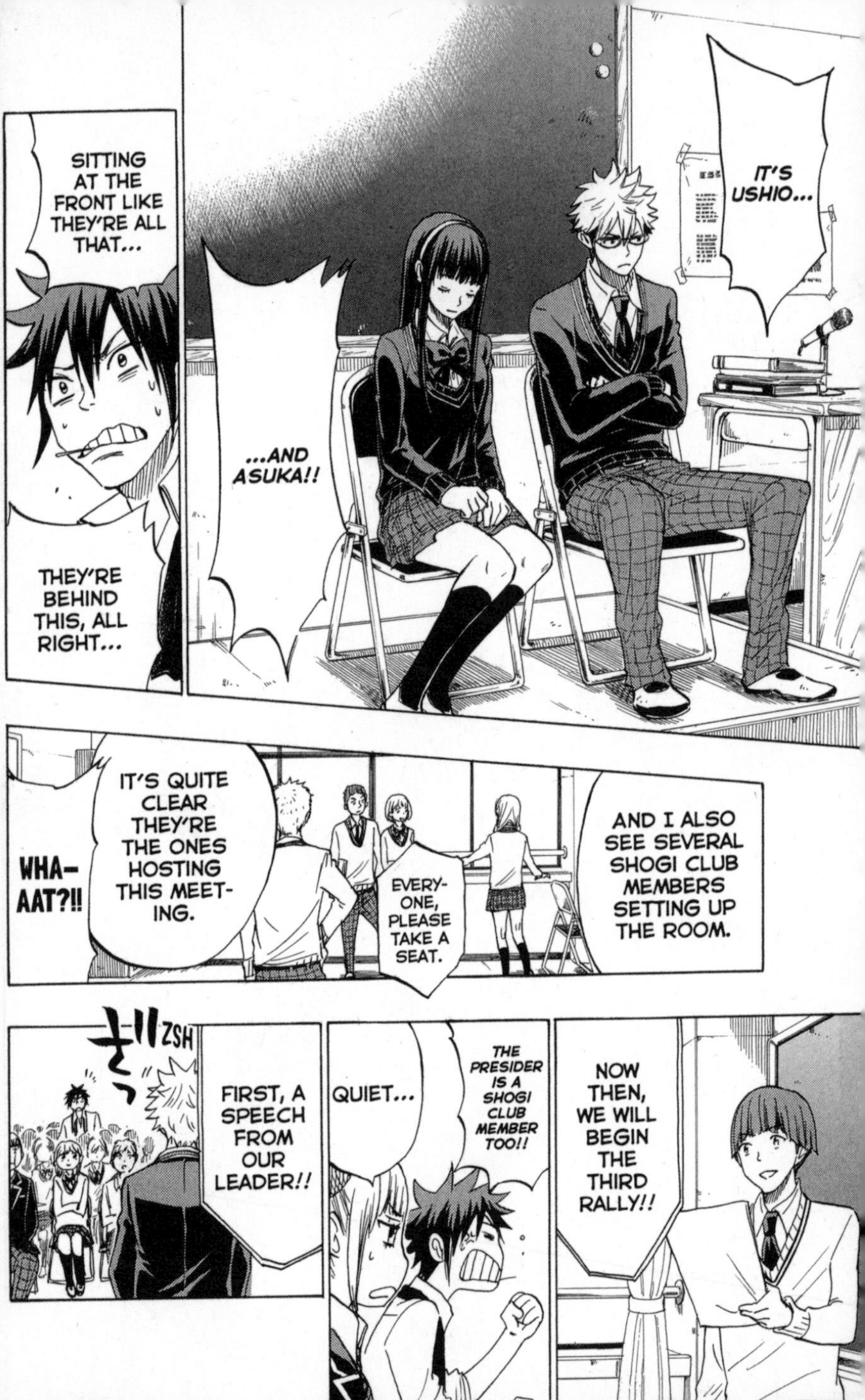
IT'S USHIO...
...AND ASUKA!!
SITTING AT THE FRONT LIKE THEY'RE ALL THAT...
THEY'RE BEHIND THIS, ALL RIGHT...
AND I ALSO SEE SEVERAL SHOGI CLUB MEMBERS SETTING UP THE ROOM.
EVERY-ONE, PLEASE TAKE A SEAT.
IT'S QUITE CLEAR THEY'RE THE ONES HOSTING THIS MEET-ING.
WHA-AAT?!!
NOW THEN, WE WILL BEGIN THE THIRD RALLY!!
THE PRESIDER IS A SHOGI CLUB MEMBER TOO!!
QUIET...
FIRST, A SPEECH FROM OUR LEADER!!
ZSH

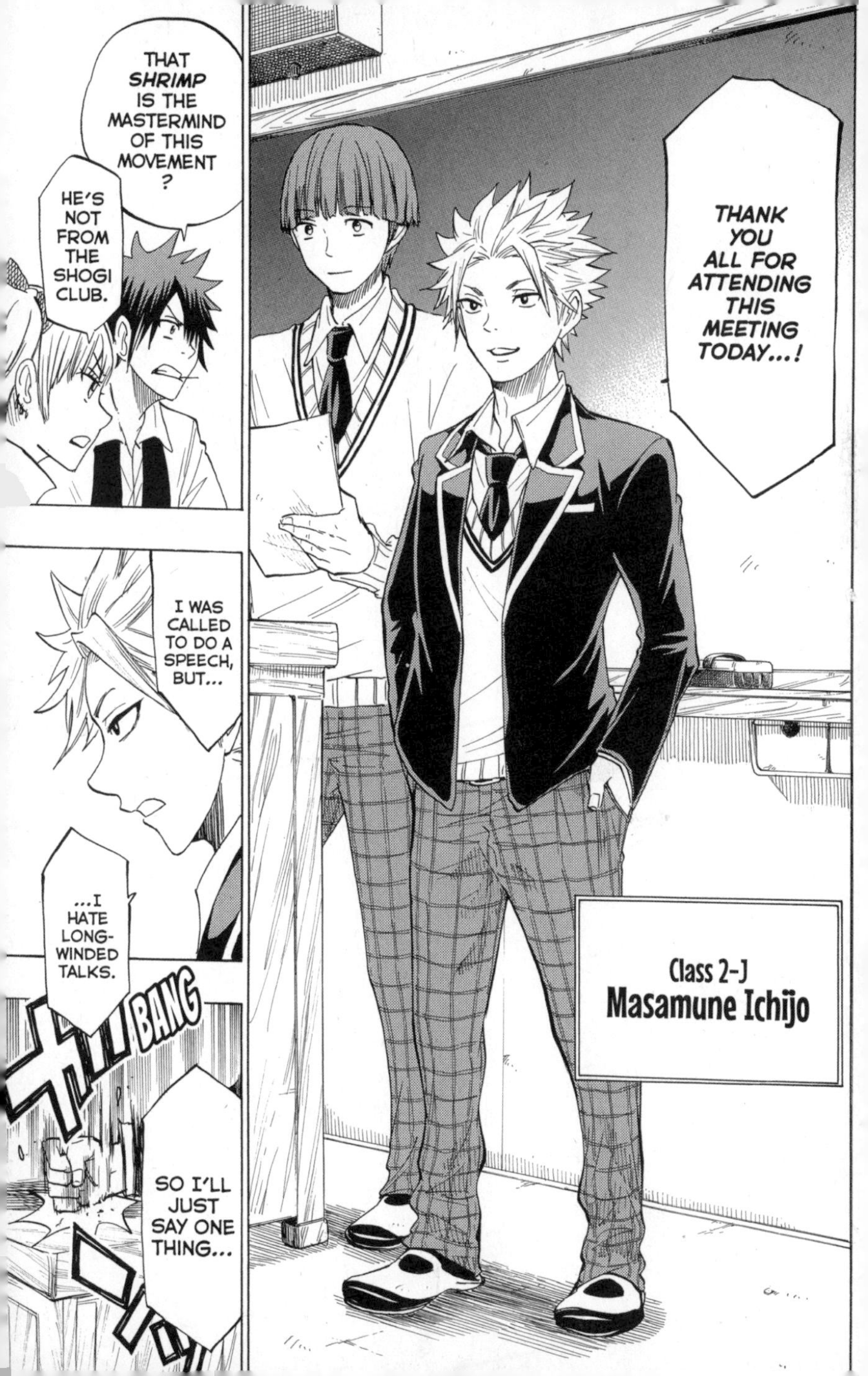
THANK YOU ALL FOR ATTENDING THIS MEETING TODAY...!
Class 2-J
Masamune Ichijo
THAT SHRIMP IS THE MASTERMIND OF THIS MOVEMENT?
HE'S NOT FROM THE SHOGI CLUB.
I WAS CALLED TO DO A SPEECH, BUT...
...I HATE LONG-WINDED TALKS.
BANG
SO I'LL JUST SAY ONE THING...

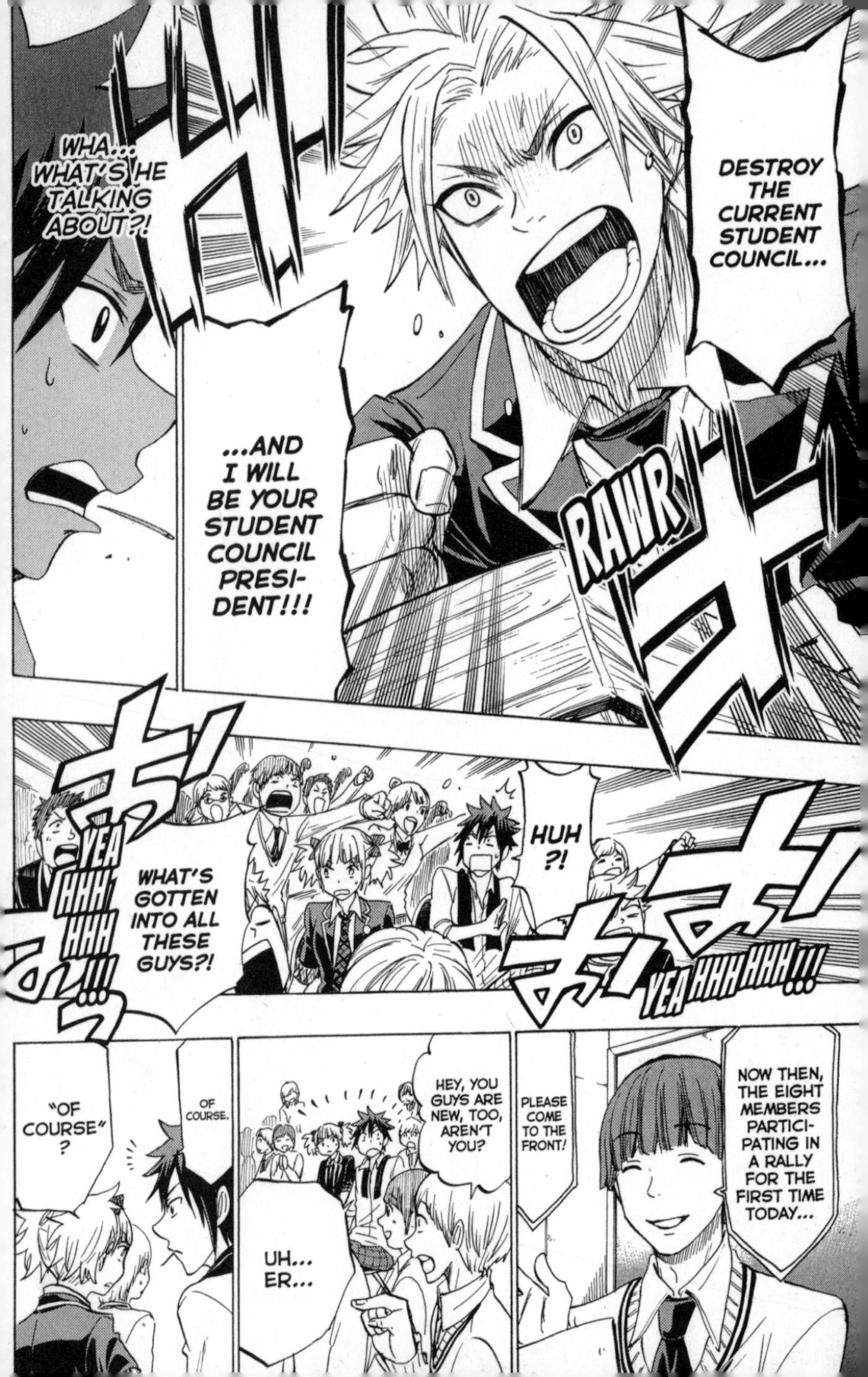
DESTROY THE CURRENT STUDENT COUNCIL...
RAWR
...AND I WILL BE YOUR STUDENT COUNCIL PRESIDENT!!!
WHA... WHAT'S HE TALKING ABOUT?!
YEAHHHHHH!!!
HUH?!
WHAT'S GOTTEN INTO ALL THESE GUYS?!
YEAHHHHHH!!!
NOW THEN, THE EIGHT MEMBERS PARTICIPATING IN A RALLY FOR THE FIRST TIME TODAY...
PLEASE COME TO THE FRONT!
HEY, YOU GUYS ARE NEW, TOO, AREN'T YOU?
UH... ER...
OF COURSE.
"OF COURSE"?

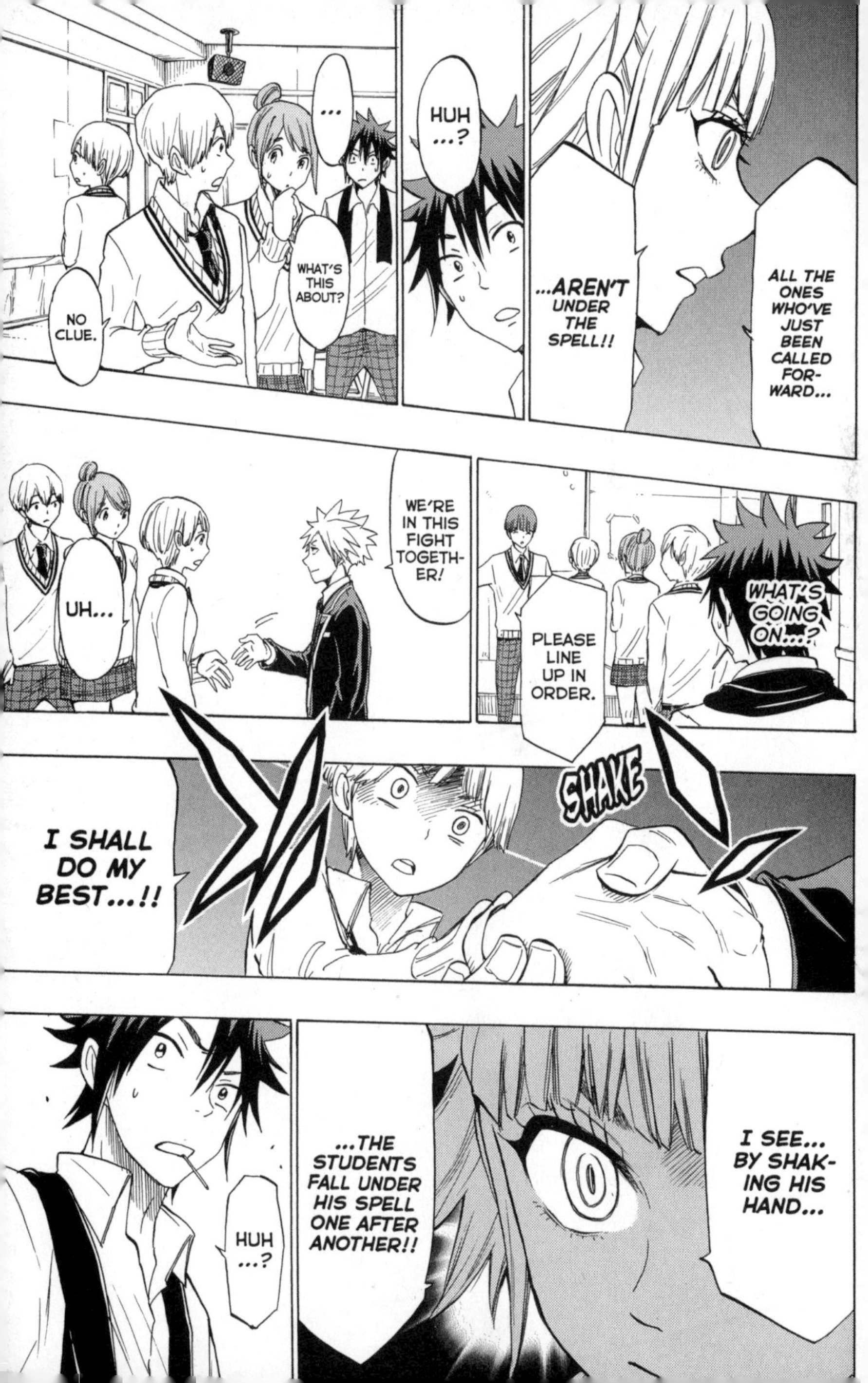
ALL THE ONES WHO'VE JUST BEEN CALLED FOR-WARD...
...AREN'T UNDER THE SPELL!!
HUH ...?
...
WHAT'S THIS ABOUT?
NO CLUE.
WHAT'S GOING ON...?
PLEASE LINE UP IN ORDER.
WE'RE IN THIS FIGHT TOGETH-ER!
UH...
SHAKE
I SHALL DO MY BEST...!!
I SEE... BY SHAK-ING HIS HAND...
...THE STUDENTS FALL UNDER HIS SPELL ONE AFTER ANOTHER!!
HUH ...?

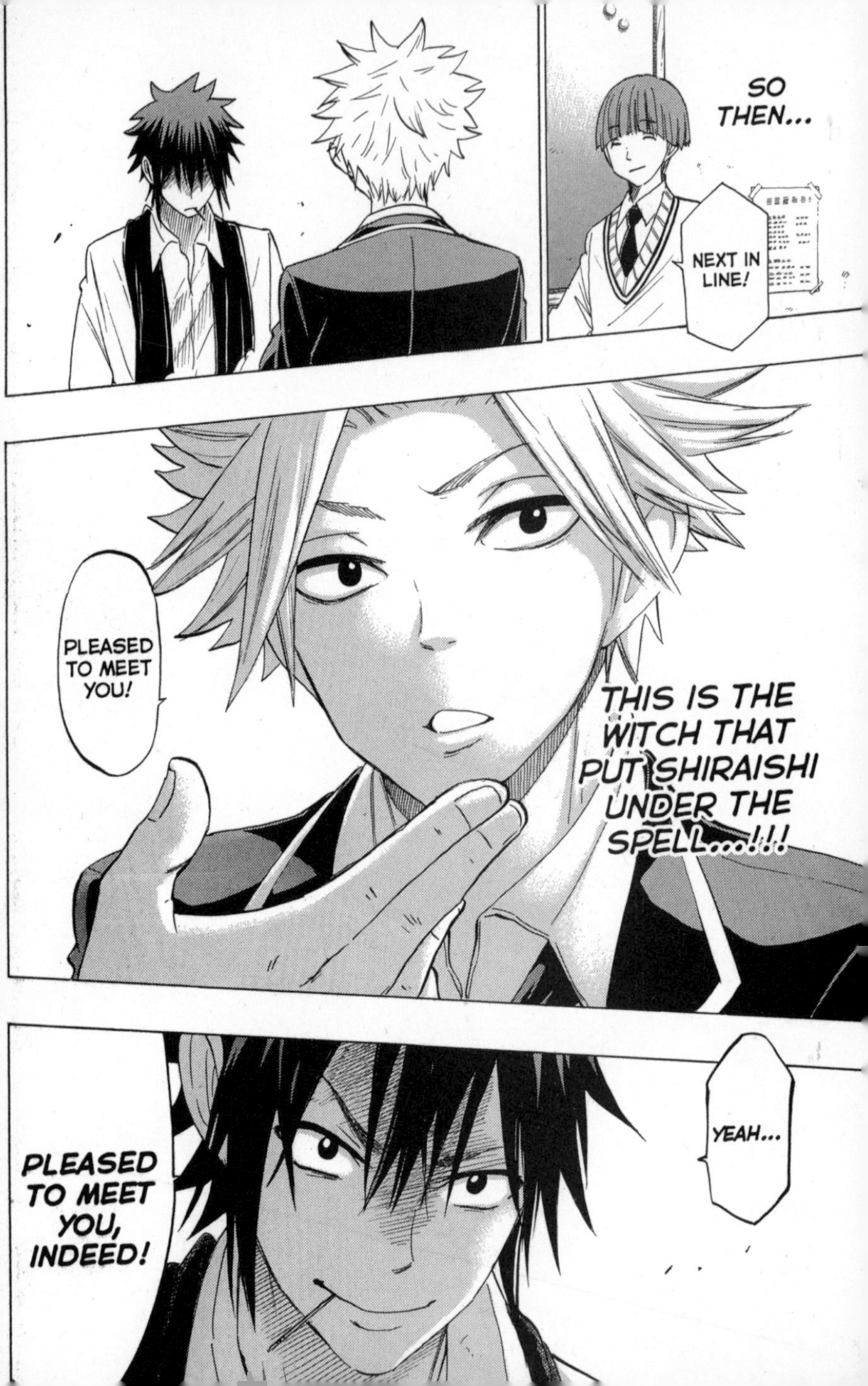
SO THEN...
NEXT IN LINE!
THIS IS THE WITCH THAT PUT SHIRAISHI UNDER THE SPELL...!!!
PLEASED TO MEET YOU!
YEAH...
PLEASED TO MEET YOU, INDEED!

CHAPTER 136: One reeeeally annoying power.

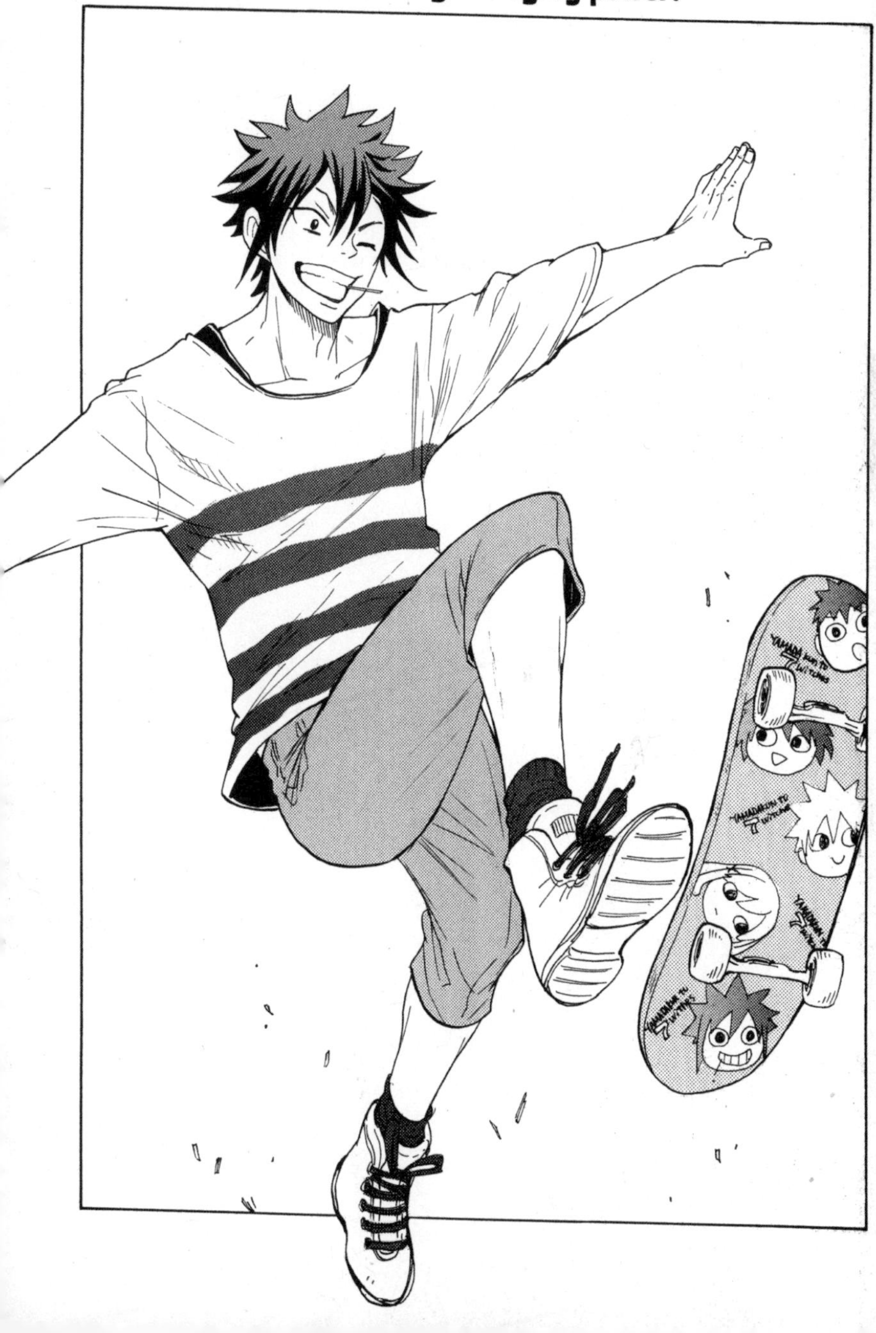

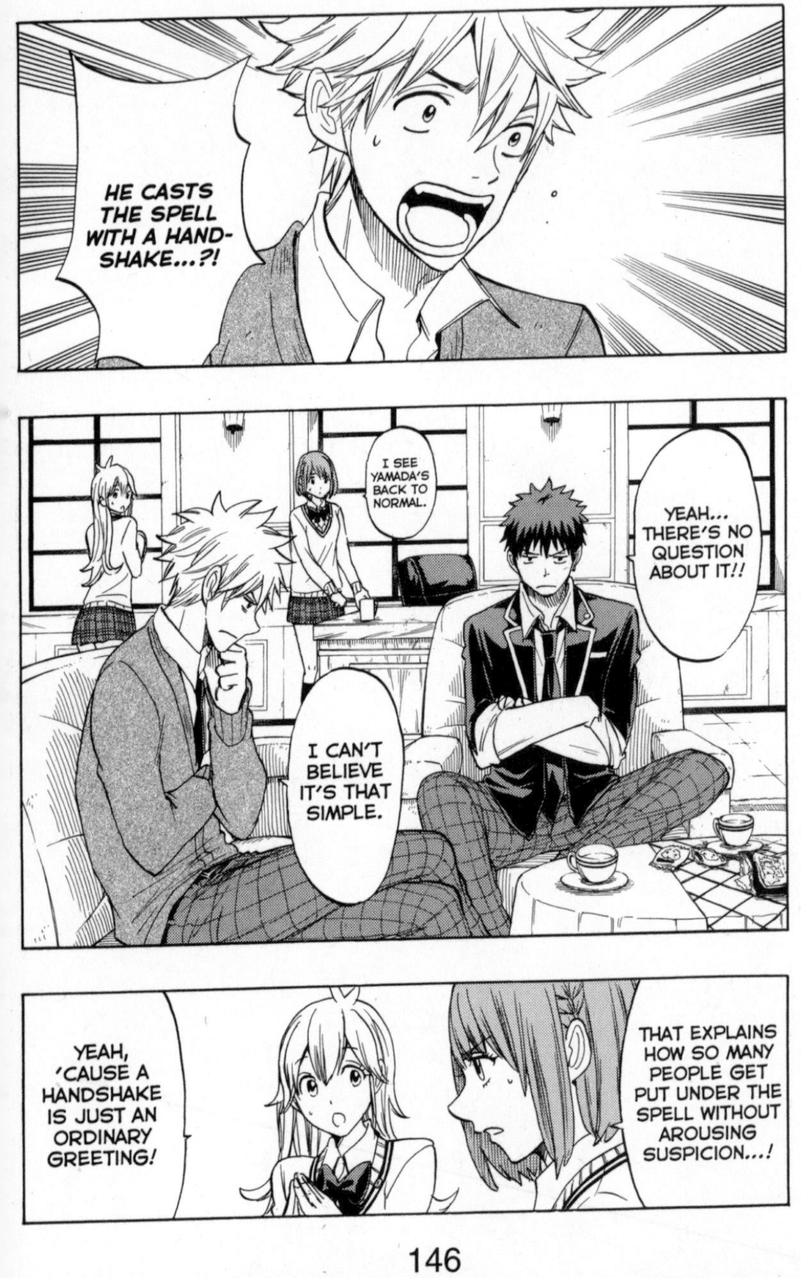
HE CASTS THE SPELL WITH A HAND-SHAKE...?!
YEAH... THERE'S NO QUESTION ABOUT IT!!
I SEE YAMADA'S BACK TO NORMAL.
I CAN'T BELIEVE IT'S THAT SIMPLE.
THAT EXPLAINS HOW SO MANY PEOPLE GET PUT UNDER THE SPELL WITHOUT AROUSING SUSPICION...!
YEAH, 'CAUSE A HANDSHAKE IS JUST AN ORDINARY GREETING!

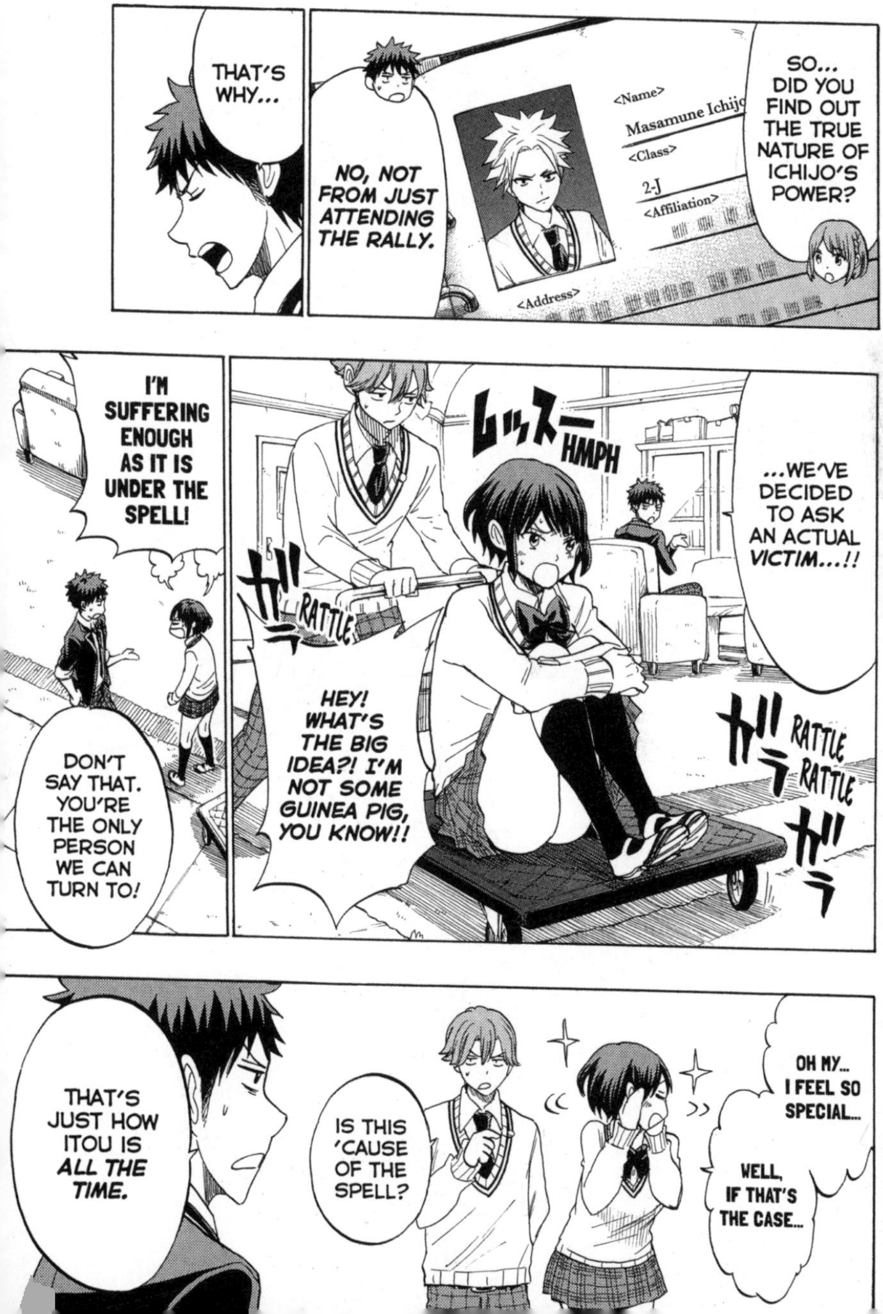
SO... DID YOU FIND OUT THE TRUE NATURE OF ICHIJO'S POWER?
<Name>
Masamune Ichijo
<Class>
2-J
<Affiliation>
<Address>
NO, NOT FROM JUST ATTENDING THE RALLY.
THAT'S WHY...
...WE'VE DECIDED TO ASK AN ACTUAL VICTIM...!!
HMPH
RATTLE RATTLE
RATTLE
HEY! WHAT'S THE BIG IDEA?! I'M NOT SOME GUINEA PIG, YOU KNOW!!
I'M SUFFERING ENOUGH AS IT IS UNDER THE SPELL!
DON'T SAY THAT. YOU'RE THE ONLY PERSON WE CAN TURN TO!
OH MY... I FEEL SO SPECIAL...
WELL, IF THAT'S THE CASE...
IS THIS 'CAUSE OF THE SPELL?
THAT'S JUST HOW ITOU IS ALL THE TIME.

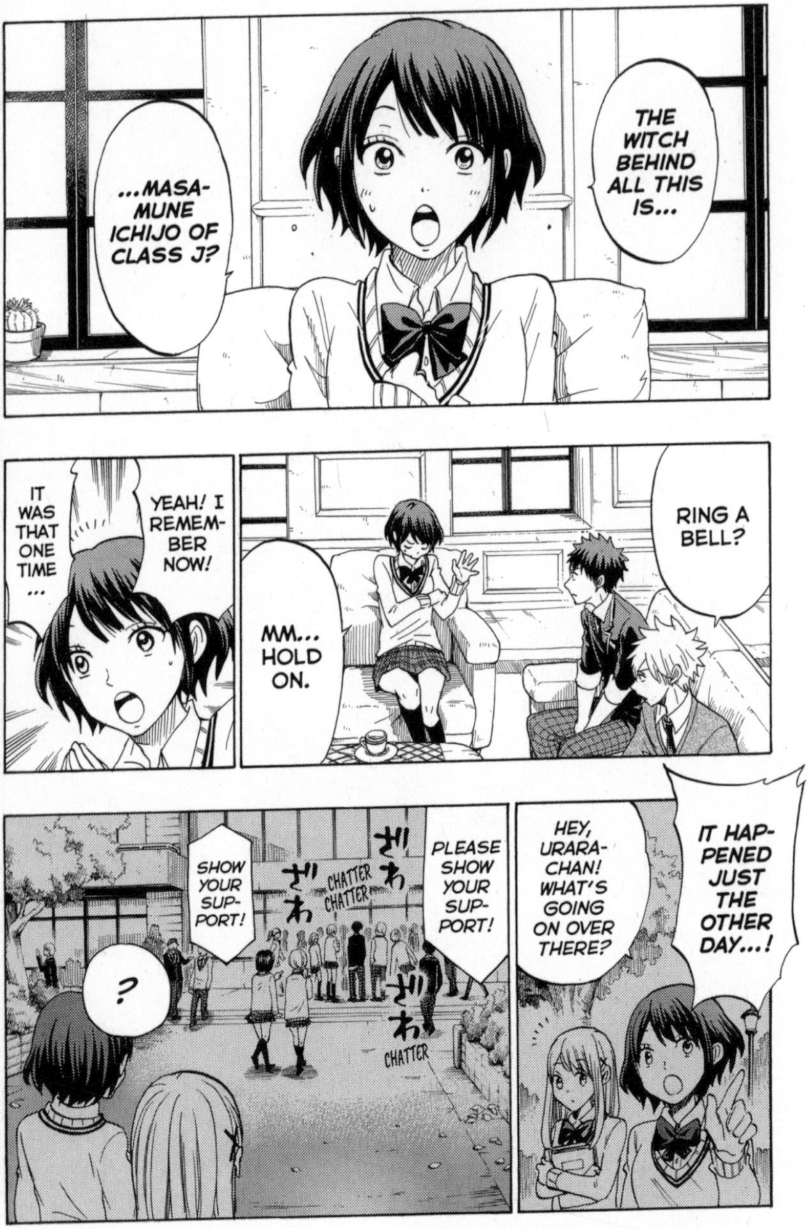
THE WITCH BEHIND ALL THIS IS...
...MASA-MUNE ICHIJO OF CLASS J?
RING A BELL?
MM... HOLD ON.
YEAH! I REMEMBER NOW!
IT WAS THAT ONE TIME...
IT HAPPENED JUST THE OTHER DAY...!
HEY, URARA-CHAN! WHAT'S GOING ON OVER THERE?
PLEASE SHOW YOUR SUPPORT!
ざわ ざわ
CHATTER CHATTER
SHOW YOUR SUPPORT!
?
ざわ
CHATTER

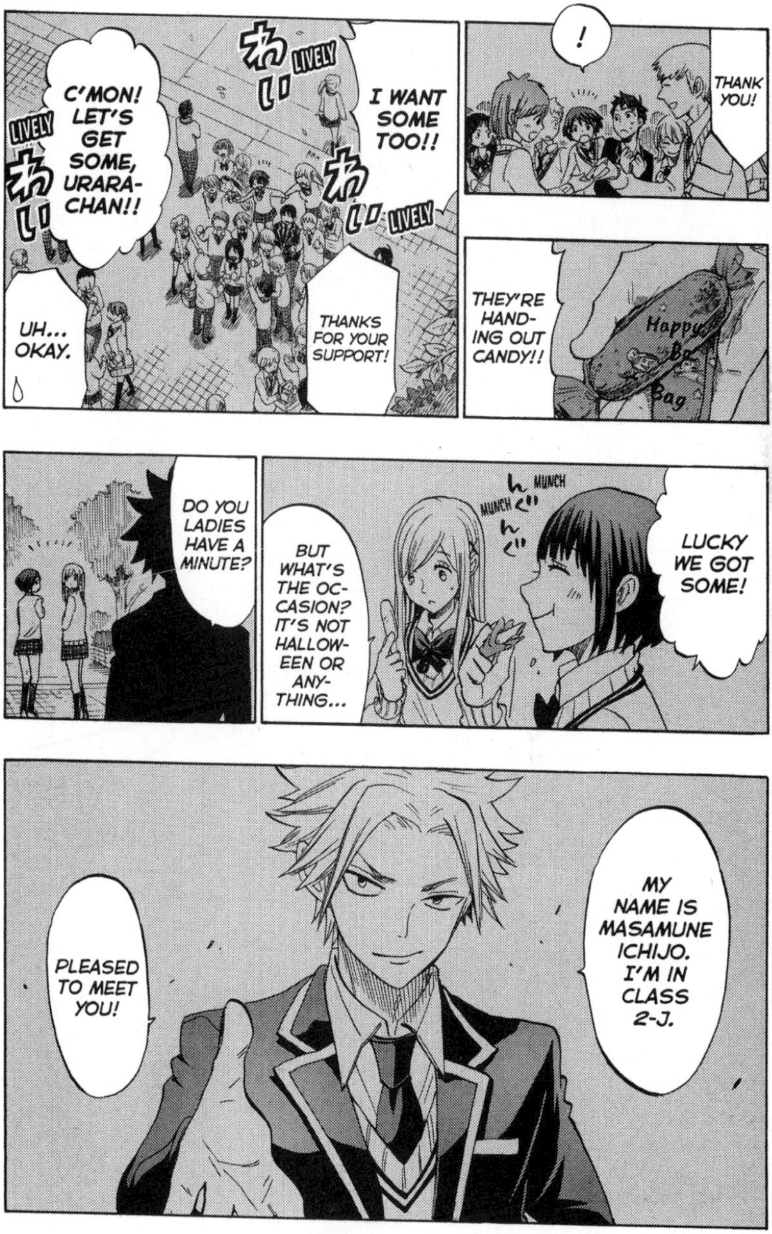
THANK YOU!
!
Happy Be Bag
THEY'RE HAND-ING OUT CANDY!!
わい LIVELY
I WANT SOME TOO!!
わい LIVELY
C'MON! LET'S GET SOME, URARA-CHAN!!
LIVELY わい
THANKS FOR YOUR SUPPORT!
UH... OKAY.
LUCKY WE GOT SOME!
んぐんぐ MUNCH MUNCH
BUT WHAT'S THE OC-CASION? IT'S NOT HALLOW-EEN OR ANY-THING...
DO YOU LADIES HAVE A MINUTE?
MY NAME IS MASAMUNE ICHIJO. I'M IN CLASS 2-J.
PLEASED TO MEET YOU!

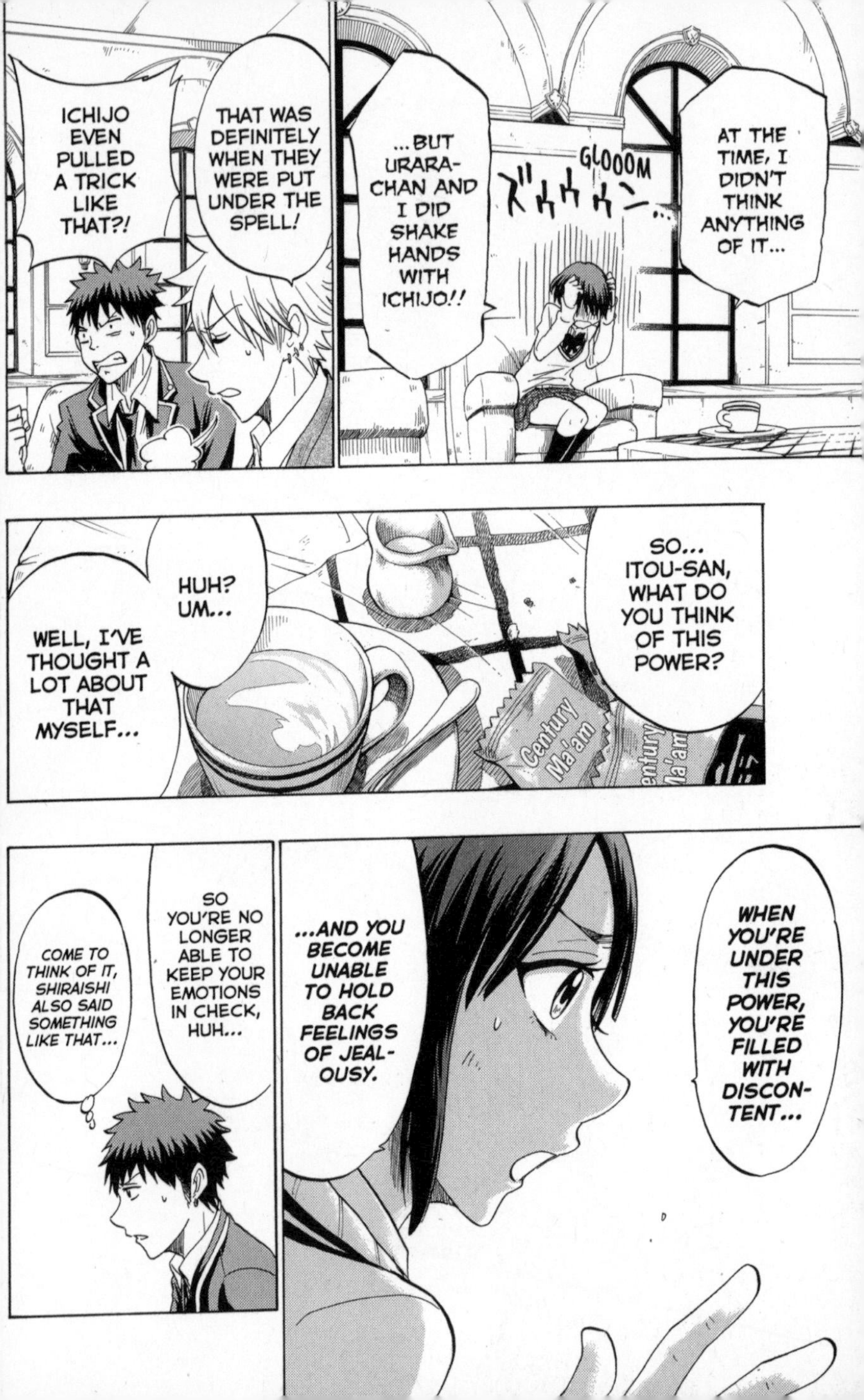
AT THE TIME, I DIDN'T THINK ANYTHING OF IT...
GLOOOM
...BUT URARA-CHAN AND I DID SHAKE HANDS WITH ICHIJO!!
THAT WAS DEFINITELY WHEN THEY WERE PUT UNDER THE SPELL!
ICHIJO EVEN PULLED A TRICK LIKE THAT?!
SO... ITOU-SAN, WHAT DO YOU THINK OF THIS POWER?
Century Ma'am
HUH? UM...
WELL, I'VE THOUGHT A LOT ABOUT THAT MYSELF...
WHEN YOU'RE UNDER THIS POWER, YOU'RE FILLED WITH DISCONTENT...
...AND YOU BECOME UNABLE TO HOLD BACK FEELINGS OF JEAL-OUSY.
SO YOU'RE NO LONGER ABLE TO KEEP YOUR EMOTIONS IN CHECK, HUH...
COME TO THINK OF IT, SHIRAISHI ALSO SAID SOMETHING LIKE THAT...

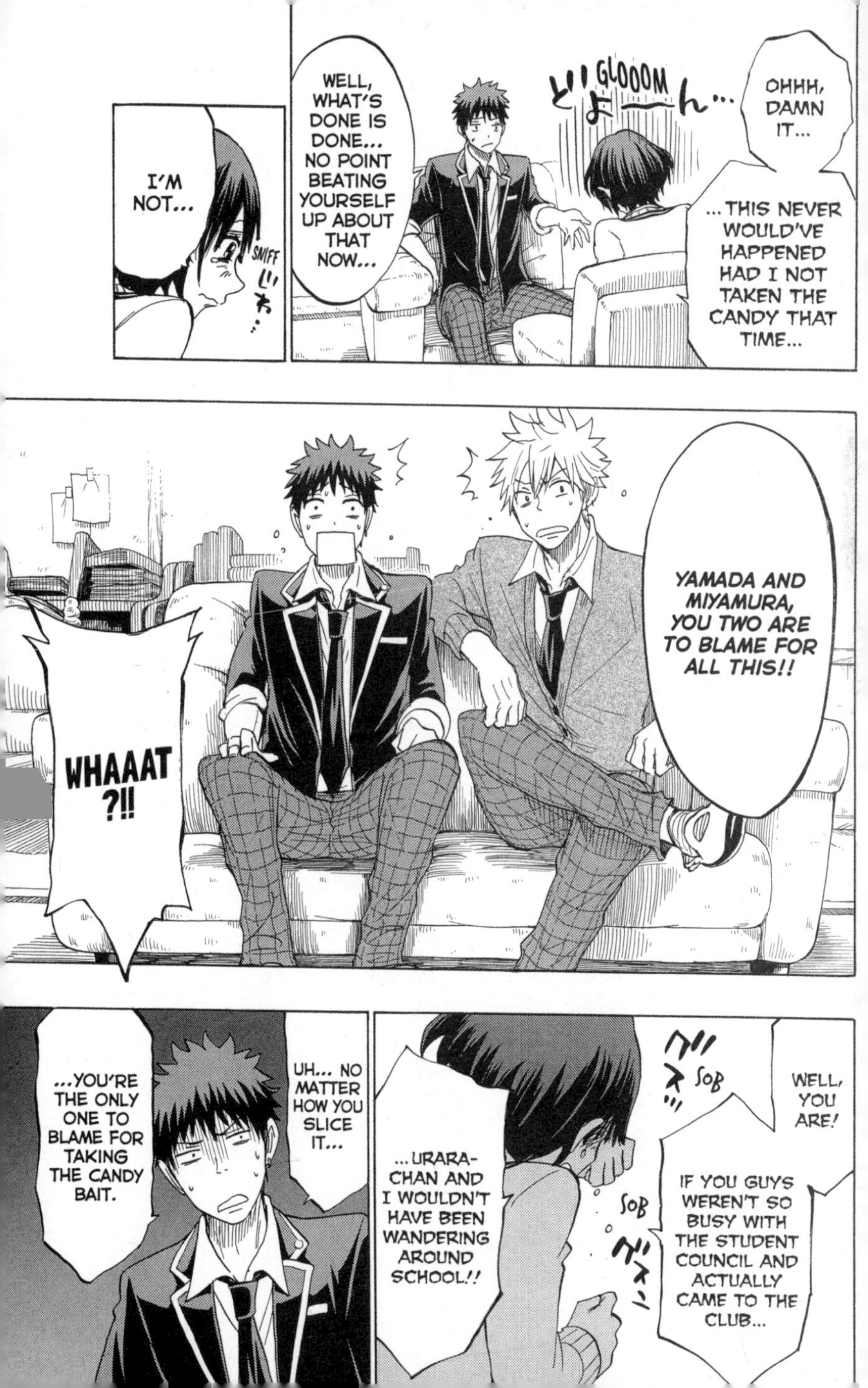
OHHH, DAMN IT...
...THIS NEVER WOULD'VE HAPPENED HAD I NOT TAKEN THE CANDY THAT TIME...
GLOOOM
WELL, WHAT'S DONE IS DONE... NO POINT BEATING YOURSELF UP ABOUT THAT NOW...
I'M NOT...
SNIFF
YAMADA AND MIYAMURA, YOU TWO ARE TO BLAME FOR ALL THIS!!
WHAAAT?!!
WELL, YOU ARE!
SOB
IF YOU GUYS WEREN'T SO BUSY WITH THE STUDENT COUNCIL AND ACTUALLY CAME TO THE CLUB...
SOB
...URARA-CHAN AND I WOULDN'T HAVE BEEN WANDERING AROUND SCHOOL!!
UH... NO MATTER HOW YOU SLICE IT...
...YOU'RE THE ONLY ONE TO BLAME FOR TAKING THE CANDY BAIT.

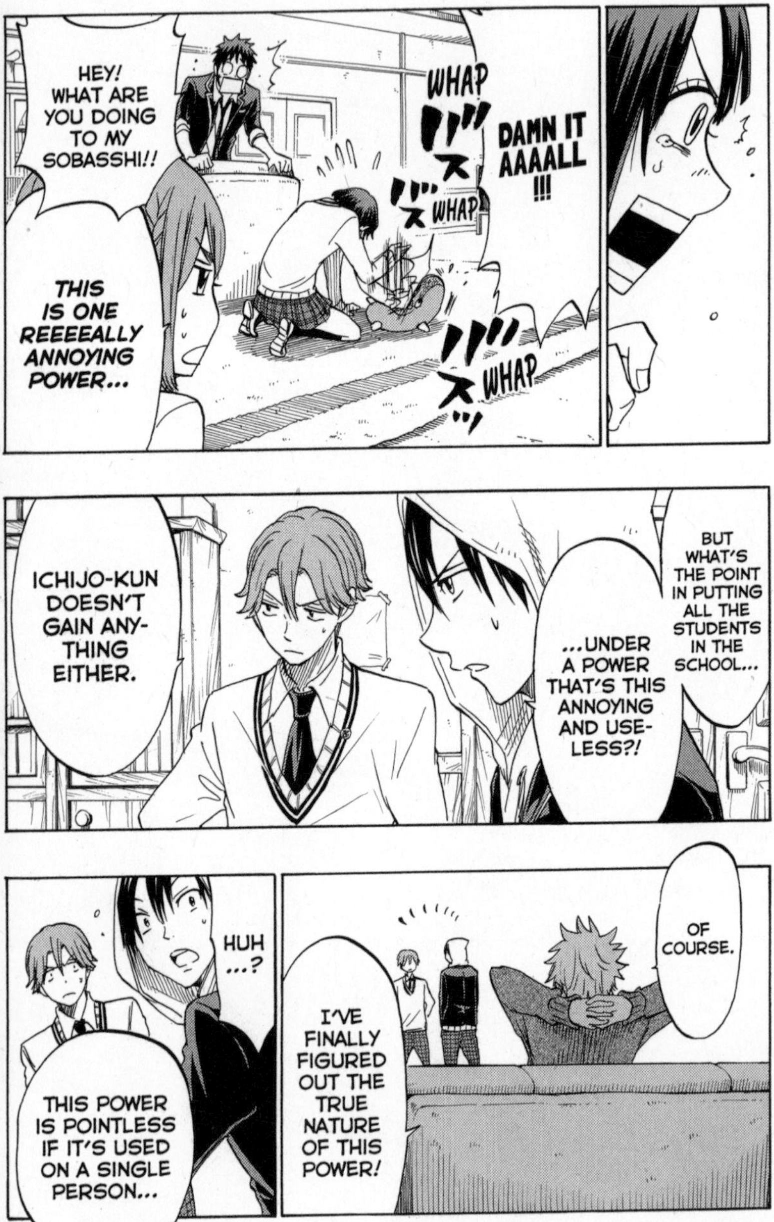
WHAP
DAMN IT AAAALL!!!
WHAP
HEY! WHAT ARE YOU DOING TO MY SOBASSHI!!
WHAP
THIS IS ONE REEEEALLY ANNOYING POWER...
BUT WHAT'S THE POINT IN PUTTING ALL THE STUDENTS IN THE SCHOOL...
...UNDER A POWER THAT'S THIS ANNOYING AND USELESS?!
ICHIJO-KUN DOESN'T GAIN ANYTHING EITHER.
OF COURSE.
I'VE FINALLY FIGURED OUT THE TRUE NATURE OF THIS POWER!
HUH ...?
THIS POWER IS POINTLESS IF IT'S USED ON A SINGLE PERSON...

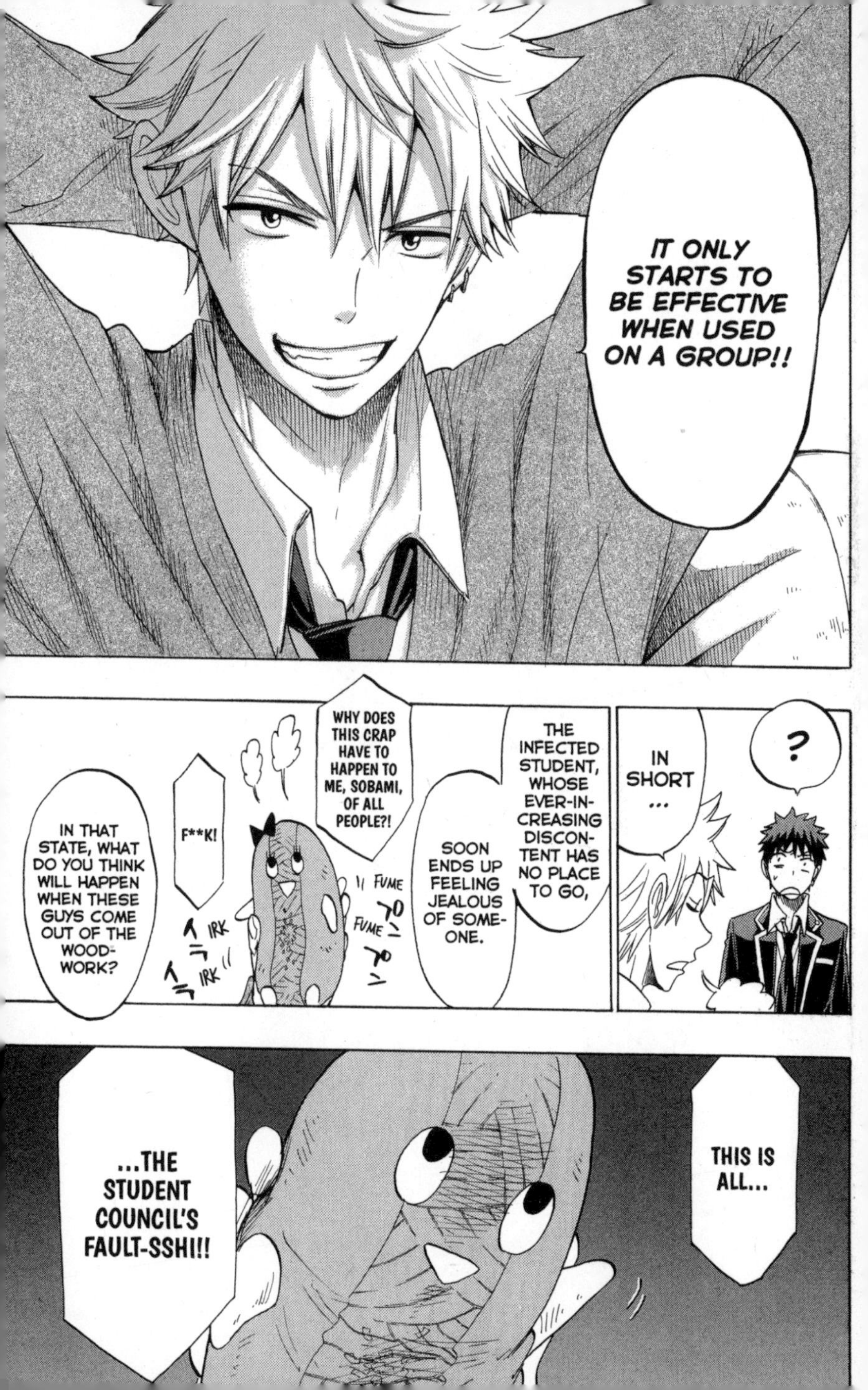
IT ONLY STARTS TO BE EFFECTIVE WHEN USED ON A GROUP!!
?
IN SHORT ...
THE INFECTED STUDENT, WHOSE EVER-INCREASING DISCONTENT HAS NO PLACE TO GO,
SOON ENDS UP FEELING JEALOUS OF SOMEONE.
WHY DOES THIS CRAP HAVE TO HAPPEN TO ME, SOBAMI, OF ALL PEOPLE?!
FUME
FUME
F**K!
IRK
IRK
IN THAT STATE, WHAT DO YOU THINK WILL HAPPEN WHEN THESE GUYS COME OUT OF THE WOODWORK?
THIS IS ALL...
...THE STUDENT COUNCIL'S FAULT-SSHI!!

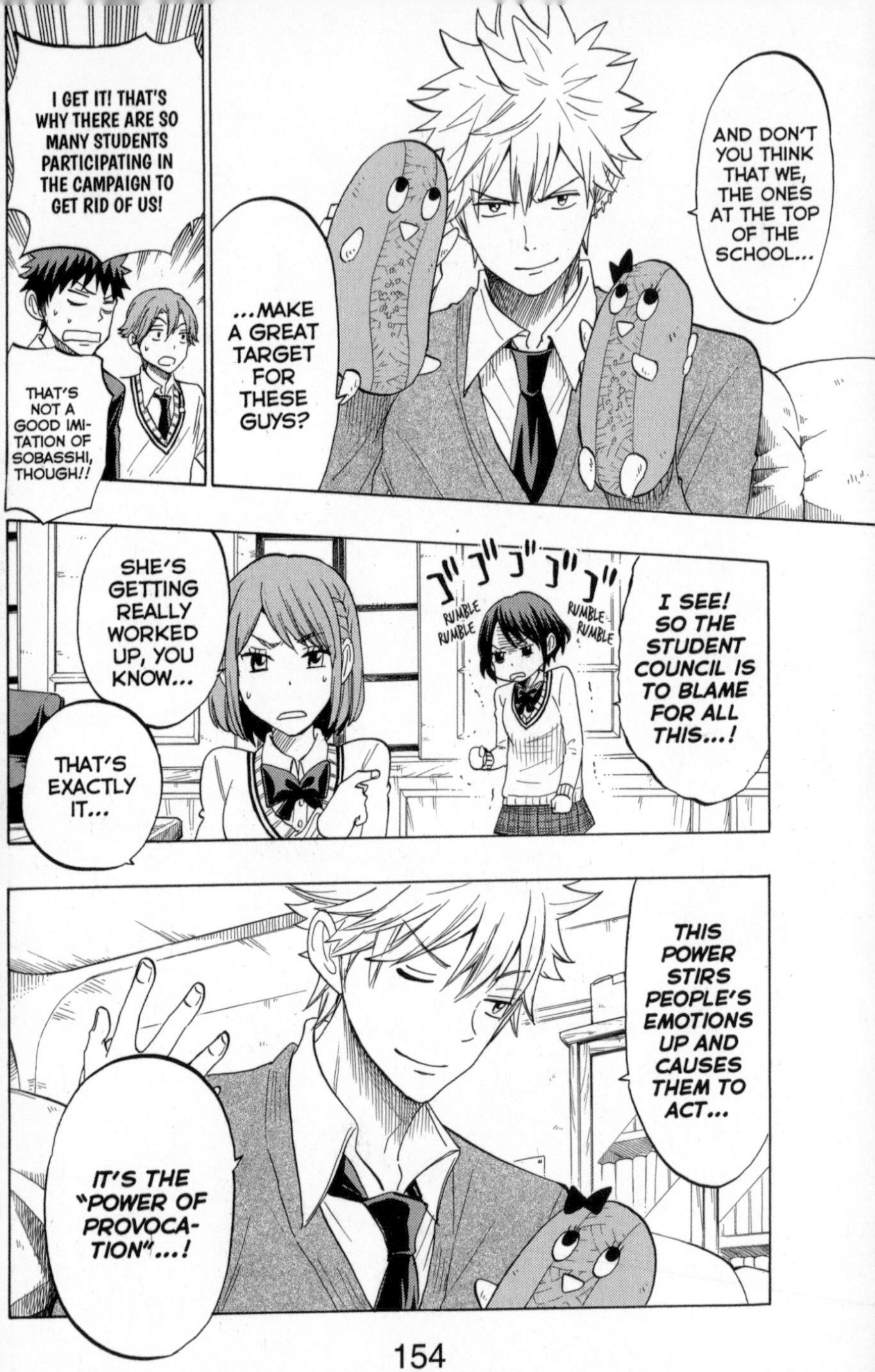
AND DON'T YOU THINK THAT WE, THE ONES AT THE TOP OF THE SCHOOL...
...MAKE A GREAT TARGET FOR THESE GUYS?
I GET IT! THAT'S WHY THERE ARE SO MANY STUDENTS PARTICIPATING IN THE CAMPAIGN TO GET RID OF US!
THAT'S NOT A GOOD IMITATION OF SOBASSHI, THOUGH!!
I SEE! SO THE STUDENT COUNCIL IS TO BLAME FOR ALL THIS...!
ゴゴゴゴゴ
RUMBLE RUMBLE
RUMBLE RUMBLE
SHE'S GETTING REALLY WORKED UP, YOU KNOW...
THAT'S EXACTLY IT...
THIS POWER STIRS PEOPLE'S EMOTIONS UP AND CAUSES THEM TO ACT...
IT'S THE "POWER OF PROVOCATION"...!

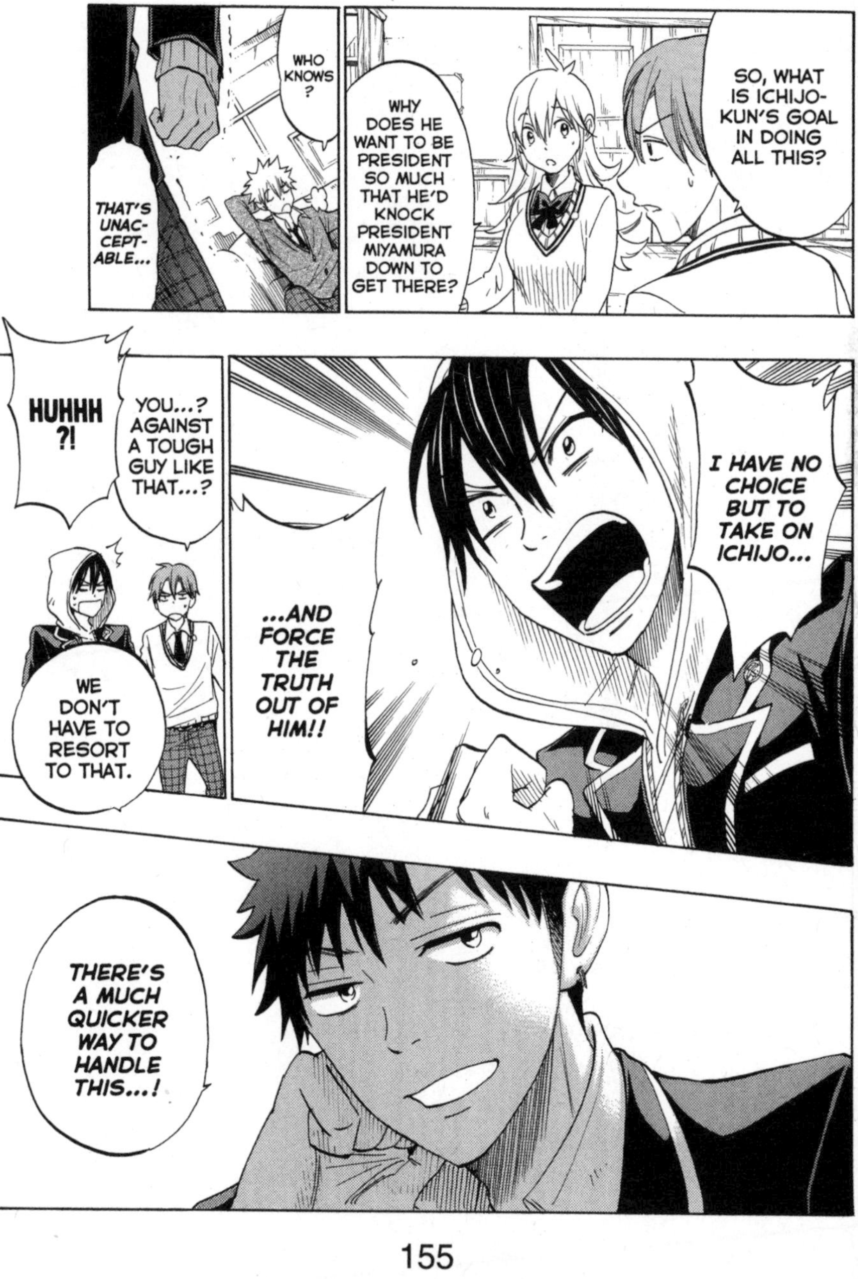
SO, WHAT IS ICHIJO-KUN'S GOAL IN DOING ALL THIS?
WHY DOES HE WANT TO BE PRESIDENT SO MUCH THAT HE'D KNOCK PRESIDENT MIYAMURA DOWN TO GET THERE?
WHO KNOWS?
THAT'S UNACCEPTABLE...
I HAVE NO CHOICE BUT TO TAKE ON ICHIJO...
...AND FORCE THE TRUTH OUT OF HIM!!
YOU...? AGAINST A TOUGH GUY LIKE THAT...?
HUHHH?!
WE DON'T HAVE TO RESORT TO THAT.
THERE'S A MUCH QUICKER WAY TO HANDLE THIS...!

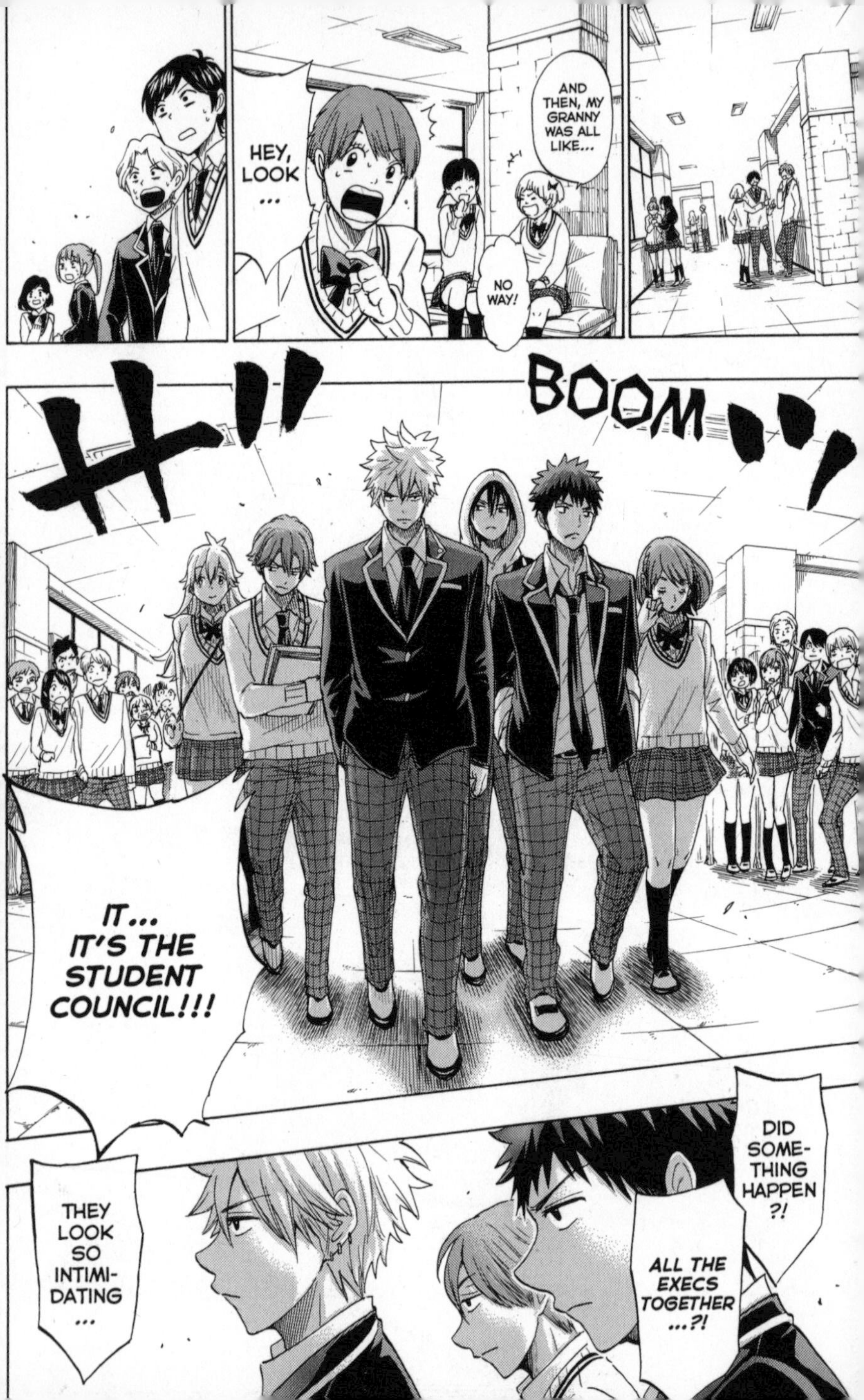
AND THEN, MY GRANNY WAS ALL LIKE...
NO WAY!
HEY, LOOK ...
BOOM
IT... IT'S THE STUDENT COUNCIL!!!
DID SOMETHING HAPPEN?!
ALL THE EXECS TOGETHER ...?!
THEY LOOK SO INTIMIDATING ...

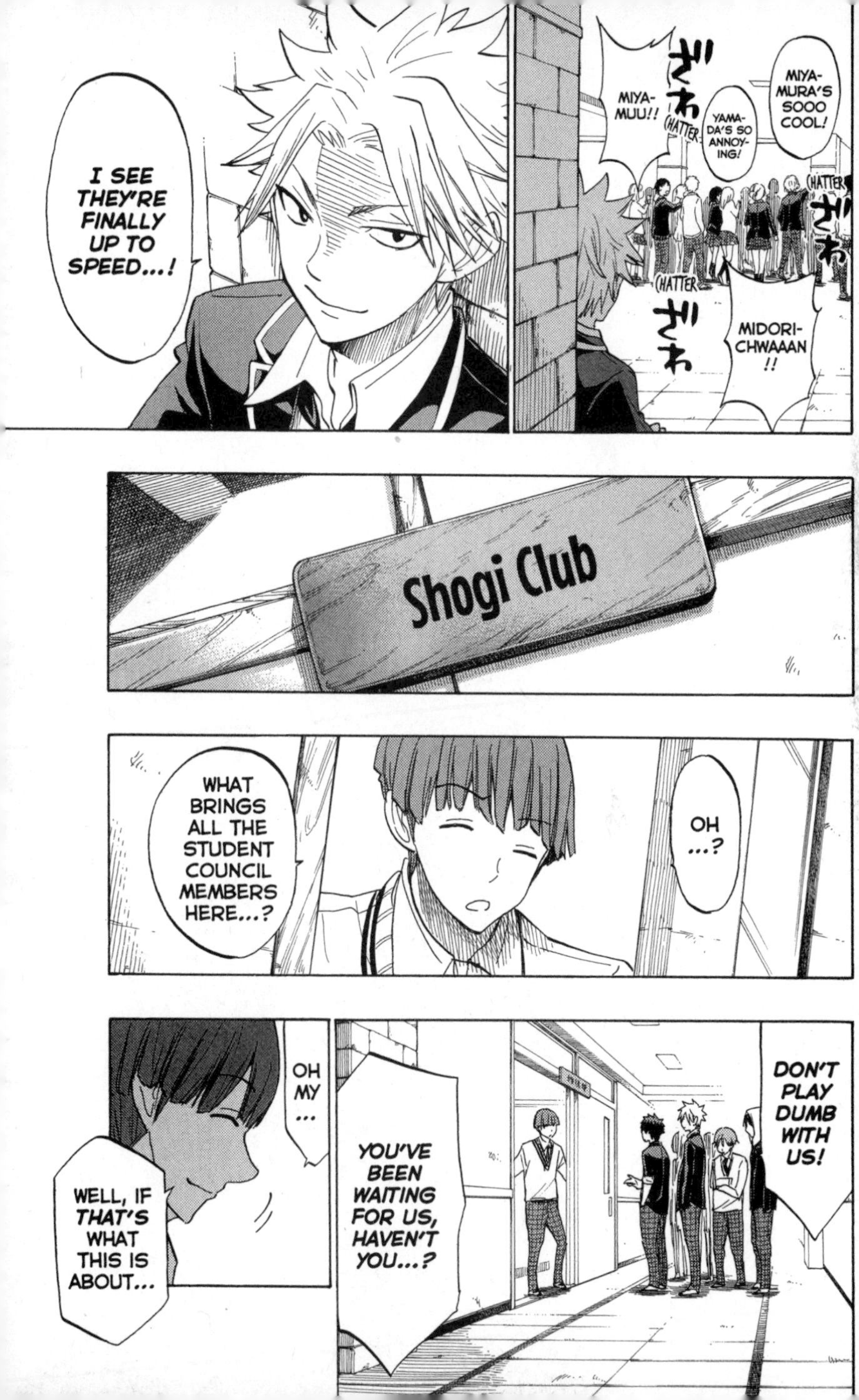
MIYA-MURA'S SOOO COOL!
ざわ (CHATTER)
YAMA-DA'S SO ANNOY-ING!
ざわ (CHATTER)
MIYA-MUU!!
MIDORI-CHWAAAN!!
ざわ (CHATTER)
I SEE THEY'RE FINALLY UP TO SPEED...!
Shogi Club
OH ...?
WHAT BRINGS ALL THE STUDENT COUNCIL MEMBERS HERE...?
DON'T PLAY DUMB WITH US!
YOU'VE BEEN WAITING FOR US, HAVEN'T YOU...?
OH MY ...
WELL, IF THAT'S WHAT THIS IS ABOUT...

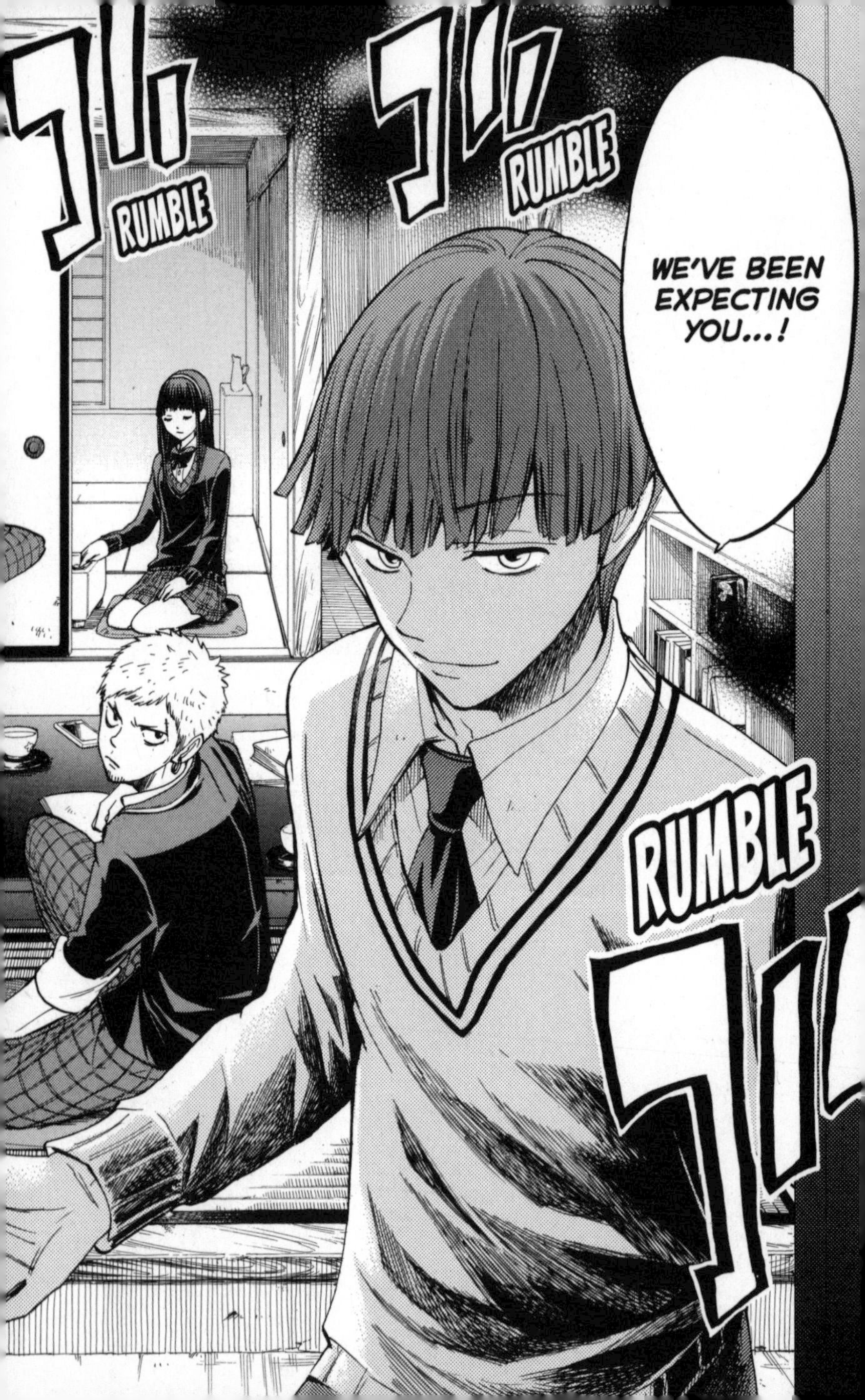
WE'VE BEEN EXPECTING YOU...!
RUMBLE
RUMBLE
RUMBLE

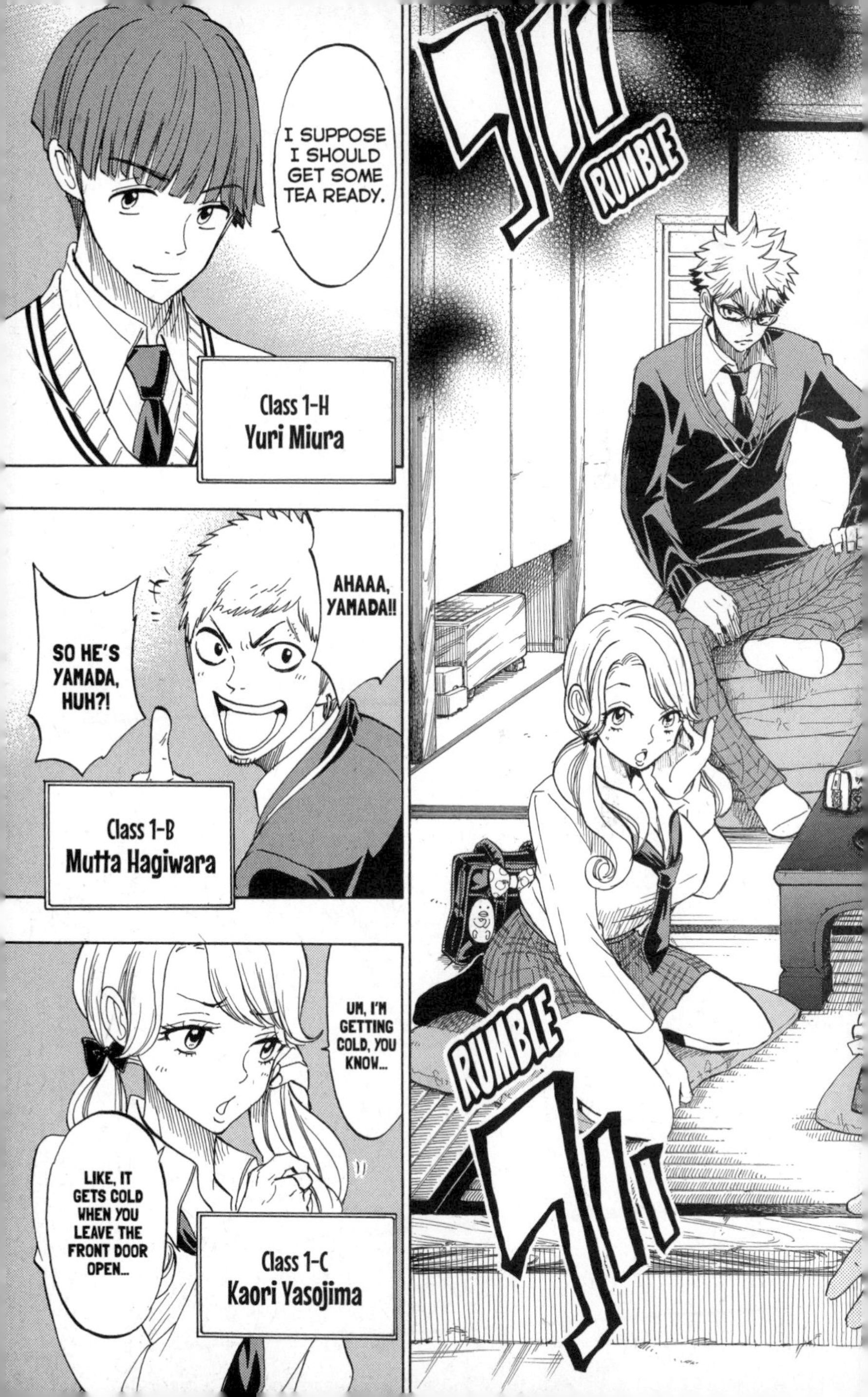
RUMBLE
RUMBLE
I SUPPOSE I SHOULD GET SOME TEA READY.
Class 1-H
Yuri Miura
AHAAA, YAMADA!!
SO HE'S YAMADA, HUH?!
Class 1-B
Mutta Hagiwara
UM, I'M GETTING COLD, YOU KNOW...
LIKE, IT GETS COLD WHEN YOU LEAVE THE FRONT DOOR OPEN...
Class 1-C
Kaori Yasojima

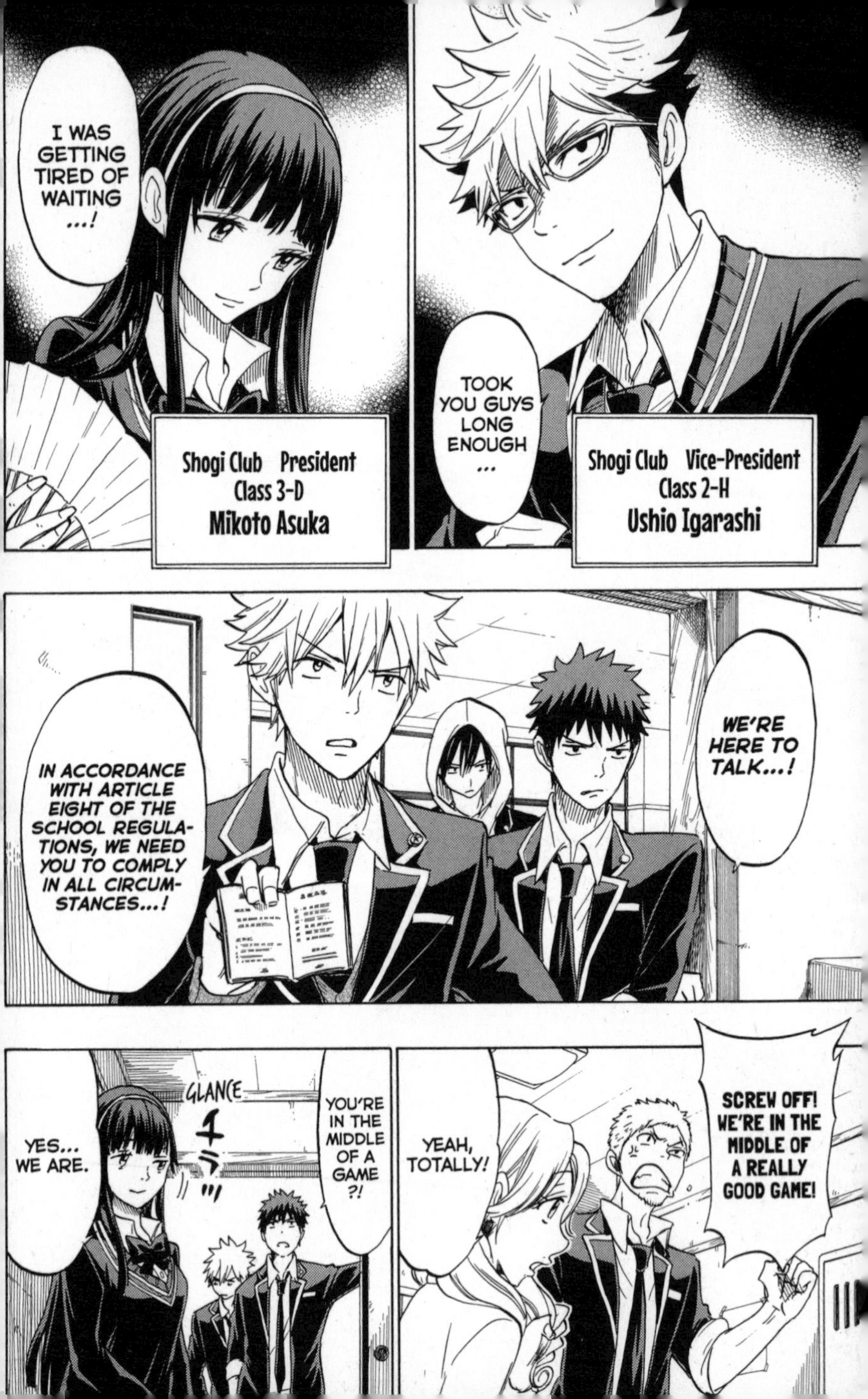
TOOK YOU GUYS LONG ENOUGH ...
Shogi Club Vice-President Class 2-H Ushio Igarashi
I WAS GETTING TIRED OF WAITING ...!
Shogi Club President Class 3-D Mikoto Asuka
WE'RE HERE TO TALK...!
IN ACCORDANCE WITH ARTICLE EIGHT OF THE SCHOOL REGULATIONS, WE NEED YOU TO COMPLY IN ALL CIRCUMSTANCES...!
SCREW OFF! WE'RE IN THE MIDDLE OF A REALLY GOOD GAME!
YEAH, TOTALLY!
YOU'RE IN THE MIDDLE OF A GAME?!
GLANCE
YES... WE ARE.

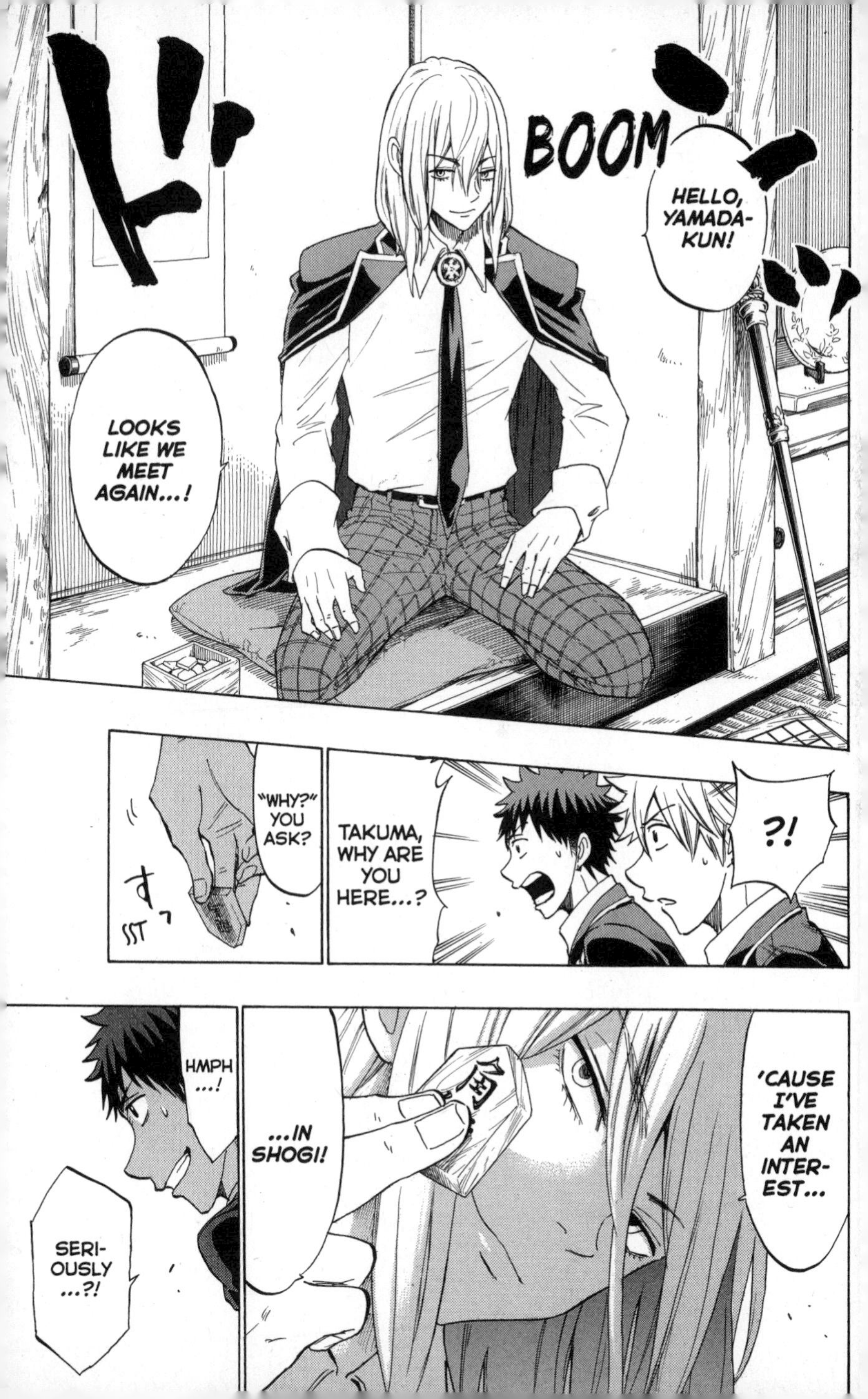
BOOM
HELLO, YAMADA-KUN!
LOOKS LIKE WE MEET AGAIN...!
?!
TAKUMA, WHY ARE YOU HERE...?
"WHY?" YOU ASK?
す
SST
'CAUSE I'VE TAKEN AN INTEREST...
...IN SHOGI!
HMPH...!
SERIOUSLY...?!

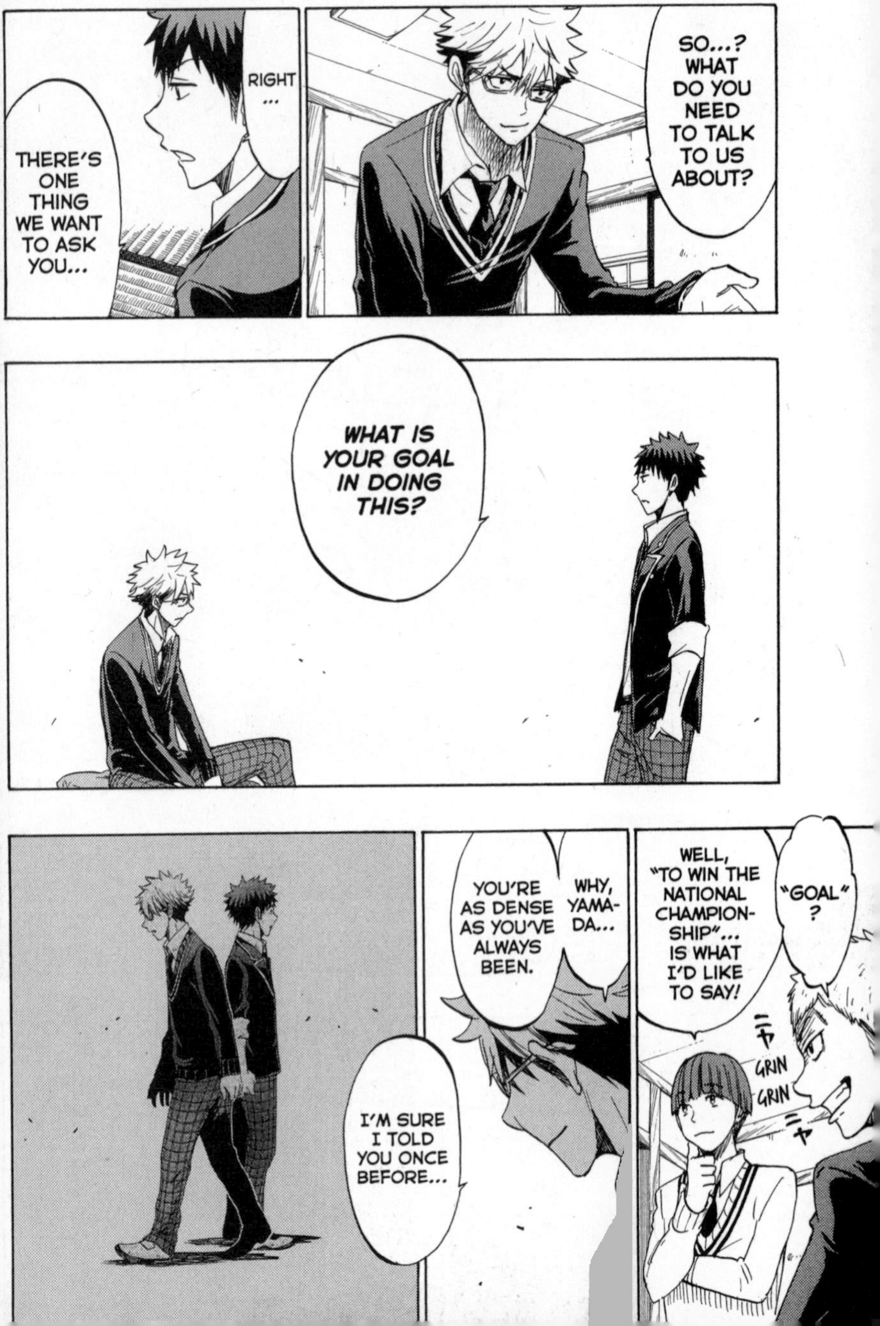
SO...? WHAT DO YOU NEED TO TALK TO US ABOUT?
RIGHT...
THERE'S ONE THING WE WANT TO ASK YOU...
WHAT IS YOUR GOAL IN DOING THIS?
"GOAL"?
WELL, "TO WIN THE NATIONAL CHAMPIONSHIP"... IS WHAT I'D LIKE TO SAY!
ニヤ GRIN
ニヤ GRIN
WHY, YAMADA...
YOU'RE AS DENSE AS YOU'VE ALWAYS BEEN.
I'M SURE I TOLD YOU ONCE BEFORE...

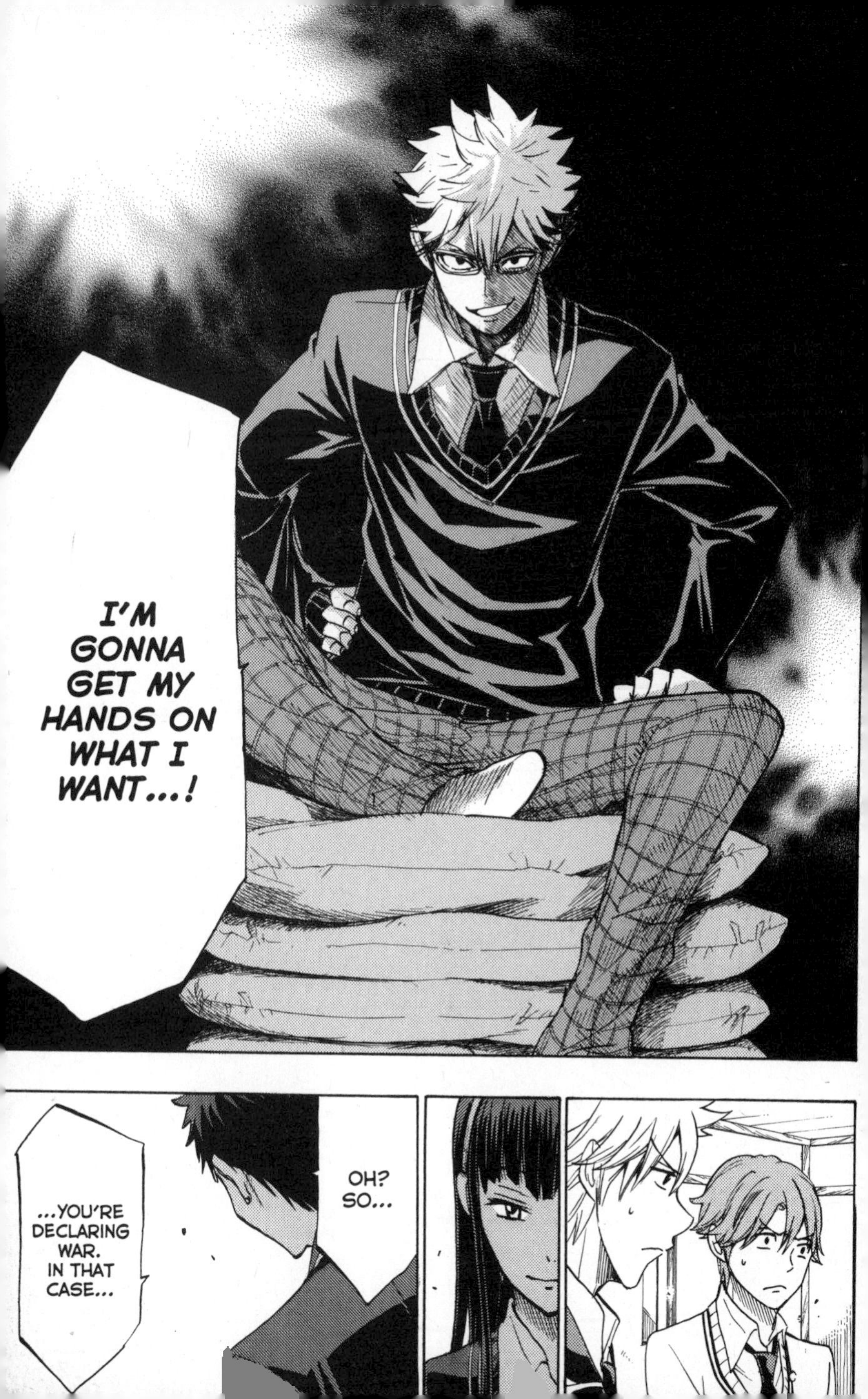
I'M GONNA GET MY HANDS ON WHAT I WANT...!
OH? SO...
...YOU'RE DECLARING WAR. IN THAT CASE...

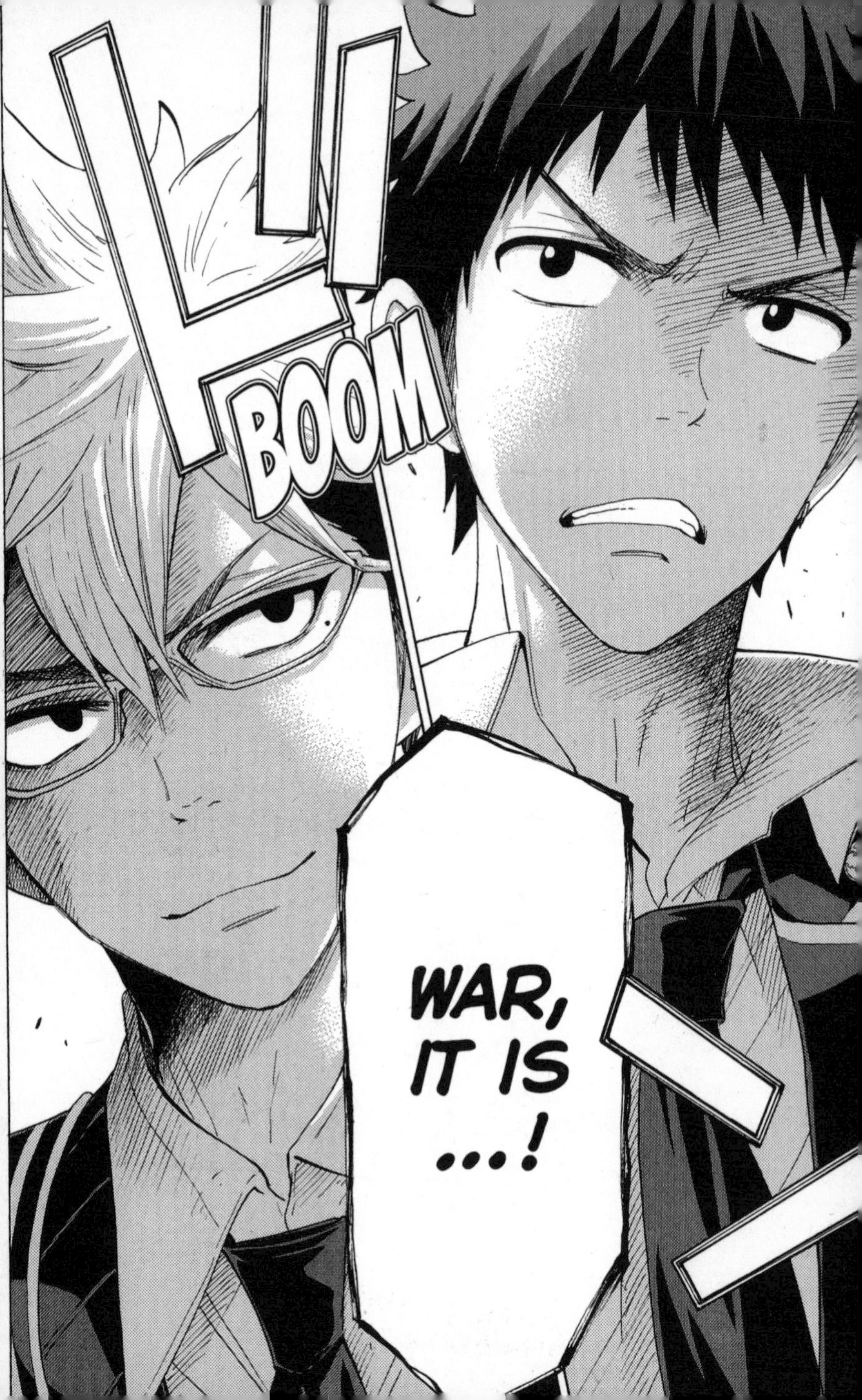
BOOM
WAR, IT IS ...!

CHAPTER 137:
I'm not so sure about that.

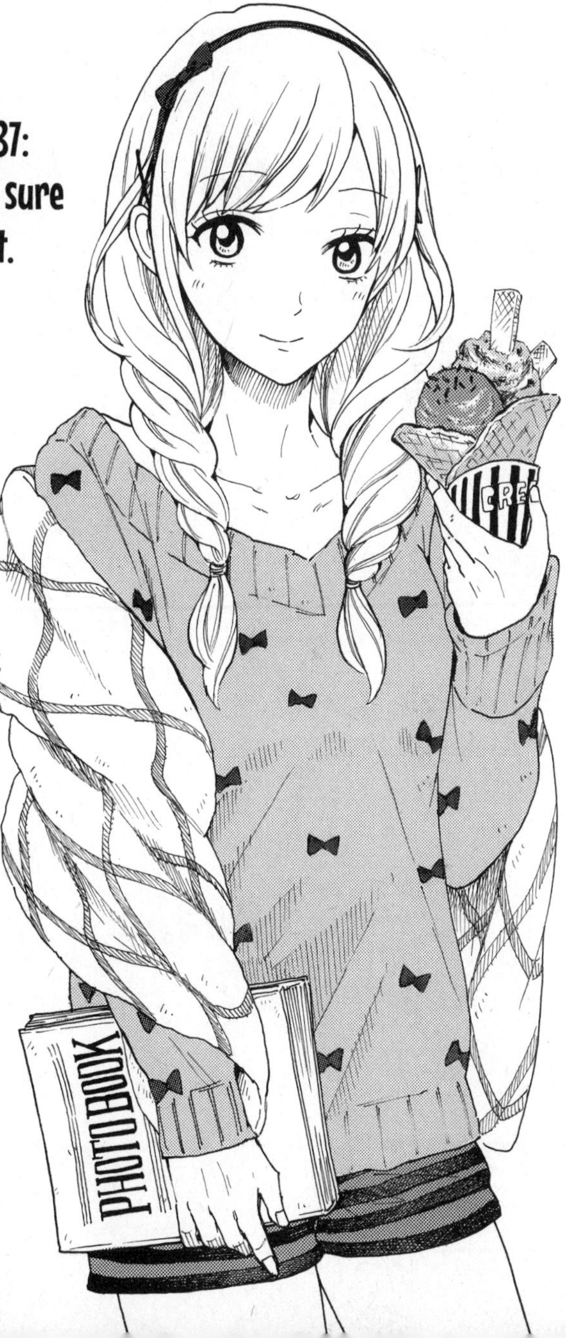
PHOTOBOOK

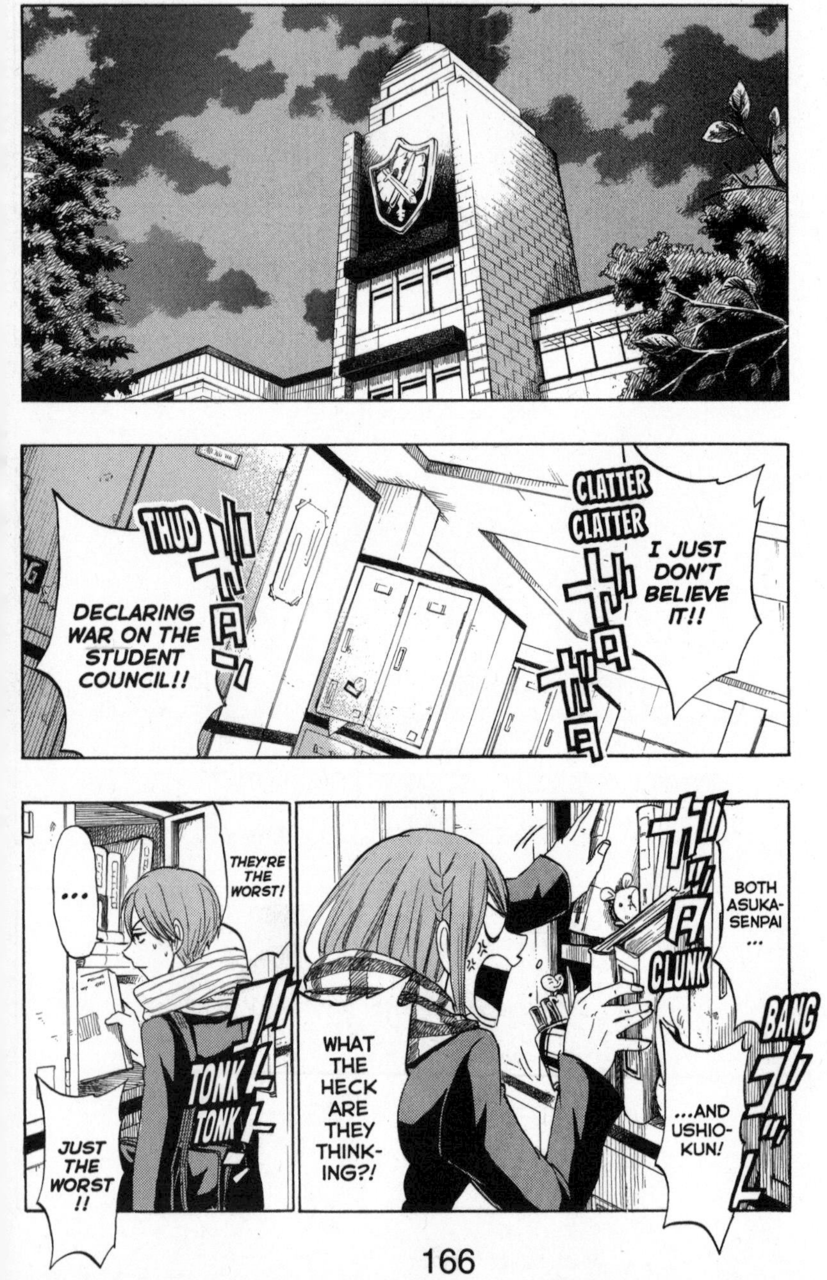
CLATTER CLATTER
I JUST DON'T BELIEVE IT!!
THUD
DECLARING WAR ON THE STUDENT COUNCIL!!
BOTH ASUKA-SENPAI...
CLUNK
BANG
...AND USHIO-KUN!
WHAT THE HECK ARE THEY THINKING?!
THEY'RE THE WORST!
...
TONK TONK
JUST THE WORST!!

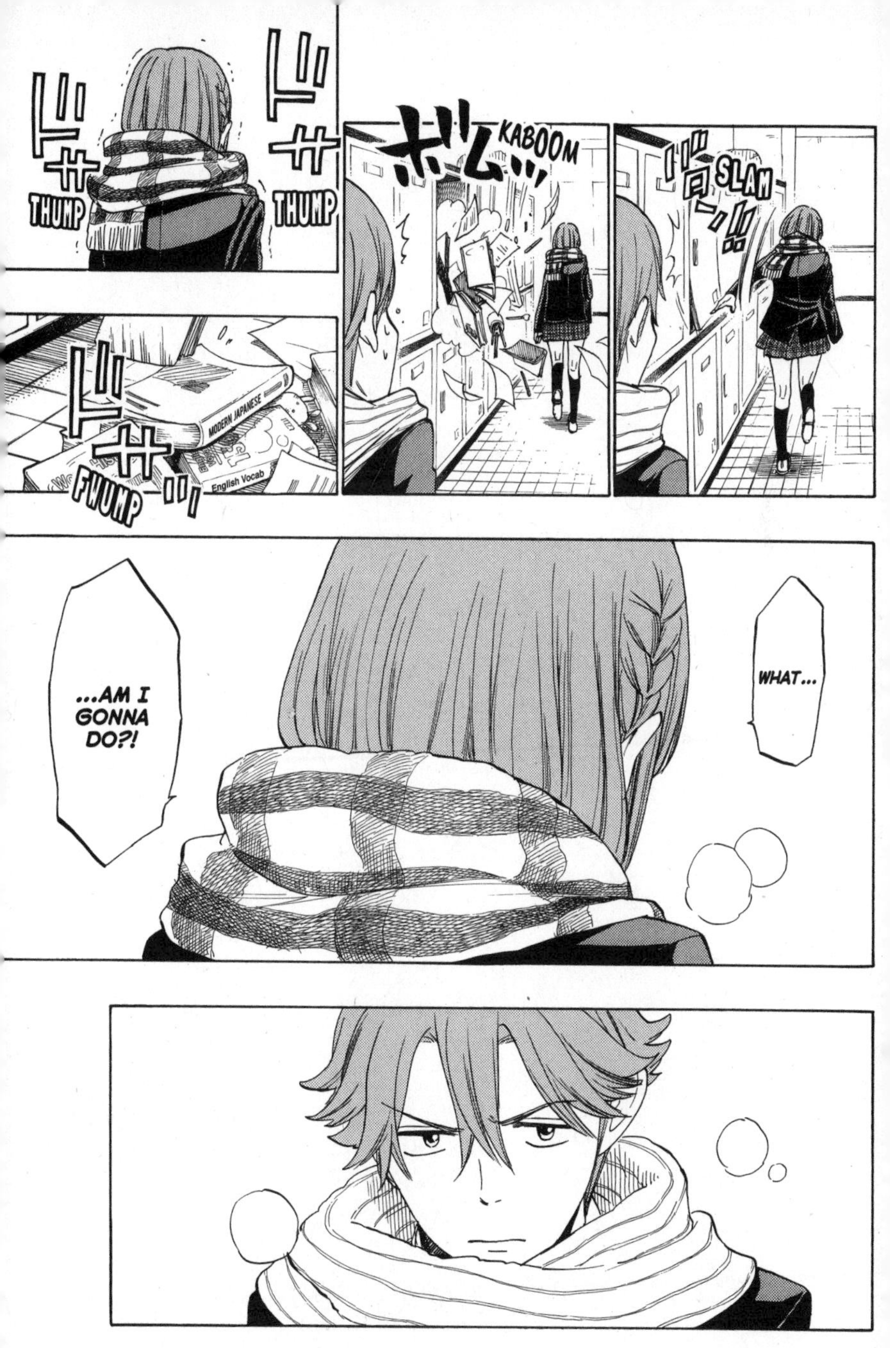
SLAM
KABOOM
THUMP
THUMP
MODERN JAPANESE
English Vocab
FWUMP
WHAT...
...AM I GONNA DO?!

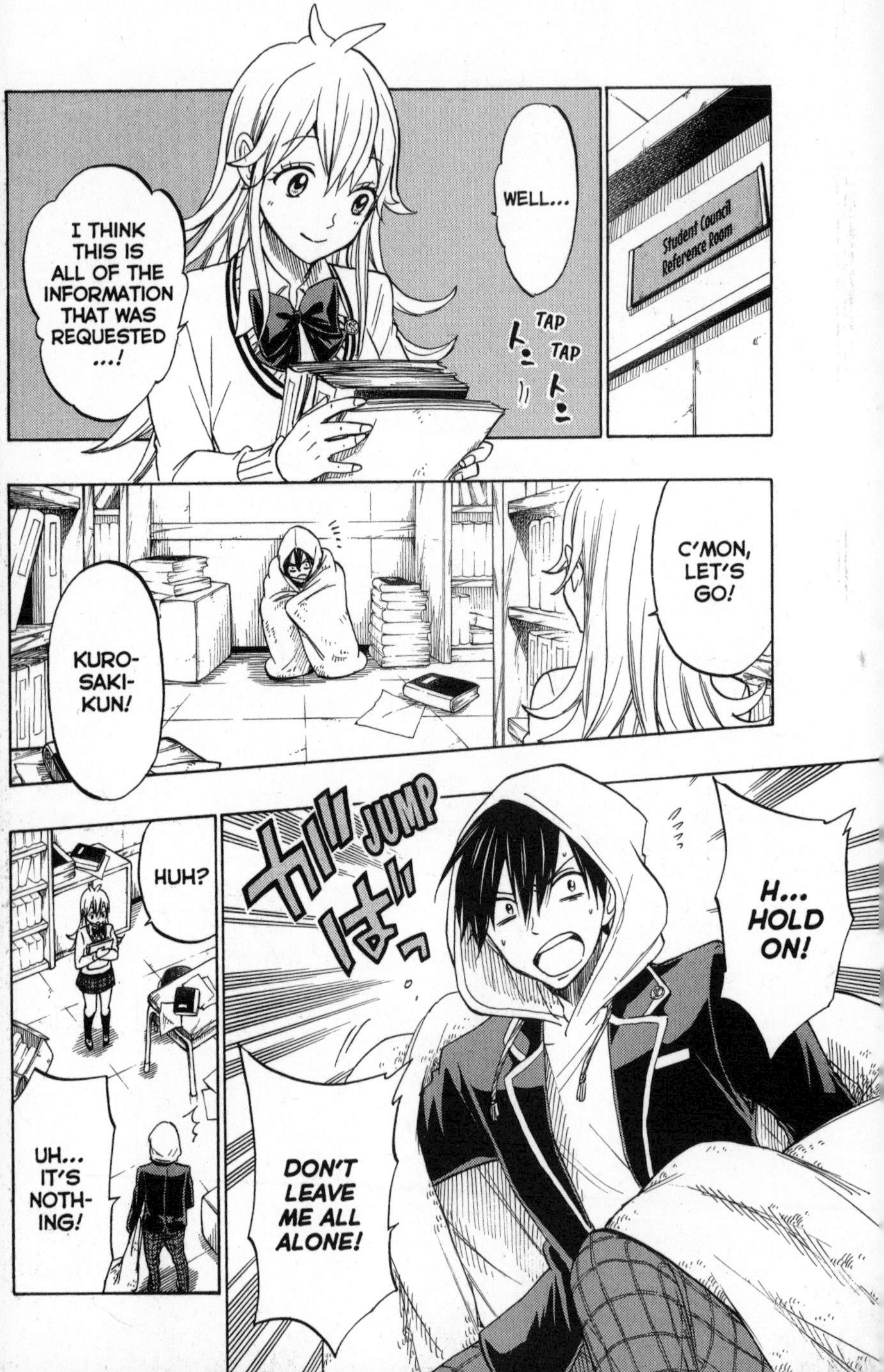
Student Council Reference Room
WELL...
TAP TAP
I THINK THIS IS ALL OF THE INFORMATION THAT WAS REQUESTED ...!
C'MON, LET'S GO!
KURO-SAKI-KUN!
H... HOLD ON!
JUMP
DON'T LEAVE ME ALL ALONE!
HUH?
UH... IT'S NOTH-ING!

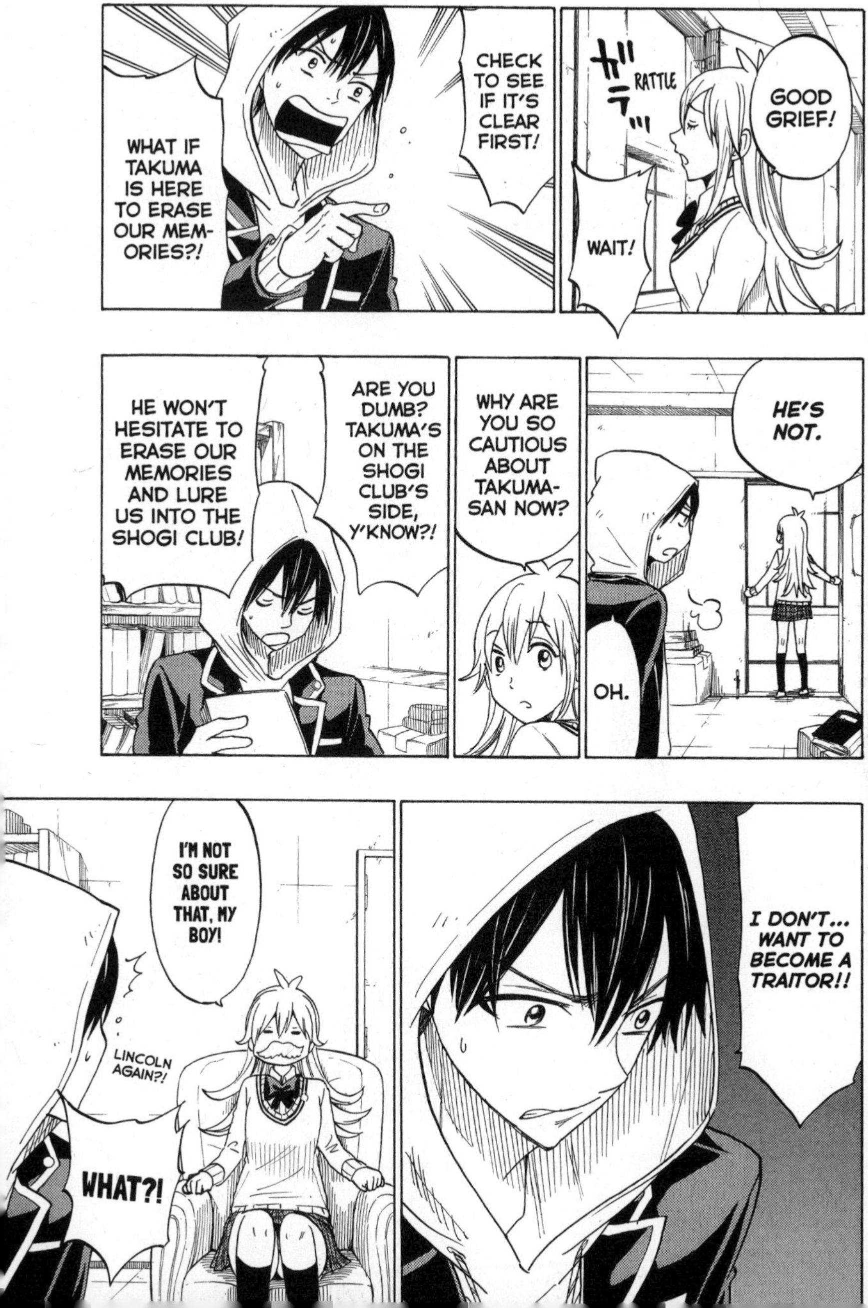
GOOD GRIEF!
RATTLE
WAIT!
CHECK TO SEE IF IT'S CLEAR FIRST!
WHAT IF TAKUMA IS HERE TO ERASE OUR MEMORIES?!
HE'S NOT.
OH.
WHY ARE YOU SO CAUTIOUS ABOUT TAKUMA-SAN NOW?
ARE YOU DUMB? TAKUMA'S ON THE SHOGI CLUB'S SIDE, Y'KNOW?!
HE WON'T HESITATE TO ERASE OUR MEMORIES AND LURE US INTO THE SHOGI CLUB!
I DON'T... WANT TO BECOME A TRAITOR!!
I'M NOT SO SURE ABOUT THAT, MY BOY!
LINCOLN AGAIN?!
WHAT?!

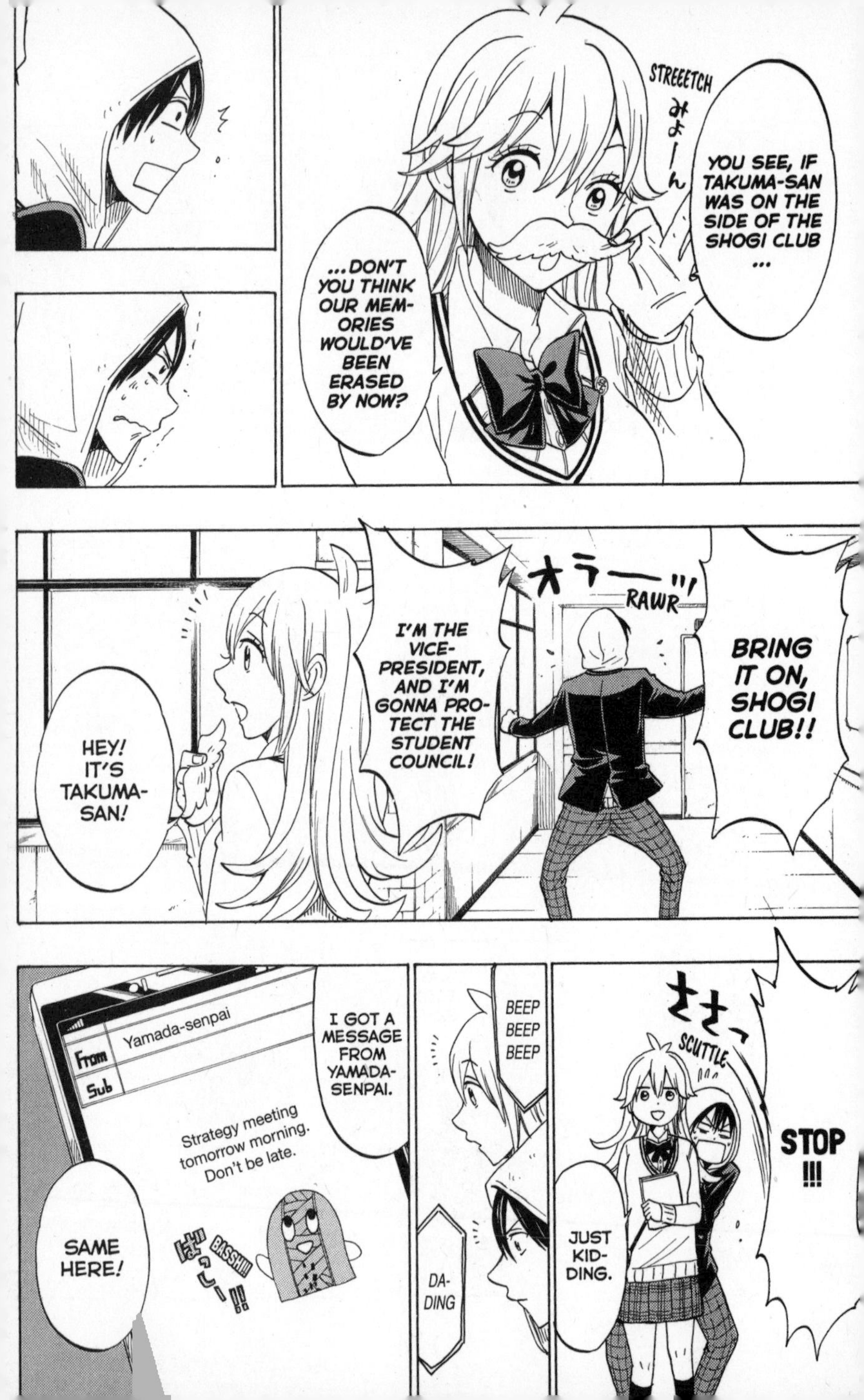
STREEECH
みよーん
YOU SEE, IF TAKUMA-SAN WAS ON THE SIDE OF THE SHOGI CLUB ...
...DON'T YOU THINK OUR MEMORIES WOULD'VE BEEN ERASED BY NOW?
BRING IT ON, SHOGI CLUB!!
オラー
RAWR
I'M THE VICE-PRESIDENT, AND I'M GONNA PROTECT THE STUDENT COUNCIL!
HEY! IT'S TAKUMA-SAN!
ささっ
SCUTTLE
STOP!!!
JUST KIDDING.
BEEP BEEP BEEP
DA-DING
I GOT A MESSAGE FROM YAMADA-SENPAI.
From Yamada-senpai
Sub
Strategy meeting tomorrow morning. Don't be late.
ばっしー!!!
BASSH!!!
SAME HERE!

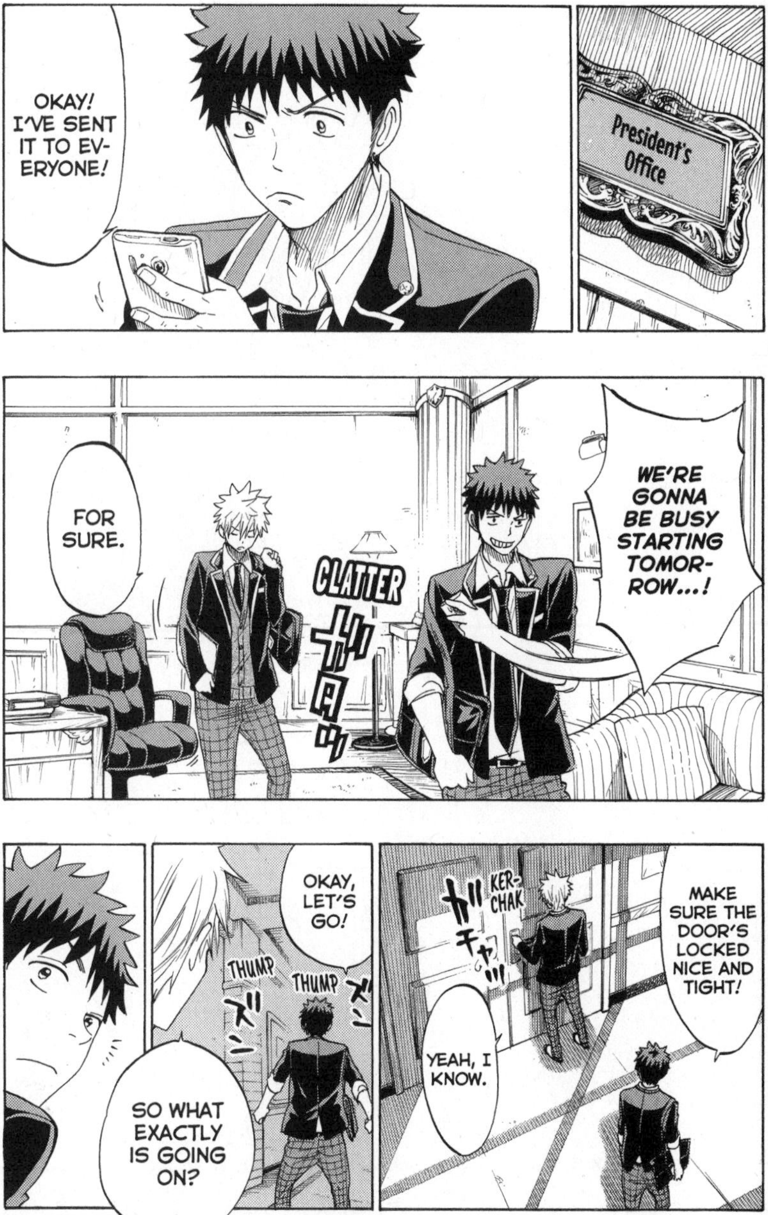
President's Office
OKAY! I'VE SENT IT TO EV-ERYONE!
WE'RE GONNA BE BUSY STARTING TOMOR-ROW...!
CLATTER
FOR SURE.
MAKE SURE THE DOOR'S LOCKED NICE AND TIGHT!
KER-CHAK
YEAH, I KNOW.
OKAY, LET'S GO!
THUMP
THUMP
SO WHAT EXACTLY IS GOING ON?

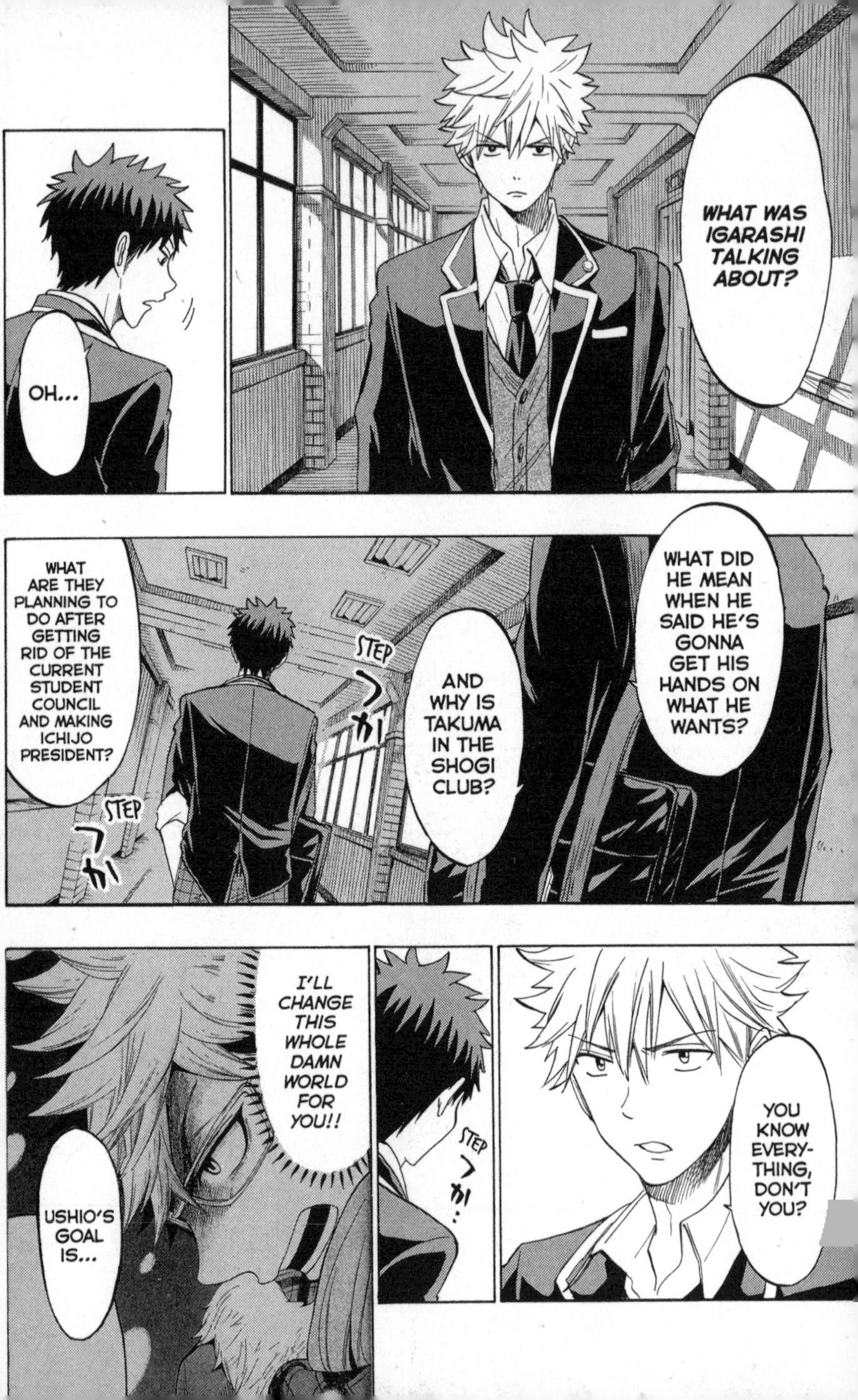
WHAT WAS IGARASHI TALKING ABOUT?
OH...
WHAT DID HE MEAN WHEN HE SAID HE'S GONNA GET HIS HANDS ON WHAT HE WANTS?
AND WHY IS TAKUMA IN THE SHOGI CLUB?
STEP
WHAT ARE THEY PLANNING TO DO AFTER GETTING RID OF THE CURRENT STUDENT COUNCIL AND MAKING ICHIJO PRESIDENT?
STEP
YOU KNOW EVERY-THING, DON'T YOU?
STEP
I'LL CHANGE THIS WHOLE DAMN WORLD FOR YOU!!
USHIO'S GOAL IS...

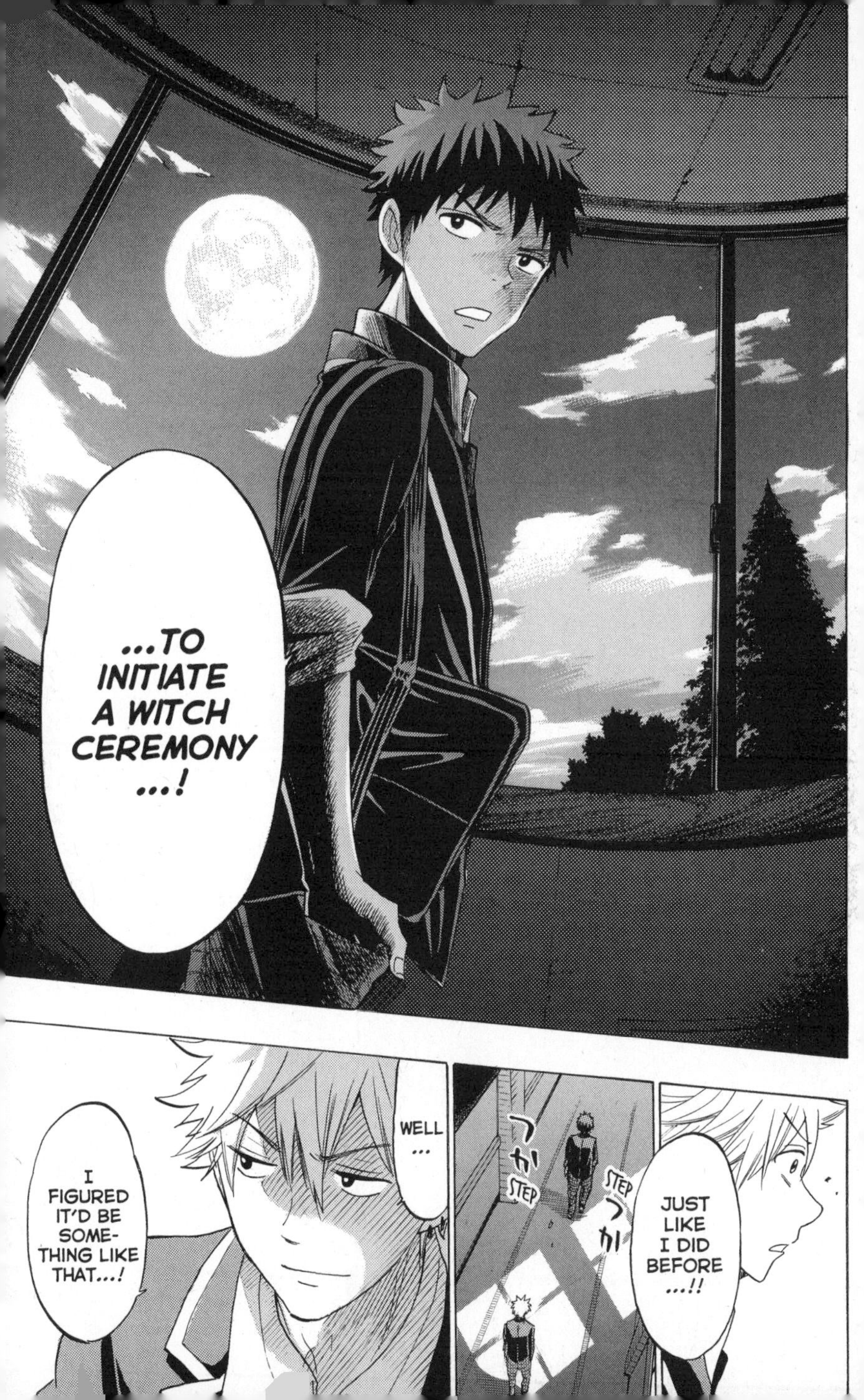
...TO INITIATE A WITCH CEREMONY ...!
JUST LIKE I DID BEFORE ...!!
STEP つか
つか STEP
WELL ...
I FIGURED IT'D BE SOME-THING LIKE THAT...!

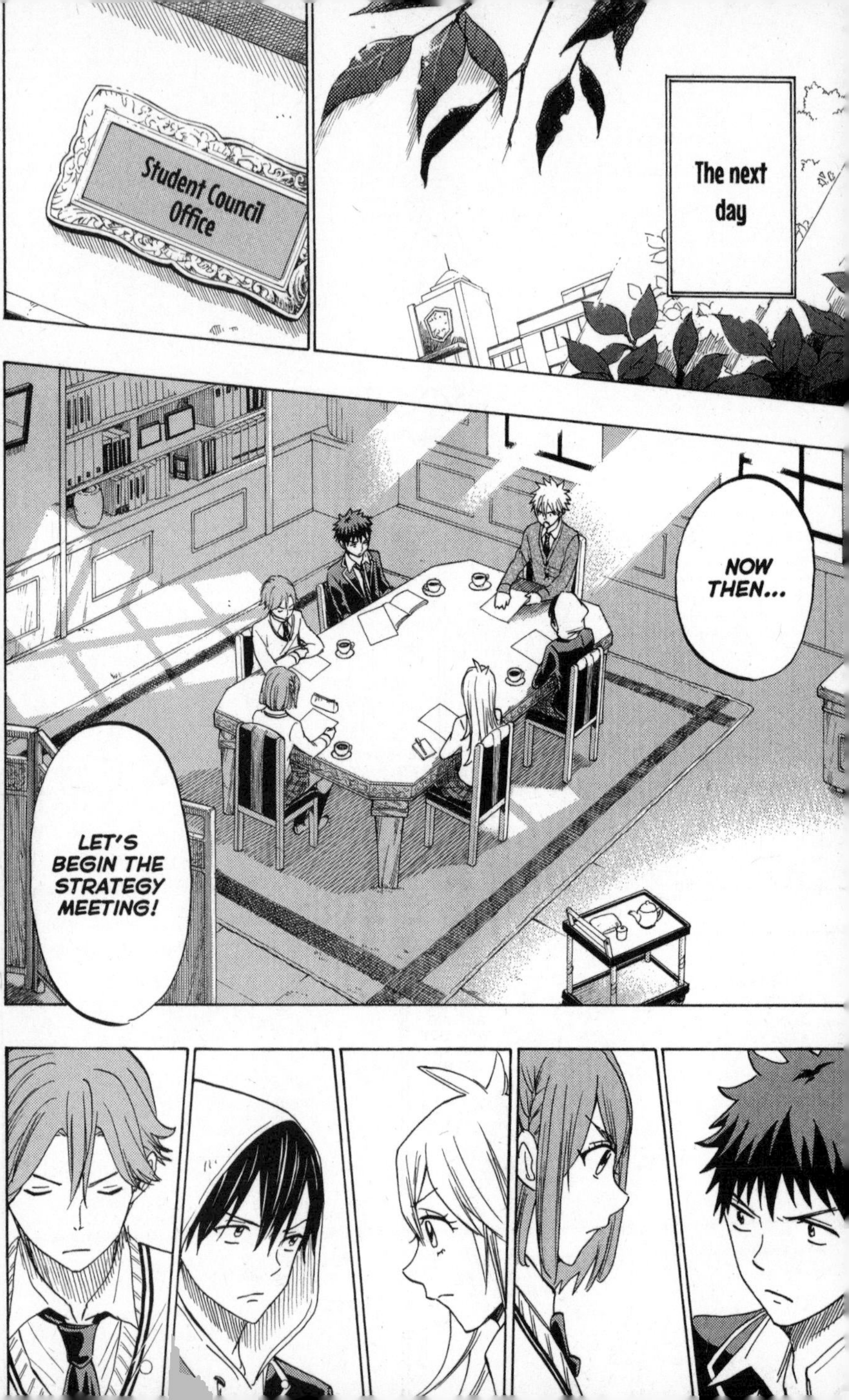
The next day
Student Council Office
NOW THEN...
LET'S BEGIN THE STRATEGY MEETING!

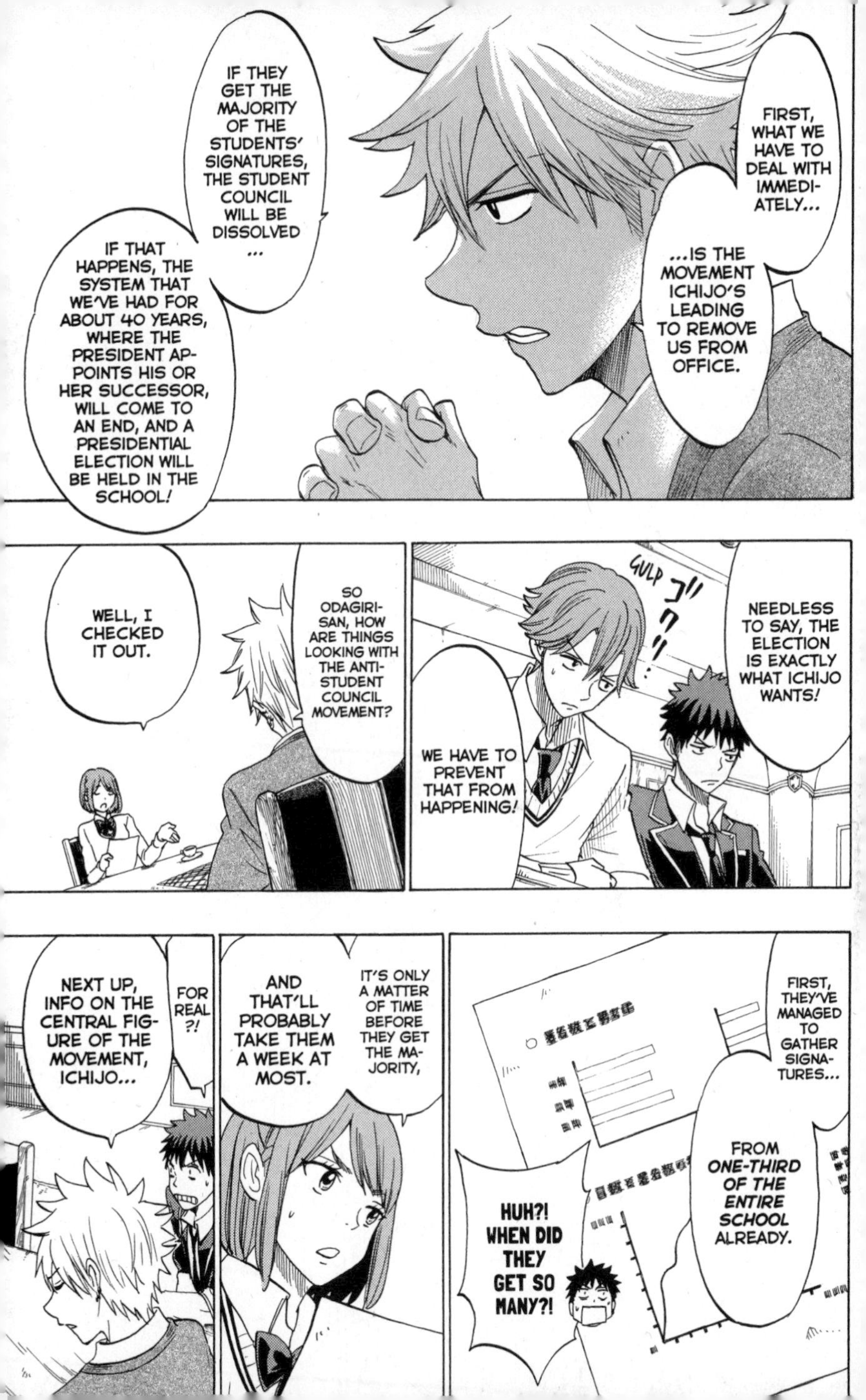
FIRST, WHAT WE HAVE TO DEAL WITH IMMEDIATELY...
...IS THE MOVEMENT ICHIJO'S LEADING TO REMOVE US FROM OFFICE.
IF THEY GET THE MAJORITY OF THE STUDENTS' SIGNATURES, THE STUDENT COUNCIL WILL BE DISSOLVED...
IF THAT HAPPENS, THE SYSTEM THAT WE'VE HAD FOR ABOUT 40 YEARS, WHERE THE PRESIDENT APPOINTS HIS OR HER SUCCESSOR, WILL COME TO AN END, AND A PRESIDENTIAL ELECTION WILL BE HELD IN THE SCHOOL!
NEEDLESS TO SAY, THE ELECTION IS EXACTLY WHAT ICHIJO WANTS!
GULP
WE HAVE TO PREVENT THAT FROM HAPPENING!
SO ODAGIRI-SAN, HOW ARE THINGS LOOKING WITH THE ANTI-STUDENT COUNCIL MOVEMENT?
WELL, I CHECKED IT OUT.
FIRST, THEY'VE MANAGED TO GATHER SIGNATURES...
FROM ONE-THIRD OF THE ENTIRE SCHOOL ALREADY.
HUH?! WHEN DID THEY GET SO MANY?!
IT'S ONLY A MATTER OF TIME BEFORE THEY GET THE MAJORITY,
AND THAT'LL PROBABLY TAKE THEM A WEEK AT MOST.
FOR REAL?!
NEXT UP, INFO ON THE CENTRAL FIGURE OF THE MOVEMENT, ICHIJO...

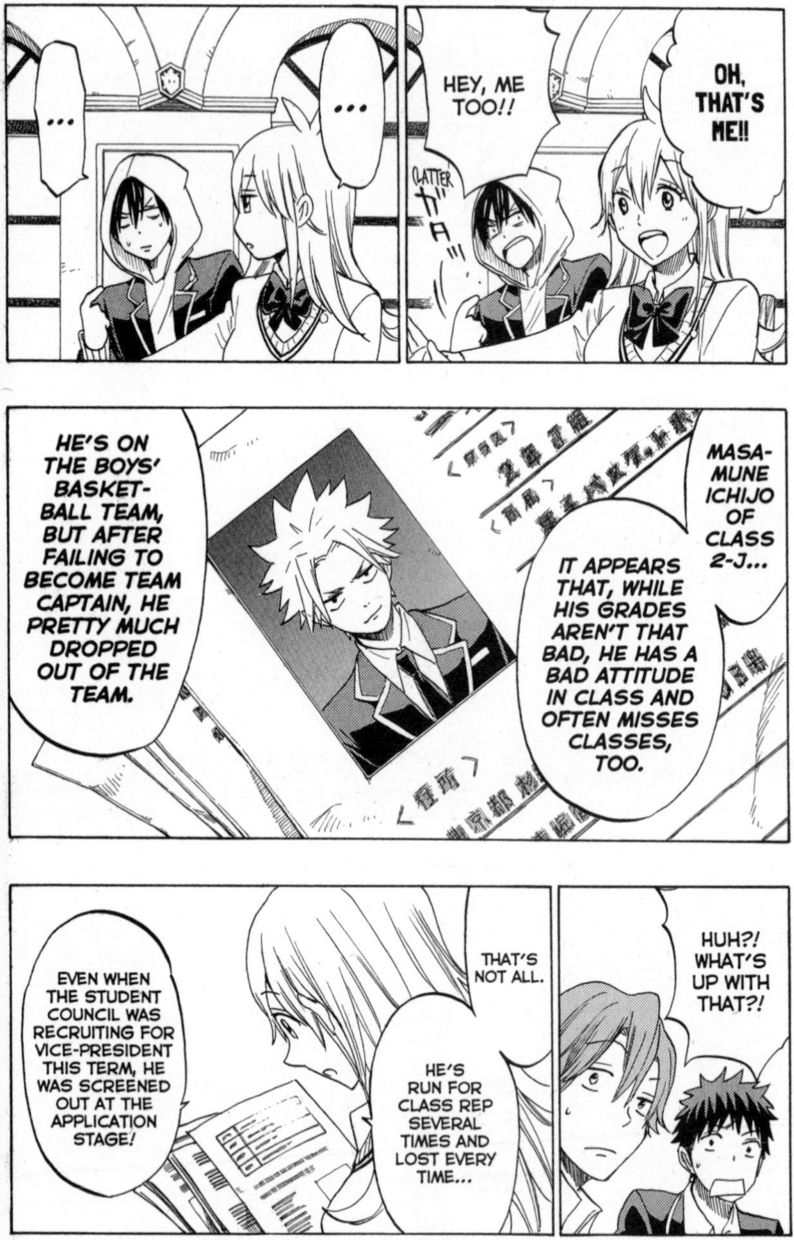
OH, THAT'S ME!!
HEY, ME TOO!!
CLATTER
...
...
MASA-MUNE ICHIJO OF CLASS 2-J...
IT APPEARS THAT, WHILE HIS GRADES AREN'T THAT BAD, HE HAS A BAD ATTITUDE IN CLASS AND OFTEN MISSES CLASSES, TOO.
HE'S ON THE BOYS' BASKET-BALL TEAM, BUT AFTER FAILING TO BECOME TEAM CAPTAIN, HE PRETTY MUCH DROPPED OUT OF THE TEAM.
HUH?! WHAT'S UP WITH THAT?!
THAT'S NOT ALL.
HE'S RUN FOR CLASS REP SEVERAL TIMES AND LOST EVERY TIME...
EVEN WHEN THE STUDENT COUNCIL WAS RECRUITING FOR VICE-PRESIDENT THIS TERM, HE WAS SCREENED OUT AT THE APPLICATION STAGE!

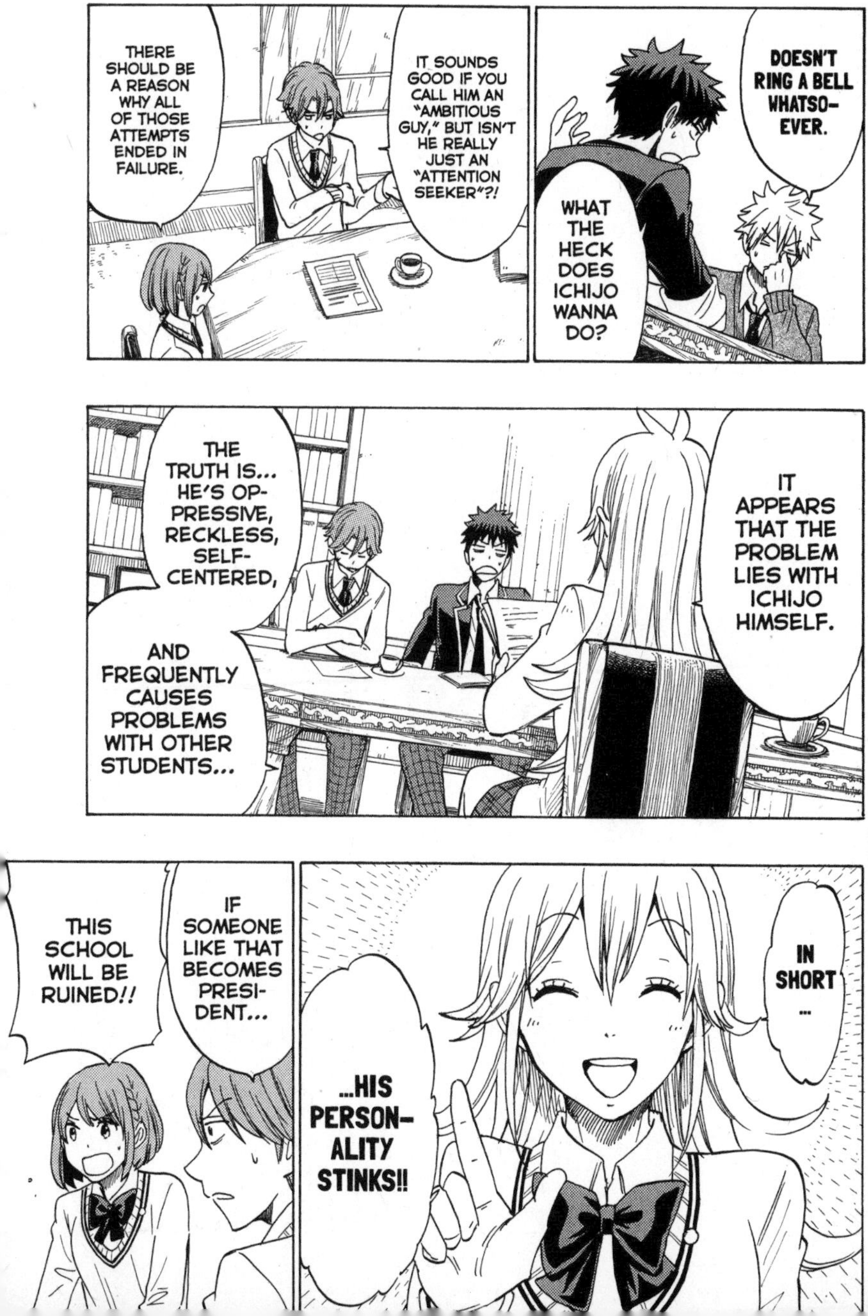
DOESN'T RING A BELL WHATSO-EVER.
WHAT THE HECK DOES ICHIJO WANNA DO?
IT SOUNDS GOOD IF YOU CALL HIM AN "AMBITIOUS GUY," BUT ISN'T HE REALLY JUST AN "ATTENTION SEEKER"?!
THERE SHOULD BE A REASON WHY ALL OF THOSE ATTEMPTS ENDED IN FAILURE.
IT APPEARS THAT THE PROBLEM LIES WITH ICHIJO HIMSELF.
THE TRUTH IS... HE'S OP-PRESSIVE, RECKLESS, SELF-CENTERED,
AND FREQUENTLY CAUSES PROBLEMS WITH OTHER STUDENTS...
IN SHORT...
...HIS PERSON-ALITY STINKS!!
IF SOMEONE LIKE THAT BECOMES PRESI-DENT...
THIS SCHOOL WILL BE RUINED!!

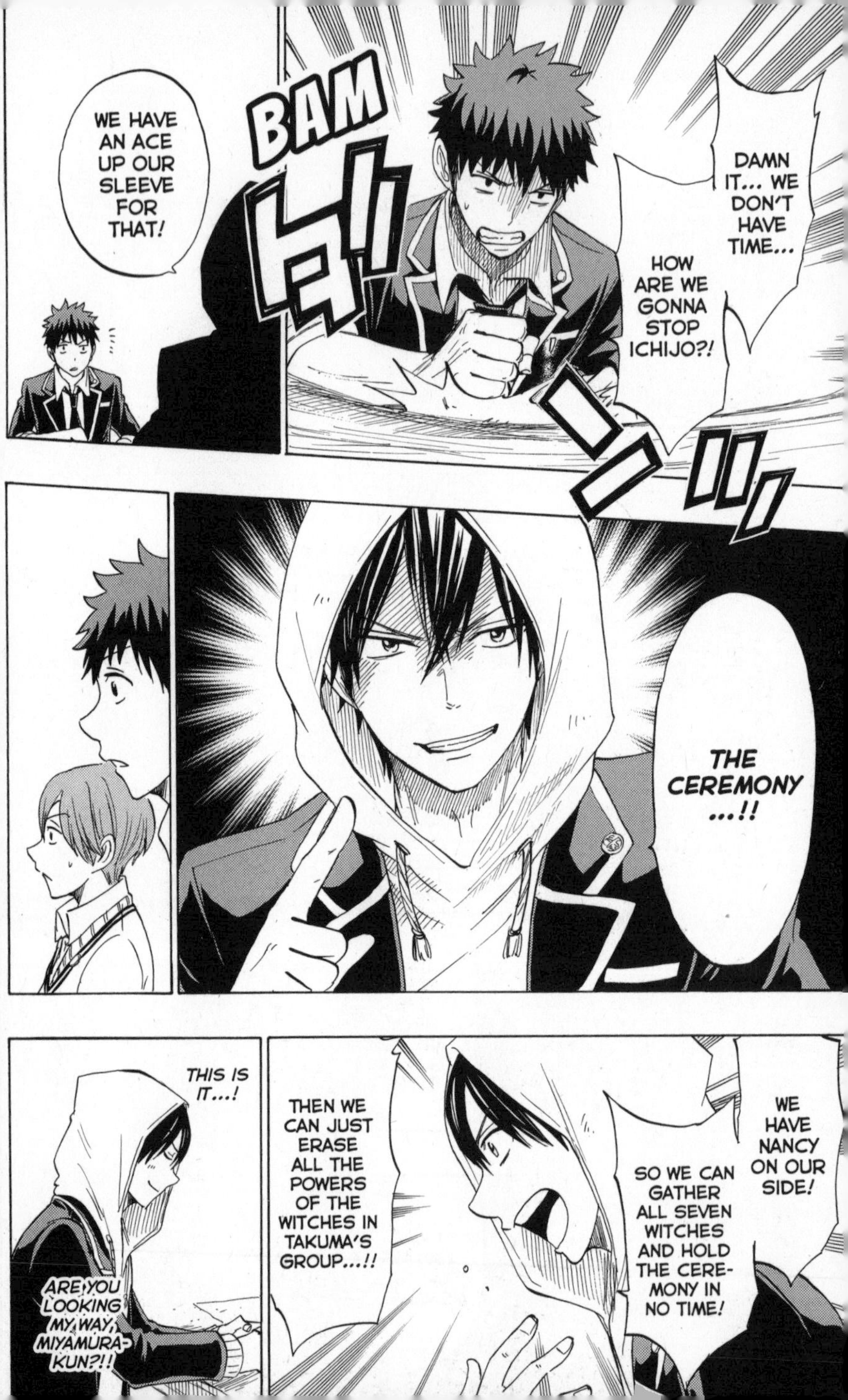
DAMN IT... WE DON'T HAVE TIME...
HOW ARE WE GONNA STOP ICHIJO?!
BAM
WE HAVE AN ACE UP OUR SLEEVE FOR THAT!
THE CEREMONY ...!!
WE HAVE NANCY ON OUR SIDE!
SO WE CAN GATHER ALL SEVEN WITCHES AND HOLD THE CEREMONY IN NO TIME!
THEN WE CAN JUST ERASE ALL THE POWERS OF THE WITCHES IN TAKUMA'S GROUP...!!
THIS IS IT...!
ARE YOU LOOKING MY WAY, MIYAMURA-KUN?!!

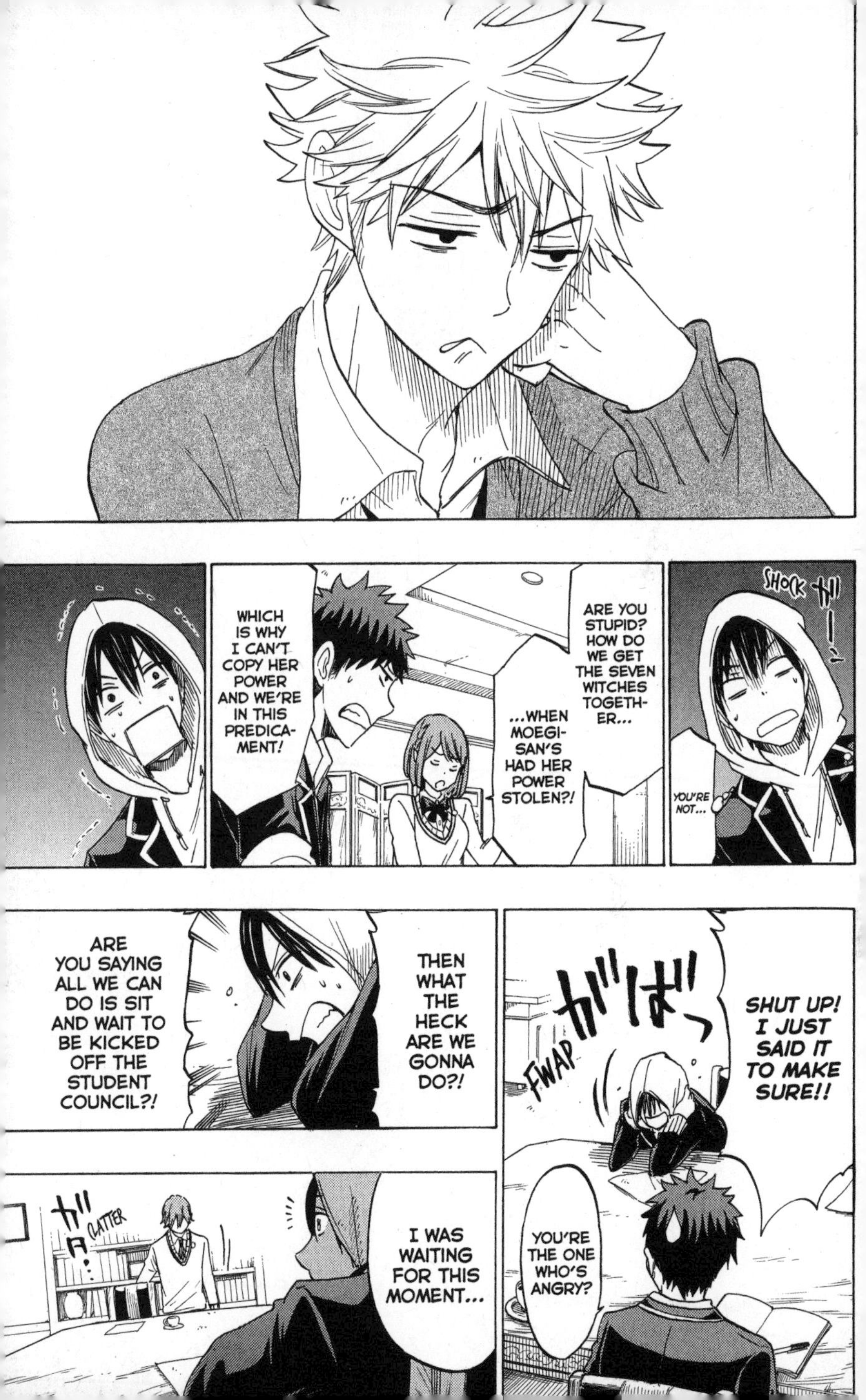

SHOCK
YOU'RE NOT...
ARE YOU STUPID? HOW DO WE GET THE SEVEN WITCHES TOGETHER...
...WHEN MOEGI-SAN'S HAD HER POWER STOLEN?!
WHICH IS WHY I CAN'T COPY HER POWER AND WE'RE IN THIS PREDICAMENT!
SHUT UP! I JUST SAID IT TO MAKE SURE!!
がばっ
FWAP
YOU'RE THE ONE WHO'S ANGRY?
THEN WHAT THE HECK ARE WE GONNA DO?!
ARE YOU SAYING ALL WE CAN DO IS SIT AND WAIT TO BE KICKED OFF THE STUDENT COUNCIL?!
I WAS WAITING FOR THIS MOMENT...
CLATTER

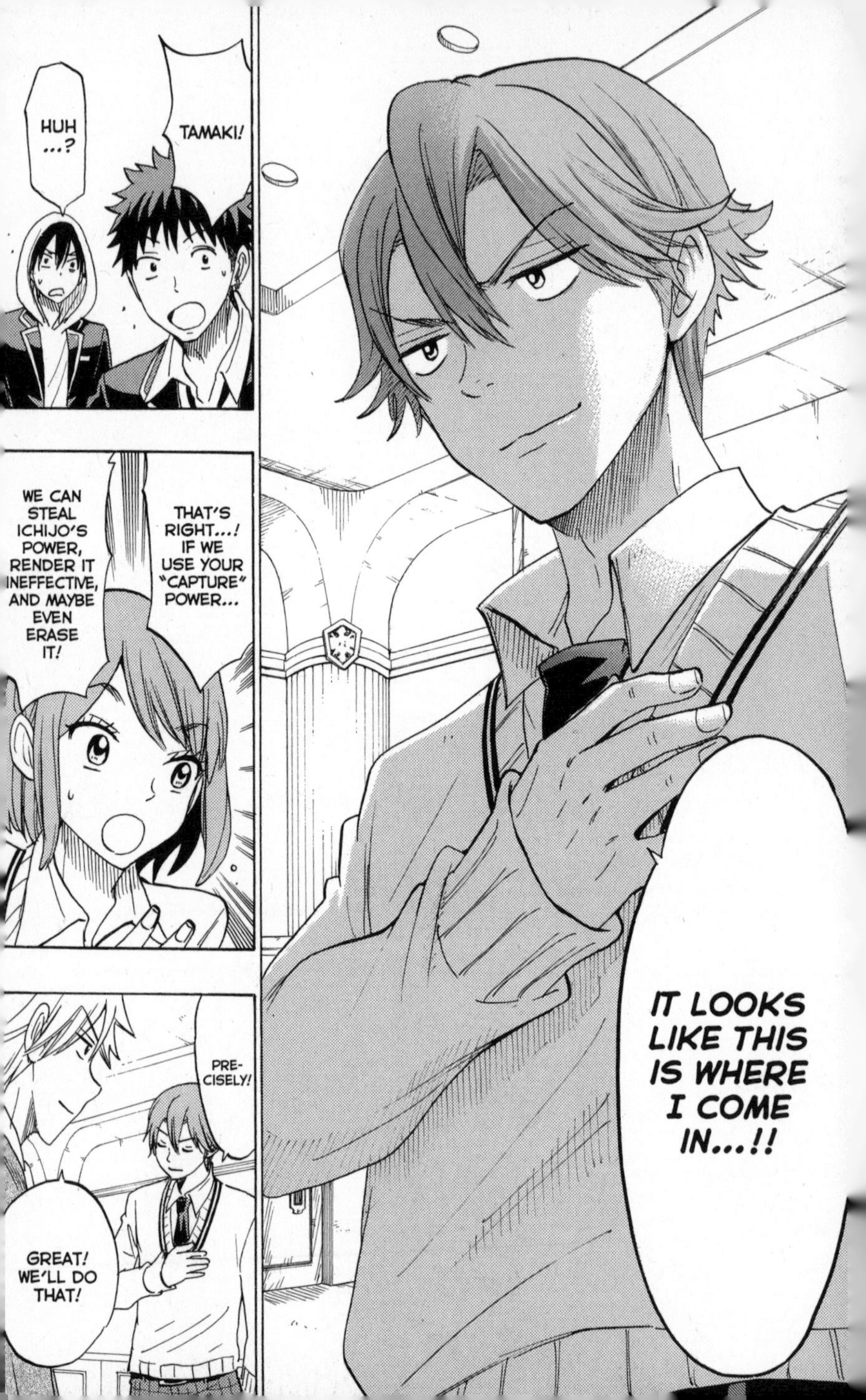
IT LOOKS LIKE THIS IS WHERE I COME IN...!!
TAMAKI!
HUH ...?
THAT'S RIGHT...! IF WE USE YOUR "CAPTURE" POWER...
WE CAN STEAL ICHIJO'S POWER, RENDER IT INEFFECTIVE, AND MAYBE EVEN ERASE IT!
PRE-CISELY!
GREAT! WE'LL DO THAT!

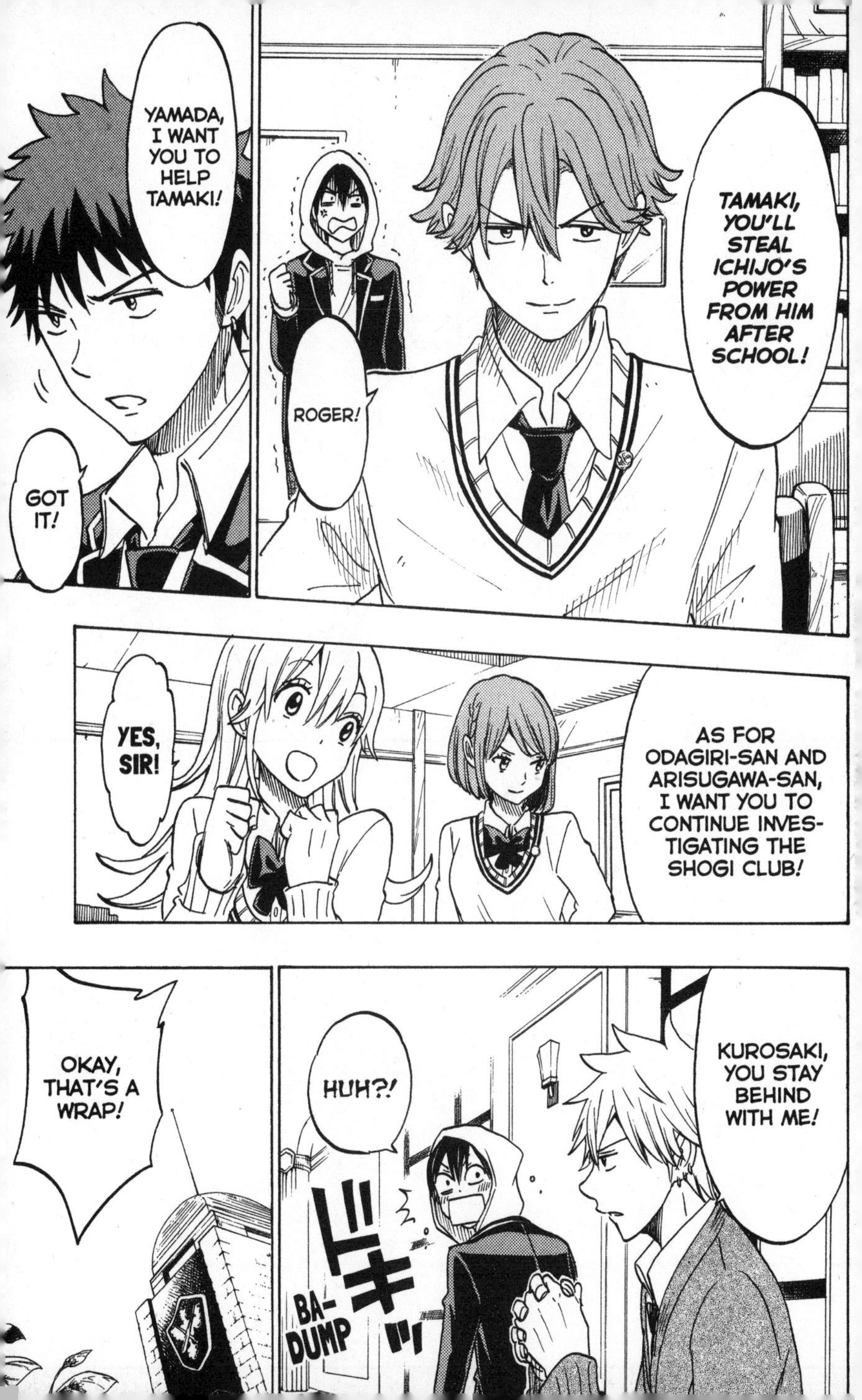
TAMAKI, YOU'LL STEAL ICHIJO'S POWER FROM HIM AFTER SCHOOL!
ROGER!
YAMADA, I WANT YOU TO HELP TAMAKI!
GOT IT!
AS FOR ODAGIRI-SAN AND ARISUGAWA-SAN, I WANT YOU TO CONTINUE INVES-TIGATING THE SHOGI CLUB!
YES, SIR!
KUROSAKI, YOU STAY BEHIND WITH ME!
HUH?!
BA-DUMP
OKAY, THAT'S A WRAP!

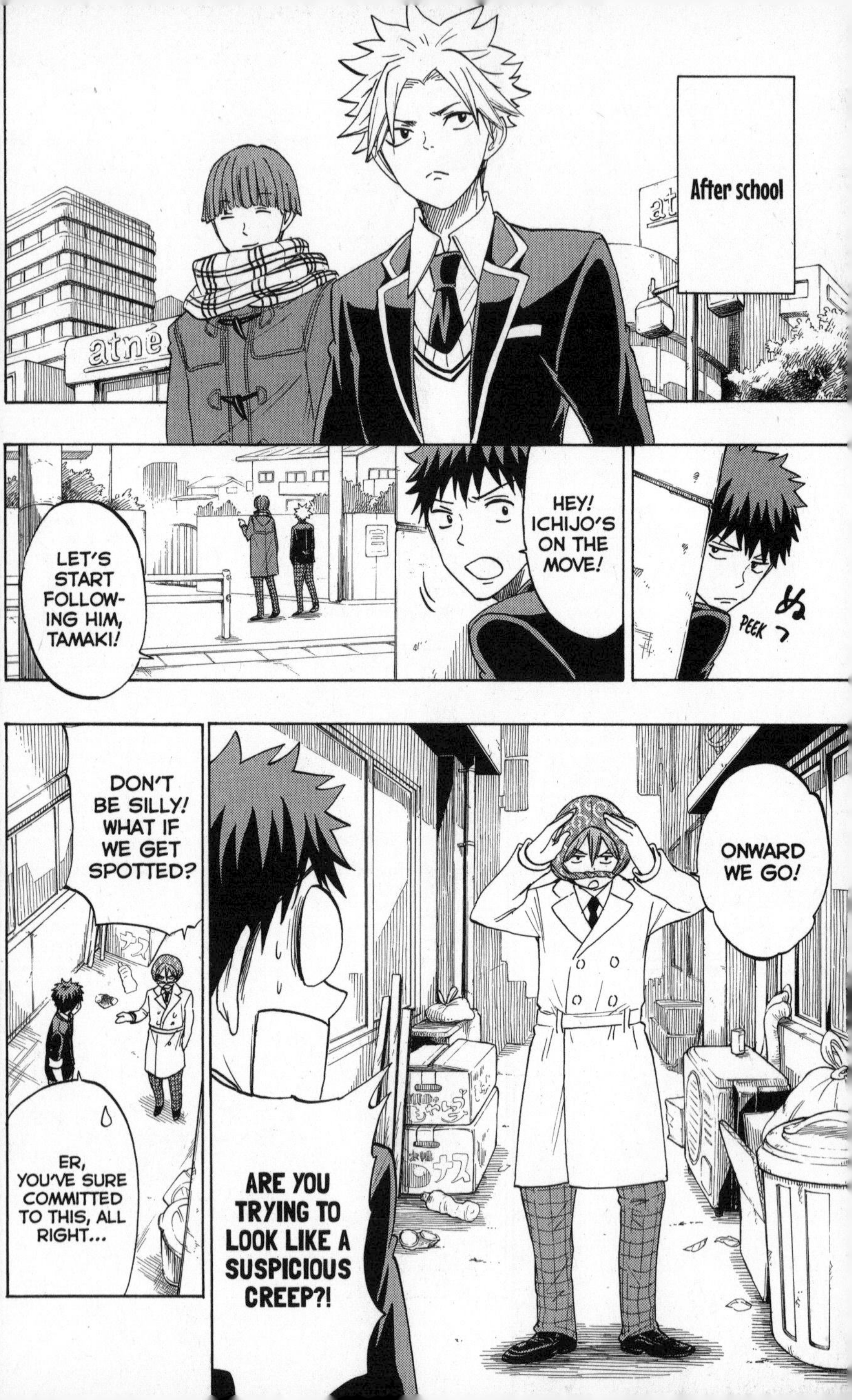
After school
PEEK
HEY! ICHIJO'S ON THE MOVE!
LET'S START FOLLOWING HIM, TAMAKI!
ONWARD WE GO!
ARE YOU TRYING TO LOOK LIKE A SUSPICIOUS CREEP?!
DON'T BE SILLY! WHAT IF WE GET SPOTTED?
ER, YOU'VE SURE COMMITTED TO THIS, ALL RIGHT...

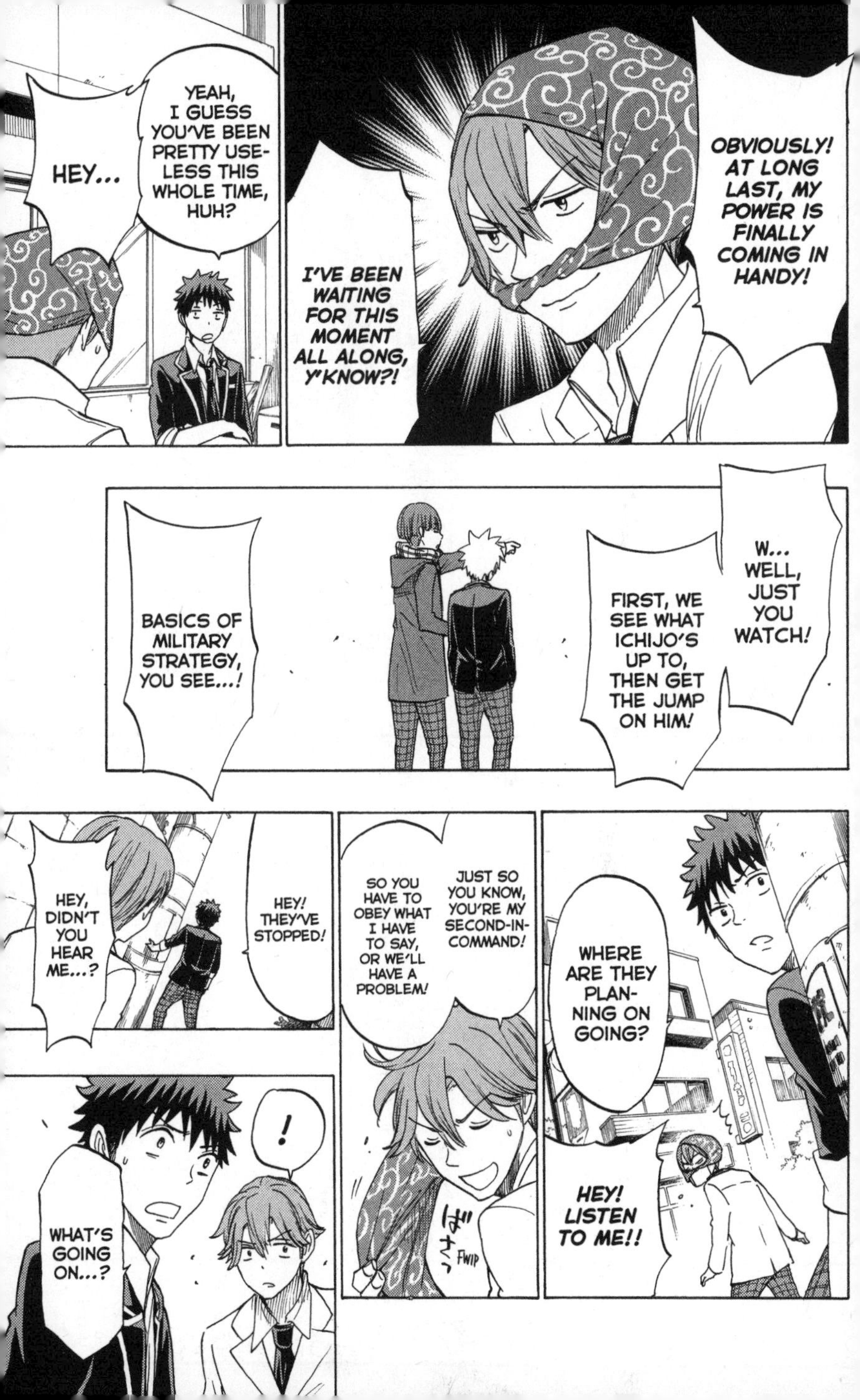
OBVIOUSLY! AT LONG LAST, MY POWER IS FINALLY COMING IN HANDY!
I'VE BEEN WAITING FOR THIS MOMENT ALL ALONG, Y'KNOW?!
YEAH, I GUESS YOU'VE BEEN PRETTY USE-LESS THIS WHOLE TIME, HUH?
HEY...
W... WELL, JUST YOU WATCH!
FIRST, WE SEE WHAT ICHIJO'S UP TO, THEN GET THE JUMP ON HIM!
BASICS OF MILITARY STRATEGY, YOU SEE...!
WHERE ARE THEY PLAN-NING ON GOING?
HEY! LISTEN TO ME!!
JUST SO YOU KNOW, YOU'RE MY SECOND-IN-COMMAND!
SO YOU HAVE TO OBEY WHAT I HAVE TO SAY, OR WE'LL HAVE A PROBLEM!
ばさっ
FWIP
HEY! THEY'VE STOPPED!
HEY, DIDN'T YOU HEAR ME...?
!
WHAT'S GOING ON...?

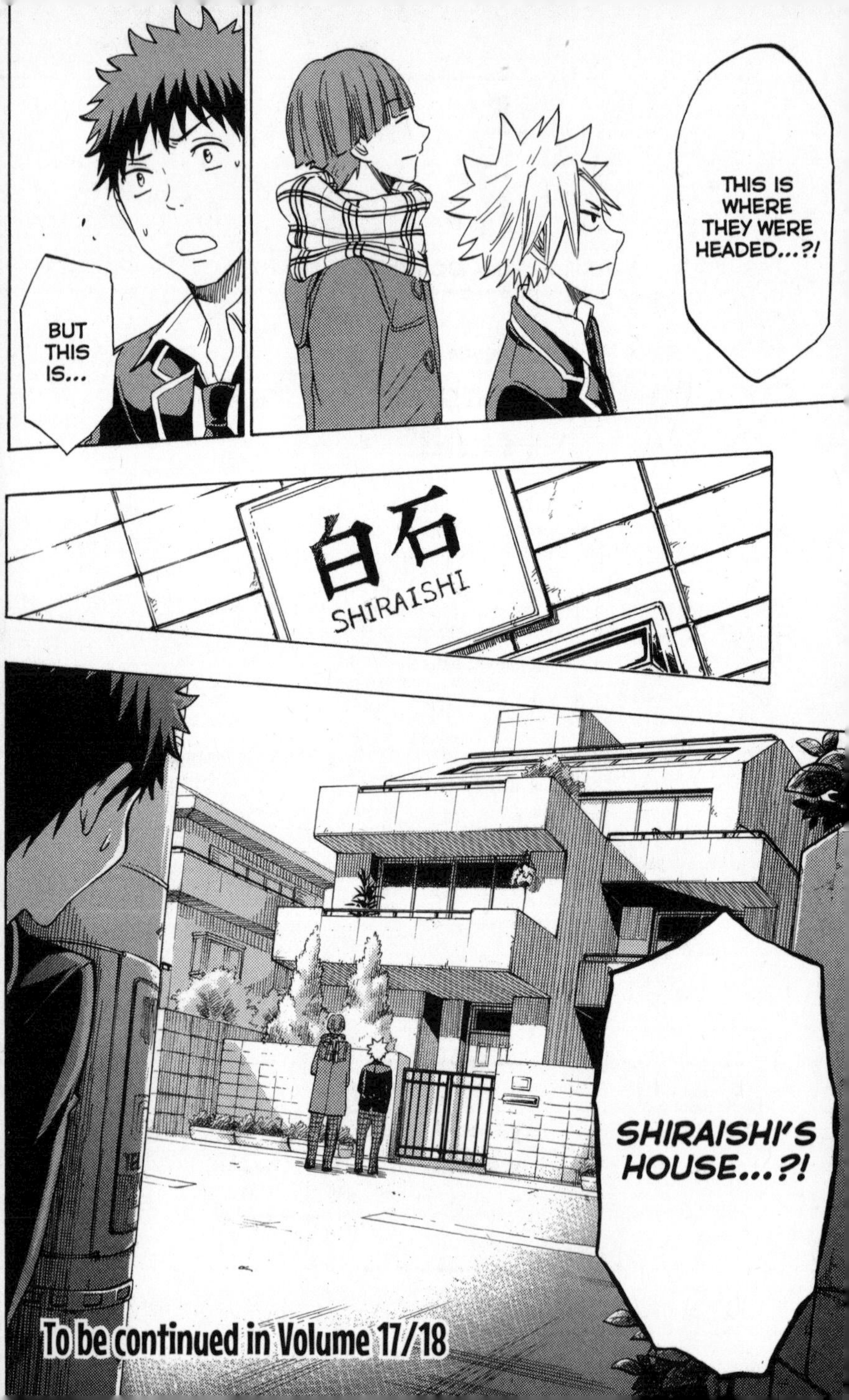
THIS IS WHERE THEY WERE HEADED...?!
BUT THIS IS...
白石
SHIRAISHI
SHIRAISHI'S HOUSE...?!
To be continued in Volume 17/18

朱雀高等学校
裏ホームページ
SUZAKU HIGH SCHOOL UNDERGROUND WEBSITE

 It's Q&A Corner #11! This time, it's...

The Toranosuke Miyamura Q&A Special!!!

 Wh...Why are we doing that?!

 Because there were so many questions that were directed towards you!! I wonder why no one ever asks about me... Wahhh!!

 Well, Itou-san, you're more the type that fans keep their eye on...like, the type that'd be fine if left alone...

 Okay, but still, that doesn't make me feel better! Whatever! Let's get started!!

 See that? Maybe it's the part of you that gets over things quickly.

Q1. I heard that Miyamu's dad is a diplomat. How does his family spend time together?

Chiba Prefecture, H.N Princess-san

Good question. My dad and mom are in England right now for work, so usually, it's just my sister, myself, and our housekeeper, Hatsue-san, at home.

Whaaat?! In that huge mansion of yours?! You have two bathrooms!! And you have a huge garden!!

I grew up in London until midway through elementary school. But once I came back to Japan, my sister and I ended up staying here. That's why my sister's Japanese sounds a little strange. And it looks like she learned her Japanese from Japanese literature.

So you're fluent in English?!

I haven't spoken it in so long... So I've forgotten it.

Q2. What kind of wallet does Miyamura-kun use?! Being wealthy, he must use a long wallet! Yamada-kun's was a coin pouch shaped like Sobasshi, though...

Tochigi Prefecture, H.N Daibutsu-san

MUCH DO YOU WANT?!
I ONLY HAVE 400 YEN!

In response to your question, this is his wallet!!

Huh?! When did you pull out my wallet?!

What the...?!
This is Gucci!! It's a brand-name wallet!!

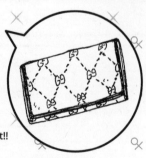

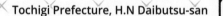

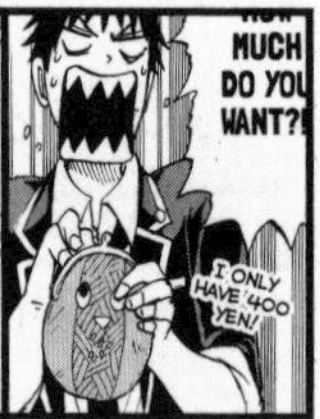

My dad bought it for my birthday last year. It's nice, isn't it?

 It's so ostentatious. (RUMMAGE RUMMAGE)
And your clothes are from Burberry!!

 Hey, hey! You better not accidentally put it in your own pocket in all the confusion!

Q3. President Yamazaki loves to use his (?) quill pen. Does Miyamura-kun not use it?

Fukushima Prefecture, H.N Airin-san

 Nah, I don't. The quill pen on the President's desk was something Yamazaki forgot to take with him. As a Student Council President, you're allowed the privilege of getting one thing that you'd need to carry out your duties, and I chose an iPad.

 You sure are a hipster who swims with the tide.
I get why girls talk about you so much.
Anyway, that's a wrap for this Q&A!

 Did you have fun with our special feature on yours truly?!
How about a special feature on Itou-san? I wonder if we'll ever get one?!

Please send your correspondence here ↓

Yamada-kun and the Seven Witches: Underground Website
c/o Kodansha Comics
451 Park Ave. South, 7th Floor
New York, NY 10016

※ Don't forget to include your handle name (pen name)!

Suzaku Gallery

This is where we'll introduce illustrations that we've received from all of you!

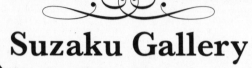

Selected artists will receive **a signed shikishi from the series creator**! When you make a submission, please make sure to clearly write your address, name, and phone number! If you don't, we won't be able to send you a prize, even if you're selected! Looking forward to all your submissions!

Urara♥

Okayama Pref., H.N. rami-san

Urara-chan has such a big smile here. You drew it with such pretty lines.

山田くんと7人の魔女
宮村家のかせいふさん。
山田NG
別名 おっかねぇかせいふ

Ehime Pref., H.N. Haaru-san

Hatsue-san is such a good person. But she doesn't seem to like Yamada.

山田竜 × 逢坂良太さん
祝アニメ化!!

Kanagawa Pref., H.N. Gonshari-san

It's Osaka-san who was the voice actor for Yamada! They seem like good friends!

おいゴラァ!宮村ァア!!!
山田くんと7人の魔女

Hyogo Pref., H.N. Teruteru-san

Huh? Why am I being yelled at in this picture?!

山田くんと7人の魔女
みやび
うらら

Fukuoka Pref., H.N. Saki-san

It's Urara and me! Super cute, and it looks like a purikura pic!

山田くんと7人の魔女

Kagoshima Pref., H.N. Ikepan☆Melonpan-san

Even a guy like me who doesn't like cats would adore a cat like this!!!

Suzaku Gallery

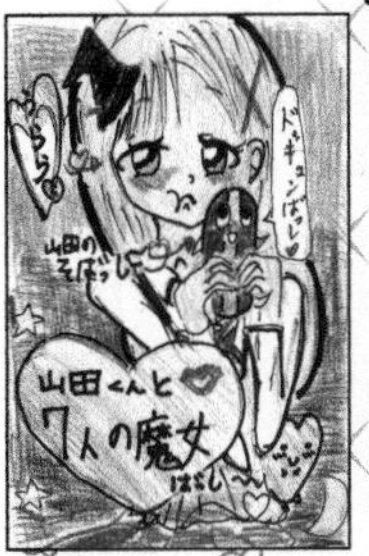
山田くんと
7人の魔女

Toyama Pref.,
H.N. Mikan-san

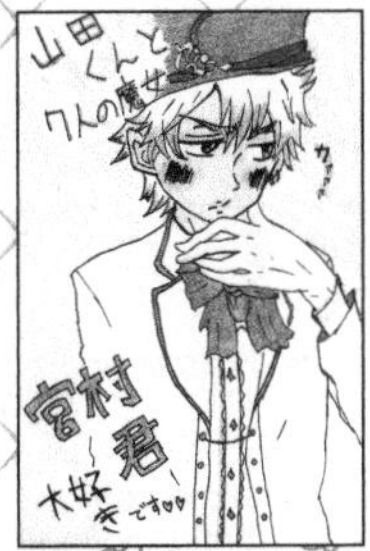
山田くんと
7人の魔女
宮村君
大好きです

Tokyo Pref.,
H.N. Mari-san

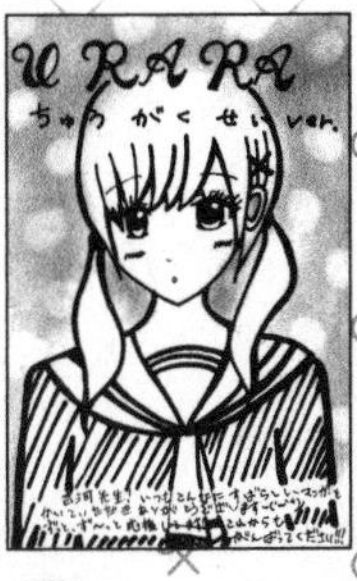
URARA
ちゅうがくせいver.

Aichi Pref.,
H.N. Tomoka Tani-san

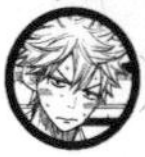
If Shiraishi-san looked at me like this, my heart would also "skip a beat-sshi"! ♥

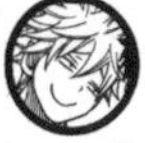
Who is this stud?! Oh, it's me.

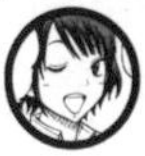
I wonder what kind of girl Urara-chan was in junior high!

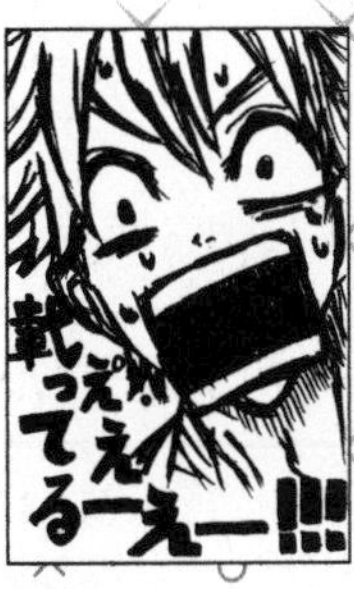
輝いってえるーえー!!!

Ehime Pref.,
H.N. Niji-san

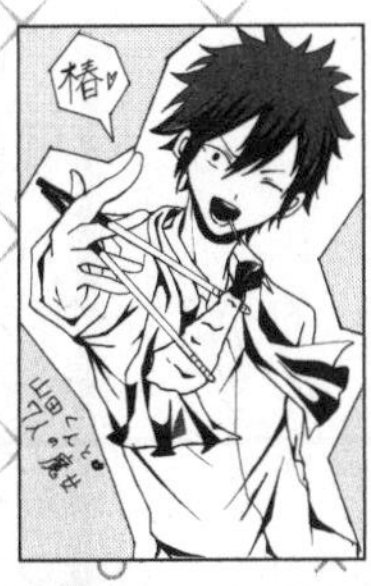
椿

Hyogo Pref.,
H.N. Anna-san

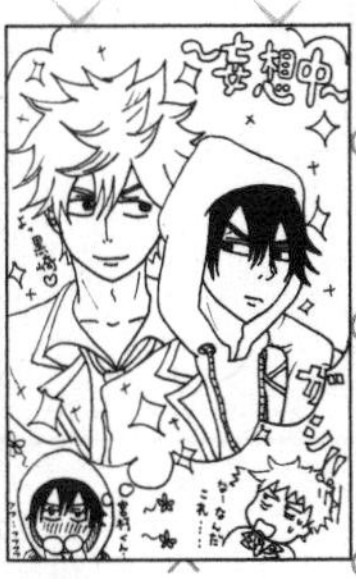
~妄想中~

Mie Pref.,
H.N. Ranranrambo-san

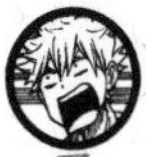
This is great!

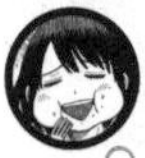
Tsubaki's cooking is dynamic, yet delicate! I wonder how his cooking tastes so good.

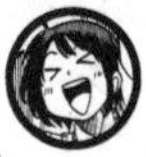
Yeah, Kurosaki! You're free to let your imagination run wild!! Go for it!

Please send your art here ↓

Yamada-kun and the Seven Witches: Underground Website
c/o Kodansha Comics
451 Park Ave. South, 7th Floor
New York, NY 10016

※ Please clearly write your address, name, and phone number. If your address, name, and phone number aren't included with your submission, we won't be able to send you a prize.

※ And if necessary, don't forget to include your handle name (pen name)!

Please send your letters with the understanding that your zip code, address, name, and other personal information included in your correspondence may be given to the author of this work.

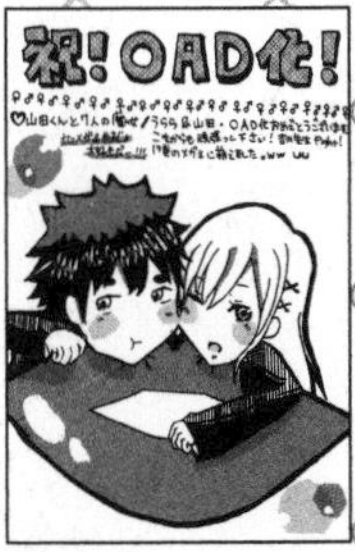
祝！OAD化！

Osaka Pref.,
H.N. Kisaragi-san

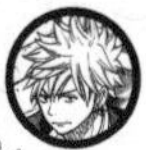
Check us out in the anime series, too!

Translation Notes

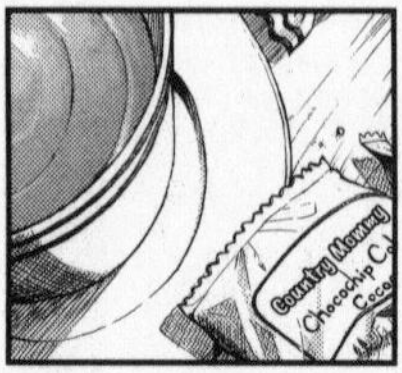
Country Mommy
Chocochip

Country Mommy and Century Ma'am, pages 27, 150

These are two separate parody versions of a Japanese soft-cookie brand called Country Ma'am.

"How do you read this character?!", page 55

This actually came up once before in a previous volume, but because the school is over 100 years old, documents created up to a certain point in time will likely use different *kanji* (Chinese characters). In Japan, more traditional and complicated forms of some *kanji* were in use until about 1950, so you could probably guess that the document Yamada and Tamaki is holding was created prior to 1950.

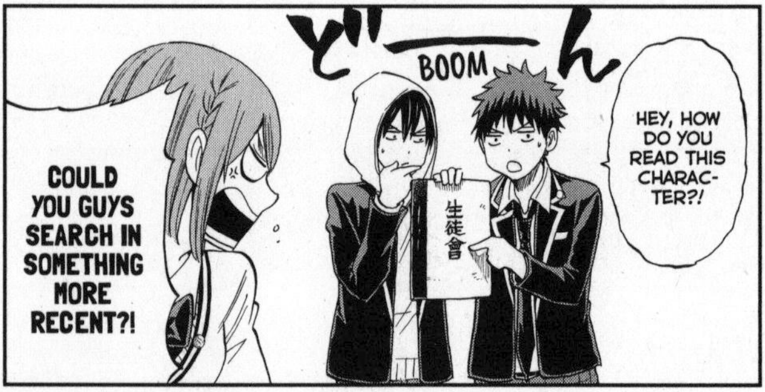
どーん
BOOM
HEY, HOW DO YOU READ THIS CHARAC-TER?!
生徒會
COULD YOU GUYS SEARCH IN SOMETHING MORE RECENT?!

"Too hot to handle, huh...", page 110

In the original Japanese, the phrase that was used here literally has Yamada wondering if Miyamura has a "cat tongue". This is a fairly common Japanese phrase that is used to define people who can't handle high-temperature foods like coffee and ramen.

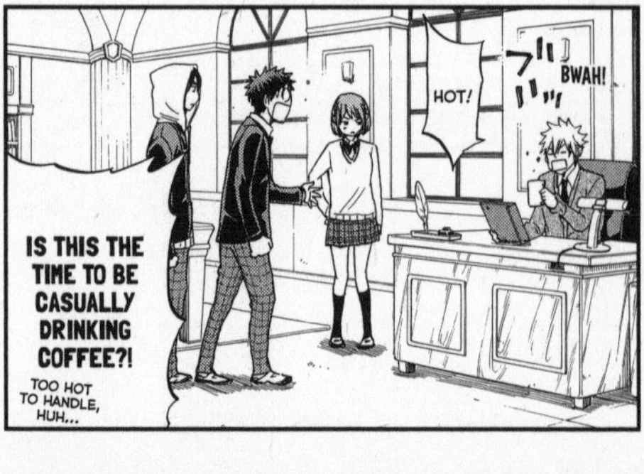
BWAH!
HOT!
IS THIS THE TIME TO BE CASUALLY DRINKING COFFEE?!
TOO HOT TO HANDLE, HUH...

Happy Bag, page 149

This is a parody of Happy Turn, a sweet and salty cracker made by Kameda Seika. It's a very common snack that is almost the equivalent of candies you'll find at your grandmother's house.

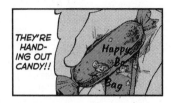

THEY'RE HAND-ING OUT CANDY!!

Happy Ba Bag

Two bathrooms, page 186

Having two bathrooms in your house may not seem like a big deal to many American readers, but it can be in Japan. First of all, the word translated to bathroom here, "*ofuro*", is basically the bath itself, and Japanese baths are typically larger and require more space than typical Western-style bathrooms. The Japanese bathroom is centered on the bath, and toilets, sinks, and other sections are usually kept separate. A house may have two or three toilets, but usually only one bath. Also, within the actual room for a Japanese bath, the flooring usually has a drain, and a shower is attached to the wall away from the bath, because you wash yourself before entering the bath. This can make the Japanese bath closer to a hot tub or pool, so you could imagine the owners of a house that had more than one of these being pretty well off.

Long wallet, page 186

In many Western countries, a bi-fold wallet is common, and this is not uncommon in Japan, but you may also see people in Japan carrying around long wallets. Long wallets keep paper currency straight and can usually carry a larger amount of money. They are more typically associated with women in Japan, but when men do carry them, they're men who are well off (or want to look like they're well off).

Yamada-kun and the Seven Witches volume 16 is a work of fiction. Names, characters, places, and incidents are the products of the author's imagination or are used fictitiously. Any resemblance to actual events, locales, or persons, living or dead, is entirely coincidental.

A Kodansha Comics Trade Paperback Original.

Published in the United States by Kodansha Comics, an imprint of Kodansha USA Publishing, LLC, New York.

Publication rights for this English edition arranged through Kodansha Ltd., Tokyo.

First published in Japan in 2015 by Kodansha Ltd., Tokyo, as *Yamada-kun to Nananin no Majo* volume 16.

ISBN 978-1-63236-583-5

Printed in the United States of America.

www.kodanshacomics.com

9 8 7 6 5 4 3 2 1

Translation: David Rhie
Lettering: Sara Linsley
Editing: Ajani Oloye
Kodansha Comics edition cover design: Phil Balsman